The Story of the World

ALSO BY SUSAN WISE BAUER

The Story of the World: History for the Classical Child
(PEACE HILL PRESS)
Volume 1: Ancient Times (Revised Edition, 2006)
Volume 2: The Middle Ages (Revised Edition, 2007)
Volume 3: Early Modern Times (2004)

*The History of the Ancient World: From the Earliest Accounts
to the Fall of Rome*
(W.W. Norton, 2007)

*The History of the Medieval World: From the Conversion of
Constantine to the First Crusade*
(W.W. Norton, 2010)

The Well-Educated Mind
A Guide to the Classical Education You Never Had
(W.W. NORTON, 2003)

Though the Darkness Hide Thee
(MULTNOMAH, 1998)

WITH JESSIE WISE

The Well-Trained Mind
A Guide to Classical Education at Home
(Revised edition, W.W. NORTON, 2009)

www.susanwisebauer.com

The Story of the World

History for the Classical Child

Volume 4: The Modern Age
From Victoria's Empire to the End of the USSR

Susan Wise Bauer

illustrations by Sarah Park

Peace Hill Press
Charles City, VA

Manufacturing by BookMasters, Inc., Ashand, OH (USA), #50006637,
September 2014
Cover design by Andrew J. Buffington
Cover painting by James L. Wise, Jr.

Publisher's Cataloging-in-Publication

Bauer, S. Wise.
The story of the world. Volume 4, The modern age :
    from Victoria's Empire to the end of the USSR / by
    Susan Wise Bauer ; illustrated by Jay L. Wise and Sarah Park.
p. cm.
Includes index.
"History for the classical child."
SUMMARY: Chronological history of the modern age, from 1850 to 2000.
Audience: Ages 5–12.
LCCN 2004112538
ISBN   0-9728603-3-9   978-0-9728603-3-8   (paper)
ISBN   0-9728603-4-7   978-0-9728603-4-5   (cloth)

1. History, Modern — 19th century — Juvenile literature.
2. History, Modern — 20th century — Juvenile literature.
[1. History, Modern —19th century. 2. History, Modern — 20th century.]
I. Wise, Jay L. II. Park, Sarah. III. Title. IV. Title: Modern age.

D299.B35 2005909.8

QBI04-200396

Print Year   2014
Printing Number   16

Peace Hill Press • 18021 The Glebe Lane • Charles City, VA 23030
www.peacehillpress.com
info@peacehillpress.com

Table of Contents

Table of Maps

Table of Illustrations

Foreword

The four volumes of the Story of the World are meant to be read by children, or read aloud by parents to children. Each of the first three volumes increases slightly in difficulty. Although older students can certainly make use of them, the primary audience for Volume 1 is children in grades 1–4. For Volume 2, the primary audience is grades 2–5; and for volume 3, grades 3–6. This volume is targeted at students in grades 4–8.

The first three volumes (which cover history from roughly 5000 BC up until 1850) are designed so that siblings can use them together; so, a first grader could certainly make use of Volume 2 if her third-grade sister were using it as well.

I wouldn't study this particular volume, though, with children younger than fourth grade. The events that shaped the twentieth century—by which I mean the events that have laid down the borders of countries and dictated the ways in which those countries relate to each other—have almost all involved violence. As an academic, a writer, a historian, and the mother of children ranging in age from four to beginning high school, I have done my best to tell this history in a way that is age appropriate. Because of that attempt, this volume is less evocative than the previous three. I have always tried to tell history as a story, to bring out the color and narrative thread of events. But with this history, I have found myself veering continually toward a more matter-of-fact and less dramatic tone. The events of the twentieth century—the bombing of Hiroshima, the purges of Stalin, to name only two—are dramatic enough. Turned into story, they would be overwhelming.

Despite their violent nature, I don't think these events should be ignored by parents of young children. A fourth grader hears the news on the car radio, on the TV, or in the conversation of his elders. He hears the words ("terrorism") and senses the worry of the adults around him. A fourth or fifth grader who has a vague idea of what is going on in the world deserves to be started on the path to understanding. The shape of the world today is not random; it has been formed by a very definite pattern of happenings. To deny a child an understanding of that pattern is truly to doom a child to fear, because war, unrest, and violence appear totally random.

Even in this book, violence is not random. It is alarming, but not random. As you read, you will see, again and again, the same pattern acted out: A person or a group of people rejects injustice by rebelling and seizing the reins of power. As soon as those reins are in the hands of the rebels, the rebels become the establishment, the victims become the tyrants, the freedom-fighters become the dictators. The man who shouts for equality in one decade purges, in the next decade, those who shout against him. Boiling history down to its simplest outline so that beginning scholars can grasp it brings this repetition into stark relief.

Again and again, while researching this book, I was reminded of the words of Alexander Solzhenitsyn, who spent eleven years in the labor camps of the Soviet Union, and who, when he became powerless, finally understood that revolution never brings an end to oppression. Solzhenitsyn wrote, "In the intoxication of youthful successes I had felt myself to be infallible, and I was therefore cruel. In the surfeit of power I was a murderer and an oppressor. ... And it was only when I lay there on rotting prison straw that I sensed within myself the first stirrings of good. ... Even in the best of hearts there remains ... an unuprooted small corner of evil. Since then I have come to understand the truth of all the religions of the world: They struggle with the *evil inside a human being*. ... And since that time I have come to understand the falsehood of all the revolutions in history: They destroy only those carriers of evil contemporary with them."

Revolution shatters the structures; but the men who build the next set of structures haven't conquered the evil that lives in their own hearts. The history of the twentieth century is, again and again, the story of men who fight against tyrants, win the battle, and then are overwhelmed by the unconquered tyranny in their own souls.

A note on accuracy: Historians vary widely on such matters as the number of war casualties in any given conflict, the sizes of armies, and even specific dates on which treaties were signed or independence declared. Since this is a basic text for young students, I have decided (fairly arbitrarily) to use *Encyclopædia Britannica* as the final authority on dates and numbers.

There is no single accepted method of transliteration for Arabic and Chinese names. I have chosen to use the Pinyin system for most Chinese names, unless another transliteration is extremely well known ("Manchuria" instead of the Pinyin "Dongbei," for example). I have generally followed *Britannica* for names in other languages.

— Susan Wise Bauer
Charles City, VA
March, 2005

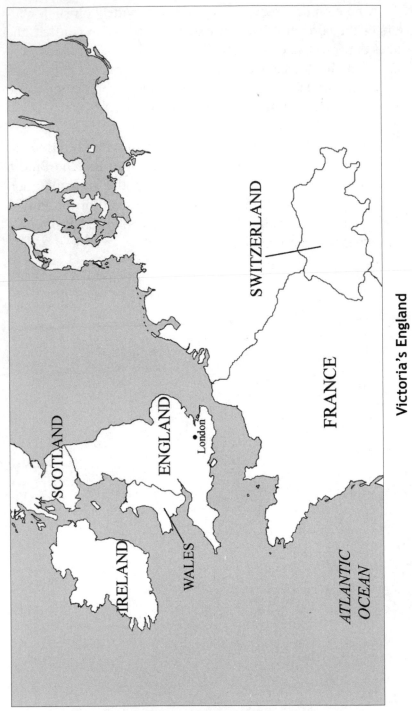

Victoria's England

Chapter One
Britain's Empire

Victoria's England

Summer had come to England. The sun poured down on the hot, soot-covered roofs and cluttered streets of London. The Thames River shone in the morning light. In an open green space at the center of the city, a huge glass box sat like a glittering toy on the grass.

Beneath the glass roof of the box, an army troop was marching in circles, beating a path on the grass. The youngest soldier looked up at the glass ceiling nervously.

"It's going to collapse any minute!" he whispered to the soldier in front of him.

"Quiet!" bellowed the sergeant at the troop's head. "Left! Right! Left, right, left! Stamp your feet! March until it falls down on your head!"

The young soldier hunched his shoulders and tramped harder. The ceiling shook—but the walls stood firm. Finally, the sergeant called his men to a halt. They had marched for an hour, and failed to shake the glass building down. Queen Victoria and her husband, Prince Albert, would be delighted!

Victoria was queen of Great Britain, a country made up of four smaller countries (England, Scotland, Ireland, and Wales) all allied together. In less than a year, Victoria and Albert planned to invite the entire world to Great Britain's capital city, London, for the biggest fair ever held: "The Great Exhibition of the Works of Industry of All Nations." Countries from all across the globe would bring their inventions, their machines, goods to this fair. But such a huge fair needed an building to hold all those exhibits.

Albert had looked at 245 different plans for buildings and had rejected all of them. Finally, he found the perfect exhibition hall: a glass building made out of almost a million feet of glass, attached to four thousand tons of iron columns and beams. This glass building had been designed by a man named Joseph Paxton, a gardener who had spent years building greenhouses. It was bigger than any building in England, and it would shine in the sun like a jewel.

But when the people of London heard about the glass building, they objected. If huge crowds milled around underneath the glass ceiling, shaking the ground with their feet, the building might collapse and kill everyone beneath.

So Joseph Paxton made a smaller model of his glass building and asked the troop of soldiers to jump and stamp around underneath it, shaking the ground. The model remained standing. Plans to build the giant greenhouse could go ahead!

There was no time to waste. The Great Exhibition was due to open in less than nine months. Every glassmaker in England was called upon to help. Thousands of sheets of glass and hundreds of iron bars and columns were brought to an open green space in the center of London called Hyde Park. There, the iron and glass were put together into a huge greenhouse that covered nineteen acres—the same space as seventeen football fields. A huge dome rose from it, big enough so that the towering elm trees in the park could fit right into the building. Paxton's building, the Crystal Palace, was ready for the fair.

Countries from all over the world brought thirteen thousand different exhibits. Vases and hats from Russia, furniture from Austria, farming tools from the United States, rich clothing and embroidery made in Prussia, fine cloth and weapons from France, and Swiss watches filled the halls. There were statues and pictures, a life-sized lead mine, the first gigantic models of dinosaurs, cuneiform tablets just discovered in the ancient land of Assyria, and a fountain hundreds of feet high.

On May 1, 1851, Queen Victoria and Prince Albert arrived in their state carriage to open the very first day of the Great Exhibition. The Crystal Palace shone in the sun. Flags waved from the roof. Sunshine flooded through the glass walls and illuminated the queen as she walked into the central dome. As she entered, a huge choir began to sing the Hallelujah Chorus.

Victoria and Albert walked through the Crystal Palace, admiring the beautiful clothing and furniture and the ingenious inventions from other countries. Later, Queen Victoria wrote in her diary, "We were quite dazzled by the most splendid [Indian] shawls and tissues ... [and] charming Turkish stuffs,

Queen Victoria, ruler of the British Empire

including very fine silks.... [And] there were 'Bowie' knives in profusion, made entirely for Americans, who never move without one."

But Albert and Victoria were the most pleased by exhibits from all parts of the British Empire—an empire that stretched around the world. Australian convicts from the British colony of Australia had sent bonnets made out of palm leaves. British New Zealand sent carved wood. British-run factories in India sent beautiful silks and cottons. The British colony of Canada sent a brand-new kind of fire engine. Throughout the Crystal Palace, visitors marveled at British machines: a huge locomotive engine, a diving bell, models of steamships, cranes, pumps, plows and reapers, and architects' models of bridges and buildings.

The *real* reason for the Great Exhibition was to show the entire world how powerful and modern the British Empire was. Britain itself was just a tiny island off the coast of Europe. But British governors were in charge of British colonies and territories in Canada, Australia, New Zealand, India, South Africa, and many more places. Victoria's empire was so big that the British said, "The sun never sets on the British Empire!" No matter where the sun's light fell as the Earth travelled around it, the rays would warm land governed by the British.

British colonies sent coal, silk, furs, and other valuable goods back to Britain itself. But the British didn't spread their empire just for money. They were sure that they could improve every part of the world—if they could just take control of it. Englishman Cecil Rhodes wrote, "We are the first [best] race in the world, and ... the more of the world we inhabit, the better it is for the human race."

The Great Exhibition made this clear! Only half of the Crystal Palace was given over to exhibits from the rest of the world. The other half was filled entirely with British goods. The six million visitors who came to the Great Exhibition could see exactly what the British thought of themselves: Britain was as powerful as the rest of the world, put together. The British historian and writer Thomas Babington Macaulay exclaimed,

"[The Great Exhibition was] a most gorgeous sight. … I cannot think that the Caesars ever exhibited a more splendid spectacle." Just like the Caesars of the Roman Empire, the kings and queens of Britain had spread their laws, their customs, and their language across the world.

But just like the Romans of old, the British would soon have to fight to keep their empire together.

The Sepoy Mutiny

Not long after the close of the Great Exhibition, Britain found itself fighting a war in India—a war in which the eighty-two-year-old emperor of India, Bahadur Shah, would be forced to hide in a tomb while fighting raged outside.

Long before Bahadur Shah was born, English merchants who wanted to buy rare silks, cotton, and tea from India asked the emperor of India, Jahangir, for permission to build little settlements called *trading posts* along the Indian coast. These settlements would be safe places for their ships to land.

Jahangir agreed. So the merchants, joining together into a group called the East India Company, began to build their trading posts. For a hundred years, the East India Company went on building trading posts throughout India. More and more Englishmen and women settled around the trading posts. The trading posts put guns on their walls to defend the settlers. The trading posts began to look more like English cities!

One of the largest of these "English cities," Calcutta, lay on India's northeast coast, in the province of Bengal. The governor of Bengal began to grow nervous about this large settlement of Englishmen with guns, right in the middle of his country. He decided that it was time for the English to leave—so he assembled an army and marched out to fight against them.

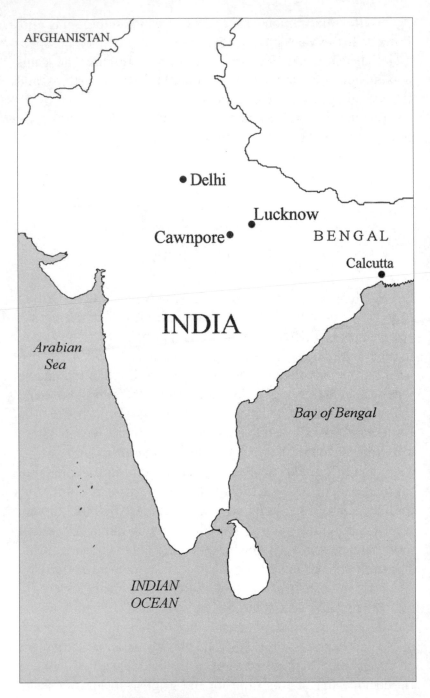

India During the Sepoy Mutiny

But the merchants of the East India Company didn't want to leave Calcutta. They hired an army of English soldiers and an English general and fought back. When they defeated the Indian army, the East India Company took control of the government of Bengal.

The merchants had become governors.

By the time Bahadur Shah was born, the East India Company had seized control of more and more parts of India. In some places, British officials actually ran the government of India. In others, they allowed local rulers to control their courts and their ceremonies—but British "advisors" told the rulers what to do. And the taxes paid by Indians on their land went to the British.

Many Indians were displeased by life under British rule. They could see that British soldiers and officers treated Indians with scorn. The British tore down Indian temples to make room for British railroad tracks. Sometimes they forced Indian Muslims to shave their beards, which symbolized their faith. And both Hindus and Muslims in India were afraid that the British were out to convert them, by force, to Christianity.

When Bahadur Shah's father finally died, as a very old man, Bahadur Shah became the emperor of India. He was already sixty years old. Even though he was emperor, he had to do exactly as the East India Company told him. The Company even paid his salary!

In 1856, when Bahadur Shah was eighty-one years old and had "ruled" India for twenty-one years, the East India Company made a very big mistake.

The Company had three large armies to help control the three hundred million people of India. The army officers were all British, but many of the soldiers were native Indians, both Hindu and Muslims, who had agreed to work for the East India Company. These native soldiers were called *sepoys*.

In 1856, the British passed a law declaring that any soldier who belonged to the British army in India could be put on a ship and sent to fight in another country. The Hindu soldiers were appalled. A devout Hindu could only keep himself ceremonially clean if he could cook his own food and draw his own water for bathing—and this was impossible on board a ship. A Hindu soldier who went on a British ship and then came home often found that his relatives and friends refused even to eat with him.

Then something even more disturbing happened. The East India Company bought a new, modern kind of rifle called the Enfield rifle, and announced that the army would begin using it. Soon, word spread through the ranks of the sepoys: "Don't use the rifle! They are trying to make us into Christians once more!"

To understand this, you have to know that in those days, when a soldier loaded a rifle, he first had to load the powder, and then the bullets. This took time! But in an Enfield rifle, the bullets and powder were folded up together in a greased-paper package called a cartridge. All the soldier had to do was bite off the end of the cartridge, pour the powder into the rifle, and slide the bullet in.

Now, the sepoys whispered to each other that the grease used to coat the cartridges had been made out of animal fat. Devout Hindus were horrified by the thought that the fat of cows might touch their lips. Cows were sacred animals, never to be eaten. The Muslims were just as sickened by the idea that they might have to put pig fat into their mouths. In Islam, hogs were unclean.

At once, the British government announced that Hindu and Muslim soldiers could make their own grease out of vegetable oil. But it was too late. The sepoys were already angry at their British superiors, who called them "pigs" and other demeaning names. Now they were convinced that the cartridges were a deliberate attempt to destroy their Hindu and Muslim faith.

The sepoys began to rebel all over the northwest of India. They announced that Bahadur Shah, now eighty-two, was their commander in chief. Bahadur Shah was too old to fight—but he watched as the rebels took control of Delhi, drove the British out of the city of Cawnpore, and then laid siege to the city of Lucknow.

But the British had no intention of losing India. The East India Company marched new divisions of well-trained British soldiers into India, and laid siege to Delhi. The rebels fought desperately to keep their city. One out of every three British soldiers who besieged Delhi was killed. But finally the British flooded over the walls. They found Bahadur Shah hiding in the tomb of his great ancestor Humayan and dragged him out to stand trial for treason. Bahadur Shah was found guilty and sent away to live, under guard, in a distant city—where he died, five years later, at the age of eighty-seven.

The British government declared that India would no longer have an emperor. But the East India Company wouldn't govern India anymore, either. Britain was fed up with the incompetent rule of the East India Company. If the Company had not treated the sepoys so poorly, perhaps the Sepoy Mutiny would never have happened.

So Queen Victoria took India away from the East India Company and announced that India was now a colony of Britain, governed directly by the Queen and Parliament with the help of a head official called the Viceroy of India. Queen Victoria promised that all the British would work to make India a better place for the Indians.

But India didn't belong to the Indians any more. It had become British. All over India, Indians went on hoping for the day when they would get their own country back.

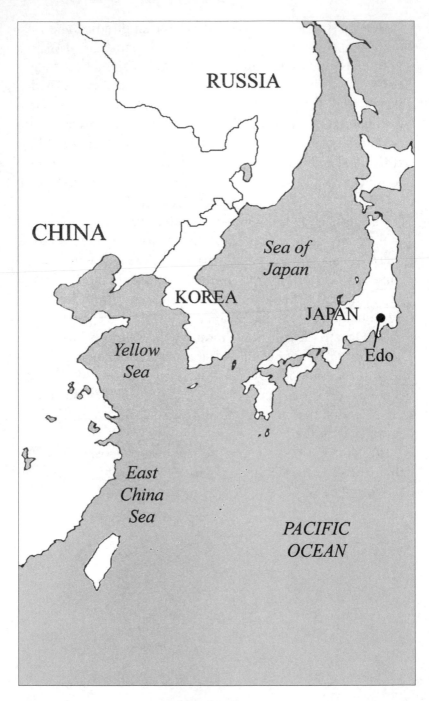

Japan Re-Opens

Chapter Two
West Against East

Japan Re-Opens

Far across the world, another island empire lay. But this empire didn't want to spread across the world. It wanted to keep the rest of the world out.

The four islands of Japan were ruled by a *shogun*, a military general who inherited his position. For two hundred years, that shogun had been from the Tokugawa family. The Tokugawa shoguns were afraid that Christian missionaries, coming into Japan, would convert the Japanese to Christianity and destroy the traditional Buddhist faith. They were even more afraid that foreign armies would follow the missionaries in and take over Japan.

The Tokugawa shoguns decided that it would be best to keep all Christians out of Japan. As a matter of fact, it would be even safer to keep anyone from Western countries (countries in Europe or the Americas) out. The Japanese had everything that they needed to live. They did not need Western ideas, or Western missionaries, or Western goods.

So the shoguns passed laws, forbidding the Japanese to travel to foreign lands. A Japanese fisherman who was blown off course and landed on a foreign shore could never come home. Western merchants could not come to Japanese ports. Only a few Dutch ships were allowed to land on an artificial island in Japan's most important harbor—and they were only allowed to do this once per year.

For almost two hundred years, the Japanese followed their own customs, fished off their own shores, and had nothing to do with the West. But even though merchants and missionaries from the West couldn't get into Japan, Western books were translated into Japanese and brought into the country. The shogun, the warriors who obeyed him (the *samurai*), and other educated people in Japan knew about Western ideas such as democracy (governments in which the people of a country rule themselves, instead of obeying a king or queen). They heard about Western technology (scientific discoveries used to make machines and other inventions). As time went by, more and more Japanese began to think that perhaps keeping Japan separate from the rest of the world wasn't such a good idea.

But before the Japanese could open their own doors to the West, the United States of America decided to break the doors down.

One hot August afternoon in 1853, the Japanese who lived near Edo Bay stood along the shores of the bay, staring out to sea. They had heard alarming rumors of four huge ships from the United States, loaded with guns, sailing their way. The ships had already been nicknamed the "Black Ships" by the Japanese fishermen who had seen them pass by.

Soon, four black specks showed themselves at the edge of the bay. As the Japanese watched, the ships grew nearer—and bigger. Two of them were brand-new, powerful steamships. The Japanese had never seen steamships before. They whispered to each other, "Two of the ships are burning!"

All four ships, bristling with cannon, dropped their anchors and lay with their guns pointing at the shores. The American sailors lined the decks, ready for action, armed with muskets and cutlasses.

What did these foreigners want? Slowly, nervously, a few Japanese boats pushed off from shore and approached the ships. But the Americans allowed no one on board. Several brave Japanese tried to swing up onto the chains that stretched down from the ships into the water, but the Americans waved their cutlasses to keep them away.

Meanwhile, the leader of the expedition, Commodore Matthew Perry, was down in his cabin, waiting.

Matthew Perry had been given a difficult job. American merchants wanted to buy fine Japanese silks and ceramics, and something even more important: coal. Steam engines needed coal to keep running, and the islands of Japan had plenty of natural coal. So the president of the United States, Millard Fillmore, sent Matthew Perry to Japan with a letter, asking Japan to open its ports to American ships.

Once before, the United States had asked Japan to trade with America. But the American captain who brought the request to Japan had been very friendly—so friendly that the Japanese decided he was too weak to take seriously. They refused to listen to him and sent him away.

Matthew Perry didn't intend to make the same mistake. He told his men to keep the Japanese away from the ships until they sent a truly important official out to see him. So the Americans told the Japanese who tried to board, "We bring a letter from the president of the United States to the Emperor of Japan. But we can only give it to a high official of the Emperor."

The Japanese went back to the shore to talk this over. They could see that the Americans did not understand how Japan was governed. Japan did have an emperor, but although the Japanese believed that the emperor was almost divine, he didn't actually rule in Japan. The shogun had all the power.

Finally, the Japanese decided to write a letter assuring Matthew Perry that the governor of a nearby town, a man named Toda, was the emperor's high official. They signed the letter in the emperor's name, and gave it to the Americans. When the Americans saw this forged paper, they agreed to come ashore and give the president's letter to Toda.

So Matthew Perry came ashore with his officers and a military band. The Japanese escorted him into a room hung with purple cloth and gauze curtains, where Toda sat, looking very serious. Matthew Perry handed over the president's letter, enclosed in a rosewood box with gold hinges. And then the Americans marched away, with their band playing "Yankee Doodle."

Toda thought the whole scene was very funny. But he and the other Japanese knew that the letter from the president was serious. Before he left, Matthew Perry warned the Japanese that he would return in one year for an answer—and that the answer had better be yes.

The Japanese knew that they could not fight back against Matthew Perry and his Black Ships. Japan had only a few cannon along the shores, and some of them no longer worked. The samurai, the warriors of Japan, were no longer the fierce soldiers they had once been. They had been taught to be government officials, not warriors. One samurai school even allowed its students to practice horseback riding indoors on wooden horses on rainy days, so that they wouldn't have to get wet!

When Matthew Perry came back to Japan in 1854, the Japanese agreed to sign a trade treaty with them. Not too long after, France, Spain, and other European countries signed their own treaties with Japan. Japan was closed to the West no more.

The Crimean War

In the same year that Matthew Perry sailed from the West to the East, a war broke out halfway between East and West.

The war started when two countries quarreled over the keys to a church. Of course, the church keys didn't actually *begin* the war. They were more like a lit match. A tiny match can't do much damage on its own—but if you shove it under a stack of dry firewood, you'll end up with a huge bonfire. The war that began in 1853 flared up because the countries involved were ready to fight with each other; there were plenty of pieces of "dry firewood" waiting to be lit.

The first piece of "firewood" was tossed onto the stack by the Turks. The Ottoman Turks ruled over the land of Palestine, where the cities of Jerusalem and Bethlehem lay, and also over the city of Constantinople (which the Turks had renamed Istanbul). All three of these cities were important to Christians. And although the Turks were Muslims, they didn't want to make the Christian nations of Europe angry by keeping Christians away from holy places. So the ruler of Turkey gave England, France, and several other countries permission to take care of different holy places in Palestine.

The second piece of "firewood" was laid down by Nicholas I, the *czar* (ruler) of Russia. Nicholas I was determined to capture the city of Istanbul (which the Russians still called Constantinople) for Russia. Russia had no way to send ships down into the Mediterranean Sea. But if Russia owned Constantinople, Russian ships could sail down from the southern coast of Russia, through the Black Sea, past Constantinople, and into the Mediterranean. Those ships could carry Russian goods—and Russian soldiers! Nicholas I was looking for any excuse to attack the Turks and take Constantinople away.

The third piece of "firewood" was England's fear of Russia. Nicholas I wanted the British to fight with him against the Turks, and he was willing to divide any land that he won with his British allies. But the English thought that Russians were wild and savage. Nicholas I visited Queen Victoria in London, hoping to impress her with his wisdom. (He was even careful to tell the Queen that Prince Albert had a "very noble air," since he knew that Victoria liked to hear her husband praised.) But after he left, Queen Victoria snapped, "He has an uncivilized mind!" And one of her government officials warned, "I believe that if this barbarous nation [of Russia], the enemy of all progress ... should once succeed in establishing itself in the heart of Europe, it would be the greatest calamity which could befall the human race."

The fourth piece of "wood" was tossed onto the pile by France. France didn't like the Turks—but at least the Turks were a weak and disorganized empire. Russia, on the other hand, had become a huge and threatening country, not very far

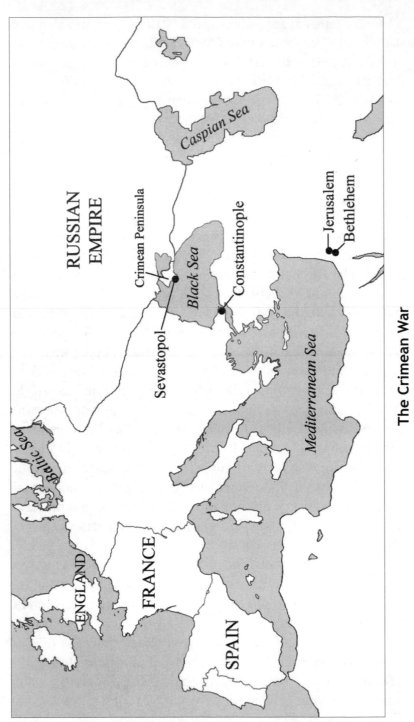

The Crimean War

away. If Russia attacked the Turks, perhaps France would be next! So the French also decided to try to make friends with the English. The king of France, Louis-Philippe, traveled to England to see Victoria, only two months after Nicholas I. The French and the English had been enemies for hundreds of years; Louis-Philippe was the first French king to visit the English monarch since 1356 (and in 1356, the French king had been dragged into England as a prisoner of war!). But Louis-Philippe managed to please Queen Victoria. She ordered a feast held for him, with the gold plates used for her favorite guests.

Now the firewood was laid. The match was ready to be struck.

Russian and French Christians started to argue with each other about who should protect the Church of the Nativity in Bethlehem, where they believed that Jesus had been born. The king of France told the ruler of Turkey that French warships would attack Constantinople if the French didn't get the keys to the church. When Nicholas I heard about this, he retorted that he would march down and attack the Turks if the French *did* get the keys!

And that is exactly what he did. The Russian army invaded the northern part of the Turkish Empire. The French, afraid that Russia would grow bigger and even stronger, launched their own attack against the Russians. And the British joined with the French.

In the first year of fighting, the French and the British managed to drive the Russians back out of the Turkish Empire. But the two countries then decided to weaken Russia even more. Together, France and Britain were determined to capture the Russian city of Sevastopol.

Sevastopol lay in the north of the Black Sea, on a little chunk of land jutting down from Russia called the Crimean Peninsula. The Russians kept their warships at Sevastopol. If the French and British armies could capture Sevastopol, Russia would never be able to sail warships down into the Mediterranean Sea.

So the British and French armies marched towards Sevastopol. But the Russians fought back fiercely. The British and French soldiers had to dig trenches, fight a battle, push a little more forward, dig more trenches, fight another battle, and push a little more forward—for months and months. They spent so much time on the Crimean Peninsula that the whole war became known as the Crimean War. And as the Crimean War went on, the British army became more and more disorganized. No one seemed to be able to get food and clothing to the troops. Supplies sent to the Crimean Peninsula sat in piles, spoiling, only miles away from hungry soldiers who were wearing shreds of disintegrating uniforms. And in one of the most famous battles of the Crimean War, the Battle of Balaklava, British officers ordered mounted soldiers to charge forward into a much bigger Russian force, instead of waiting for reinforcements. The soldiers obeyed—and almost all of them were killed. Their charge was later made famous in the poem, "The Charge of the Light Brigade":

> Someone had blundered.
> Theirs not to make reply,
> Theirs not to reason why,
> Theirs but to do and die.
> Into the valley of Death
> Rode the six hundred.

But although the British weren't very organized, the Russians didn't do much better. Nicholas's chief general made horrible mistake after horrible mistake. Finally, Nicholas's son Alexander fired the general and appointed another one. When Nicholas I heard what his son had done, he had a stroke from anger—and died not long afterwards.

Only a few months after Alexander took control of Russia, the British and French finally managed to capture Sevastopol. More than one hundred thousand Russians had been killed or wounded defending it! Alexander knew that it was time for Russia to give up fighting. So in 1856, he agreed to sign a peace treaty called the Peace of Paris. Russia would get Sevastopol back, but only after returning Turkish land to the Turks. And Russia had to promise not to keep any warships in the Black Sea.

Russia could no longer dream of sailing a Russian fleet into the Mediterranean Sea. Russia's ambitions had been quenched—for the moment.

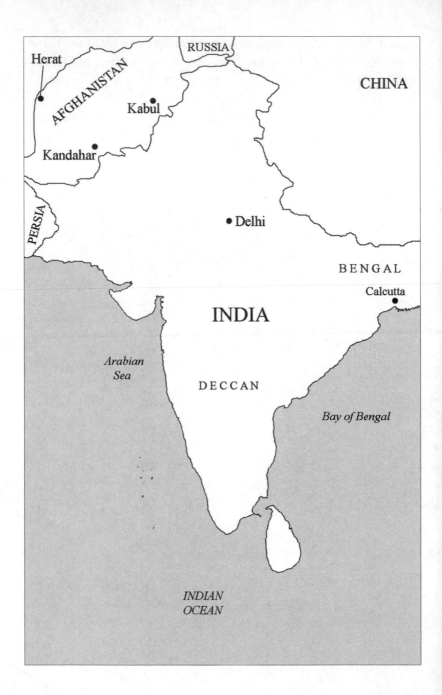

The Great Game

Chapter Three
British Invasions

The Great Game

Just three years after the Second Opium War ended, another king, in another country, managed to drive the British and all other foreign invaders out of his homeland. The king's name was Dost Mohammad Khan, and he ruled in Afghanistan, a rocky, parched country that lay sandwiched between Russia to the north and India to the south.

By the time that Dost Mohammad became its leader, Afghanistan had already been invaded over and over again. First, the Mongols had taken the country over. Then, a prince of India named Babur had added part of Afghanistan to his Indian Empire. Persia, which lay along Afghanistan's western border, moved in to take over the rest of Afghanistan.

Two hundred years later, a heroic Afghan chief named Mirwais Hotoki Khan drove the Persians out. At first, Mirwais Khan had worked for the Persians. He even lived at the Persian royal court. But then the Persian *shah* (king) assigned a cruel, ruthless Persian governor to run Mirwais Khan's home, the eastern city of Kandahar. Mirwais Khan saw his people suffering, arrested, and killed for no reason. So he invited the governor and his bodyguard to a country picnic—and had them both killed. Then, Mirwais Khan led an army into Kandahar and drove the Persians out of his country.

But when Mirwais Khan died, after six years of rule, the Persians invaded Afghanistan once again.

Another hero arose to push back the foreign invaders. He was a native Afghan who had served in the bodyguard of the Persian *shah*. He fought against the Persians, pushed them back out of his country, and ruled for twenty-six years over all the different tribes who lived in Afghanistan. He became known as Durrani, which means *pearl*, because his rule was as valuable as a jewel to the people of Afghanistan.

But then Durrani died, and the tribes began to quarrel about who should be king next. Finally, one soldier managed to take control of Kabul, the largest, most important city in Afghanistan. His name was Dost Mohammad Khan.

At first, Dost Mohammad Khan was *khan*, or chief, only in the city of Kabul. But he spent the next ten years fighting to spread his power around the surrounding countryside. Finally, the other leaders of Afghanistan agreed to recognize him as their leader. They gave him the title of *Amir*, or Commander, because it would be his job to lead the Afghan people in war against their enemies.

Dost Mohammad was a skilled warrior and general; a tall, keen-eyed, energetic man who preferred plain soldier's clothes to fancy court costumes. But he soon learned that fighting alone would not protect Afghanistan from invasion. To keep his country independent, Dost Mohammad would have to scheme and plot.

You see, Afghanistan lay right between Russia and British-run India. Russia and Britain were enemies. Neither country wanted the other to control the country between their two borders. So Russia and Britain each tried to convince Dost Mohammad to sign an alliance. The Russian and British strategies to get control of Afghanistan became known as the Great Game.

The first move in the Great Game came from Russia. The Russian government convinced Persia to join Russia in an invasion of western Afghanistan. The combined Persian-Russian army could easily overcome the west of the country and then march on towards Kabul, where Dost Mohammad ruled. But when the British saw this army on the move, they sent a message to the Shah of Persia. The message warned the Persians that, if the invasion continued, Persia would be considered an enemy of Britain—and would suffer the consequences.

The Shah of Persia wasn't particularly afraid of Dost Mohammad. But he didn't want to make enemies of the entire British Empire! So the Persian soldiers all withdrew from Afghanistan. Britain had won the first match in the Great Game.

Now the British tried a move of their own. They planned to lend a lot of money to Dost Mohammad, so that he could use it to hire soldiers to fight against the Persians and the Russians. This would keep the Russians out of Afghanistan. It would also put Dost Mohammad in debt. "A loan of money," one British diplomat wrote, "would give us a great hold upon him!"

Instead of taking the money, Dost Mohammad decided that he too would join in the Great Game. He told the British government that Afghanistan would be a friend and ally to Great Britain—as long as British soldiers would help him drive out the Indians who still lived in the southern parts of Afghanistan.

When the British government refused, Dost Mohammad asked the Russians for help instead. At this, the British grew angry. "It is time," one British official announced, "to interfere decidedly in the affairs of Afghanistan."

Instead of helping Dost Mohammad drive the Indians out of Afghanistan, the British sent *sepoys* (Indian soldiers under British command) and English soldiers from India northward into Afghanistan. This Indian-British army marched through the wilds of Afghanistan until they reached the fortress city that protected Dost Mohammad's kingdom. Dost Mohammad had put his son in control of this fortress—but his son had neglected to wall up all of the fortress's gates. When the Indian-British army discovered that one of the gates was not bricked up, they blew it up, captured the fortress, and then stormed on towards the center of Dost Mohammad's kingdom, the city of Kabul.

Dost Mohammad wanted to stand and fight, but his soldiers, seeing the overwhelming British force, had begun to desert him. He had to flee into India!

Meanwhile, the Indian-British army occupied the city of Kabul—and grew more and more unpopular. They ate food that belonged to Afghans, took whatever they wanted from the markets, and treated the people of Kabul with contempt.

Finally, the Afghans had had enough. In Kabul, angry Afghans killed a British official before soldiers could arrive to protect him. Then they besieged the army's headquarters. When another British official arrived to settle things down, the rebels killed him as well.

The British-Indian army decided that it was time to leave Kabul. But now winter had come. The soldiers marched south towards India in freezing cold, with Afghan fighters following them and attacking from behind. Four days into the journey, over four thousand British soldiers had died. Only 120 were left. As this tiny remainder approached the border, the rebels made a final attack against them. Only one wounded man escaped. The army that had invaded Afghanistan had been completely destroyed.

The British gave up the idea of conquering Afghanistan. But they were angry over the massacre of their army. Troops of British soldiers marched into Afghanistan, burning, killing, and looting. When they had destroyed dozens of villages and killed hundreds of Afghans, they withdrew. Their revenge was over.

Now Dost Mohammad returned from India. His kingdom had shrunk. The Persians had taken advantage of the chaos to invade the west. Other warlords had seized bits of the country for themselves. All Dost Mohammad had left was the city of Kabul.

But Dost Mohammad was a patient man. He spent over fifteen years slowly rebuilding his kingdom. And because he knew that another war with Britain would only weaken Afghanistan more, he decided to make peace with his enemy.

In 1855, twelve years after the disastrous British invasion of Afghanistan, Dost Mohammad signed a treaty with Britain. This treaty promised that he would not attack the British, and that the British would stay out of Afghanistan. When the Sepoy Mutiny broke out in India, two years after the treaty was signed, Dost Mohammad kept to his part of the treaty. He did not go down into India and join the sepoys against the British. "Had Dost Mohammad turned against the British," one British general said later, "I do not see how any part of the country north of Bengal could be saved."

Meanwhile, Dost Mohammad kept on expanding his territory. He added Kandahar to his kingdom, and gave it to one of his sons to rule. Then, in 1863, he drove the remaining Persians out of the west.

Finally, Afghanistan was free of invaders.

Two weeks later, Dost Mohammad died, late one night, in his own bed. He had ruled over an independent Afghanistan for fourteen days.

Wandering Through Africa

Far away from Afghanistan, a Scottish missionary was about to find out about the continent of Africa. His love for Africa would pave the way for yet another invasion.

It was a chilly spring night in Scotland, and David Livingstone was tired of studying for his medical degree. He stood up, stretched, and looked around his tiny room. He was ready for a break.

Just down the street, a missionary was giving a special talk on Africa. Livingstone knew nothing about this mysterious, unexplored continent. He decided that he'd go down and listen to the missionary's adventures before he went back to his books.

The missionary, Robert Moffat, told story after story of his life in Africa, as David Livingstone sat fascinated. Moffat had been living for years in a town called Kuruman, five hundred

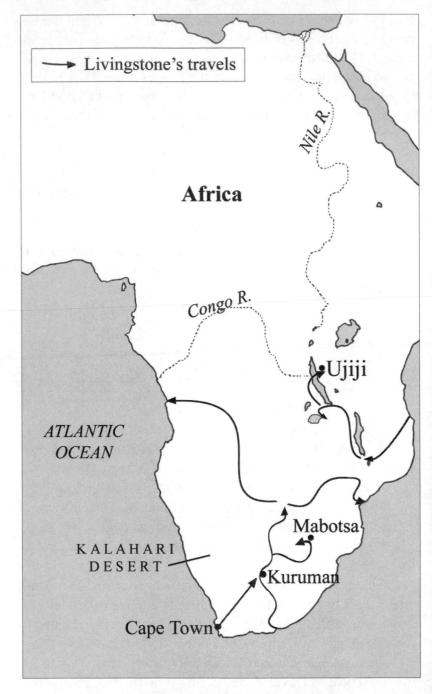

Livingstone's Travels in Africa

miles from the southern coast of Africa. In the far south of Africa, the Dutch and British and other Europeans were already living and trading; they had built a busy city called Cape Town on the coast, and had settled all around Cape Town as well.

But north of Kuruman lay the rest of the huge continent of Africa: hundreds and hundreds of miles that no European had ever seen. "Often, as I have looked to the vast plains of the north," Robert Moffat told his audience, "I have, in the morning sun, seen the smoke of a thousand villages where no missionary has ever been!" As he heard those words, David Livingstone was filled with a great desire to visit those thousand villages, to care for the sick and to preach Christianity.

A year later, Livingstone had finished his studies and become a doctor. He boarded a ship and sailed for Africa. When he arrived at the port of Cape Town, he found hundreds of Europeans, building trading posts and settlements along Africa's coast. But Livingstone was anxious to move away from Europeans, towards the mysterious heart of Africa. He travelled slowly northward, learning to survive like an African. He ground flour for his bread by hand, ate boiled caterpillars and locusts, and enjoyed one of the great delicacies of Africa: an enormous frog that lived in the earth and croaked loudly right before rain. "It is nearly as large as a chicken!" Livingstone wrote in his journal.

As he learned more and more about Africa, Livingstone came to hate the slave trade (the practice of taking Africans from Africa, and selling them as slaves to other countries). Even though the slave trade was illegal, slave traders were still visiting the coast of Africa and taking Africans away into slavery.

David Livingstone hoped to stop the slave trade. He thought that if he went on exploring Africa, he might find rivers and other trade routes that ran into the center of Africa. If Europeans could reach the center of Africa easily, they could come in and trade with the Africans for ivory, salt, and other goods—instead of for slaves.

Livingstone's explorations almost killed him. Three years after his arrival, he was living in Mabotsa, a town just east of the burning sands of the Kalahari Desert. For weeks, the people of Mabotsa had been losing their cows to lions that broke into their cattle pens. Livingstone agreed to go out with his African companions to drive the lions away.

But as he was loading his gun, a lion crept up behind him, unnoticed. It leaped on Livingstone, knocked him to the ground, grabbed his shoulder and shook him back and forth. Later, Livingstone wrote, "[The shaking] caused a sort of dreaminess, in which there was no sense of pain, nor feeling of terror ... a stupor similar to that which seems to be felt by a mouse after the first shake of the cat."

Two of Livingstone's African friends shot the lion with their rifles. The lion turned and attacked them—but before it could kill either man, it staggered and collapsed.

Livingstone's arm was badly broken. But he refused to return home. He wanted to keep on looking for those trade routes that would bring the slave trade to an end.

In 1857, the same year as the Sepoy Mutiny, Livingstone wrote a book about his explorations called *Missionary Travels*.

David Livingstone, attacked by a lion on the African savannah

He returned to England so that the book could be published. It was a tremendous success. Thousands and thousands of copies were sold. The British were happy to forget about the troubles in India for a little while, and read about an exciting new continent instead. David Livingstone became famous.

A year later, in 1858, the government of Great Britain gave David Livingstone the official job of finding trade routes into Africa for British traders. The papers that made Livingstone a *consul* (a British government official) told him to go on exploring Africa, so that Great Britain could "promote commerce and civilization [in Africa], with a view to the extinction of the slave-trade."

So David Livingstone set sail for Africa once more, this time with the support of his country.

For the next fifteen years, he would go on exploring Africa, mapping out its rivers and lakes, and learning about its dozens of kingdoms: the land of the Oromo, of the Masai, the Burundi, the Luba, and many, many more. Livingstone spent so many years in the center of Africa that many people began to wonder whether or not he was still alive. Finally the American newspaper the *New York Times* sent one of its journalists, Henry Morton Stanley, to find the missing explorer.

Stanley travelled across Africa for weeks until he found the famous missionary at Ujiji, a village just east of the Congo River. He saw a man whose face was carved with deep lines and tanned brown as leather by the sun. The skin seemed to stretch tightly over his bones. A branch had snapped back into one of his eyes and injured it. His left arm hung at his side, twisted and almost useless.

Stanley was so awed in the presence of this great man that he decided to display the best American manners he could. He walked up to David Livingstone, took off his hat, and said, "Dr. Livingstone, I presume?"

Stanley offered to take Livingstone back home to England, but the missionary refused. He had decided to remain in Africa for the rest of his life. Two years later, David Livingstone died in a hut in central Africa. His African friends took out his heart and buried it under a tree, according to African tradition. Then they wrapped his body in bark and canvas, tied it to a pole, and carried it to the coast so that a European ship could take David Livingstone home.

David Livingstone had hoped to make Africa stronger. But his maps of Africa would make it easier, years later, for England and other European countries to come into Africa and to treat it just as India had been treated: like a land to be captured, conquered, and used.

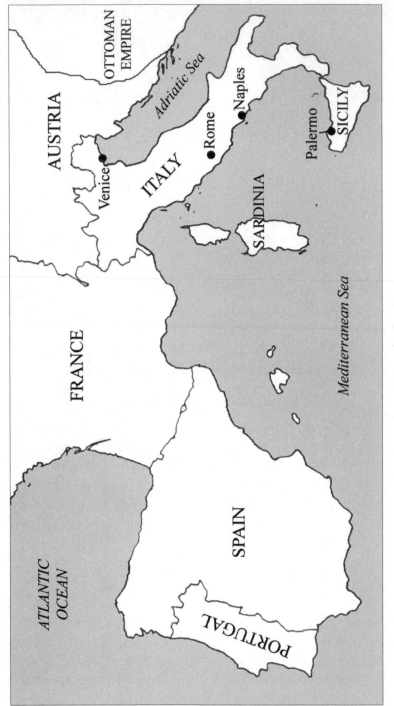

The Nation of Italy

Chapter Four
Resurrection and Rebellion

Italy's "Resurrection"

In 1850, if you were an American, your leader was the president of the United States. If you were Spanish, you spoke the language of Spain and saluted the Spanish flag. And if you were French, you swore allegiance to the leader of France.

But in 1850, to be "Italian" simply meant that you lived on the rocky peninsula that stretched down into the Mediterranean Sea like a boot. On that peninsula, over a dozen different states jostled each other. Each had its own laws, its own borders, and its own prince. Most of those states belonged not to a country called "Italy," but to the country of Austria. There *was* no Italy. "Italy," one Austrian nobleman remarked, "is merely a geographic expression!"

But in the years between 1820 and 1860, the people who lived in the Italian states began to believe that "Italy" should be more than a "geographic expression." *Italy* should be a *nation*.

All over the Italian peninsula, men who hoped to shake free of Austria and unite the Italian states into one country began to meet together in secret societies. These societies had names like "Sublime Perfect Masters" and "the Carbonaria." They had secret passwords and codes, mysterious rituals, and underground meetings. Their members grew long hair and bushy beards. The police who patrolled Italian streets watched for these rebels, hoping to arrest them. Then the police would drag them off, not to jail—but to the barber's, for a haircut.

If Italy was ever going to be free of Austrian rule, the secret societies would have to do more than hold meetings and grow long hair. But although the different societies all wanted the Italian states to be united into one nation, each society had a different idea about what this nation should be. Some wanted Italy to be a republic—a country in which the Italians themselves would elect their leaders and make their own laws. Others wanted the Italian states to join together under the leadership of the pope, the leader of the Roman Catholic Church, who lived in the Italian city of Rome. Still others thought that Italy should be ruled by a king—perhaps the king of Piedmont-Sardinia, the powerful Italian state in the north.

In 1831, the secret society called "the Carbonaria" managed to join all of these disagreeing societies together in an open revolt against Austrian rule. But Austria sent soldiers to break up the rebellion. Hundreds of secret society members were arrested. The ringleaders were sentenced to be hanged or shot.

One of the ringleaders, Giuseppe Mazzini, escaped. He watched in horror as the other leaders of the Carbonaria were put to death—but he wasn't willing to give up the fight for independence. Instead, he formed another society, called Young Italy. Every Young Italian was under forty and had to own a rifle, a dagger, and fifty bullets. The Young Italians knew that two hundred years earlier, back in the days of the Renaissance, the Italian states had been free and powerful. They hoped to make the states free and powerful once more—but this time, united into one Italian republic. This movement became known as the *Risorgimento* (the "rising again," or "Resurrection," of Italy).

The princes of Italy and the noblemen of Austria were frightened of Mazzini. He believed that God had told him to free Italy. He always wore black, saying, "I am in mourning for my country." And he preached that it was moral and right to assassinate tyrannical leaders. One of his heroes was Brutus, the Roman senator who had helped to kill Julius Caesar. Soon, Austria declared that membership in Young Italy was a crime punishable by death.

But Young Italy continued to grow. Soon a young sailor named Giuseppe Garibaldi joined Mazzini's Young Italy.

Garibaldi would soon become Mazzini's right hand man in yet another revolt against Austrian rule.

This revolt began in 1848. Fighting spread north as far as the powerful state of Venice, and south all the way down to the city of Rome. As the fighting grew bloodier, the pope fled from Rome into Naples, the southern kingdom of Italy, which was still under Austrian control. He sent out messages to Roman Catholic kings all over Europe, begging them to send their armies to drive the Young Italians out of Rome.

France answered the pope's call. Soon, French soldiers were sailing towards the coast of Italy, expecting to land near Rome and march into the city without much resistance. But as soon as they landed, they found themselves attacked by an army made up of Young Italian volunteers. The army was commanded by Giuseppe Garibaldi—and fought fiercely. "They were as wild as dervishes!" one French officer exclaimed. "They were even clawing at us with their hands!"

But the French troops were well-trained soldiers, unlike Garibaldi's inexperienced revolutionaries. They pushed on towards Rome. For three weeks, Garibaldi resisted. But finally he was forced to flee, along with the rest of his men.

Up north in Venice, the revolt had fared no better. The Austrian army was marching against the rebels. They had cannons, better guns, and even the very first bombers; Austrian soldiers sailed over Venice in balloons and dropped bombs on the revolutionaries below!

Before long, Venice was forced to surrender. Mazzini escaped capture and hid in the city of London. Garibaldi fled to the United States. Austria reclaimed the Italian states, and the pope returned to Rome. The republican revolution had failed.

The revolutionaries had not given up hope, though. Once again, they began to plan for a war of independence. It took them ten years to regain their strength. But a decade after the failed revolt in Rome and Venice, the Italians tried once again to fight for their freedom.

This time, they had decided to abandon the idea of an Italian republic. Instead, they would bring the Italian states together into a kingdom, under the reign of an Italian king. This king, Victor Emmanuel II, had just come to the throne of the northern state Piedmont-Sardinia.

Victor Emmanuel and his advisors remembered the disastrous revolt of ten years before. So he and his advisors promised the king of France that, if French soldiers would change sides and fight *for* Italy this time, Victor Emmanuel would give the French king part of his own kingdom.

The French king agreed. So the rebels formed an army in the north. Soldiers came from all over Italy to join. Giuseppe Garibaldi sailed back from America and became a major general. Once again, the Austrians and the Italians clashed. This time, the Italians had the French army behind them. But not for long! After less than a year of fighting, so many French soldiers had died that the king of France decided to withdraw from the war. He made peace with the Austrian government.

The rebellions in Rome and Venice had failed. The revolt in Piedmont-Sardinia seemed doomed. So Giuseppe Garibaldi collected over a thousand soldiers together, put them onto leaky ships, and sailed down through the Mediterranean Sea to the south of Italy. He would invade Naples, the southern kingdom of Italy, and make one last attempt to fight for freedom.

Garibaldi landed his ships on the shores of Sicily, the large island at the tip of the Italian peninsula. He marched his men towards Palermo, one of Sicily's most important cities. An army under Austrian command was already on its way over from Naples to fight against him.

But Garibaldi convinced the poor farmers and peasants of Sicily that he would be able to free them from Austrian oppression. In tens, and then in hundreds, the Sicilians flooded into Garibaldi's army. When the two armies met at Palermo, Garibaldi's men won the battle.

Garibaldi then sailed his men over to the shores of Naples. His army had grown to thirty thousand soldiers.

Less than three months after his arrival in the south of Italy, Garibaldi's thirty thousand revolutionaries met the soldiers of Austria and Naples at the Volturno River, in the center of Naples. The Battle of Volturno was the final fight of the Risorgimento—and Garibaldi's army was victorious! When Victor Emmanuel travelled down south to celebrate the triumph, Garibaldi greeted him with the words, "I salute the first king of Italy!"

The following year, 1861, Victor Emmanuel was crowned king of Italy—the first king of the *nation* of Italy. Italy was not a republic, as Mazzini had hoped that it would be. But at last, Italy was *Italian.*

The Taiping Rebellion

In China, a new kind of war had already begun—a war not between countries, but between the rich and poor of the same nation.

China would not be the only country where rich and poor fought. But in China, the war was led by a man who believed that God had ordered him to overthrow the emperor of China.

The emperor belonged to the Qing dynasty, which had ruled in China for more than two hundred years. At first, this family of emperors had tried to be both powerful and virtuous. The early Qing rulers wanted to be just and wise. One of the first Qing emperors had even written out rules that should govern the life of every virtuous man, and had done his best to follow those rules himself.

But as time went on, the Qing emperors had grown less virtuous. By 1850, the royal court was filled with luxury, waste, and corruption. Government officials had begun to take advantage of the poor, and to use tax money to make themselves rich.

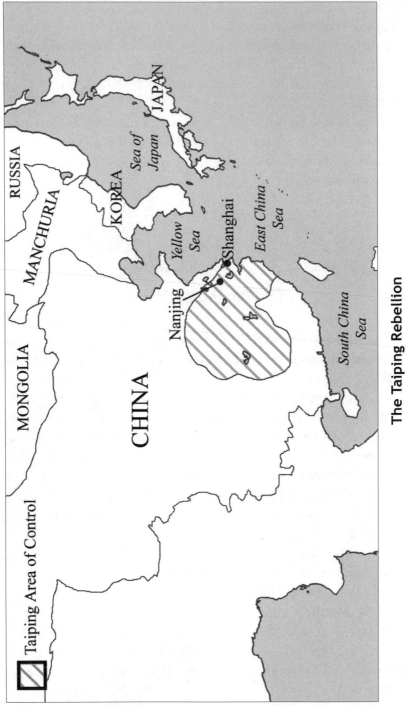

The Taiping Rebellion

Meanwhile, China was growing. Between the year 1700 and the year 1850, the population of China *doubled*—from 150 million to 300 million people! By 1850, all of those extra people were moving away from the crowded cities of China towards the more distant farmland in the north and west. Soon, groups of newcomers to the far areas of China began to quarrel and fight with the people who already lived there. Government officials in these distant parts of China sometimes treated the newcomers harshly, taxing them or driving them away.

And China was growing poorer and poorer. British merchants had brought the drug opium to Chinese ports. "Opium eaters" had beautiful dreams, but they couldn't stop taking opium. Millions of Chinese became addicted. Chinese opium users gave British merchants tremendous amounts of money for opium. But the British didn't spend nearly as much of *their* money on Chinese goods, so more money was leaving China than was coming into it. The country was becoming poorer. Chinese workers could find no work—and often, no food. And taxes were rising.

The poor people of China were desperate, hungry, and hopeless. They were ready to follow anyone who would promise them a better life.

The leader who arose was named Hong Xiuquan.

Hong came from Huaxian, far south of China's two great rivers. He had studied for a long time to take the examination that would allow him to become a government official. As a matter of fact, he studied so hard and so long that he collapsed in exhaustion! While he was unconscious, he had an odd dream. He dreamed that an elderly man with white hair gave him a special sword and ordered him to fight against demons, and that an older brother joined him to fight at his side.

When he woke from his dream, Hong was sure that God had spoken to him in his dream. Hong had learned a little bit about Christianity from Western missionaries in his home town. So he decided that the elderly man in his dream was God the Father, that the older brother was Jesus Christ—and that Hong himself was the younger, Chinese brother of Jesus, called to fight against the evils that made the poor people of China miserable.

Hong began to tell his friends of his new calling. He began to collect a following around him. Soon, he had over two thousand disciples—poor farmers, mineworkers, charcoal burners, ex-soldiers, and peasants. They called themselves the God Worshippers. They gathered together, agreed not to use opium or alcohol, and put all of their belongings into a common treasury.

By 1850, the God Worshippers had grown to a group of almost twenty thousand people. This huge gathering of peasants made the wealthy land owners in the area very nervous! So the land owners joined with soldiers from the Qing dynasty and attacked the God Worshippers.

Hong decided that this attack on his followers simply proved that he was indeed fighting against evil. He announced that he would now call himself the Heavenly King, and that his followers were citizens of the Heavenly Kingdom of Great Peace—in Chinese, the *Taiping Tianguo*.

Hong's followers, now called the Taipings, fought back against their attackers successfully! As a matter of fact, they captured a little, walled city called Yongan, a little to the west of Hong's home town. They made Yongan their military headquarters, organized themselves into a regular army with commanders and soldiers, and got ready for war. Hong told his followers, "Men and women officers must all grasp the sword! Together, rouse your courage; together, slay demons! Golden bricks and golden houses await you. Even the lowest shall wear silks and satins!"

These were wonderful promises for poor peasants to hear. Inspired by Hong's words, the Taipings began to march north towards Nanjing, a large Chinese city far to the northeast. They planned to fight against the corrupt Qing officials, and destroy the government that stole from the poor. To show that they were enemies of the Qing, they grew their hair long instead of wearing the traditional queue (pigtail) of the Qing. People who saw them pass called them the "longhaired rebels."

Probably no one thought that this odd little army would amount to anything. But something amazing happened. It took the Taipings a little less than a year to march to Nanjing. And in that year, over one million Chinese peasants joined them!

As they marched, the growing army of the Taipings attacked and killed unjust landlords and greedy government officials. They burned tax papers and destroyed government offices. "Every time they entered a rich house," wrote one man who saw the Taipings with his own eyes, "they dug into it to find treasure. But they did not take from the peasants. Instead, they gave clothes and other goods that they had taken from the rich to the poor."

Now the Taipings were no longer a little rebel group. They were revolutionaries. They had great ideas as to how China should be run once the Qing were overthrown. They planned to divide the land up evenly, with men and women getting equal shares. Each family would grow crops and keep as much as they needed for themselves. They would put the rest into a public store. In this new country, all men and women would be brothers and sisters. Later, one Taiping leader would even suggest that China hold elections for its leaders, like Western countries.

When the Taipings reached Nanjing, they conquered it and made it their capital. Then they sent out an army to attack Beijing, where the Qing emperor lived. They weren't able to capture Beijing—but the Qing soldiers who poured out to meet them weren't able to retake Nanjing either. The two forces simply went on fighting for years.

By 1860, the Taipings were marching towards Shanghai. For a little while, it seemed that this city, too, might fall to the rebels.

But then the war began to turn against them. Great Britain had signed a treaty with China that would open up more Chinese ports to British merchants, just as soon as the rebellion was put down. So the British began to help the Qing fight back against the Taipings. British steamships helped to move Qing armies up and down the coast. Some British soldiers even joined with the Qing in battle!

By 1864, the Taiping rebellion was doomed. Nanjing was captured. As the Qing army flooded into the city, Hong Xiuquan killed himself. As many as thirty million Chinese had died during the Taiping Rebellion.

But once the revolt was over, the advisors who surrounded the Qing emperor did make some changes. The Chinese government would now help peasants who had to move to new areas by giving them tools and seeds, and helping them to build irrigation systems. Taxes were lowered. Corrupt officials were removed from power.

The Qing dynasty had barely survived the rebellion. But thanks to these reforms, the Qing would sit on the Chinese throne just a little bit longer.

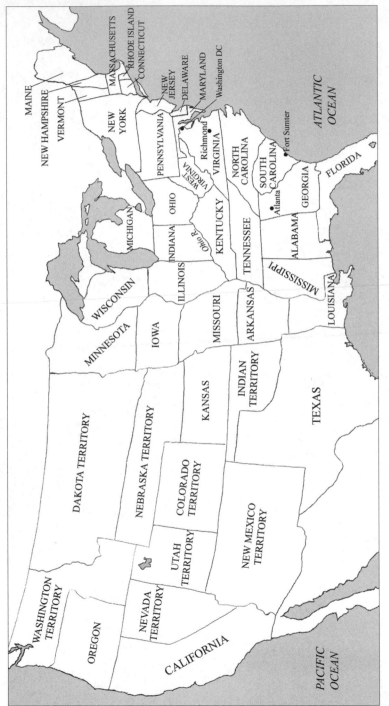

America in 1862, During the Civil War

Chapter Five
The American Civil War

South Against North

On a cold April night in 1861, only a month after Victor Emmanuel was crowned king of Italy, the president of the United States sat in the White House, reading the handwritten page that lay before him. *I, Abraham Lincoln, president of the United States ... hereby do call forth, the militia of the several States of the Union ... seventy-five thousand ...*

He sighed, rubbing a weary hand across his face. The next morning, this proclamation would be published in newspapers across the country. And seventy-five thousand American men would pick up guns and bayonets, and set out to fight against their neighbors.

But Abraham Lincoln felt that he had no choice.

Two months earlier, seven of the United States—South Carolina, Mississippi, Florida, Alabama, Georgia, Louisiana, and Texas—had announced that they would no longer belong to the United States. Instead, they would form their own country, the Confederate States of America.

The Confederate States demanded that United States soldiers who were stationed at Fort Sumter, a military base in South Carolina, leave and turn the fort over to Confederate soldiers. But the United States refused to give up Fort Sumter.

Two days earlier, in the still dark just before sunrise, Confederate soldiers had begun to fire round after round of cannonballs and shot at the walls of Fort Sumter. After a full two days of firing, the besieged U.S. commander inside the fort had finally hauled down the American flag. Now, the flag of the Confederate States flew over Fort Sumter's walls.

Abraham Lincoln had to decide how the United States would respond. He chose to fight. The United States would use force to bring the seven rebel states back into the U.S.

The next morning, Lincoln published his proclamation. People all over the United States gathered together, cheering, making speeches, and singing *The Star-Spangled Banner*. But not every state was pleased that Lincoln was going to war. Two days later, Virginia joined the Confederate States. A month later, three more states—Arkansas, Tennessee, and North Carolina—left the United States for the Confederacy as well. And along the border between North and South, the states of Kentucky, Missouri, West Virginia, Maryland, and Delaware sent a message to the president. They would not join the Confederacy, but they refused to fight for the U.S. The governor of Missouri told Lincoln that the war against the South was "illegal, unconstitutional … inhuman and diabolical." And the governor of Kentucky snapped, "Kentucky will furnish no troops for the wicked purpose of subduing her sister Southern States."

The United States was less than a hundred years old—and already the country had broken apart into civil war.

Lincoln had been elected president the year before, in 1860. And in the United States of 1860, every state was allowed to decide for itself whether or not some people could hold others as slaves. Down in southern states such as South Carolina and Georgia, slavery was legal. Farmers made their living by growing huge fields of tobacco and cotton. And tobacco and cotton needed plenty of hands to weed, tend, and pick them. Farmers could only grow these crops if they had plenty of cheap help. Without slaves, the farms of the South would collapse.

In the northern states, slavery was illegal. But states such as New York, Pennsylvania, and Massachusetts didn't have huge fields of crops that needed tending. They had factories, mills, and ironworks instead. "It's easy for northerners to say that slavery should be against the law," Southerners complained. "The north doesn't need slaves to survive!"

For decades, southern and northern states argued about slavery. But the argument didn't turn into war until new states began to join the U.S.A. The southern states wanted slavery to be legal in these new states, so that the northern states would be outnumbered. And the northern states wanted slavery to be *illegal* in the new states, so that slave-holding states wouldn't overwhelm the rest of the U.S.

Even before he became president, Abraham Lincoln was firmly on the side of the north. When he was asked why he didn't want new states to have slaves, Lincoln retorted, "If there was a bed newly made up, to which the children were to be taken, and it was proposed to take a batch of young snakes and put them there with them, I take it no man would say there was any question how I ought to decide." Lincoln believed that slavery was as poisonous as a nest of snakes.

So as soon as Lincoln became president, the slave-holding states of the South began to get ready to leave the United States. When they finally left, or *seceded*, Lincoln declared war.

At first, both Lincoln and his generals thought that the war would be short. Government officials and their wives even went to the earliest battles of the war to watch, as though they were seeing a play. They were sure that the play would end with the blue-coated United States soldiers (called *Union soldiers* because they were fighting to keep the states *unified*) crushing the gray-uniformed Confederates.

But in just months, Lincoln realized that the war would not be won so easily. He tried inviting Giuseppe Garibaldi over from Italy to lead his army; after all, Garibaldi had just won an enormous victory against a fierce enemy! But Garibaldi decided to stay in Italy. Eventually, Ulysses S. Grant became Lincoln's general instead.

In the South, the Virginia general Robert E. Lee led the Confederate soldiers into battle. Robert E. Lee didn't approve of slavery, but when Virginia seceded, he had chosen to be loyal to his home state.

A year after the Civil War began, Abraham Lincoln announced that all slaves in the Confederacy would be declared free on January 1, 1863. This announcement was known as the "Emancipation Proclamation." Of course, Lincoln had no power in the Confederacy—so his proclamation didn't actually change anything for the slaves in the South. But by making this proclamation, Lincoln had announced to the whole world that the Civil War was no longer about keeping the United States together. Now, the war was being fought to end slavery.

Abraham Lincoln, sixteenth president of the United States

Lincoln needed to assure the people of the U.S. that the war was important—because hundreds of thousands of men were suffering and dying. In the Battle of Gettysburg, in 1863, over fifty thousand men were wounded and killed in just three days of fighting. Hundreds of towns and cities were burned and destroyed, including the cities of Richmond, Virginia and Atlanta, Georgia.

On April 9, 1865, Robert E. Lee realized that his Confederate army was out of food and too weak to fight on. He agreed to surrender to Ulysses S. Grant in the little Virginia town of Appomattox. After four years of fighting, the war was over.

The Confederacy fell apart. The southern states were forced to rejoin the Union, without their slaves. But over five hundred thousand men had been killed—more than in any other war the United States has ever fought, even in the twentieth century. In the South, a whole generation had been wiped out.

The Civil War had saved the Union, but it had also changed the United States forever.

After the Civil War

Just days after Robert E. Lee surrendered his forces to Ulysses S. Grant, Abraham Lincoln woke up late at night, gasping with fear. He sat up and looked around him. He was in his bedroom at the White House. The nightmare he'd woken from was just a dream. It wasn't real.

But instead of feeling relief, Abraham Lincoln was haunted by dread. The dream had been so vivid! He had been wandering through the White House. Every room was empty; every hall was deserted. But he could hear wails and groans. "The silence was broken by … pitiful sobbing," Lincoln told his wife, when she asked him why he was frightened. "But the mourners were invisible. I went from room to room; no living person was in sight, but the same mournful sounds of distress met me as I passed along."

Finally, Lincoln dreamed that he arrived at the East Room of the White House. There he saw a coffin, resting on a stand, guarded by soldiers. But the face of the man who lay in the coffin was covered.

"Who is dead?" Lincoln asked. The nearest soldier answered "The president. He was killed by an assassin." The crowd all around the coffin raised their voices in weeping. And then Lincoln woke up. "I slept no more that night," he told a friend, the next day. "Although it was only a dream, I have been strangely annoyed by it ever since."

But Lincoln tried to shake the dream away. Only a few days later, on April 14th, Lincoln spent the day meeting with his advisors, planning out how the defeated Confederate states should be brought back into the Union. It was Good Friday (the Friday just before Easter on the Christian calendar), and that same night he and his wife were supposed to go out and see a play.

Lincoln didn't want to go. He was still disturbed by his dream, and his day of dealing with war matters had made him both weary and mournful. But people in Washington were celebrating the end of the war, and the newspapers had already announced that Lincoln would be at the play. The rest of the audience was looking forward to sharing the theater with the president.

So Lincoln decided to go. He and his wife rode a carriage through the dim, cool night to Ford's Theatre. They arrived just before the play began, around nine o'clock in the evening, and walked to their box—a special private balcony where Lincoln could sit in a rocking chair and watch the play in comfort.

A police officer named John Parker had been assigned to stand at the door that led from the hallway into Lincoln's box. He was supposed to keep anyone from coming through. But after half an hour or so, Parker got so interested in the play that he left his post, and wandered down to the main floor and sat with the audience! Abraham Lincoln's box was unguarded.

Outside of it hid a man who hated Lincoln and the United States.

He was an actor named John Wilkes Booth. Although he had been born in Maryland, he thought of himself as a Southerner. Instead of fighting in the Civil War, he had gone on acting in plays. He felt guilty because he had not defended the South. So now he had formed a plan: He would redeem himself by fighting the greatest fight of all—against Lincoln, the enemy of the southern states.

Now, John Wilkes Booth crashed through the door of Lincoln's box and fired a pistol directly at the president. Lincoln slumped down in his chair. Booth leaped up onto the side of the box, ready to jump down onto the stage below. He planned to dash across the stage and out the side door of the theatre. In the alley outside the door, he had left a horse, saddled and ready to ride away.

But a Union flag hung on the balcony's side. Booth's heel caught it. He twisted in the air and broke his leg as he landed.

Dragging his leg behind him, he limped from the stage and out the door and clambered onto his horse. He rode south into Virginia, expecting to be welcomed as a hero by Virginians. But although he stopped at several farms, the owners wanted nothing to do with him. Booth rode deeper and deeper into the Virginia countryside, his leg aching with each jolt of his horse's hooves.

Back at the theater, a doctor was trying to revive Lincoln. But it was too late. Lincoln was still breathing, but he was unconscious. Early the next morning, he died without ever awakening again. His body was laid out in the East Room, where soldiers guarded it and crowds came to weep, just as in his dream.

Twelve days later, Union soldiers who had been searching the countryside for Booth finally found him. He was hiding in a barn in Virginia, on a farm near the Rappahanock River. The soldiers set the barn on fire to drive him out, and shot him as he came to the front door.

On the day he was shot, Lincoln had told another government official, "If we are wise and discreet we shall reanimate the States and get their governments in successful operation, with order prevailing and the Union re-established. ... I hope there will be no persecution, no bloody work after the war is over. ... Enough lives have been sacrificed."

But although the war was over, it would be many years before the United States was healthy again. Lincoln's assassination showed just how much hatred remained in the country. Many Southerners still hated the northern states. And even worse, many whites still hated blacks.

In December of 1865, eight months after Lincoln's death, the United States passed the Thirteenth Amendment to the Constitution. This meant that the Constitution of the United States now included these words: "Neither slavery nor involuntary servitude, except as a punishment for crime whereof the party shall have been duly convicted, shall exist within the United States, or any place subject to their jurisdiction." In other words, no one could be held prisoner and forced to work unless he had been convicted of a crime and sent to jail. And the states could no longer decide for themselves whether or not slavery should be legal. It was illegal in every state of the Union!

The years after the Civil War were called a time of "Reconstruction" for the southern United States. But not very much "rebuilding" went on. Although the Constitution said that slaves were to be freed, the government of the United States did not help these slaves to get any land where they could live. Nor did the slaves win any payment for the years they had spent working for their masters. Instead, the free blacks of the South, penniless, had to try to earn their own living, usually on farms owned by white farmers—farmers who were bitter that the United States had taken away their slaves. These free blacks were often treated just as badly as they had been during slavery.

Slavery had ended. But it would be many more years before African-Americans were given all of the freedoms and privileges of whites.

The War of the Triple Alliance

Chapter Six
Two Tries For Freedom

Paraguay and the Triple Alliance

The Civil War had just ended in North America. But in South America, an equally bloody war was about to begin.

In 1865, Francisco Solano López had just come to power in Paraguay. Paraguay was a little country in the center of South America, sandwiched between the much larger countries of Argentina and Brazil. López had inherited his power from his father, Carlos Antonio López. Carlos Antonio had worked hard to make Paraguay a strong country; he had built up the army and prepared his oldest son, Francisco Solano, to inherit his power. But he spoiled Francisco, treating him like a hero when he was still a teenager, and even making him a general when he was only eighteen years old.

In 1853, when Francisco was twenty-seven, his father sent him to France to buy weapons for Paraguay's army. Francisco looked around him at the sprawling French Empire and thought, "This is the kind of empire I, too, would like to rule!"

Carlos Antonio López warned his son, "We have a strong army now. But when you become ruler, try not to fight. Instead, try to negotiate with the countries around you. Be diplomatic!" But when his father died in 1862, Francisco Solano López set out to make Paraguay one of the most influential countries in Latin America—even if that meant taking on the armies of Argentina and Brazil.

López had a difficult task. He had to fight not only with Argentina and Brazil, but also with those who disagreed with him within his own country. Like most of the countries of Latin America, Paraguay was populated by three different groups of people: descendents of slaves, native South American Indians, and *creoles*. Creoles were Spanish colonists who had been born *in* South America, rather than in Spain. Fifty years before López came to power in Paraguay, the creoles of South America had helped lead their colonies to independence, freeing them from Spanish and Portuguese rule. By 1830, the Spanish and Portuguese colonies had become independent countries: Brazil, in the center, was one of the largest. Argentina stretched down almost to the tip of the continent. To the west lay Chile and Peru, and to the north a handful of smaller states.

Once the colonies had become countries, the creoles took power. The other people of Latin America—the native South Americans, and descendents of African slaves who had been brought to South America by the Europeans—were poor and often badly treated. They resented their creole overlords. Among themselves, the creoles fought with each other to become dictators of their own countries. And the South American countries fought with each other as well. As a matter of fact, the Italian revolutionary Giuseppe Garibaldi had helped the little country of Uruguay, sandwiched between Brazil and Argentina, to fight against an Argentinian dictator who wanted to control it.

Only two years after Francisco Solano López came to power in Paraguay, Uruguay was once again the center of trouble. Two politicians were vying for control of Uruguay. Brazil wanted one of the politicians, a soldier named General Flores, to win the struggle, because he would then become an ally and friend of Brazil. So the Brazilian army helped Flores gain power in Uruguay.

At this, López grew indignant. Like Uruguay, Paraguay was sandwiched between the larger countries of Brazil and Argentina. López didn't want Brazil to decide the fate of the smaller countries of South America! He asked Argentina to join with him in a fight against Brazil. When Argentina refused, López turned to his army. In 1865, he marched fifty thousand soldiers down the Paraguay River into Argentina.

War had begun. Brazil, Argentina, and Uruguay—now under the control of General Flores, who owed both his power and his loyalty to Brazil—united against Paraguay. This war became known as the War of the Triple Alliance.

López, outnumbered by the three hostile armies, intended to get control of the rivers that led into Argentina and Brazil so that he could sail down and attack these countries. So he began to plan a sea battle to take control of an important river port held by Brazil. This was a bold move. Brazil had thirty-three steamships and twelve sailing ships. López had only two gunboats and fifteen other small boats. But he knew that Brazil's navy had been designed to sail on the ocean off Brazil's coast, not on the river. The steamships ran on propellers and needed deep water. López hoped to surprise Brazil's army at low tide, when the water would be shallow and the huge Brazilian fleet would be less able to maneuver.

He collected his little fleet together, along with six barges loaded with cannon that he planned to tow into the battle. At nine o'clock, on the morning of June 11, 1865, the Paraguayan navy attacked. The little Paraguayan ships zipped in and out of the narrow river channels, avoiding the guns of the larger, slower Brazilian ships.

But as the battle wore on, the Brazilian cannon began to find their mark. A Paraguayan ship sank into the river mud. Cannonballs smashed the boilers of one of the steamships. Another boat was rammed by an iron-clad Brazilian ship.

Four hours after it began, the battle ended. The Paraguayan fleet had been all but destroyed. The commander of the Paraguayan fleet had been wounded, and died a few days later. Brazil blocked up the rivers that led into Paraguay. Now, López could not get out of his country by water. He was landlocked.

In the next year of fighting, Francisco Solano López lost almost twenty thousand of his men. A deadly disease called cholera was spreading among them, killing more. He was starting to run out of guns, food, and medicine. And the Triple Alliance was better armed than the Paraguayan soldiers; López's army only had old-fashioned flintlock muskets, which didn't always fire, but the Triple Alliance army was using the new Enfield rifles, just like the British army in India.

Soon, López had been pushed back into his own country. Then, the Triple Alliance invaded. Now, López was fighting to defend his own land! His army made a stand at Humaitá, a fortress on the southern tip of Paraguay. For three years, the Paraguayan army resisted the besieging Triple Alliance. But in 1868, they were finally forced to surrender the fortress. They retreated back north, towards the capital city of Asunción. The Brazilian and Argentinian forces marched into Paraguay. Asunción fell to the Triple Alliance in 1869.

Still, López refused to give up. He collected a new army and went on fighting. Many people thought that he had now grown insane. He suspected his officers, his army, and even his family of treason. He ordered thousands of Paraguayans arrested and put to death—including many of his bravest officers, his own sisters' husbands, and even both of his brothers!

A year later, on March 1, 1870, López led the ragged remnants of his army out to face a Brazilian attack in Cerro Corá, far up in the north of his country. He was killed in the attack. Finally, the war was over. Brazil and Argentina each took a piece of Paraguay's land; Brazilian soldiers occupied the rest of Paraguay.

Hundreds of thousands of men had died. Brazil alone had lost one hundred thousand soldiers, with another sixty-five thousand injured. Half of the population of Paraguay had died: killed in battle, executed by López, or wiped out by hunger and disease. Farmland had been destroyed as the armies had stormed through Paraguay. Starvation loomed. Paraguay, once strong, had become powerless.

Even today, Paraguayans disagree about López. Was he a patriot, fighting for the freedom of his country against the schemes of Argentina and Brazil? Or was he an insane dictator—as one of his own officers called him, a "monster without parallel"?

The Dominion of Canada

Far to the north of South America, another country reached for independence.

Canada became free in 1867, just two years after the end of the American Civil War. But the story of Canada's independence actually begins three hundred years earlier, when French and English colonists both settled in the northern reaches of North America. As the settlements grew, France and Britain struggled over who would control them. In 1763, after bitter fighting, the French surrendered their colonies to British rule.

The British divided their new Canadian colony into two parts. The French-speaking colonists were in Lower Canada, today called Quebec; the English-speaking colonists lived in Upper Canada, later known as Ontario. Both parts of Canada were governed by English-speaking officials of Great Britain. But the French Canadians kept their language and their French customs, even under British rule.

When war between Great Britain and the United States broke out in 1812, neither Upper nor Lower Canada joined in the fight. Most Canadians *wanted* to remain part of Great Britain.

But after the War of 1812 ended, more and more Canadians began to complain that Great Britain was not giving them the chance to govern themselves.

These complaints were the loudest in Lower Canada. French Canadians had their own elected group of leaders, the Assembly of Lower Canada. But by law, the English governor of Lower Canada had the final word in all matters of law. And he ignored all of the Assembly's suggestions! A tall, handsome, dark-haired Frenchman named Louis Joseph Papineau

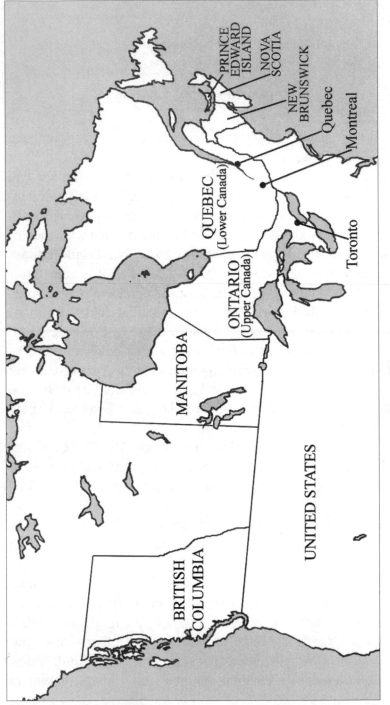

The Dominion of Canada

believed that the governor should be forced, by law, to pay attention to the elected Assembly. The French Canadians who agreed with him formed into a group called the Patriotes.

Papineau travelled through Lower Canada, exhorting French Canadians to protest the power of the English governor. His speeches worked a little too well. By 1837 the Patriotes had whipped up so much indignation that masses of French Canadians were planning on arming themselves and rebelling, just as the Americans had done. Papineau went through the countryside again—but this time, he was pleading with French Canadians to stop and think before they began to fight.

His pleas didn't work. French Canadians under the leadership of the Patriotes set up their headquarters in a stone-walled village called St. Denis, on the banks of the Richelieu River. On November 23, 1837, British soldiers marched down from Montreal, intending to invade St. Denis and arrest the Patriote leaders. But after less than a day of fighting, the Patriotes had driven the attackers away.

The British weren't about to give up so easily. More soldiers came flooding down from Montreal, poured over the walls of St. Denis, and burned the village down.

Immediately, a short, red-headed Canadian in Upper Canada saw his chance.

William Lyon Mackenzie, the son of a Scottish family, had been loudly complaining for years that the governor of Upper Canada didn't listen to the Assembly of Upper Canada—any more than the Lower Canada governor listened to the Assembly of *Lower* Canada. Now, Mackenzie realized that all of the soldiers stationed in Upper Canada had gone down to fight in Lower Canada. It was the perfect time for Upper Canadians to rebel!

Mackenzie managed to gather a little crowd of discontented Upper Canadians around him. The tiny army set off to attack Toronto. But most Upper Canadians didn't want to fight a war against the British. As Mackenzie's group of rebels approached Toronto, thousands of Upper Canadians loyal to Great Britain gathered against them.

The "army" fell apart immediately. William Mackenzie ran away. He knew that he would be arrested as soon as the British could find him, so he dressed his short body in skirts and women's shawls and sneaked across the border into the United States. Down in Lower Canada, the tall, aristocratic Papineau also fled across the border into the United States.

Britain had kept hold of its Canadian colonies. But the rebellion had frightened British officials. They sent a nobleman named the Earl of Durham to go to Canada and find out how to prevent another revolt. When the Earl of Durham returned from Canada, he reported that the Canadians would probably never rebel again—as long as the Assemblies were given the power to govern their own country.

So the British decided to rearrange the government of Canada. Lower and Upper Canada would become one colony with one British governor. Each one of the separate areas, or "provinces," in Canada would also have its own leader—a "lieutenant-governor" who would help the British governor. Each province would also have its own elected Assembly. All of the provinces together would send elected representatives to a bigger Assembly—the Assembly of the United Canadas.

The British had given the Canadians plenty of elected Assemblies. But none of the Assemblies had the power to overrule either the governor of all Canada, or the lieutenant-governors of the provinces. So Canadians kept on writing, speaking, and arguing about their right to govern themselves.

Finally, the lieutenant-governor of the province of Nova Scotia agreed to let the Assembly of Nova Scotia choose all of his advisors. These advisors would tell him how to govern. Now the Assembly of Nova Scotia, not the governor, held the greatest power in the province.

Before too long, the governor of Canada and the Assembly of the United Canadas followed the same procedure. Over time, the elected Assemblies had managed to gain the power to govern Canada.

By the 1860s, the Canadian provinces were talking about joining together into a "federation." This federation would still be loyal to Great Britain, but it would have its own constitution, its own Canadian House of Commons, and its own Canadian Senate.

Canadians had good reasons for wanting a federation. Many Canadians were afraid that the western territories of Canada—the areas not yet formed into provinces—would be taken by the United States, unless Canadians could join together and claim those territories for a strong, united Canada. Most Canadians didn't want to belong to the United States, especially since the horrible Civil War had just ended. One nineteenth-century poster, urging Canadians to join together in a federation, had a British flag on one side with the words, "Loyalty to Great Britain. Protection … !" On the other side, these words were written across a faded American flag: "Yankee Grit … Annexation! Ruin!" (*Annexation* meant that the United States would take Canadian territories for its own.)

The provinces argued and argued about forming a federation. Smaller provinces, like Prince Edward Island, were afraid that a federation would give the larger provinces too much power. But finally Quebec, Ontario, Nova Scotia, and New Brunswick decided to join together. A new law, called the British North America Act, formed these four provinces into a new country called the Dominion of Canada. The British North American Act also explained how the western territories of Canada could be formed into provinces, and then drawn into the Dominion of Canada.

The Act took effect on Monday, July 1, 1867. Cannons and fireworks were shot off. Canadians threw parties all over the new Dominion of Canada. Parades and speeches celebrated the birth of this new country.

In the next three years, three more provinces decided to join the Dominion of Canada: Manitoba, British Columbia, and Prince Edward Island. By 1900, the Dominion of Canada stretched all the way to the west coast of North America. The western territories of Canada would never belong to the United States.

Victoria, the Queen of England, was still the queen of Canada. But just as England was really governed not by Victoria but by the British Parliament, so Canada would now be governed by its own House of Commons and Senate. Canada wasn't free from Great Britain—but it was independent.

France—Republic and Empire

Chapter Seven
Two Empires, Three Republics, and One Kingdom

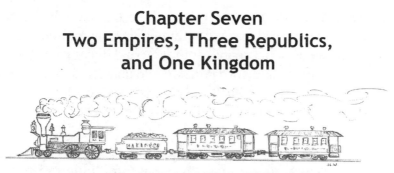

Two Empires and Three Republics

Like Great Britain, France was an empire that ruled colonies across the world. But France had not always been an empire. As a matter of fact, by the year 1871, France had been a monarchy once, an empire twice, and a republic three different times! And the two empires and three republics had all come within a hundred years of each other.

Before we visit the French Empire, let's look back at this unstable history. Until the year 1789, France was a monarchy, governed by kings who belonged to the royal Bourbon family—and who claimed that God gave them the right to rule exactly as they pleased. But the French wanted to be a republic, like the brand-new United States of America. They wanted to elect their own leaders, not submit to the tyranny of kings.

So in 1789, the French revolted. During the French Revolution, the king was executed (along with thousands of aristocrats), and France became a republic for the first time. But the first French Republic was filled with bloodshed, unhappiness, and unrest. When an army general named Napoleon Bonaparte seized control of the government and had himself crowned Emperor, the First Republic of France ended. But many French were simply grateful that someone was willing to bring order to the chaos of France! Now Napoleon had become Emperor Napoleon I, and the First French Empire had began.

After Napoleon, two kings from the Bourbon family reclaimed the throne of France and continued to rule over the

First French Empire. But the second of these kings, Charles X, returned to the old bad ways of ruling France. He refused to listen to the wishes of the people of France, and did as he pleased. He even told newspapers what they could and couldn't publish.

Once again, the French revolted! This revolution was known as the Three Glorious Days, or *Les Trois Glorieuses*, because it only lasted from July 27 to July 29, 1830. In Paris, indignant Frenchmen turned over wagons and carts in the streets and piled paving stones, small trees, and iron railings ripped from the fronts of houses over them to make huge barricades. They hid behind these barricades, shooting at the French army, which was trying to clear the barricades away and arrest the rebels. Charles X was forced to flee to England!

But the revolutionaries disagreed about who should take Charles' place. Many Frenchmen, like the Marquis de Lafayette, wanted France to be a republic again. Lafayette had helped the American colonists fight for their own independence from the British king. Now he wanted to see France free from kings as well.

But another, stronger group of Frenchmen wanted France to become a *constitutional monarchy*, like Great Britain. France would still have a king, but this king would have to obey a written set of laws, instead of doing whatever he pleased.

Finally Lafayette decided to help end the revolution by agreeing to a constitutional monarchy. He went before his followers, wearing the flag of the French kings around his shoulders like a shawl, and convinced them to join with the other revolutionaries to put a king back on the French throne.

So one of the republican leaders, Louis-Philippe, became the new king of France. Louis-Philippe wasn't supposed to be an absolute ruler, like the Bourbon kings. Instead, he was called the "Citizen King," because he was supposed to act only by the wishes of the people. "He reigns," one of his supporters explained, "but he does not govern."

The First Empire still existed, but now Louis-Philippe, the Citizen King, was at its head. But all the time that Louis-Philippe reigned, the French revolutionaries who had wanted a republic kept on complaining, writing, and speaking about the dangers of a king. Two revolutionaries even tried to assassinate him by planting a gunpowder bomb on the street where an official parade was due to pass by. When the bomb exploded, the courtiers and soldiers around it were killed—but Louis-Philippe survived.

After eighteen years of Louis-Philippe's reign, his enemies planned a huge gathering in Paris. They hoped that the crowd would decide to throw the Citizen King out, and bring a republic back to France. When Louis-Philippe saw the enormous mass gathering, he ordered that the gathering be cancelled and sent the French army out to disperse the meeting.

The crowd that had gathered was furious! Once more, their king was trying to use force against them, in order to get his own way. They stormed the palace gates and broke in, flooding through halls, smashing royal dishes, pulling all of the gold coating off the furniture, and taking turns sitting on the royal throne. Louis-Philippe jumped into a horse-drawn carriage and drove out of Paris. When he was stopped, he announced that his name was Mr. Smith. He got out of the city, and, like Charles X before him, sailed for England.

The year was 1848. The Citizen King was gone, and so was the First Empire. Now the Second Republic would begin.

The leaders of the Second Republic started out by writing a new constitution—one that looked very much like the American constitution. It said that every man in France would be allowed to vote for a president, and also for representatives who would gather together in an assembly and make laws. The president would only be able to govern for four years. That way, no one man could gain too much power in France.

But when the first elections for president were held, something very alarming happened. The winner of the election turned out to be Louis-Napoleon Bonaparte, the nephew of the first French emperor, Napoleon himself!

Was the Emperor Napoleon's nephew the right man to be president of a French republic? Many people were skeptical—but Louis-Napoleon had gotten millions more votes than any other candidate. So he was sworn in as president of the Second French Republic.

But Louis-Napoleon couldn't convince the elected assembly of France to do what he wanted. The assembly wouldn't give him all the money he wanted. And they wouldn't agree to let him run for president a second time.

On December 2, 1851, Louis-Napoleon made his move. He arrested seventy French leaders who had disagreed with his plans. He then announced that France had a new constitution (which he had helped write). This constitution took power away from the assembly, gave it to the president, and made Louis-Napoleon president for ten more years. When the people of Paris objected, Louis-Napoleon brought out the army and arrested thousands and thousands of protestors. A year later, he had himself declared Napoleon III, the Emperor of France.

The Second Republic had lasted only five years. Now the Second Empire had begun.

Napoleon III was not a royal-looking man. Like his famous uncle, he was very short; his beautiful wife Eugenie was much taller than he was. He wore huge, long mustaches, and a tiny little chin beard called an "imperial." But despite his looks, Napoleon III was determined to behave like an emperor. He travelled to Great Britain and promised Queen Victoria that he would help the British fight the Crimean War against Russia. And after France and England triumphed in the Crimea, Napoleon III declared war on Prussia, the country just to his east.

Napoleon had worked hard to make the French army strong—but he didn't realize how quickly the Prussians would react to his declaration of war. Prussian armies stormed into France even before the French army could organize itself for battle. Napoleon himself had been ill with painful stones (calcium deposits) in his kidneys and bladder. Aching and sore, he rode out to the east, towards the approaching Prussian army.

Napoleon III and his soldiers met the Prussians in the city of Sedan, in northeast France, on September 1. Napoleon soon realized that his army was outmatched. He threw himself into the center of the fighting, hoping to be killed in battle. But on September 2, he was taken prisoner along with almost one hundred thousand of his soldiers.

Messengers quickly took the news to Paris. On September 4, the people of Paris heard that their emperor had been captured. They celebrated! Finally, France could be a republic again. The Second Empire had ended, and the Third Republic could begin.

The leaders of the Third Republic made peace with Prussia, which released the sick, powerless Napoleon III. He, too, went to live in England. He hoped that he might be able to collect an army, land on the shores of France, and reclaim his throne.

But instead he died, old and sick, without ever returning to France. From 1870 on, France remained a republic. Napoleon III was the very last emperor of France.

The Second Reich

Just as France was becoming a republic, Prussia was becoming a kingdom.

Prussia was a German state—but not part of "Germany." In 1870 there was no such country as "Germany." Instead, thirty-eight different German-speaking states lay across the land east of France. These states were joined together into a loose group called a *confederation*.

You've already heard the word "confederation." Remember, in the American Civil War, the Southern states left the Union to form a *confederacy*. In a confederacy, the states agree

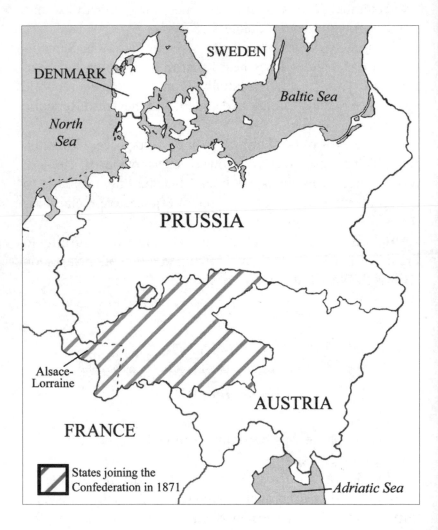

The Second Reich

together to elect officials who will be in charge of dealing with foreign countries and other matters that affect all of the states. But each state stays independent, with its own government and its own identity.

Prussia belonged to the German Confederation. It was just one German state among many. But in 1847, a square-shouldered man with a determined jaw was elected to the Prussian assembly. His name was Otto von Bismarck, and he was determined to make Prussia the ruling state of the confederation.

Otto von Bismarck served in the Prussian government for fifteen years. For those fifteen years, he nursed his wish to make Prussia great. He wanted the German confederation to become a single German country, led by a powerful Prussian king and protected by an invincible Prussian army.

But the king of Prussia was far from strong. As a matter of fact, he had had a stroke—and could no longer speak or see.

In 1861 the sick king died. His brother Wilhelm became king, or *kaiser*, in his place. Wilhelm appointed Otto von Bismarck to be his chancellor (prime minister). Now that he was chancellor, Bismarck set about making Prussia the leader of the German states. If this meant war, Prussia would fight! In a stirring speech to the Prussian assembly, Bismarck announced that Prussia would become the strongest of the German states not "by speeches and majority votes, but by blood and iron." This speech earned Bismarck the nickname of the "Iron Chancellor."

Soon it became clear that the Iron Chancellor had more power than the king of Prussia. Wilhelm was a polite, sensible man, a good soldier, and a careful king. But he was not as bold as Bismarck. More than once, when the king and the chancellor disagreed, Bismarck threatened to quit—and Wilhelm quickly agreed to follow Bismarck's wishes. Bismarck's leadership became known as the "chancellor dictatorship."

Under Bismarck's "dictatorship," Prussia fought two wars before turning to attack France. In 1864, Prussia joined with the large German state of Austria and attacked Denmark, capturing the southern part of Denmark's kingdom. Prussia then insisted on controlling this newly captured land. When Austria objected, Prussia turned and attacked Austria as well!

The Prussian army was victorious. At the end of the short, violent war, Bismarck announced that Prussia would now form a *new* confederation of German states—a North German Confederation that *didn't* include the state of Austria. Prussia wanted no other state competing to lead the Confederation.

Then Prussia turned to confront Napoleon III and France. When Napoleon III was forced to surrender, Prussia claimed the northeast corner of France, an area called Alsace-Lorraine, as its own. And four more German kingdoms offered to join the triumphant Prussia in the North German Confederation.

In 1871, the year after the war with France, Otto von Bismarck convinced the other German states in the confederation to declare Wilhelm of Prussia the "German Emperor." The states agreed—with some reluctance. They wouldn't allow Wilhelm to call himself the "Emperor of Germany," because none of the German states wanted to belong to a country called "Germany." Each state wanted to keep its own princes, dukes, and assemblies. But they allowed Wilhelm to take the title "German Emperor"—which meant that he was the most important of all other German rulers. And the Confederation became known as a kingdom, or Reich.

At last, Prussia was the strongest state in a German kingdom. This kingdom was known as the "Second Reich." Germans liked to think that they were the heirs of the Holy Roman Empire, which they called the "First Reich." Of course, the Holy Roman Empire had not been a Prussian-led kingdom. But by claiming that their new German kingdom was a successor to the Holy Roman Empire, Bismarck and the Prussians implied that Wilhelm was the successor to the Holy Roman Emperor!

But Otto von Bismarck, not Wilhelm, was the most powerful man in the Second Reich. Wilhelm made Bismarck the royal chancellor, which meant that Bismarck appointed government officials and decided how the Second Reich would act towards the other countries in Europe. And the Reich's actions were most often warlike. "Better pointed bullets than pointed speeches," Bismarck once remarked.

Bismarck's dedication to war was very Prussian. Other German states were more interested in art, or in science, or in learning. But the noblemen of Prussia had always been more interested in war. As a matter of fact, Prussia spent five-sixths of its money on its army!

The whole kingdom of Germany was becoming more and more Prussian. Wilhelm's son Friedrich (who happened to be married to Queen Victoria's oldest daughter) was disturbed by the overwhelming Prussian influence on the German states. He wrote in his diary:

> In this nation of thinkers and philosophers, poets and artists, idealists and enthusiasts, the world will recognize nothing but a people of conquerors and destroyers. ... [The Germans are] the foremost people of the world in civilization, yet at the moment ... we are neither loved nor respected, but only feared. We are deemed capable of every wickedness, and the distrust felt for us grows ever more and more pronounced. ... Bismarck has made us great and powerful, but he has robbed us of our friends, the sympathies of the world, and our conscience.[1]

If Friedrich had inherited the German throne after his father, perhaps the German Empire would have become a little less "Prussian." But as his father grew older, Friedrich began to grow ill. He had cancer, but he was never properly treated. When Wilhelm died, Friedrich became emperor. He was emperor for less than a hundred days before he too died.

His son, Wilhelm II, became the third German emperor. Wilhelm II was a violent, quarrelsome, quick-tempered bully. He wanted the Second Reich to conquer other lands, to claim colonies around the world, and to have a navy even larger than

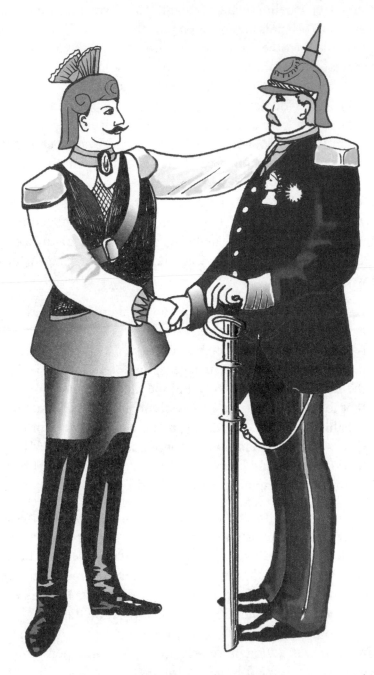

Two years after inheriting the throne,
Wilhelm II (left) forced Bismarck (right) to resign.

Great Britain's huge and powerful fleet. Wilhelm II soon decided that even Bismarck was too cautious and careful. Two years after inheriting the throne, Wilhelm II forced Bismarck to resign.

The Second Reich was set on a path of war and destruction. But it would follow this path without the man who had helped to make it into a kingdom. Bismarck went to live in a small German town, where he spent his time writing out his memories of his years of service to Prussia. He died eight years later, before he could see the collapse of the Second Reich—a collapse that would shake the whole world.

---

1. Friedrich II of Prussia's diary, reprinted and translated in *The Age of Bismarck: Documents and Interpretations*, ed. Theodore Hamerow (HarperCollins, 1973).

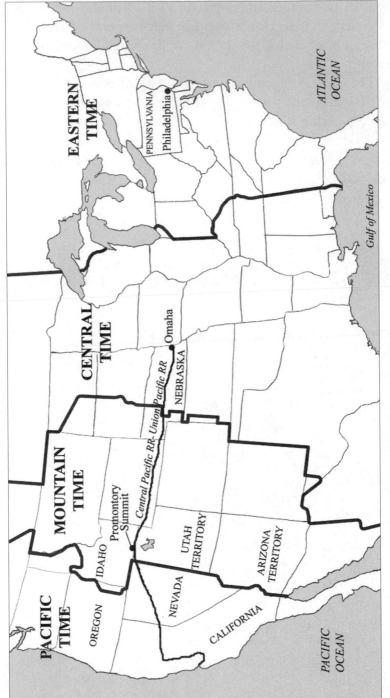

Railroads and Time Zones

Chapter Eight
Becoming Modern

Rails, Zones, and Bulbs

On a warm spring morning in Utah, a crowd of men and women milled around two vast train engines, sitting nose to nose on a brand-new railroad track. But they weren't worried about the engines crashing. These two engines, nicknamed "Jupiter" and "Engine 119," had been driven towards each other on the same track, one from the east and one from the west. They met each other at Promontory Summit, Utah, on May 10, 1869, and stood facing each other over a gap in the track. A single piece of track was missing—the piece that would finish the first railroad track to run all the way across the entire United States.

Two railroad officials stepped forward to help lay the last railroad tie. It was a special tie, made of polished California laurelwood, with four holes drilled in it for the last four spikes: a golden spike made by the railroad company, two silver spikes donated by the states of Arizona and Nevada, and a last gold spike sent by a newspaper in San Francisco, California.

The officials slipped the four spikes through four holes in the laurelwood tie, and tapped them in with a special silver hammer. But the laurelwood tie wouldn't stand up to the weight of a train, so immediately the special tie and spikes were taken out and sent to a museum. A regular old pine railroad tie was put in its place. The two officials took turns swinging a *real* hammer at the last iron spike. The first official took a huge swing and hit the tie, missing the spike altogether. Then the second official took a swing and missed both the spike *and* the tie! An experienced rail worker had to pick up the hammer and knock the spike in instead.

The railroad across the United States was finished. For seven years, twenty thousand men from as far away as China had been building for twelve hours a day, blasting passes through mountains with dynamite and stretching bridges across rivers and valleys. Now the railroad ran unbroken from coast to coast. Before the railroad was built, a businessman from New York who wanted to travel to California had to take a month-long journey by stagecoach, or sail in a steamship all the way around the coast of South America. Now he could reach the opposite coast in just five days!

Soon more and more railroads were built across the west. Trains carried people to cities where they might never have settled. Companies made tremendous amounts of money from shipping grain, cattle, coal, and other loads to far-away places of the United States. Railroad tracks crisscrossed the wild prairie lands.

And railroads also changed the way people kept time.

For as long as anyone could remember, cities all over the world set their own clocks by looking at the sun. When the sun was at its highest point in the sky, it was noon. But because the surface of the earth curves, noon for a city on the East Coast comes sooner than noon for a city a little further west. In 1869, when clocks in New York City read twelve o'clock noon, clocks in Boston read 12:12. And in a city in California, it might be 8:32 a.m.—or 8:47. How could trains, moving quickly across the hundreds of miles between cities, ever be able to tell passengers when they would arrive?

Ten years after the last spike was driven at Promontory Summit, a Canadian railroad engineer named Sir Sandford Fleming suggested that it might be a good idea to divide the world into twenty-four time zones. Each one of the zones would stretch from the North Pole down to the South Pole, like a thin slice of an apple. In each time zone, clocks would be set to the same time. Now, Boston and New York would reach noon at exactly the same moment. And when you travelled from one time zone to the next, you would move exactly one hour ahead or behind. Noon in Virginia would always be exactly nine a.m. in *every* city in California—not 9:13 or 9:21.

Railroad engineers welcomed Fleming's idea. On November 18, 1883, cities all across the United States reset their clocks to match the new time zones. Time had become *standardized*—kept according to the same rules across the whole United States (and, eventually, across the whole world).

Railroads and time zones began to change the way people in the American west thought about the world.

The world no longer seemed quite as large as it once had. Making and selling goods to as many people as possible was becoming easier and easier. Local towns and small villages were changing, thanks to the ideas and inventions that came to them from large cities. And it seemed simpler than ever to come up with inventions that would make life better and better. The United States, along with the other countries of the West, was becoming *modern*.

One more invention joined with railroads and time zones to make the world more modern. In 1879, the scientist Thomas Edison unveiled his new creation: a light powered by electricity.

Edison had tried for years to come up with a way to use electrical currents to light up homes and businesses after dark. He and his assistants had tried three thousand different designs! Edison was so obsessed with his experiments that, on his wedding day, he forgot he had gotten married and went to his lab—leaving his new wife at home alone.

Finally Edison managed to seal a *filament* (a strand that could be made to glow with electrical energy) into an airtight glass bulb. As long as no air reached the filament, it wouldn't burn up. It would just shine with power.

Edison's first "light bulbs" only lasted for a few hours. But Edison kept on testing different kinds of filaments—thousands of them. He tried hickory wood, cedar wood, flax stalks, bay wood, and boxwood. He sent off to tropical lands for new and different kinds of wood. At last Edison's bulbs would stay lit for fifteen hundred hours before the filament burned out.

Next, Edison and his lab helpers worked on developing a whole system to run these lights: wires, cable, generators, light sockets, and everything else needed to light up a whole building—or a whole city. At first, Americans were suspicious of these new lights. When the storekeeper John Wanamaker decided to put electric lights into his huge Philadelphia store, shoppers wouldn't go through the doors. They were sure that the bulbs would go off like little bombs at any moment! But the bulbs didn't explode, and soon more and more stores, factories, and even homes were using electric lights.

The human invention of the railroad had conquered space; now, it didn't matter if a company was hundreds of miles away from the people who bought its goods. The human invention of time zones seemed to have conquered the challenge of time; now, people set their clocks according to time zones, not according to the sun. And electric lights had conquered the dark. Dusk was no longer the end of the working day. Now, men could go on laboring, long after sunset!

Japan's Meiji Restoration

With the help of railroads, time zones, and electric lights, the United States was moving towards modern times. The country of Japan was beginning the same journey.

In 1854, fifteen years before the engines met at Promontory Summit, Matthew Perry had convinced Japan to open its ports to American trade. But many Japanese were unhappy that the shogun had allowed his officials to sign the trade treaty. The treaty gave the United States plenty of privileges in Japan—but it didn't do much for the Japanese. Four years later, when a Japanese official signed another agreement allowing Americans to settle down and live in Japan, a group of samurai ambushed him and cut his head off as punishment.

But although the Japanese didn't want the United States to take advantage of Japan, most Japanese also knew that Japan could no longer stay isolated from the West. It seemed that the Tokugawa shogunate, which had ruled Japan for over 250 years, just couldn't manage to deal with the problems of a modern Japan.

Twelve years after the treaty was signed, the Tokugawa shogun died. A young man of twenty-nine, Tokugawa Yoshinobu, became shogun in his place. He could see that the power of the shogunate was tottering. At once, he started to make changes. He tried to strengthen Japan's navy, and promised that he would throw all foreigners out of Japan. But it was too late for the shogunate. Rebellious *daimyo* (Japanese noblemen) had already gathered, demanding that Yoshinobu resign and end the Tokugawa shogunate for good.

Yoshinobu could see that a civil war would only weaken Japan, and make his country even less able to stand up to the United States and the other countries of the West. So in 1868, he agreed to resign. He was marched off to his house and put under guard. In his place, the daimyo put the seventeen-year-old emperor on the throne of Japan—the emperor who had been completely powerless as long as the shoguns governed in Japan. Edo, the city where the shoguns had once ruled, was renamed Tokyo and became the emperor's imperial city.

For a year, Japanese loyal to the shogunate fought with Japanese who were loyal to the emperor. Finally the last army of shogunate loyalists—over twenty thousand men—were driven back into a castle and surrounded by thirty thousand of the emperor's troops. Then the emperor's army destroyed the castle with guns and cannon that they had bought from the West.

Now a new time had begun in Japan. The daimyo who had helped the emperor regain his throne called it the "Meiji Restoration," because they insisted that the traditional imperial rule of the emperor was being "restored." But in reality, the emperor had no more power than before. Now Japan was ruled by the educated daimyo who surrounded him and told him what to do.

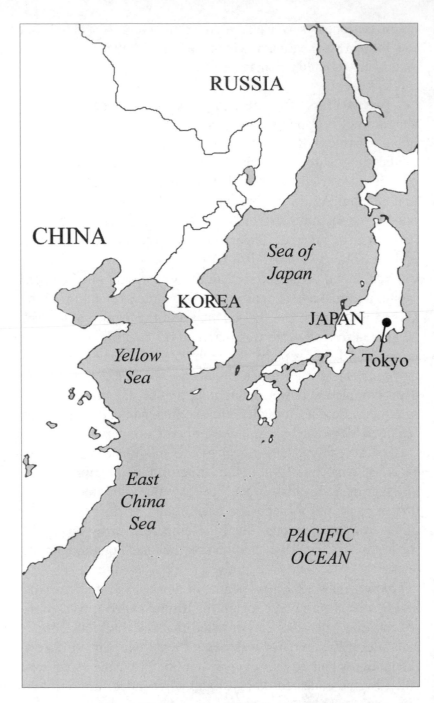

Japan During the Meiji Restoration

These daimyo wanted to know the ways of the West so that Japan could stand as an equal to any Western nation. So they sent young men to Europe to go to school. They hired French experts to come to Japan, build a dockyard, and teach the Japanese to build ships and repair them. American miners were hired to show the Japanese how to dig coal mines. British factory experts were brought in to build a spinning factory and to train spinners. By 1872, all Japanese were told that they needed to wear Western clothes, not Japanese robes, at all official ceremonies and meetings.

And an even more startling change came next. Less than ten years after the end of the shogunate, in 1876, the samurai were told that they could no longer carry swords in public at all. At this, they revolted.

The samurai knew that giving up their swords meant that their whole way of life was ending. For centuries, Japan had been a *feudal* society—a society in which each person served someone else in return for privileges and favors. The shogun promised to protect the noblemen of Japan, the daimyo, and granted them land to live on; in return, the daimyo promised to provide the shogun with food and all his needs. Then the daimyo gave castles to the samurai, the warriors; in return, the samurai fought to protect them. The samurai were the only Japanese men who had this special job of protecting the daimyo, and so they were the only men allowed to carry swords.

But now there was no shogun. Instead, Japan had an emperor—and now, a new army. This army would be made up of *conscripts* (men ordered to serve in the army, in exchange for money), not samurai. Like armies in Western countries, soldiers in Japan were now supposed to fight in return for a salary, not because they owed a feudal obligation to a nobleman!

The samurai didn't want to lose their power—or their right to live in the castles of the daimyo. So when they were told they could no longer wear their swords, they gathered together in a samurai army to fight against this new army of peasants with guns. They were led by a samurai warrior famous for his strength, Saigo Takamori.

The new army of conscripts was called out to face the samurai. But the peasants with guns were more powerful than the trained Japanese warriors with their swords. Rank on rank of samurai fell as the guns boomed. When he saw that the samurai were doomed, Saigo Takamori killed himself. His rebellion, the Satsuma Revolt, had lasted less than a year.

By 1884, Japan had a new constitution. It had been written by a Japanese statesman who admired Bismarck so much that he had travelled to the new German state to see how it was run. The constitution that he wrote made Japan's government much like the German government. Japan's emperor was the "head of state" in Japan, just as Wilhelm II was the king of the German state, but a "cabinet" (a group of advisors, such as a prime minister) actually made policies for the country. Japan would also have two assemblies, made up of educated and intelligent Japanese representatives. These assemblies would pass laws for Japan.

Does this sound familiar? It should. Japan was beginning to adopt the form of government used in the West. Even though this time in Japan's history is known as the Meiji Restoration, the power of the emperor wasn't really "restored" at all. The emperor was little more than a symbol—a symbol of faithfulness and loyalty to Japan.

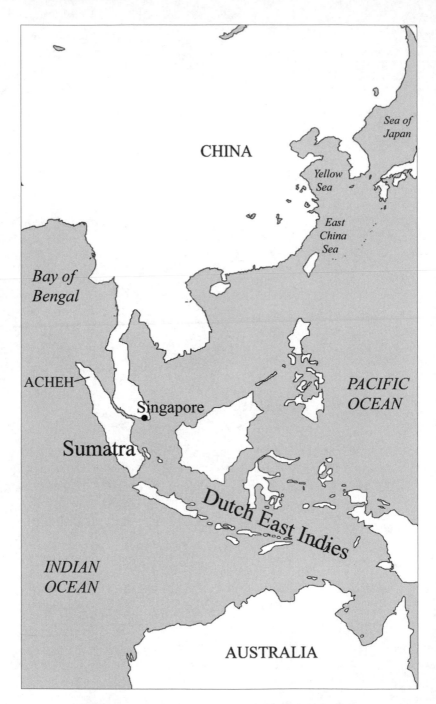

The Dutch East Indies in the Time of Dien

Chapter Nine
Two More Empires, Two Rebellions

The Dutch East Indies

As France and Germany struggled to become strong, two other empires were fighting to keep the land they had claimed for themselves.

Far south of Japan, six good-sized islands lie among a thick scattering of tinier ones. Today, this cluster of islands is called the Indonesian *archipelago* (group of islands). But a hundred years ago, the islands were known as the "Dutch East Indies."

Why were these islands in southeast Asia called "Dutch"? Two hundred years earlier, merchants from the Netherlands formed a trading company to build trading posts in the east, so that Dutch ships could land and buy cinnamon, nutmeg, and pepper. Like the British East India Company, the United Dutch East India Company built some trading posts in India. But most of the Dutch trading posts were built further east, on the islands called the "East Indies."

Before long, the government of the Netherlands took over the control of the ports from the United Dutch East India Company. And at the same time, the Dutch government also took control of most of the East Indies. The East Indies would become part of the Dutch Empire.

The Dutch also wanted to claim the island of Sumatra, which lay north of the East Indies. But the British also wanted Sumatra. Great Britain had already seized Singapore, the city that lay on the very southern tip of the peninsula that jutted down from the mainland of Asia, almost touching Sumatra. If the Dutch were in Sumatra, they would be far too close to British territory!

In 1824 the two countries came to an agreement. The Dutch would promise never to attack Singapore, and they would give the British all of the Dutch ports and settlements in India. In return, the Dutch could have Sumatra as their own.

But there was a catch: the Dutch had to allow the kingdom of Acheh, on the northern end of Sumatra, to stay independent. That way, Acheh would be like a "neutral zone" (an area that neither country could claim) between the British in Singapore and the Dutch in Sumatra.

At first, this arrangement seemed to work. The East Indies poured money into Dutch pockets. The islands were rich in all sorts of wonderful things: gold, rubies and sapphires, coal for running steam engines. The warm damp fields were perfect for growing coffee, tea, and rubber plants. Under Dutch rule, the farmers of the East Indies had to set apart one fifth of their land to grow crops for the Dutch. And they had to spend three days a week working on this land, rather than on their own. The Dutch knew that farmers would be reluctant to spend so much time working for their foreign rulers. So they promised mayors and chiefs in every part of the East Indies part of the profit from these "official" crops.

Many of the local officials saw a chance to get rich. They agreed—and even forced their people to work harder than the Dutch asked. In some communities, the farmers worked on the Dutch land for two hundred days every year! The chiefs and mayors grew rich, the Dutch had more money than they knew what to do with—and the farmers who were laboring their lives away grew angrier and angrier.

Small revolts broke out here and there. Soon the government of the Netherlands realized that the little independent kingdom of Acheh was encouraging these rebellions. One Dutch official fumed, "Acheh is nothing but a pirate's den!"

But the Dutch didn't want to anger the huge British Empire by attacking Acheh. So in 1871, the Dutch negotiated another treaty with Britain, called the Sumatra Treaty. In the treaty, Britain gave the Dutch permission to take over Acheh as well.

In 1873 the Dutch invaded Acheh with three thousand men. They didn't realize that the fighting would go on for more than thirty years.

The people of Acheh refused to yield. Muslim leaders, army captains, city chiefs, and even women fought fiercely to keep the Dutch from conquering their country. A young woman named Tjoet Njak Dien became one of Acheh's fiercest warriors. Her father and her husband were both soldiers in Acheh's army. When the Dutch seized Acheh's capital city, Dien, her father and her husband fled into the jungles. There, they began a *guerrilla war* (a war fought from hiding, rather than with an organized army on regular battlefields). When her husband and her father were killed, Dien took over the job of guerilla commander. She married another guerilla leader. They fought side by side. In the middle of the war, Dien gave birth to a baby girl—and carried her into battle too.

Dien and her husband knew that in order to resist the Dutch, the guerillas needed better weapons and more ammunition. So together, they formed a plan. Both of them came out of hiding, found a camp of Dutch soldiers, and walked right into the middle of it. "We want to surrender!" they said. "We were wrong to fight against you. Please, let us help you in your war against our rebellious countrymen."

The Dutch were so pleased by this "surrender" that they gave Dien's husband a medal, and put him in command of an entire army unit. The people of Acheh were horrified. Dien and her husband seemed to be traitors to their country. But the two were carefully studying Dutch strategy, learning to use Dutch weapons, and listening carefully to Dutch plans. One by one, they recruited Achenese soldiers into the Dutch unit. But these soldiers were really freedom fighters, guerillas from the jungle who were only pretending to be loyal to the Dutch.

As soon as there were enough Achenese in the unit, Dien's husband led his unit off to battle—and never returned! He took all of the guns, ammunition, and cannon with him, and gave them to the Achenese. With the help of these new supplies, the guerrilla fighters managed to drive the Dutch soldiers back.

But even so, the war dragged on for years and years and years. For twenty-four years, the husband and wife fought on. Finally, Dien's husband was killed. By now, Dien was fifty-one years old and had spent most of her life fighting in the jungle. She was beginning to weaken from illness. She had lost most of her eyesight, and now she had lost her husband. But she refused to give in.

In 1901, after almost thirty years of war, Dien was captured by the Dutch. They sent her to live under guard, far away from her home. Even in exile, she came to be known as *Ibu Perbu*: The Queen.

Two years later, in 1903, the Dutch finally gained control over Acheh. But the long war had been so expensive that the Dutch government had been forced to spend all the money it had made from the East Indies.

Note: This country's name is now spelled Aceh, but in the nineteenth century, it was known as Acheh.

The Sick Man of Europe

It was a cold, dark morning in the Russian city of St. Petersburg. The wind howled over the crowded roofs, whisking snow from the wooden tiles and whirling it along the icy cobbled streets. It was ten degrees below zero—cold enough to freeze the fingers and toes of the British *ambassador* (an official messenger or representative that one country sends another). But the ambassador was waiting in the audience room of the Winter Palace, where a huge fire had been built in the cavernous hearth. The fire had warmed the room until it was almost uncomfortably hot.

The ambassador heard a cough from the door. He stood up. The czar of Russia was hobbling towards him, an attendant on each side.

The czar, Nicholas I, settled himself carefully in a chair near the fire. He had been sick with a high fever for several days, but he had decided to get up out of bed to greet the ambassador.

For a little while, the two men talked of small matters. But Nicholas I had something more serious in mind. He leaned forward.

"We have a sick man on our hands," he said.

For a moment, the British ambassador was puzzled. Was the czar speaking of himself?

"A sick man," the czar repeated, "a man gravely ill. It will be a great misfortune if one of these days he slips through our hands, especially before the necessary arrangements are made."

Now the ambassador understood. The czar was speaking of the Ottoman Empire—the sprawling country just south of Russia, that stretched from the Tigris and Euphrates Rivers, all the way across Asia Minor, into the Greek peninsula. The Russians wanted to take part of the Ottoman Empire for itself. And they hoped that Britain would be their ally, not their enemy, as they made the "necessary arrangements" to conquer the Turks.

Why did the czar call the Ottoman Empire a "sick man"? For many years, the Ottoman Turks had been growing weaker and poorer. The *sultans* who ruled over the Ottoman Turks had spent so much money that they had to borrow money from other countries just to pay the soldiers in the Turkish army. And although the sultan still claimed to rule over a vast empire, at least three parts of that empire had started to ignore the sultan. The people who lived in the mountainous land north of Greece, which the Turks called the "Balkans" (the Turkish word for "mountain"), were doing exactly what they pleased. So were the people of Anatolia, right in the middle of Asia Minor. And so were the Lebanese, on the eastern coast of the Mediterranean.

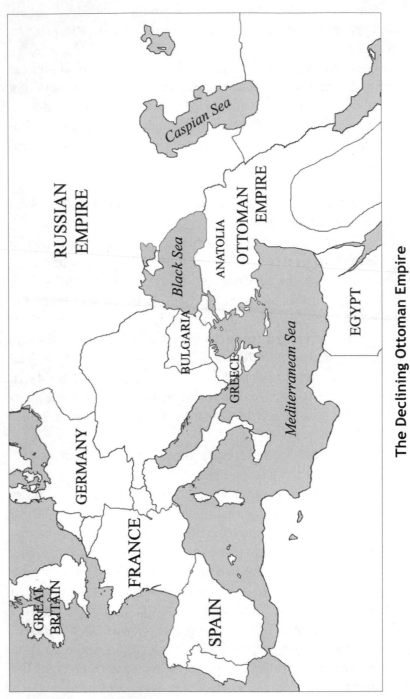

The Declining Ottoman Empire

The Ottoman Empire was certainly sick! And the British ambassador knew exactly what the czar was saying—that it was time to take over the Ottomans. But he also knew that Russia would grow larger and stronger if it added Ottoman land to its own territory. His job was to tell Russia what the British government would think of this idea; and Great Britain didn't want Russia to grow larger.

The ambassador smiled at the czar. "A sick man should be taken care of by a physician," he said. "He should be helped to recover—not have his limbs amputated by a surgeon!"

After this, Nicholas I knew that Great Britain would not help the Russians fight against the Turks. As a matter of fact, Great Britain was more likely to fight *against* Russia. Do you remember reading about the Crimean War? In 1853, the Russians had marched south into Ottoman territory, hoping to claim some of it for their own. But the British and the French had forced Russia to give up all of the land it took from the Turks. Neither country wanted Russia to get any bigger—or any more powerful.

But the Russians had not given up the idea of attacking the Ottoman Empire, the "sick man of Europe," again.

In 1876, Russia got its chance.

The sultan of the Ottomans, a big, cheerful man named Abdul Aziz who enjoyed parties and good eating, was having trouble with Bulgaria. Bulgaria lay just south of the Russian border, on the western coast of the Black Sea. It had been part of the Ottoman Empire for more than four hundred years, but the Bulgarian people had never been content with their Ottoman overlords. They called the Ottoman rule "the Turkish yoke."

Now, young revolutionaries in Bulgaria were busy preaching that Bulgaria should be independent. The Young Bulgarians, like the Young Italians who fought with Garibaldi, wanted their country to be free from the Turks. Instead, they wanted Bulgaria to have a modern constitution, like the constitution of the American states.

In April 1876, the Bulgarian revolutionaries picked up weapons and rebelled against the Turks. But these revolutionaries weren't as well organized as the revolutionaries of Italy. They were scattered all over Bulgaria in little groups. Abdul Aziz and his officials didn't hesitate. They ordered the Turkish army to march into Bulgaria, kill the revolutionaries—and kill anyone who had helped them.

The soldiers obeyed their orders. Many Bulgarians who didn't even *know* the revolutionaries were murdered. Sixty villages were wiped out. By the time the army had finished putting down the April Uprising, almost twelve thousand Bulgarians were dead.

The rest of Europe was shocked by this bloodshed! Over in Germany, Bismarck told the German people that the Turks should no longer be treated as part of Europe. In Italy, Giuseppe Garibaldi condemned the sultan for his cruelty. The prime minister of Britain announced that European countries should rise up together and drive the Turks out of Bulgaria.

Meanwhile, Abdul Aziz was in trouble. His own people had turned against him. On May 30, a little more than a month after the bloodshed in Bulgaria, Turkish rebels marched into the palace in the middle of the night. Abdul Aziz ran out of his room in his huge nightshirt, waving a sword! But when he realized that he was outnumbered, he agreed to give up his throne.

Four days later, Abdul Aziz was dead. His doctor said that he had committed suicide—but a British doctor who saw Aziz's body said that he had been murdered.

The Ottomans needed a new sultan. So they chose Murad V, the nephew of Aziz. Murad had never been either clever or brave. When he heard about Abdul Aziz's death, he fainted, and then spent two days throwing up. Afterwards he sat on his new throne for hours, rubbing his chin with his right hand. Before long, it became clear that Murad V had lost his wits.

So after just ninety-three days, the Turks sent Murad V away for a long rest.

Murad's brother, Abdulhamid II, became the new sultan of the Ottoman Empire. He knew that the empire was bankrupt, filled with rebellion, and threatened by the other countries of Europe. He did his best to make the "sick man of Europe" better. He announced that the empire would have a constitution, like the modern Western countries. The Ottoman Turks would even have an assembly that would meet together to make laws.

Abdulhamid worked hard for his country. Even the British ambassador praised him, calling him a man with "kindliness of disposition and enlightened views." But even Abdulhamid could not keep the Russians away. Russia had long wanted Ottoman land—and now the Russian army had the perfect excuse to invade. The czar pointed out that when the Turkish army had wiped out Bulgarian villages, Muslim soldiers had killed many Bulgarian Christians, and that the Christians of Russia were obliged to help protect their fellow believers. The Russian army began to march south towards the Ottoman borders. Thousands of Bulgarians flooded to join them and to fight against their Ottoman oppressors. Four months after fighting began, the Russians had taken away much of the Ottoman land, and were getting close to Istanbul itself.

By January of 1878, the Ottoman forces had begun to crumble. By March, it was clear that Russia had won the war. Abdulhamid was forced to sign a treaty that would give Bulgaria its independence. Russia took part of Anatolia (the area we sometimes call "Asia Minor") for itself. Under the treaty, the Ottoman Empire lost half of its territory!

Abdulhamid still sat on the Ottoman throne. But the sick man of Europe had had most of his limbs amputated, just as the Russians wanted. The Ottoman Empire would never again be a world power.

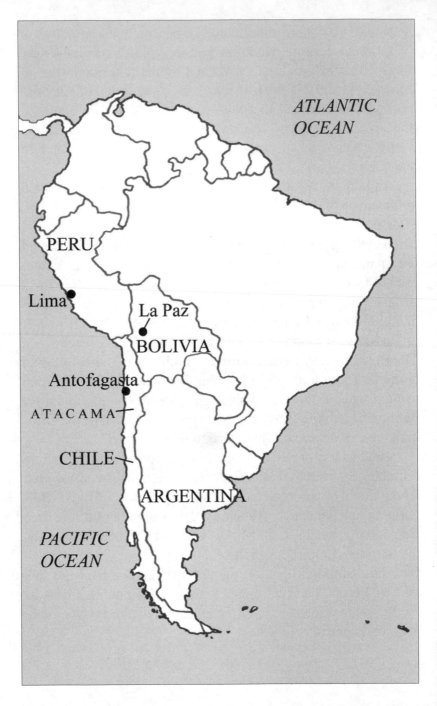

The South American Coast After the War of the Pacific

Chapter Ten
A Canal to the East and a Very Dry Desert

The War of the Pacific

Down in South America, a five-year war was about to start—a war fought because two countries quarreled over the driest place on earth.

In Chapter Six, we read about the War of the Triple Alliance, between the three-way partnership of Brazil, Argentina, and Uruguay, fighting against the country of Paraguay. In 1879, fourteen years after the War of the Triple Alliance began, another war broke out, between three more South American countries.

This time, the three countries were on the other side of South America, along the western coast. The country of Peru was the farthest to the north. It lies just below the equator (the imaginary line that runs around the center of the earth). On the west side of Peru, the Pacific Ocean laps up against hundreds of miles of beaches. But not far inland, the ground rises suddenly up into mountains. The Andes Mountains, rocky and covered with snow, run right down the middle of Peru like a backbone.

Just below Peru is the shorter, rounder country of Bolivia. Like Peru, Bolivia had a coastline along the Pacific Ocean. But Bolivia stretches into the middle of South America. Farmland, valleys, and even tropical jungles are inside its borders.

Just below Bolivia lies Chile, a long, skinny country running all the way down the coast. Bolivia is shaped like an orange, but Chile is shaped like a noodle! The country of Chile is ten times as long as it is wide. If you laid Chile sideways on top of a map of the United States, it would stretch from the

East Coast all the way over to California. But it would only be as tall as the state of Pennsylvania.

The war started with a quarrel between Chile and Bolivia over the Atacama Desert—a bleak, empty stretch of sand that covered the southern part of Bolivia and the northern edge of Chile. The two countries had never really decided on a boundary that ran across the desert. Why would they bother? The ground of the Atacama Desert is made of salt, sand, and hardened lava. It is fifty times drier than Death Valley. The Atacama Desert is the driest place in the whole world!

This South American desert is so dry because it lies in a "rain shadow." A rain shadow is a stretch of earth behind a mountain, shielded from the wind. When a storm blows towards a rain shadow, it hits the mountain first. The air of the storm rises up higher and higher, trying to get over the mountain. As it rises, the air grows cooler. All of the water in the air condenses and falls out. By the time the air reaches the other side of the mountain, all the water has fallen out of it. There is no rain left to fall in the rain shadow. Scientists who have tested the soil of the Atacama Desert say that it is as barren and lifeless as the soil on Mars!

The Atacama Desert may not have water or life. But it does have chemicals and minerals in it. Copper lies below the sand. So does saltpeter, used to make gunpowder. And so does a chemical called *sodium nitrate*. Sodium nitrate comes from a disgusting place; it often forms when bat and seabird droppings decay. But it is very useful for making fertilizer—and for making bombs.

Miners from Chile went into the Atacama Desert to dig for copper and for sodium nitrate. But Bolivia claimed that, since part of the desert belonged to Bolivia, the miners should pay taxes *to* Bolivia when they sold the copper and sodium nitrate that they found.

The two countries quarreled about the desert. They quarreled about the taxes. They quarreled about where the boundary line between Chile and Bolivia should be drawn. Finally,

Bolivia got so exasperated with the quarrelling that Bolivian officials seized all of the buildings, tools, and minerals of a Chilean mining company that was working in the Atacama Desert. Bolivia announced that everything the mining company owned would be sold at auction.

On the day that the auction was supposed to be held, Chilean soldiers marched up to the city of Antofagasta and took control of it. Antofagasta was a Bolivian city on the coast of the desert. Merchants who wanted to load up on the copper or sodium nitrate being mined in the desert could dock their ships at Antofagasta and fill their holds. By claiming the port city, Chile was claiming the right to control the Atacama Desert—and everything dug out of its sands.

Two weeks later, Bolivia declared war on Chile!

But Bolivia wasn't alone in its fight against Chile. Six years earlier, Bolivia and the country of Peru had signed a treaty with each other. This treaty promised that the two countries would always be each other's allies—especially against Chile. Now, Bolivia called Peru to come help in the desert war.

But it is very hard to fight in a desert so dry that not even snakes can survive. Instead, the three countries fought their war in the waters of the Pacific, just off the coast. And even though Bolivia and Chile had started the war by quarrelling over the Atacama Desert, the war at sea—the War of the Pacific—ended up being mostly between Chile and Peru.

Chile, which had so many miles of coastline, had one of the strongest navies in South America. But Bolivia had no navy at all, while Peru had a navy with two iron warships in it, the *Huáscar* and the *Independencia*.

Right at the beginning of the war, the commander of the *Independencia* was chasing a smaller wooden ship from the Chilean navy. He chased the smaller ship right over the top of a sharp reef—and tore the bottom of his iron ship right off! In one stroke, Peru had lost half of its iron battleships.

The commander of the *Huáscar*, Admiral Miguel Grau, was more successful. For six months, Miguel Grau sailed up and down the coast of Chile, attacking Chilean ships and keeping merchants away from Chilean ports. But finally the Chilean navy managed to corner the *Huáscar* in a violent sea battle. Miguel Grau was killed. His men tried to open the drains in the *Huáscar* to sink it, but Chilean sailors swarmed on board in time to save the *Huáscar* and take it for Chile.

Now Chile's path to Peru was clear. The Chilean army invaded Peru. The War of the Pacific had moved onto land!

Peru's president fled from the country. Chilean soldiers invaded Lima, Peru's capital, and burned the southern part of the city to the ground.

But Peru refused to surrender for three more long, destructive years of war. Finally, Peru had to agree to sign a peace treaty that gave the southern part of its coastline to Chile. Bolivia also had to give up land—its entire coastline! From that day on, Bolivia was "landlocked." It had no way to get to the sea. And Chile had won the rights to the Atacama Desert and all of its mines. In years to come, Chile would make a great deal of money by selling sodium nitrate to countries who needed to make explosives for war.

Peru had suffered terribly from the War of the Pacific. The country was deep in debt and had lost thousands and thousands

One of Peru's iron warships, the *Huáscar*

of soldiers during the fighting. After the treaty was signed, the people of Peru were so angry and unhappy that civil war broke out, and went on for seven years.

And Bolivia was angry that it had lost its land along the Pacific Ocean. In the year 2004—more than a hundred years after the War of the Pacific had ended—the president of Bolivia was still insisting that Chile and Bolivia should talk about who really owned the land along the sea.

The Suez Canal

In the same year that the War of the Pacific began, the ruler of Egypt lost his throne.

When you think about Egypt, you probably picture mummies, buried deep beneath the sloping sides of pyramids. You imagine hieroglyphs written on temple walls, reed boats sailing down the Nile River, and pharaohs wearing their cobra crowns.

But it had been hundreds of years since a pharaoh ruled over Egypt. The country of Egypt had become part of the Islamic empire in the Middle Ages. By the middle of the 1500s, the Ottoman Turks had taken over the Islamic empire. Egypt became a far-away part of the Ottoman Empire—a part that no one really paid very much attention to.

In 1805, an officer in the Ottoman army seized the throne of Egypt. This officer, Muhammad Ali, claimed that he was ruling in the name of the Ottoman sultan. But the Ottoman sultan was so weak that Muhammad Ali could pretty well do whatever he wanted. And what he wanted was to make Egypt a little more like the countries of Europe. He brought university professors from Europe into Egypt, to teach Egyptian students about the West. He tried to make Egypt bigger, by taking over part of the Sudan (the country that lay just south of Egypt).

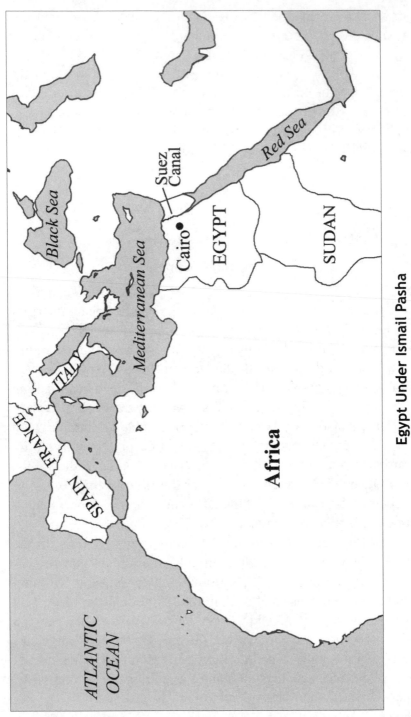

Egypt Under Ismail Pasha

He hired French soldiers to come down to Egypt and train the Egyptian army.

Egypt was growing stronger, more modern—and more like the West.

After Muhammad Ali died, his son Said Pasha became the ruler of Egypt. Like Muhammad Ali, Said Pasha claimed to be loyal to the Ottoman Empire. Again the Ottoman Empire paid very little attention to him.

But Said Pasha made a decision that would soon attract attention to Egypt from all over Europe. He gave a French company permission to start digging a canal (a man-made river leading from one body of water to another) from the southern banks of the Mediterranean Sea, down to the left-hand tip of the Red Sea.

Naturally, the countries of Europe were very interested in this canal—the Suez Canal. The canal could change the way that European countries traded with China, Japan, and the other countries of the Far East. Instead of travelling all the way down the coast of Africa, around the tip of that enormous continent, and then heading east, European ships could sail from the Mediterranean Sea straight down into the Red Sea and then turn east. When the canal was finished, it would be a hundred miles long, about twenty-six feet deep, and it would make the trip from Europe to the East six thousand miles shorter!

The Suez Canal took ten years to finish. By the time it was opened, Said Pasha had died. His nephew, Ismail Pasha, had taken control of Egypt.

Ismail's reign started out well. In 1867, four years after he became the ruler of Egypt, the sultan of the Ottoman Empire (which still claimed to own Egypt, even though the Ottomans didn't have very much power over Egypt) gave him the title of *khedive*. This title came from the ancient Persian word for lord; in Turkish it meant "king" or "sovereign ruler." For Ismail to be called the khedive of Egypt was a great honor!

Two years later, Khedive Ismail invited leaders from all over the world to come celebrate the official opening of the

Suez Canal. The Empress of France, the Crown Prince of Prussia, the Emperor of Austria, and dozens of other rulers and ambassadors arrived to watch the first ship sail through the canal. "It was a gorgeous and glittering scene," wrote a British nobleman who saw the opening with his own eyes. "There were fifty men-of-war [warships] flying the flags of all nations of Europe, firing salutes, playing their bands, whilst the sandy [land near the canal] was covered with tented Arabs and Bedouin from far and near who had come with their families, on horseback and camel, to join in the greatest festival that Egypt had seen since [ancient] days." There were fireworks and speeches, blessings from Christian priests and Muslim leaders, fireworks and feasts. Ismail Pasha even planned to have an opera performed for the distinguished guests. The Italian composer Giuseppe Verdi was writing an opera called *Aida*, about a heroic soldier of ancient Egypt. It would have been perfect for the celebration of the Suez Canal, but Verdi didn't finish it in time. Instead, the guests got to hear his opera about an Italian clown—*Rigoletto*.

The rule of Ismail Pasha, the khedive of Egypt, seemed to be flourishing. He had great plans to make Egypt even stronger. He wanted to make the schools better, so he opened new classrooms for girls. He built new roads and railroads. He oversaw the building of new factories and cotton mills; since the Civil War had destroyed the cotton plantations of the United States, Egyptian cotton was in great demand. He marched down into the Sudan, south of Egypt, and took over even more of it, so that Egypt's borders stretched down along the coast of the Red Sea.

But Ismail Pasha spent too much money on his projects. He had to start borrowing money from France and Great Britain. Under his rule, Egypt borrowed over ten million dollars! Finally, Ismail had to sell control of the Suez Canal to the British to raise extra money.

But even this money didn't pay off Egypt's debts. France and Great Britain demanded control over Egypt's treasury so that they could get their money back. That was the beginning of the end for Ismail Pasha. Now that he had lost control of Egypt's money, he had lost control of Egypt's government.

Four years later, the British and French told the Ottoman sultan that Ismail Pasha would have to go.

The Ottoman sultan had just lost his war with Russia. He wasn't strong enough to defy France and Great Britain. He ordered Ismail to leave his position. Ismail couldn't resist the sultan, the French, or the British. In 1879, he left his home, his palace, and his country, and went to live in exile in Italy.

Ismail's son Tawfiq became the khedive—a khedive who had to obey British orders. The Egyptian army grew more and more unhappy with the British control over their country. Egyptian army officers tried to lead a rebellion—but the British marched into Egypt with an army and captured Cairo, Egypt's capital city. Now Egypt was an occupied territory. And soon Britain extended its rule down over the Sudan as well.

Like India, Egypt had now become British. The empire where the sun never set had grown a little bit larger.

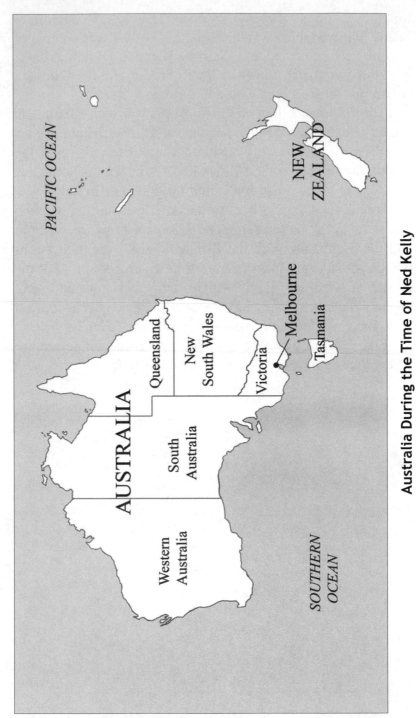

Australia During the Time of Ned Kelly

Chapter Eleven
The Far Parts of the World

The Iron Outlaw

On a stifling hot June evening, five men were putting on home-made armor. They buckled on breastplates made from plow parts, and pulled on helmets made from buckets with holes cut for eyes. They looked as though they were pretending to be knights in armor for a costume party.

But the five men weren't getting ready for a party. They were about to fight a desperate battle with the Australian police. At the end of it, four of them would be dead—and one would be dragged away to be hanged for murder.

Australia was part of the British Empire. But in those days, people in Great Britain thought of Australia as the bottom of the world—so far away that most of them would never visit it. And many of the people who lived in Australia were either condemned criminals or the children of criminals. Decades earlier, Great Britain had decided that British prisons were too crowded for any more prisoners. Instead, the British prisoners were put onto ships and sent far, far southeast, to the continent of Australia. There, watched over by British guards and British governors, the prisoners planted fields, built houses, and grew food.

At first, the prisoners struggled to survive under the scorching Australian sun. But as time went on, they learned what crops would grow in the cracked, dry ground. Many earned their freedom, settled down on land of their own, and raised families. Free men and women sailed from Great Britain to join them. In England, a poor man had no chance to grow rich. But in Australia, he might be able to own a farm of his own.

When gold was discovered in Australia, thousands of gold miners came from all over the world to dig in the red Australian earth. Many of the miners grew even poorer as they desperately searched for gold, but others found unbelievable wealth. They loaded gold nuggets into their shotguns and fired them off for fun. They sprinkled gold dust in their Christmas dinners! One gold nugget dug up in Victoria weighed a hundred and fifty pounds—as much as a man.

Two years after the gold rush began, the British government decided that it would no longer send convicts to Australia. Australia was growing richer—and stronger. Instead, the settlements of Australia would become regular British colonies.

But the Australian colonies were filled with trouble. Rich men with gold and power took the best land of Australia and pastured their sheep on it. Poor working farmers often had to survive on tiny, dry patches of ground. And many Australians believed that government officials and policemen didn't care about the rights of the poorest sheep-farmers and cattle-herders.

Desperate men hid along the roads, holding up the wagons that took gold from the mines into the towns. Some of these bandits, called "bushrangers," became as famous in Australia as Robin Hood was in England. Martin Cash was called the Gentleman Bushranger because he was so polite to the men he robbed at gunpoint. "Captain Thunderbolt" stole money from inns. "Captain Moonlite" robbed banks.

But the most famous bushranger of all was Ned Kelly.

Ned Kelly's father was a prisoner who had served his time and earned his freedom. But when Ned was eleven, his father died. His mother Ellen had to raise her seven children and farm eighty acres of wild Australian land alone.

Ned Kelly started getting in trouble at a very young age. But it isn't always clear whether he had really done all of the things the police accused him of. When he was only fourteen, he was arrested for robbing a traveller, but there wasn't enough evidence to convict him. A year later, he was arrested again for helping a bushranger. This time, he was sent to jail for six months. Just a few weeks after he was released from jail, he was arrested again—this time, for accepting a stolen horse from a friend. Ned protested, "I didn't know the horse was stolen!" But the judge sent him back to jail, this time for three years.

Not too long after Ned Kelly got back out of jail, a policeman arrived at the Kelly farm late one warm afternoon. The policeman announced that he was there to arrest Ned's little brother, Dan, for stealing horses.

Nobody knows exactly what happened next. The policeman went back to the police station and said that Ned had shot at him, and that Ned's mother Ellen had attacked him with a shovel. But neighbors of the Kellys said that Ned was miles away at the time. And Ellen Kelly said that she hadn't attacked the policeman with a shovel at all. In fact, she had offered to feed him dinner!

But the police decided to arrest Ned and Dan Kelly and charge them with attempted murder. The two boys ran away from home and hid in the wild bush lands of Australia. So the police arrested Ellen Kelly instead—and sent her to jail for three years.

Ned Kelly, out in the bush, was furious. He believed that poor farmers such as himself could never be treated fairly by the police. He believed that the government would always be on the side of the rich.

When a band of four policemen came after Ned and Dan Kelly, the two Kellys fought back. In a gun battle fought at Stringybark Creek, three of the policemen were killed.

Ned claimed that he had shot the policemen in self-defense. "I was compelled to shoot them," he wrote in a letter defending himself, "or lie down and let them shoot me!" But the government said that Ned and Dan, along with two friends who had joined them in the wilderness, were guilty of "wilful murder." There was a reward of 800 pounds for the capture of these four outlaws! And anyone who saw them could shoot them on sight without asking questions first.

For almost two years, Ned Kelly, his brother, and his two friends roamed through southeastern Australia with a gang of followers. They robbed banks and hid from the police. But to many poor Australians, Ned Kelly and his gang were heroes because they had fought back against cruel and unjust police and government officials.

In June of 1880, Ned Kelly and his gang planned to blow up the railroad tracks near the little town of Glenrowan. They captured a hotel in Glenrowan and set up their headquarters there. Before they could plant dynamite beneath the track, police surrounded the hotel.

Ned Kelly and his gang were prepared for a shootout. They had made themselves iron armor out of plow parts! Each suit of armor weighed fifty pounds or more and would stop a bullet. Ned, his brother Dan, and three other gang members armed themselves in iron before the police attacked.

But Ned Kelly didn't have any armor on his legs! During the gun battle, he was shot in the legs. He collapsed while he was trying to save his brother and the rest of his gang. The outlaws were killed—except for Ned. He was captured by police and taken to the city of Melbourne. There, Ned Kelly was put on trial for murder.

During his trial, Ned Kelly claimed that he had always fought only to defend himself. He told the judge, "I am the last man in the world who would take a man's life!" When the judge said, "You are accusing the witnesses against you of lying!" Ned Kelly answered, "I dare say. But a day will come, at a bigger Court than this, when we shall see which is right and which is wrong."

Ned Kelly was sentenced to be hanged. Thirty thousand Australians signed a petition, asking the governor of Melbourne to save Ned Kelly from death. But the governor refused. In 1880, Ned Kelly was executed.

For a hundred years, Australians wrote stories and poems about Ned Kelly. Some Australians insisted that Ned Kelly was just a common criminal. But others believed that Kelly was a brave man, fighting against unjust laws that Great Britain forced Australians to obey.

Twenty-one years after Ned Kelly's death, Australia became the Commonwealth of Australia. Like Canada, Australia would remain part of the British Empire—but the Australians would have the right to make their own laws and elect their own leaders.

Carving Up Africa

Australia was far away—but the mysterious jungles and plains of Africa seemed just as distant. As far as Great Britain, Germany, France, and the other countries of Europe were concerned, Africa was a wild, mysterious, distant land.

After David Livingstone, other explorers had followed his tracks. They had travelled down the Nile River to its source and sailed across the wide Congo into Africa's unknown center. They found hundreds of miles of wealth: elephants with ivory tusks, ground filled with gold and silver to be mined, limestone waiting to be quarried, rubber plants, wide fields perfect for cotton, coffee, and tea. No European had ever laid claim to this land. So, as far as the explorers were concerned, *no one* owned it.

France, Germany, and Great Britain—not to mention Spain, Portugal, and Russia—all built more and more trading posts around the coasts of Africa. By the end of the 1870s, there were plenty of European traders and missionaries in Africa. But most of the African continent itself was still under the control of African chiefs and kings.

Then, two countries began to push for more.

Leopold, the king of Belgium, seized the most land. Even before he inherited the throne of Belgium, Prince Leopold

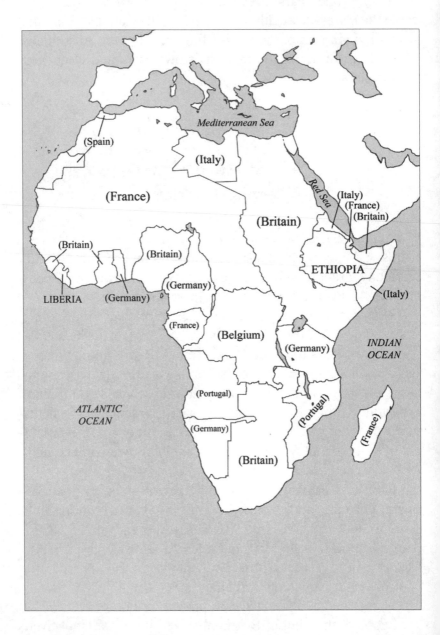

European Control in Africa After the Scramble

wanted his tiny country to grow larger by claiming colonies all around the world. Five years before becoming king, he told his people, "I believe that the moment is come for us to extend our territories. I think that we must lose no time, under penalty of seeing the few remaining good positions seized upon by more enterprising nations than our own." And, just one year later, he told his countrymen, "Imitate your neighbours; extend beyond the sea whenever an opportunity is offered. You will there find precious outlets for your products, food for your commerce, … and a still better position in the great European family."

When Prince Leopold became King Leopold II, he tried to convince the Belgian Parliament to claim the center of Africa, the "Congo Basin," for its own. Parliament refused. So Leopold announced that he was going to found a new charity, the "International African Association," which would bring modern science and trade into Africa. He hired Henry Stanley, the explorer who had gone into Africa and looked for Livingstone, to help him map out trade routes into the Congo. Henry Stanley mapped out a route a thousand miles long! Leopold II built trading posts and little medical offices all along this route, in the name of the International African Association. And then he announced that all unclaimed land along the route was actually his own, private, personal colony in Africa.

The German states were not far behind. In 1880, only nine years after the German states had reluctantly agreed to recognize Wilhelm as the "German emperor," the Second Reich was claiming lands in both the east and the west of Africa for "Germany."

The other countries of Europe didn't intend to be left behind, while Belgium and Germany took the riches of Africa for their own. Portugal claimed the southeastern African coast. The French took control of lands in the west, southwest, and north, and also convinced chiefs in the Upper Congo to sign treaties of peace, in exchange for bolts of cloth and barrels of alcohol. Italy signed a treaty of alliance with Ethiopia, in the northeast of Africa. And Great Britain claimed pieces of the southeastern coast, the southern tip of Africa, and a few scattered kingdoms along Africa's western coast.

All of these countries wanted still more. The years after 1880 became known as "The Scramble" because so many countries were elbowing each other to gain control of African land. Every country in Europe believed that whatever country held the most foreign territory could claim to be the greatest.

In 1884, Germany invited the rest of Europe to a conference in the German city of Berlin. At this "Berlin Conference," representatives from a dozen different countries decided that it would be best for everyone if France, Germany, Portugal, Italy, and all the other countries of Europe didn't *fight* over Africa. After all, wars were expensive. It would be simpler to just agree on some way to divide the land fairly. After all, there was a *lot* of Africa to go around.

So at the Berlin Conference, the countries of Europe agreed that, if any country built trading posts and missionary stations in any area of Africa, that country had "occupied" the area and could claim it. No other country would try to claim, or attack, that territory.

Everyone signed the agreement and went home, pleased with their civilized and peaceful solution. But this very civilized and peaceful solution ignored the African tribes who had *lived* in these occupied countries for thousands of years. Most Europeans thought that the Africans who lived in the plains and jungles of their continent weren't fully human—certainly not smart enough to control their own land. For Europeans, Africans were like children who had to be watched over, guided, and controlled.

Although the Berlin Conference was supposed to prevent war, it actually *caused* a hundred years of unhappiness and unrest in Africa. When a European country "occupied" part of Africa, it drew lines around its new "colony" and gave it a name, like "British Somalia" or "Rhodesia." But long before Europeans started drawing lines around colonies, African tribcs had been making alliances and fighting wars with each other. When European countries started laying out new borders for new countries, they often drew lines that divided friendly tribes from each other and locked hostile tribes together inside the same country borders.

By 1900, every mile of Africa—except for Ethiopia, on the eastern coast, and the little country of Liberia, on the western coast—had been claimed by a European country. The enormous continent of Africa had been divided: Germany, Italy, Britain, Portugal, Spain, and France had taken every square inch.

An African-American writer named W. E. B. Du Bois was in his teens when the Berlin Conference ended. He watched the changes that Europeans brought to Africa, as they built trading posts and missionary stations and took Africa for their own. As a grown man, he wrote, "The invading investors who wanted cheap labor at the gold mines, the diamond mines, the copper and tin mines, the oil forests and cocoa fields, followed the missionaries. The authority of the family was broken up; the authority and tradition of the clan disappeared; the power of the chief was transmuted into the rule of the white district commissioner.... By the end of the nineteenth century, the degradation of Africa was as complete as organized human means could make it."

Ireland During the Potato Famine

Chapter Twelve
Unhappy Unions

Ireland's Troubles

While Great Britain was claiming African land for itself, it was having troubles much closer to home. The island of Ireland, just off the coast of England, was demanding the right to rule itself—and the British were refusing.

The quarrel between Ireland and England had been going on for hundreds of years. In 1541, the English king Henry VIII had claimed Ireland as his own. Even though Henry VIII became a Protestant, most of Ireland remained Catholic.

The Protestant kings and queens who came after Henry VIII did not treat the Catholics of Ireland well. Protestant rulers took land away from Catholics and gave it to Protestants. Catholics were told they couldn't buy land, or even inherit it from their relatives. Catholics weren't allowed to join the army. And even though Ireland had its own Parliament, only Irish Protestants were allowed to be in it.

In 1801, the British government dissolved Ireland's Parliament. From now on, the Irish would have to send their representatives to the British Parliament. Ireland had lost even more of its independence—but even worse times were coming.

In 1845, reports of a strange new problem were beginning to spread across Europe. Potato plants in Holland had begun to blacken and wither. Beneath the stems, the potatoes were rotting in the ground. Soon, potato plants in France and Britain were rotting too.

The farmers of Ireland called this potato rot the "murrain" or the "blight." They hoped desperately that the rot wouldn't spread into Ireland. Hundreds of thousands of Irish farmers were actually living on farms owned by British landlords who lived in England. They grew wheat and oats for their landlords—and potatoes for themselves. The wheat and oat crops were shipped off to England to be sold. Only the potatoes remained in Ireland. If the potatoes rotted, the Irish would have very little to eat.

One September morning in 1845, an Irish farmer in his field pushed his hand into the ground to check on his potatoes. His fingers found only soft, rotten mush. Desperately, he began to dig. A horrible stench rose up out of the ground. All of the potatoes beneath the thick stem had rotted away in the ground.

The blight had come to Ireland.

Most people didn't realize that the potatoes were dying because of disease. Some thought that electricity or train smoke had somehow poisoned the ground. Others blamed the rot on bird droppings. But what everyone did see was that Ireland had no potatoes to eat—and none to plant for the next year.

The potato crop failed again the following year, and the year after that, and the year after that. No one knew how to stop the potato plague. People in Ireland began to die of hunger in the hundreds, and then in the thousands, and then in the hundreds of thousands. So many people died in one town that the town's church built a coffin with a false bottom. When the coffin was carried to a grave, the body would drop out of the bottom of the coffin into the ground—so the coffin could be reused. Travellers throughout Ireland found dead men and women in houses, fallen beside the road, and lying in fields.

But over in England, many of the English members of Parliament didn't believe that the Irish were really starving. After all, the Irish were always making a big fuss over nothing! British landlords paid no attention to the suffering of the farmers who rented their lands. When the starving men couldn't pay their rent, the landlords evicted them (forced them to leave their homes).

Many landlords were doing something even more cruel. Even though the potatoes were rotting, the wheat and oat crops were still growing. But instead of allowing the hungry farmers to eat this food, English landlords insisted that it be shipped out of Ireland and sent to England, just as always. One Irishman who lived during the potato plague, John Mitchel, wrote about standing on the shore of Ireland, surrounded by starving people—and weeping as ships filled with food sailed away towards England.

Not all Englishmen ignored the plight of Ireland. The prime minister of England, Robert Peel, knew that something had to be done. He believed that Ireland needed to be able to buy cheap food from the United States and other countries, so that the Irish could survive until the potato plague was over.

But there was a problem. Thirty years before, the British Parliament had passed laws called the "Corn Laws." These laws said that anyone in Ireland or England who bought food from another country had to pay a huge tax on it. The Corn Laws were meant to protect British farmers. Since grain grown in Ireland and Britain was so much cheaper than grain brought from another country, British merchants would be more likely to buy from British farmers.

Robert Peel thought that a famine was a very good reason to *repeal* (get rid of) the Corn Laws. Surely, he thought, Parliament would see that the Irish needed to be able to buy cheap food from other countries. But Parliament refused. The members of Parliament told Robert Peel that England should just leave Ireland alone to work out its own problems.

Robert Peel kept on insisting that the Corn Laws should be repealed. At last, he won the fight. Parliament agreed to get rid of the tax. But before very much grain could reach Ireland, Robert Peel lost his position as prime minister. His help for Ireland had made him very unpopular. And the next prime minister wasn't as concerned for the Irish as Robert Peel. As a matter of fact, he remarked that the Irish were starving because they weren't working hard enough to help themselves.

Five years after the plague began, farmers began to see healthy potatoes in their fields. By 1850, the blight was over. But Ireland was changed forever. Almost a million Irish were dead. Another million had left their homes and gone to other countries; over eight hundred thousand had gone to the United States. In Ireland itself, hatred of English rule had grown even stronger. More and more Irish began demanding the right of home rule—the right to make their own laws and to hold their own Parliament, just as Canada and Australia did.

Once again, the British Parliament resisted. This time, they were joined by many Irish Protestants. Protestants were afraid that an Irish Parliament would be mostly Catholic—and that Protestants would suffer. They wanted Ireland to stay under the Protestant government of England.

For years, the debates went on and on.

In 1886, the prime minister of Britain, William Gladstone, finally asked Parliament to vote on a law that would give Ireland home rule. This law, the "Home Rule Bill," wouldn't make Ireland independent from Great Britain. But it would allow the Irish to have control over their domestic affairs (issues that had to do with life in Ireland, and that only affected the Irish).

Gladstone and his supporters hoped that the Home Rule Bill would help to heal some of the hatred between Ireland and England. A famous cartoon published in a newspaper, just before the British Parliament voted on the Home Rule Bill, shows a tall beautiful woman named "Britannia" (representing the British Empire) standing at a crossroads beneath two road signs. One sign says "Home Rule" and points down a road where William Gladstone is standing. Gladstone is holding an olive branch of peace, with a label tied to it that says "Freedom, Friendship."

But above Britannia's head, another sign points in the opposite direction. It says "Perpetual Coercion." This meant that if the British kept on running Ireland's affairs from England, they would always have to use force to make the Irish follow their English laws. On the road to Perpetual Coercion stands another politician, a man who was against Home Rule—holding a pair of handcuffs.

When the Home Rule Bill came up before Parliament, the members of Parliament voted against it. Great Britain had chosen the road of Perpetual Coercion. And that decision would lead to a hundred years of chaos, unrest, and violence in Ireland.

The Boers and the British

It was a hot February night in the South African town of Mafeking. The shabby, tin-roofed buildings lay quiet. Moonlight glinted from the metal roofs and fell down over a deep, black trench dug around the town, with an earthen wall thrown up on the other side. Beyond the earthen wall, the tents of a besieging army stretched out, almost as far as the eye could see.

Inside his headquarters—a wooden building with a plain tin roof—the British commander of Mafcking sat, writing out instructions. He had been in this little town for almost four months. The soldiers camped outside weren't letting any food through. And the people of Mafeking had very little left to eat.

So it was vital that the horse that had died that afternoon be used properly. The commander, Robert Baden-Powell, was listing all of the ways in which the horse could be eaten. He wrote:

1. Send the mane and tail to the hospital for stuffing mattresses and pillows.
2. Send his shoes to the foundry, to be melted down into bullets.
3. Boil the skin, head, and feet all day, and then chop it up and add flavoring to it. Then we can eat it. We'll call it "brawn."

The Boer War

4. Mince up all of the horseflesh, stuff it into the intestines, and cook it; then we'll have sausages to feed the men.
5. Boil the bones into soup, and serve the soup to the townspeople.
6. After the bones are boiled, pound them up into powder and mix them with the flour—it'll make the flour last longer.

Robert Baden-Powell laid down his pen and leaned back in his chair. He could hear the boom of guns from outside the walls. The siege might go on for months yet. But if the people of Mafeking could eat horses, perhaps they would survive until the British army arrived to rescue them.

Why was Mafeking under siege?

To understand this, let's go back a few years. Do you remember the "Scramble" for Africa? In the years after 1880, European countries decided to divide up Africa among themselves. Most European governments ignored the African tribes who were already living there, and simply claimed the land for themselves.

But down in the south of Africa, Europeans had already been living for over a hundred years. These Europeans, called "Boers," were descendents of Dutch men and women who had once worked at the Dutch trading port called Cape Town. These Dutch settled down to farm South African land for themselves and established a Dutch colony called Cape Colony.

A hundred years later, the British marched into Cape Colony and occupied it. Now, Cape Colony was British territory and had to follow British laws. But one of those laws made the Boers angry. The British government decreed that every slave in Cape Colony would be set free, and that free Africans would be allowed to own property.

Many of the Boers believed that God intended all Africans to be slaves to whites. They refused to live in a colony where blacks would be living right beside whites, as free men and women. Thousands of Boers left Cape Colony, travelled north, and settled down in two new South African colonies called the Free State and the Transvaal. They began to call themselves *Afrikaners*, instead of Boers, to show that they were no longer Dutch settlers, but rather Africans of European descent.

Great Britain was too busy dealing with its other colonies to worry about the Free State and the Transvaal, so the British government agreed to recognize the Free State and the Transvaal as independent South African countries. Anyway, this land that the Boers had claimed didn't seem to be very valuable. It was dry and rocky.

But one day a boy, minding sheep along the banks of the Orange River, got bored and wandered along the bank, picking up pretty rocks. He put one shiny rock in his pocket to take home and show his parents. His mother gave the pretty rock to a neighbor who admired it.

The rock turned out to be a huge diamond.

When prospectors went to look at the banks and riverbed of the Orange River, they found more diamonds, scattered throughout the dirt and washed up between the stones. An enormous mine called the Big Hole was dug on the farm of two brothers named Nicolaas and Diederick de Beer. Thousands of diamonds were brought up out of the Big Hole. Today, the De Beers Consolidated Mines company is still the most famous diamond company in the world. The Big Hole is now a museum, where you can go down into the ground and see the diamond that started it all—now called the "Eureka Diamond."

The diamond rush brought thousands and thousands of miners to the fields and riverbanks of South Africa. The land where the diamonds were found lay right between the two Boer colonies, the Free State and the Transvaal, and the British-run Cape Colony. Neither the Boers nor the British had claimed it, so the British announced that the land would belong to the British Empire. Now, the British controlled Cape Colony *and* the diamond-filled fields of South Africa. British power was growing!

In the year 1886, not too long after the diamond fields were discovered, miners found gold in the Boer country Transvaal. Soon, the Boer government of Transvaal realized that the gold deposits were enormous—almost half of the gold known to exist in the whole world.

But it would cost a lot of money to build mines huge enough to get all of that gold out of the ground. No one in the Transvaal had quite that much money. So the government of the Transvaal made a deal with the British. British prospectors and business-men could come into the Transvaal and mine the gold, as long as the people of the Transvaal got to keep part of it.

Only four years after the agreement was made, the Brit-ish governor of the Cape Colony, Cecil Rhodes, sent British officials up north of the Transvaal and the Free State to build another colony—a British colony named Rhodesia, after him-self—on the other side of the Boer states. Now, the Transvaal and the Free State would be squeezed between two British pow-ers. British businessmen were already in the Transvaal, mining gold and meddling in local politics. And then Cecil Rhodes gave his officials permission to invade the Transvaal itself.

The people of the Transvaal could see that the British in-tended to take over their country and the Free State as well. So in 1899, the Afrikaners in both the Transvaal and the Free State declared war on Great Britain. The British called this war the "Boer War."

Two days after the war began, Afrikaner soldiers surround-ed the little town of Mafeking. Mafeking was a railroad town that lay in the British territory of Cape Colony, just over the line from the Transvaal. The British commander at Mafeking, Robert Baden-Powell, was surprised by the invasion. He only had a thousand men with him, and the Afrikaners were fierce fighters. But he was determined not to surrender. He ordered his men to dig trenches around the town, and to throw the dirt up into walls to protect Mafeking. When the Afrikaners started to shoot into the town, Baden-Powell had fake forts built inside the trenches, so that the Afrikaners would shoot at the fake forts instead of at the buildings that had people inside them. He sent his men out at night to shout at the Afrikaner camps with a tin megaphone, so that no one could sleep! And because he needed all of his men to fight, he recruited young boys from the town's inhabitants to act as messengers and helpers. These "boy scouts" were the beginning of the modern Boy Scouts.

Outside Mafeking, the war was going badly for the British. In December, after two months of fighting, British soldiers lost three huge battles in one week. At Mafeking, the siege went on, and on, and on—for 217 days! It went on so long that both sides agree to make Sundays cease-fire days. On Sunday, no one would shoot at anyone else. That way, both sides could rest, cook food, and play games.

After seven months, British reinforcements finally reached Mafeking, drove away the Afrikaners, and set the people of Mafeking free. Back in England, the British were so delighted that parties were held all night, all over Great Britain. For years afterwards, the British used the verb "to maffick" to mean "to rejoice with great noise and riotous celebration."

Now the tide of the battle had turned. The Afrikaners began to surrender. The British took control of cities in the Transvaal and in the Free State. The war was about to end.

But as it came to an end, Great Britain behaved in a way that made many British ashamed of their government. Even though fighting between the Afrikaner army and the British army had officially ended, small groups of Afrikaner guerillas roved through the countryside, attacking British camps and soldiers. These attacks went on for two years. The British seemed unable to halt them.

So the British government ordered that all families who lived in the areas where the guerillas roamed be rounded up and put into camps. British officials suspected that these families were supplying the guerillas with food, water, and weapons. These "concentration camps" put all Afrikaners who might support the guerillas in one small area where the British could watch them.

There were sixty-six of these "concentration camps" for whites, and fifty for blacks. Life in the camps was horrible. None of the Afrikaners were fed very much, but the black camps were worse; each day, the British spent less than a penny per person on food for their black prisoners. Diseases like measles, chickenpox, and pneumonia swept through the camps, killing thousands. Twenty thousand white Afrikaners died in the camps. According to British records, fourteen thousand black Africans died as well—but the British didn't keep careful track of all of the deaths in the black camps. Probably, many more died.

In 1902, the Afrikaners and the British signed a treaty called the Peace of Vereeniging. This "peace" united all of the colonies together into one nation, under British control, called the Union of South Africa. But within this Union of South Africa lived three groups that hated each other—white British, white Afrikaners, and black Africans. The Peace of Vereeniging formed a South African nation in which there would be very little peace.

Brazil Under the Reign of Pedro II

Chapter Thirteen
The Old-Fashioned Emperor
and the Red Sultan

Brazil's Republic

While the Boers and the British were fighting in South Africa, the South American country of Brazil was kicking out its emperor.

Brazil had been ruled by only two emperors in its short history. The first emperor of Brazil, Pedro I, was the son of the king of Portugal. When Pedro was a little boy, Brazil wasn't even a country. It was a Portuguese colony.

Pedro grew up in the colony of Brazil. When he was twenty-three, his father (the king of Portugal) gave him the job of governing Brazil. A year later, Pedro led Brazil in declaring independence from Portugal—and from his father. He became Pedro I, the first emperor of an independent Brazil.

The new country of Brazil was filled with rich slaveholders, powerful plantation owners, Portuguese noblemen, ambitious military officers, and politicians who wanted more power for themselves and less for the emperor. No matter what Pedro did, someone criticized him. Pedro I managed to rule this restless country for only nine years before riots broke out in the streets of Brazil's capital city, Rio de Janeiro. Unhappy Brazilians yelled that Pedro I was still too loyal to Portugal, and that he wasn't giving his people enough freedom. Pedro I collected his money, his belongings, and most of his family, caught a British warship in the port, and sailed away. Brazilians said afterwards that Pedro I had left only one silver spoon in the whole palace!

But Pedro I had left more than a silver spoon behind. He had left his ministers of state—and also his five-year-old son. The little boy had a name bigger than he was: Pedro de Alcontâra Joso Carlos Leopoldo Salvador Bibiano Francisco Xavier de Paula Leoc dio Miguel Rafael Gabriel Gonzaga, By the Grace of God and Unanimous Acclamation of the People, Constitutional Emperor and Perpetual Defender of Brazil. For short, Pedro II.

At five, Pedro II wasn't exactly ready to be the Constitutional Emperor and Perpetual Defender of Brazil. So three of his father's ministers formed a committee to help him rule until he was older. They made sure that he was properly looked after and educated. Little Pedro II worked hard at his studies. He learned French, Hebrew, Arabic, and other languages. He loved to read and write. And he was particularly fond of studying science.

In 1841, at the age of fifteen, Pedro II took control of his country.

Like his father, Pedro II found that Brazil was a very difficult country to rule. Brazil had five different kinds of people living in it. Most of the land and most of the money was owned by families who were descended from Portuguese settlers. The South American Indian tribes who had lived in Brazil before the Portuguese arrived had lost most of their land; most of them worked as poor laborers for the rich Portuguese. And because slavery was still legal in Brazil, the hardest work was done by thousands of African slaves.

These three groups of people had been joined by a fourth group: immigrants from Europe. Poor Europeans had been coming to the New World for years, looking for a better life. Many of them went to North America and settled in the United States. But many others went to South America. German, Italian, and Polish settlers had moved into Brazil and settled down—and more were coming every year.

After the American Civil War ended, a fifth group of settlers arrived in Brazil—American cotton planters who had lost their plantations. They travelled down from the American South to try their luck at growing cotton in Brazil. Even today, you can still visit the town of Americana in Brazil. Americana was founded by an Alabama cotton planter who took his family down to Brazil to start a new life. Today, you can find Brazilians in Americana who have American last names like Norris and Jones. In June, they have a huge festival called *Junino* in which a Brazilian band plays Brazilian music with Southern banjos, while young Brazilian men and women square dance.

Pedro II believed that Brazil could only prosper if all five groups of people had the opportunity to work, to earn a good living, and to get an education. He encouraged Brazilian companies to build modern factories and railroads. He started new schools. He begged skilled workers from other countries to come and settle in Brazil. He travelled to other European countries to see their scientific inventions and their factories. He even came to the United States. In Philadelphia, he went to see the new telephone invented by Alexander Graham Bell. When Bell invited him to use the telephone, Pedro II picked up the receiver and said into the mouthpiece, "To be, or not to be." He was probably the first citizen of Brazil to ever use a telephone! He was so pleased with the new invention that, when he went home, he had a telephone put into his summer house.

But most importantly of all, Pedro II set out to get rid of slavery.

Pedro's father had hated slavery, calling it a "cancer" on Brazil. Pedro II was a great admirer of the American president Abraham Lincoln, and he agreed with Pedro I. Slavery would have to go.

But many of the powerful plantation owners in Brazil used slaves to run their farms and harvest their crops. They weren't willing to give up their free help. Pedro II had to get rid of slavery very slowly. Nine years into his reign, Pedro II and his government made slave trade to Brazil illegal, so that no more slaves could be brought to Brazil from Africa Twenty one years later, the Brazilian government began to declare

137

the slaves of Brazil free. Seventeen years after that, in the year 1888, Pedro's government signed a law making slavery illegal.

By 1888, Pedro II had been the emperor of Brazil for forty-seven long years. During most of his reign, he had been a popular ruler. The people of Brazil were more prosperous than when he had first taken the throne. Pedro's new schools had also done their job. More men and women had learned how to read and write in Brazil than in any other country.

But now more and more Brazilians began to complain about their emperor. The plantation owners didn't like giving up their slaves. The soldiers in the Brazilian army thought that they weren't being paid enough. And the prosperous farmers, merchants, and shopkeepers of Brazil had begun to believe that no modern country should have a king. Instead, Brazil should be a republic, with a constitution of its own.

In 1889, the year after slavery was made illegal, Pedro II realized that he would not be able to keep his throne any longer. He was now sixty-two years old. He had spent his life working to make Brazil a rich, free, well-educated, modern country—a modern country that no longer wanted to be ruled by an old-fashioned emperor.

Late one evening, Pedro II called his Council of State together. He told them that he was going to bed. In the morning, he wanted to hear their final decision: Should he stay in Brazil, and keep his crown?

When Pedro got up the next morning, the Council of State had made up its mind. It was time for Brazil to become a republic. The emperor and his family should leave the country, but they could have twenty-four hours to get their possessions together.

"I am leaving," Pedro II answered, "and I am leaving now." Immediately he collected his family and sailed away from Brazil, heading for the city of Paris.

Two years later, the old emperor caught the flu. He died a few days before Christmas, in the year 1891. Brazil had just finished writing its new constitution when Pedro II was buried in Portugal.

In 1971, Pedro II's body was brought back to Brazil and buried in a place of honor. Brazil was finally ready to praise the second emperor for all of the years he had spent serving his country. He had become a Brazilian hero—even though the age of emperors was gone.

Abdulhamid the Red

The last time we visited the Ottoman Empire, in the year 1878, the sultan Abdulhamid II sat on the throne. The empire had just lost over half its territory. The officials who were supposed to run the empire were more interested in living comfortable, luxurious lives than in doing their jobs. Once the most powerful empire in the East, the Ottoman Empire was now known as the "Sick Man of Europe."

Although it was sick, the Ottoman Empire still covered all of Asia Minor, stretched over the ancient land of Mesopotamia and down along the Persian Gulf, and controlled the entire eastern coast of the Red Sea. It was still an empire, and Abdulhamid II wanted to make it a *great* empire once more.

But Abdulhamid had a problem. With half of his mind, he agreed with the new, modern ideas about the people of a country having the right to rule themselves. But with the other half of his mind, he liked the idea of the sultan as the unquestioned ruler of the Ottoman Empire, a powerful man who could decree what the empire would do—without opposition.

When we read about Abdulhamid before, we read about his willingness to allow the Turks to have a constitution and an assembly like a Western parliament. But the Turkish constitution did not last very long. There were two problems with

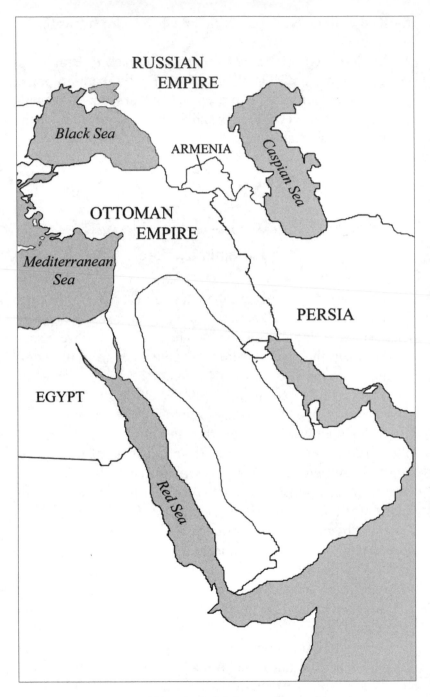

Massacre in Armenia

the constitution. First, Abdulhamid insisted that the constitution include a paragraph called "Article 113." This said that the sultan could *deport* (send out of the empire) anyone he thought "harmful to the state." This meant that Abdulhamid could send anyone who disagreed with him to another country and forbid him from coming back. Second, for centuries, the Ottoman sultan had been honored and obeyed as the ultimate power on earth. Even though many Ottoman Turks wanted a more Western government, when their Sultan made a decree, it was very hard for them to ignore it!

The Ottoman constitution lasted for exactly one year. Then Abdulhamid ordered it dissolved. Now he would rule like an old-fashioned sultan, with no constitution or parliament to limit his power.

At first, Abdulhamid used his old-fashioned power to make many Western-style improvements to the empire. He ordered railroads laid down, and had lines strung so that the Ottomans could use the new Western invention, the telegraph. He improved the great university of Istanbul. He changed some of the laws of the empire to make them more modern.

But Abdulhamid also ruled with an iron fist. He organized a huge spy network that listened for any talk of rebellion or revolt; anyone who criticized the sultan could expect a visit from the dreaded secret police. He ordered his soldiers to march in and attack rebels against the sultan in several different places within the Empire—particularly to the east.

One of these rebellions broke out in the country of Armenia.

Armenia lay up north of Asia Minor, between the Caspian Sea and the Black Sea, just south of the Russian border. Several hundred years before, the country of Armenia had been captured and divided between the Ottoman Empire and the Persian Empire. Then the Russians took away the Persian section of the country. That meant that people who called themselves Armenians lived partly under Russian rule, and partly under the rule of the Ottoman sultan. But the Armenians who lived in the Ottoman Empire were not always treated well.

They were Christians, not Muslims. The laws of the Ottoman Empire meant that they had to pay more taxes than Muslims. They didn't have the same rights as Muslims. And the Ottoman officials in charge of Armenia often treated Armenians badly, driving them from their homes and seizing their land. The Armenians hated this treatment. In 1894, they picked up weapons to fight back.

Russia wanted Abdulhamid to respond to the rebellion by giving the Armenians better protection and more rights. But Abdulhamid didn't like Russia telling him what to do. He believed that Russia was scheming with Great Britain and other European countries to encourage rebellions against him. The countries of Europe, he fumed, had already managed to "cut off the feet and hands" of the Ottoman Empire. Now, if they encouraged the rebellion in Armenia, they would "cut out the country's insides."

He wasn't about to let this happen.

So Abdulhamid sent his soldiers into Armenia and ordered them to fight against the rebels. He also ordered them to put an end to the revolt by killing Armenians not just in Armenia, but wherever they were, all through the empire. In his mind, Armenians were traitors. They were more likely to be loyal to Russia than to the Turks. Their disloyalty was like an illness that would infect the rest of the Ottoman Empire.

Many Armenians were killed by Abdulhamid's soldiers. Others were forced to march out of the Turkish territory, and died of starvation and weariness on the long walk. The killing went on for three years. No one knows exactly how many Armenians were killed, but at least a hundred thousand men, women, and children died.

Abdulhamid had not learned from the fate of Abdul Aziz! Once again, he made the countries of Europe certain that the Turks were savages, unwilling to enter into the modern age. A few years before, the British ambassador had praised Abdulhamid for his "kindliness of disposition and enlightened views." No one in Great Britain would agree with that now!

Abdulhamid had agreed with some Western views—but the Armenian massacre made it very clear that he still held onto the ideas of the past. He was determined to keep hold of his territory, and to rule it with absolute authority.

Although he wanted to keep the Sick Man of Europe from getting any sicker, his harsh methods not only made the empire sicker, but came close to killing it. Abdulhamid's iron fist and his reliance on fear and spying to keep his power had already made him unpopular with Turks who wanted their country to be more modern—particularly with university students who were learning about the ideas of the West. And when Abdulhamid ordered the Armenian massacre, he became even more

Abdulhamid the Red

unpopular with these forward thinkers. Many Turks called Abdulhamid "Abdulhamid the Red," because he had shed so much blood.

In 1889, medical students began to form a plot to get rid of Abdulhamid. They wanted to change the laws of the Ottoman Empire so that, instead of being a country under the power of an Islamic sultan who ruled by Muslim law, the empire of the Ottoman Turks would instead become a country called "Turkey." This country would be ruled by secular laws (laws not based in religious belief). The people of Turkey would be loyal to their country, not a sultan. Their slogan was "Liberty, Justice, Equality, Fraternity"—ideas they had learned from the French and American revolutions. Soon, they recruited other students at Istanbul University and other colleges to join them. They called themselves the "Committee of Union and Progress." But others called them the "Young Turks."

Abdulhamid wasn't going to put up with the revolt of the Young Turks any more than he had put up with the rebellion in Armenia. Soon, his secret police were planning to arrest the leaders of the movement. The leaders of the Young Turks had to flee from their country.

But they went to Geneva and Paris, cities where other Ottoman Turks who had been exiled from their country by Article 113 lived. They organized the Turks who no longer lived in the Ottoman Empire into a movement that wanted to change the empire—and get rid of Abdulhamid, the Red Sultan.

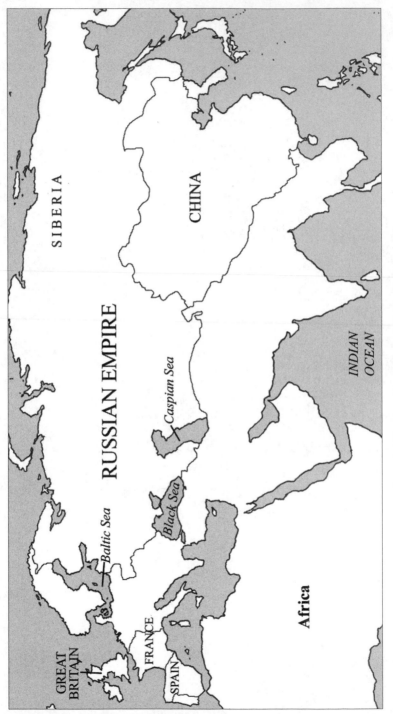

Russia Under the Rule of Alexander III

Chapter Fourteen
Two Czars and Two Emperors

The Next-to-Last Czar of Russia

Like the sultan of the Ottoman Empire, the czar of Russia still clung to his power as the absolute ruler of his huge country.

In 1889, the year that the last emperor of Brazil left his country and sailed to France, the czar of Russia was Alexander III of the royal Romanov family. He had inherited the throne of Russia from his father, Alexander II.

Alexander II was the czar who had sent Russian soldiers down to attack the Turkish Empire and take Turkish land away. But although he was a warlike czar, Alexander II had also tried to make Russia a little bit more Western, and a little bit more modern. He built railroads and new schools. He gave newspaper editors and writers more freedom to say whatever they wanted. He gave the towns of Russia permission to govern themselves. He even decreed that anyone accused of a crime had the right to be tried by a jury (a group of ordinary people, just like them), rather than being sentenced by a judge; that way, powerful, corrupt judges could not convict innocent men unjustly.

But only three years after the Russian victory over the Turks, Alexander II was killed by two assassins, who threw a bomb into his horse-drawn carriage as he was being driven through the streets of St. Petersburg.

Alexander III became czar in his father's place. He was thirty-six years old, a huge man—six foot four—with wide shoulders and a big dark beard. He had seen his father killed by his own people, and for his entire reign, Alexander III was afraid that he too would be assassinated.

As soon as he became czar, Alexander III began to take away the new freedoms of the Russian people. He cancelled Alexander II's decree that towns could govern themselves. He gave the noblemen of Russia special powers, including the right to oppress the poor peasants who worked on their land. Anyone who opposed him or criticized him was sent to the frozen north of Russia—the dreaded land of Siberia, where temperatures dropped to thirty degrees below zero in the winter, and didn't get above freezing even in August. Later, it was said, "Alexander set out to undo everything that his father did."

The noblemen of Russia approved of Alexander's unlimited power. In the year 1891, after Alexander III had reigned for ten years, one of his officials wrote a long essay in praise of his greatness. In the essay, the nobleman quoted an old poem:

> Our White Czar is a king above kings …
> All the hordes have bowed down to him,
> All the tribes have submitted to him,
> Because the White Czar is king over kings.

Then he wrote, "[The czar possesses] the unseen favor of a bright and spiritual power, creating and maintaining all [that is] around him. … Russia is the source and center of an invincible might … the most precious of our national traditions—autocracy." He was saying that the unlimited power of the czar (*autocracy*) was what made Russia great.

Naturally, the noblemen of Russia were happy to believe that the czar had divine power, and that his power should be unlimited. Under the rule of Alexander III, the noblemen had privileges, riches, and power!

But the poor people of Russia were wretched.

To the peasants, farmers, and workers of Russia, Alexander III was a cruel tyrant. The Russian writer Mary Antin, who lived in a Jewish village between the Baltic and the Black Sea, wrote that even the children knew about the cruelties of Alexander—but no one criticized the czar, because they were afraid of Alexander's police:

In your father's parlor hung a large colored portrait of Alexander III. The czar was a cruel tyrant—oh, it was whispered when doors were locked and shutters tightly barred, at night... and yet his portrait was seen in a place of honor in your father's house. You knew why. It looked well when police or government officers came on business. The czar was always sending us commands—you shall not do this and you shall not do that—till there was very little left that we might do, except pay tribute and die. One positive command he gave us: You shall love and honor your emperor. In every congregation a prayer must be said for the czar's health, or the chief of police would close the synagogue. On a royal birthday every house must fly a flag, or the owner would be dragged to a police station.... The czar always got his dues, no matter if it ruined a family.

The Jews of Russia were treated even worse than other poor Russians. They paid more taxes; they were forced to live in certain areas of Russia, and weren't allowed to move wherever they pleased. Very few Russian Jewish children were allowed to go to school, and those who were found that "their school life was one struggle against injustice from instructors, spiteful treatment from fellow students, and insults from everybody."

Alexander III had been czar for seven years when assassins tried to kill him, just like his father. He was riding in the royal railroad coach with his family when a bomb went off beneath the tracks. The railroad coach lurched off the rails, tottered, and fell, the roof collapsing inwards and the windows shattering. For a moment, nothing moved in the wreckage. And then the crumpled roof shuddered and began to rise. Alexander's huge figure rose out of the ruined coach, his wide shoulders braced beneath the roof. He held it up until his family could crawl out from beneath the twisted metal. Not a single person was killed!

But doctors think that the bruises and the strain of lifting the roof damaged Alexander's body. He was czar for six more years, but he grew slowly weaker and sicker. When he died in 1894, he left behind him a Russia filled with poor, starving peasants, proud, overbearing noblemen, and unhappy workers.

His son Nicholas II inherited the throne and a country of discontented subjects. Some Russians wanted a Western government of elected representatives, like the United States and Canada had. Others wanted the working people of Russia to be able to control the land and government of their own country.

How would Nicholas II deal with this troubled Russia?

He had no idea! When he learned of his father's death, Nicholas grew pale. "What will I do?" he said to the messenger who brought the news. "I am not prepared to be the czar. I know nothing about the business of ruling!"

Maybe Nicholas II wasn't prepared to be the czar—but he had no choice. He shouldered the job of ruling Russia. He didn't know that his father Alexander III had been the next-to-last czar.

Ethiopia and Italy

By now, most of Africa was under the rule of European countries. Great Britain, France, Germany, Portugal, and Belgium had seized most of the continent for themselves. Only two African countries remained free from European rule. On the western coast, Liberia, a country formed by the United States as a home for freed slaves, had the right to govern itself. But Liberia was a *protectorate* of the American government, which meant that anytime Liberia wanted to deal with another country, it had to get permission from the United States. So although Liberia wasn't ruled by another country, it wasn't truly independent.

All the way across the vast Sahara Desert, on Africa's eastern edge, lay the country of Ethiopia—the only part of Africa that remained truly free.

Ethiopia, filled with mountains and high plains, was sometimes nicknamed "the roof of Africa" because it was so much higher than the lands around it. Right down the middle of Ethiopia runs a huge valley called the Great Rift Valley. And although most of Ethiopia is so high, the lowest land on the earth's surface is also found in Ethiopia, at one end of the Great Rift Valley. Here, the ground has thinned and sunk and thinned and sunk until it is 371 feet below sea level—so far down that lava boils just below the surface and bubbles up through the earth. This low place, called the Danakil Depression, is too hot for a normal thermometer. A thermometer would explode before it could register a temperature! The dirt itself is colored green and blue and orange by the minerals in the ground. One European, gazing into the Danakil Depression in amazement, called it "the hell-hole of creation"!

But most of Ethiopia, far from being a "hell hole," was a prize that at least one European country was anxious to win. The Italian government had its eye on the only free African country.

Ethiopia would soon have to protect itself against Italian invasion. But before the Ethiopians could face this threat, they had to solve a problem of their own: Their country had two emperors.

One of these emperors, named Yohannes IV, came from a northern part of Ethiopia called Tigre. The other, Menelik II, came from the center of Ethiopia, an area named Shewa. Both Yohannes and Menelik claimed that, by right, *he* was the emperor of Ethiopia, the man who deserved the traditional Ethiopian title "King of Kings."

But Yohannes and Menelik didn't dare start an open war with each other. Italy was hovering on Ethiopia's borders. Down south, Great Britain was growing stronger and stronger. Just to the west, the country of Belgium was greedily expanding

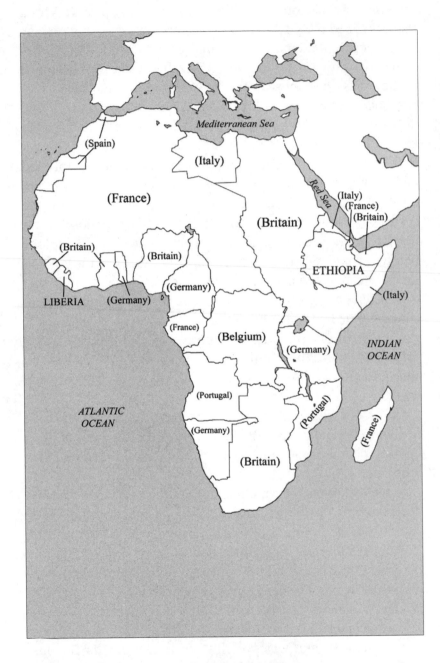

Ethiopia and Italy

its territory in Africa. If a civil war began in Ethiopia, with the Ethiopians spending their money and energy fighting each other, these European countries could just swoop in and take over.

Both Yohannes and Menelik had already tried to make alliances with different European countries. British soldiers had helped Yohannes get rid of the Ethiopian emperor who came before him—so that he could seize the throne. And Menelik had been buying weapons from both Italy and France. He even sent an Ethiopian Christian priest to these two countries, to help him negotiate good prices for guns.

Yohannes and Menelik both knew that these alliances would make it easier for European countries to take control of Ethiopia. So they made a deal with each other. They decided that Yohannes would have the title King of Kings. But Menelik would get to be the king of the center of Ethiopia. And both men agreed to be allies and fight side by side if a European army invaded.

During his rule as King of Kings, Yohannes managed to fight off an Egyptian invasion of Ethiopia, keeping his country free from the control of the Egyptians to the north. Meanwhile, Yohannes and Menelik ruled their own territories. They were polite to each other. They plotted against each other, while trying not to get caught. They made deals with Italian and British army officers in order to get more weapons. And each one hoped that the other would drop dead.

In 1889, Menelik got his wish. Yohannes IV led his soldiers into battle against invaders from the west—and was shot. As he died, he whispered, "Make my son king!"

Menelik didn't have any intention of allowing Yohannes' son to become King of Kings. Instantly, he declared himself emperor. Yohannes' army, which had fallen apart after Yohannes was shot, was too disorganized to prevent him.

Menelik began his reign by trying to protect his country from the Italians. Only months after Yohannes IV died, Menelik made a deal with the Italians. He promised them that they could take a tiny coastal area as an Italian colony, as long as they agreed to respect Ethiopia's independence.

But Menelik had been tricked. The treaty he signed with Italy had two different versions. The version written in Menelik's language said that if he wanted to, Menelik could ask Italy's advice on dealing with other countries. But the version written in Italian said that he *had* to ask Italy's permission before dealing with any other country.

This treaty had turned Ethiopia into a protectorate of Italy. It would make Ethiopia like Liberia—a country that wasn't truly free. The Italians sent copies of this treaty to Great Britain, Germany, and Belgium in order to prove that Italy now controlled Ethiopia. When Menelik appealed to Queen Victoria of England for help, she refused to deal with him—because the European countries had agreed not to interfere with each other's territories.

Menelik had only one choice. He had to go to war to reject the treaty.

The Italians assembled their soldiers on the coast that Menelik had given to Italy as a colony. They marched into Ethiopia, not expecting much opposition. The whole Italian army had less than fifteen thousand men in it.

But Menelik was ready for them. He had already traded African ivory to European gun dealers in exchange for modern weapons. Now he used these weapons to arm his own soldiers—and assembled an army of over a hundred thousand men.

When the Italians met the Ethiopians at a mountainous place called Adowa, they were horrified to see that they were outnumbered more than five to one! They had such bad maps that they didn't know where to hide, or how to get away from the huge Ethiopian army. And as the battle began, a huge rain storm poured down and confused the Italians even further.

Almost three quarters of the Italian army was killed. The others fled. Menelik's men began to chase them, but Menelik called them back. He allowed the Italian survivors to return to the coast. Menelik knew that the Italians would be too embarrassed to attack again.

Thcy were. In fact, the Italian government in Rome agreed to sign a *real* treaty recognizing Ethiopia's independence. Menelik also convinced Great Britain and France to sign similar treaties. Now, all three of these countries would watch each other. If Italy, Great Britain, or France tried to invade Ethiopia, the other two would stop it—because none of these countrics wanted any of the others to gain any more power in Africa.

The Battle of Adowa, in 1896, proved to be the only time that an African country was able to fight off European invaders. Alone in Africa, Ethiopia had kept its power. And Menelik II had earned the title "Lion of Africa."

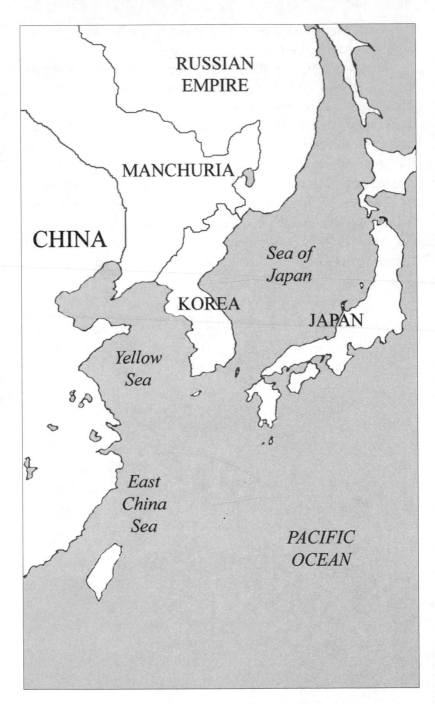

Country Borders Before the Sino-Japanese War

Chapter Fifteen
Small Countries With Large Invaders

The Korean Battleground

You may be thinking that there is a war in almost every chapter of this book. That's very close to the truth! Wars have been part of history since the beginning. But in the modern age, when countries all over the world began to build railroads and roads, and began to use steam to power trains and ships, it became much easier to move large numbers of soldiers and weapons around. The wars between countries began to get bigger. More soldiers crowded the battlefields, with more powerful weapons—and caused much more destruction.

The next war of the modern age exploded between the vast country of China and Japan, just off China's eastern coast. The last time we visited China, the enormous Taiping Rebellion had just ended, and the Qing emperor had (just barely) managed to hang onto his power. And when we last read about Japan, the shogun had just been removed from power; the Meiji emperor had taken back his throne, but the country had also elected an assembly to help him rule and had written a constitution, just like a Western democracy.

Although China was much bigger than Japan, Japan had been growing steadily stronger, and the Qing dynasty of China had been growing weaker and weaker. In 1894, Japan challenged China's power, and a war began. But the war wasn't fought in Japan or China. It was fought in Korea.

The little country of Korea lay between these two hostile neighbors, on a peninsula that jutted down from the Chinese province of Manchuria, into the Sea of Japan. The king of Korea, King Kojong, ruled with the help of his wife Queen Min.

As a matter of fact, many people thought that Queen Min was the real ruler of Korea. Kojong, the twenty-sixth king of the royal Chosun dynasty of Korea, became king when he was only eleven years old. Because he was so young, he had a regent to rule for him. The regent took control of the country, and of Kojong. Young Kojong became very used to doing as he was told.

When he was fourteen, he was told that it was time for him to get married. His bride had already been picked out for him. She was a fifteen-year-old lady of the court named Min.

Kojong did as he was told. Min turned out to be very different from the placid, obedient Kojong. She was a strong-willed, intelligent young lady, and she was much more ambitious than her fourteen-year-old husband.

Min didn't like the regent who was ruling for King Kojong. She didn't like the way he treated her husband, and she didn't like his ideas about how the country should be run. For many years, Korea had treated China as an "older brother" or a "father" country. Korea traded only with China, and sent ambassadors only to China—not to any other country. Korea became known as the "Hermit Country" because it would deal only with China. King Kojong's regent wanted to keep this old-fashioned arrangement. But Min, along with many other Koreans, thought that the time had come for Korea to start trading with other countries, and especially with Japan.

For the first seven years of her marriage, Min did her best to make sure that as many of her relatives as possible got positions in the Korean government as ministers, army officers, and other officials. When she was twenty-two, Min convinced her husband that it was time for him to take power. All of her relatives agreed. The regent had no choice but to step down. King Kojong now ruled in his own name—but Queen Min was the most powerful leader in the palace.

Very soon, King Kojong and Queen Min signed a trade treaty with Japan, so that Japanese ships could dock at three Korean ports to buy Korea's iron and coal. But Korea also wanted to remain friends with China. So China and Japan made a deal with each other. Since neither country wanted the other to take control of Korea, they agreed that Korea would be

Korea's Queen Min

protected by both China and Japan, and that neither Japan nor China could send soldiers into Korea without the agreement of the other country.

For a little while, this agreement seemed to work. But in 1894, King Kojong was faced with a problem. A new religious group called the Tonghak, in the south of Korea, started to collect weapons and plan a rebellion. Like the Taiping Rebellion in China, the Tonghak Rebellion was started by poor peasants who were miserable with their lives and angry with their leaders. King Kojong didn't want the Tonghak Rebellion to swell into an enormous civil war. So he sent a message to China, asking for Chinese soldiers to help defeat the rebels.

The Qing emperor agreed. China borrowed a British warship, loaded soldiers onto it, and sent them out into the ocean to sail south towards Korea. When the Japanese found out that China was sending soldiers into Korea without Japanese approval they were indignant. China had broken its agreement with Japan! The Japanese believed that the Chinese were out to capture Korea for themselves—and so Japanese soldiers sank the British ship with the Chinese soldiers on board.

This meant war.

By August 1, 1894, China and Japan had declared war on each other. The "Sino-Japanese" (Chinese-Japanese) War had begun. But the war didn't take place in China or in Japan. Chinese and Japanese soldiers met in Korea, and fought on Korean soil.

China's army turned out to be no match for Japan's modern soldiers, armed with Western weapons. In less than eight months, Japan had marched from southern Korea up into China itself. China had to agree to sign a peace treaty that gave Korea total independence from China, and also gave the Japanese large territories once held by China. European countries such as Germany, France, Russia, and Great Britain took advantage of China's weakness to seize other bits of China for themselves. This time is sometimes called the "Scramble for China."

Meanwhile, what about Korea?

Although Korea was now completely independent from China, there were plenty of Japanese soldiers still occupying Korean land. Many Koreans were pleased to see the Japanese in Korea, because they believed that Japan would become a strong ally of Korea. But Queen Min was worried about Japan. She doubted that Korea would remain free. Instead, she feared, Japan would first seize her country, and then rule over it.

Queen Min sent messages to Russia, asking the Russians whether they would become Korea's allies against *both* China *and* Japan. When the Japanese and the pro-Japanese Koreans heard about Queen Min's attempt to get Russia on her side *against* Japan, the Queen's fate was sealed.

Early on an October morning in 1895—only weeks after the war had ended—three assassins broke into the Queen's palace. They killed Queen Min and then escaped to Japan. When other countries protested that Japan should punish the assassins, the Japanese tried the culprits in a public court, and then announced that there was just not enough evidence to convict them.

Fifteen years after Queen Min died, Japan made Korea part of the Japanese Empire. Queen Min's fears had come true; Korea had lost its independence, and Japan had taken over her little country.

The Spanish-American War

Off the coast of China, south of both Japan and Korea, lay another small country: a gathering of islands called the Philippines. There, a small boy named José Rizal was born to a very wealthy family. José's parents wanted to give him the best of everything, including the best education. So when José was old enough he went to the most prestigious college in the Philippines. Afterwards, his parents sent him to university in Spain.

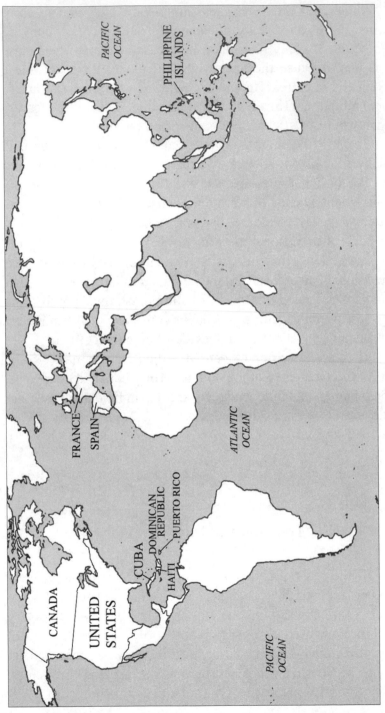

The Spanish-American War

Why in Spain? Because the Philippines were part of the Spanish Empire.

As José Rizal grew, read, and studied, he began to believe that the Spanish rule over the Philippines was unfair. Why should this European country, so many thousands of miles away, tell Filipinos how to run their country? The people of the Philippines—like the people of Canada, Acheh, Ireland, Ethiopia, and many more countries—had the right to govern themselves.

José Rizal didn't start a revolution, or organize rebels into a secret society that would oppose the Spanish. Instead, he wrote a novel called *Touch Me Not*. If you picked up this novel to read it, you might think that it was simply a love story about a young man named Crisostoma Ibarra and a beautiful girl named Maria Clara. But the novel had a hidden message in it. In *Touch Me Not*, José Rizal described the Spanish government as cruel, unjust, and oppressive. Filipinos who read Rizal's novel began to think, like Rizal, that the Philippines should be independent, ruled by Filipinos and not by Spain.

José Rizal's novel wasn't read only by Filipinos. On the other side of the world, other Spanish-ruled colonists read *Touch Me Not*. These colonists lived in Cuba, an island country that lay south of the United States, just below the state of Florida. Cuba was also governed by Spain. The Cuban colony was important because so many fields of sugarcane grew there. Cuba supplied Spain with a good part of its sugar, and the sale of Cuban sugar to other countries made Spain richer.

But many Cubans, including those who read Rizal's novel, began to think that they, too, should be independent from Spain. Cubans who were unhappy with Spanish rule began to argue, write, and talk about Cuban independence. A few decided that talking and writing weren't enough. Cubans would have to fight for their freedom! These violent revolutionaries announced that their slogan was "*¡Independencia o muerte!*" ("Independence or death!").

These Cubans believed it was better to be dead than to be ruled by Spain. And some of them began to die when Spain sent soldiers into Cuba to fight against the revolutionaries.

People in the United States of America knew what was happening in Cuba. Many Americans were sympathetic to the Cuban revolutionaries. After all, the United States had fought a revolution to win freedom from Great Britain. As the fighting to the south went on, the United States Congress declared, on behalf of the people of the United States, that Cuba should be free and independent from Spain. American newspapers printed articles about the "Cuban crisis" on their front pages, day after day.

Sometimes, these newspapers made the Cuban crisis sound even worse than it was. The largest American newspapers, just before the year 1900, were the *New York Journal*, owned by a businessman named William Randolph Hearst, and the *New York World*, owned by Joseph Pulitzer. Today, a very distinguished prize given to newspaper reporters who do excellent work is named after Joseph Pulitzer—the "Pulitzer Prize."

Hearst and Pulitzer discovered that, on days when stories about Cuba were printed on the front pages of the *New York Journal* and the *New York World*, people bought more newspapers. So both newspapers began running stories about Cuba, even when there wasn't much news coming out of the "Cuban crisis." Sometimes these stories about Cuba were exaggerated. Sometimes, they were just plain lies! The newspapers even made up interviews with make-believe "eyewitnesses" who claimed that they had seen Spanish soldiers and officials treating Cubans with terrible cruelty. William Randolph Hearst sent an artist named Frederic Remington to Cuba, and told him to send back drawings of events so grim and ghoulish that Americans would beg the United States to go to war on Cuba's behalf. When Frederic Remington protested that the Spanish weren't actually treating Cubans quite *that* badly, and that there was no need for a war to begin, Hearst replied, "You furnish the pictures and I'll furnish the war."

Why were Hearst and Pulitzer eager for war? Because during wars, hundreds of thousands of people bought newspapers to find out what was happening.

Hearst and Pulitzer were willing to do anything to sell newspapers, including inventing stories and making up interviews and pictures. Some smaller newspapers copied them. But other editors were disgusted. One said that journalism (newspaper writing) had simply become "a varied assortment of new lies."

Then something true and newsworthy truly *did* happen. On February 15, 1898, after the "Cuban crisis" had been going on for several years, a United States battleship called the *Maine* blew up in a Cuban harbor. Two hundred and sixty Americans died. Spanish officials said the explosion had been an accident. Something inside the *Maine* must have caught fire and blown up the ship. But American officials insisted that the *Maine* had been blown up by a bomb, planted by a Spanish spy.

To this day, no one knows exactly what destroyed the *Maine*—although most experts think that it probably wasn't a Spanish bomb. But in 1898, most Americans were ready to believe that the Spanish had deliberately blown up an American ship. The newspapers saw a wonderful chance to sell more copies. Paper after paper printed stories about how the Spanish had attacked United States soldiers. The stories called for the United States Congress to declare war on Spain. Headlines read, "Remember the *Maine*!" The *New York Journal* printed a million copies of its newspaper, urging the United States to attack Spain.

On April 19, 1898, the United States Congress voted to go to war with Spain. This war wouldn't just take place in Cuba. Instead, United States ships would attack the Spanish navy all over the world, wherever Spanish warships sailed.

This included the Philippines!

The Assistant Secretary of the Navy, the man who would help direct the United States battleships as they organized their attacks, was a man named Theodore Roosevelt. (He would later become president.)

Theodore Roosevelt ordered American ships to sail to the Philippines, attack the Spanish fleet docked there, and destroy the Spanish ships. Meanwhile, American and Spanish soldiers fought with each other in Cuba. Theodore Roosevelt himself led a band of soldiers nicknamed the Rough Riders into Cuba. The most famous battle fought by the Rough Riders took place on July 1, when Roosevelt and his men charged up a hill called San Juan Hill, driving the Spanish army back.

The Philippines and Cuba weren't the only places where Americans and Spanish were fighting. The United States also sent eighteen thousand soldiers to land on the island of Puerto Rico, near Cuba. Puerto Rico was also part of the Spanish Empire.

But before much fighting could take place in Puerto Rico, Spain agreed to surrender. On December 10, 1898, Spain and America signed a treaty called the Treaty of Paris. This treaty decreed that Puerto Rico, Cuba, the Philippines, and another small island called Guam would no longer belong to Spain. But none of these countries were given independence. Instead, they would be ruled by the United States of America!

The people of the Philippines were particularly angry about this. They declared that they wouldn't be ruled by the American president. Instead, they wanted their own president, a man named Emilio Aguinaldo. Aguinaldo told the United States that America was acting in a way that was "violent and aggressive" against the people of the Philippines. When the United States refused to give the Philippines complete independence, Emilio Aguinaldo declared that the Philippines were now at war with the U.S.

But Aguinaldo's forces were not strong enough to withstand American troops. In 1901, American soldiers invaded the Philippines and captured Aguinaldo. He had to agree to take an oath of loyalty to the United States, and to retire as president of the Philippines. In return, the American Congress agreed that the Philippines would be ruled by two groups of lawmakers. One group would be made up of Filipino leaders, elected by the people of the Philippines. The members of the other group would be selected by the American Congress.

In the Spanish-American War and the fighting that followed it, over two hundred thousand Filipinos died. The Philippines were free from Spain and had their own government. But this government existed in the shadow of a larger, stronger country—the United States.

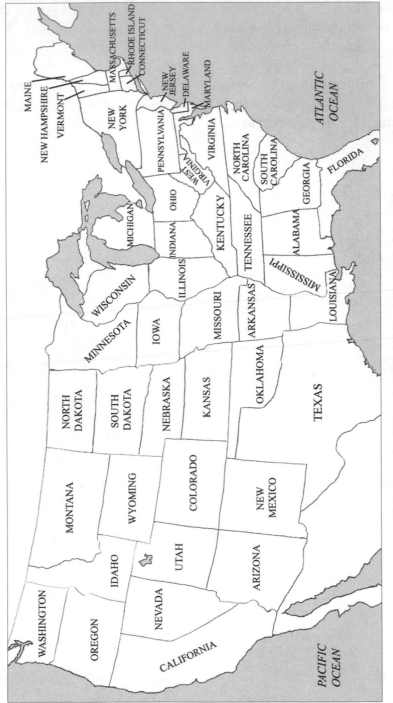

Claiming the West in the United States of America

Chapter Sixteen
The Expanding United States

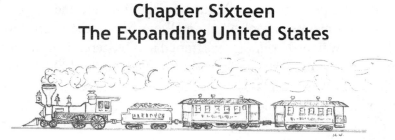

Moving West

Imagine that you and your family live in Pennsylvania, in the eastern United States, not long before the Spanish-American War. You've always lived in Pennsylvania. It's the only home you know. But your father is having trouble finding work, and your parents have heard that out in the vast western territories of the United States, settlers can begin a new life.

So they decide to pack up and head out to Oregon, all the way on the other side of North America.

You'll travel to Oregon in a wagon pulled by oxen. Horses can't live on the prairie grass out west, but oxen can. That way, you won't have to take as much food for the animals. Most of the wagon will be filled with food for your family instead. In order for you, your parents, and your older brother to reach Oregon safely, you'll need to take a thousand pounds of food with you—more than will fit in the back of a large pick-up truck today.

If you're like most families heading to Oregon, you'll soon discover that you've brought too much stuff. The more belongings you pack into your wagon, the heavier the wagon is, and the slower your oxen walk. As you ride along, you see that the families travelling ahead of you have begun to toss things out of the wagons as they go: clothes, toys, books, pieces of furniture, even cast-iron stoves.

So many families took the wagon route to Oregon to begin a new life that the path west became known as the Oregon Trail. Today, you can still see marks in the ground where thousands of wagon wheels rattled through the trail. The trip was hard. In large families, not everyone could fit into the wagon, so family members took turns walking beside the oxen. Often, they walked barefoot, on scraped and blistered feet, in the rain. Some *pioneers* (people travelling west in the 1800s) died when they were struck by lightning! Others got bruised by giant pieces of hail, the size of grapefruits. Many got sick. If they caught the mysterious, deadly illness called cholera, they might die in just a few short hours. Their families would bury the dead by the side of the trail—and move on.

Every night, the pioneers camped by the side of the trail. Every morning, they got up before sunrise and made a fire. Without a fire, there would be no hot breakfast. But by the time the wagons reached the vast western plains, there were few trees and branches to make a fire with. Sometimes, pioneers might find a chair or table that another wagon had tossed out, and build a fire with the furniture. But more often, they had to collect dried buffalo dung, which the settlers called "buffalo chips." The dung burned almost as well as wood.

A pioneer family on the Oregon Trail

Sometimes even buffalo chips couldn't be found. Then, settlers ate their food raw. A minister named Samuel Parker, who followed the Oregon Trail out west, wrote, "Dry bread and bacon consisted our breakfast, dinner and supper. The bacon we cooked when we could obtain wood for fire; but when nothing but green grass could be seen, we ate our bacon without cooking."

The trip out west took six months. But despite the long, hard journey, thousands and thousands of Americans decided to take the Oregon Trail. The eastern cities and states, from Atlanta, Georgia, to Boston, Massachusetts, were filling up. In many cities, it was hard for workers to find jobs. And in the countryside, it was hard for young farmers to find land to buy. People from Boston, New York, Philadelphia, Richmond, Charleston and a dozen other cities began to move west.

The U.S. government wanted these American settlers to claim the west for the United States. So, as people went west, government officials went with them and divided the huge western lands into areas called *territories*. When sixty thousand people had settled down in a particular territory, they could send a message to Congress and ask that their territory become a state. Once a territory became a state, the settlers who lived there could elect representatives to Congress and have a voice in their own government. After Texas (which had been claimed by the United States from the Spanish), the first western territory to become a state was Iowa, in 1846—long before the Civil War! The last was Arizona, which became a state in February of 1912.

But there was a problem. The western territories to which the settlers were travelling weren't empty. Native Americans, nicknamed "Indians," had been living there for centuries. As a matter of fact, many of the names of western states and towns come from Indian words. "Nebraska," for example, comes from a word used by the Oto tribe, meaning "flat water." "Minnesota" comes from a word used by the Dakota tribe that means "sky-tinted water."

At first, Native Americans were mostly friendly to the settlers. But as more and more pioneers arrived, the Native Americans began to see that this huge invasion would deprive them of their land. They began to defend their villages and their hunting grounds against the newcomers.

In response, the U.S. government sent an army—soldiers with guns to fight against the Native American tribes with their horses, bows and arrows. Skirmishes and battles were fought all over the west. But the sheer size of the U.S. army eventually drove the Native Americans out of the lands where they had always lived. Instead, the United States marked off certain areas of land called "reservations" and told the Native American tribes that they could only live in these "reserved places."

Even after the reservations were set up, Native Americans continued to resist. In the territory that is now Montana, the Native American leader Crazy Horse, head of the Lakota "Indians," refused to allow his people to be driven into the reservations. Instead, he called his warriors to join him near the Little Bighorn River and fight back. The U.S. soldiers who were sent to attack Crazy Horse and his men were commanded by a famous soldier named George Custer. Custer had fought in the Civil War. He was the youngest man to ever be made a general in the United States Army. But he had fewer than seven hundred men under his command—and he did not know that almost four thousand Native American warriors had answered Crazy Horse's call. When Custer led his men into the Battle of Little Bighorn, he was killed, along with hundreds of his men.

Another famous Native American warrior, an Apache chief named Geronimo, actually led a band of Apaches in an escape from their reservation. "I was born on the prairies where the wind blew free and there was nothing to break the light of the sun," he told his followers. "I was born where there were no enclosures." Instead of accepting imprisonment on a reservation, Geronimo and his band broke out. For a whole year, they fought a guerilla war against the U.S. soldiers in the territories that now belong to the states of New Mexico and Arizona. But finally Geronimo was taken prisoner. He died twenty-three years later without ever returning to his home.

The western part of the United States no longer belonged to the Native Americans. Instead, the new western states became home not only to Americans from the east, but also to people who came from all over the world. People from Sweden moved to North and South Dakota. People from Ireland moved to Montana. People from China came to California.

America was now a huge country, spreading over a vast continent. Farmers and cattle ranchers who raised grain and cows on the western plains needed a way to get their wheat, corn, and meat to hungry city-dwellers in the East. So American businessmen built large railroads. Soon, the railroad tracks crossed the continent. The buffalo that had once roamed through the plains began to disappear. Western settlers killed thousands of them—sometimes shooting buffalo from railroad cars as the trains puffed by the herds. Buffalo Bill Cody, a famous outlaw and soldier, earned his nickname because he shot more than four thousand buffalo in a little over a year. The buffalo became an endangered species—a kind of animal that is in danger of disappearing from the earth.

The American West had changed forever.

Stocks, Philanthropists, and Outlaws

Imagine for a minute that you are very, very good at making chocolate candy. Every morning you get up and start work. You mix cocoa powder, sugar, butter, and milk. You stir the mixture over the stove until it is thick and creamy. Then you pour the warm chocolate mixture into candy molds. You add marshmallow centers to some of the candies, peanuts to others,

173

butterscotch pieces to yet another tray. When the candies cool, you dip some of them in a white chocolate coating, and drizzle caramel over others. Then you take your chocolate candies out in a tray and walk through your neighborhood, shouting, "Candy for sale!" Your neighbors come out and buy the candies for twenty-five cents each. When all the candy is gone, you walk home, counting your money. You have enough money to buy ingredients for the next day's candy—and enough extra to buy yourself food for the day and a new pair of shoes.

Now imagine that someone else builds a chocolate factory down the street. Ten workers measure and dump the ingredients into ten vats, where machines stir until the chocolate is thick. The vats dump the chocolate out into molds, where ten more workers add peanuts, marshmallows, and butterscotch pieces. As soon as the chocolate cools, the molds turn over automatically and the chocolates fall out onto a conveyor belt. Two more factory workers pick the broken chocolates out, and put the others into fancy boxes.

The factory owner makes so many chocolates that he can buy huge amounts of cocoa, sugar, butter, and milk. Because he buys huge amounts, he gets a special deal and pays less for each ingredient than you do. And because machines do some of the work, he can make many more chocolates than you can, without having to pay too many helpers. As a matter of fact, his factory makes so many chocolate candies that he can sell them for ten cents each and still make a profit.

When you walk down the road with your candies, you find out that all of your neighbors have already bought cheap candy from the factory. You can't sell a single piece of chocolate! And if you lower your price to ten cents a piece, you won't make enough money to buy food and shoes for yourself.

What can you do?

You give up your chocolate making and go work in the factory. All day long, you add peanuts to candies. No matter how many candies you fill with peanuts, you earn the same amount of money for every hour that you work. By the end of the year, the factory has made seven thousand dollars in profit. But all of the profit for making extra candy goes to the factory owner, not to you!

But then something else happens.

The factory owner thinks to himself, "If I could buy ten more vats and ten more conveyer belts, I could make even more candy. It would cost me three thousand dollars. But as soon as the vats and conveyer belts were working, I could make so much more candy that I would soon earn back much more than three thousand dollars in extra profit! Where can I get three thousand dollars?"

The factory owner decides to go talk to three rich friends. He tells the rich friends that if each one of them will give him a thousand dollars, he will give them one-tenth of the factory in exchange. Of course, he can't chop off one-tenth of his factory! But he offers to give each friend one-tenth of the factory's profit at the end of the year.

The three friends agree. Each hands over a thousand dollars. At the end of the year, the factory has made fifteen thousand dollars in profit! Each friend gets one tenth of this—fifteen hundred dollars. The factory owner gets $10,500. He's richer because the factory is bigger—and his friends have gotten fifteen hundred dollars in exchange for the thousand dollars they invested at the beginning of the year.

Everyone is happy!

Except, maybe, for you. You're still making exactly the same salary as you did back when the factory only made seven thousand dollars in profit.

This is what began to happen in the United States as the year 1900 approached. Two hundred years before, most people made money by working in their homes and selling what they made. But when factories came along, they made the same goods—lace, cloth, plows, hammers, bread—more cheaply than home workers could. The home workers were forced out of business and had to go work in the factories.

Then the factory owners wanted more machines, more workers, and bigger buildings. So they asked rich men, called "investors," to give them money to make improvements in exchange for part of the profits at the end of the year. This share in the profits was called "stock," and the rich men became "stockholders."

In our story, the rich friends who gave the chocolate-factory owner money each "bought stock" in the factory. Because they were now "stockholders," they got part of the profits at the end of the year. And the chocolate factory was no longer a business owned by a single businessman. It was a "corporation"—a business in which more than one person had the right to share in the profits.

The practice of "buying stock" grew more and more common. An investor could make a tremendous amount of money, if he were both smart and lucky. If he spent $100 buying stock in a business that was about to make a huge amount of money, he might get back $1,000 at the end of the year. But if he invested $100 in a business that wasn't very well run, he might only get $10 from the tiny profits at the year's end. He would lose $90 instead of making $900!

Stockholders who owned part of the profits in six or seven different businesses could become incredibly wealthy. Some of these rich stockholders used their money to buy yachts, marble bathrooms with gold faucets, and diamond necklaces. But others believed that it was important for those who had profited from buying stock (the "stock market") to give money to those who were less wealthy.

One of the most famous of these rich men was named Andrew Carnegie. Andrew Carnegie was born in Scotland, but his parents brought him to settle in Pennsylvania when he was thirteen years old. Andrew started working in a cotton factory right away! But he was determined to become more than a factory hand. He went to night school and worked hard at every job he had. By the time he was in his thirties, Andrew Carnegie owned the largest steel company in the United States. In the year 1900, the Carnegie Steel Company made forty million dollars in profit. And since Andrew Carnegie owned more stock in the company than anyone else, he got over half of the profit—twenty five million dollars for one year's salary!

Andrew Carnegie believed that he should give away as much of this money as possible. He wrote that it was actually good for society for some men to become unbelievably wealthy—because then they could do good for others. "This, then, is held to be the duty of the man of Wealth," he wrote, "… [to become] sole agent and trustee for his poorer brethren, bringing to their service his superior wisdom, experience, and ability to administer—doing for them better than they would or could do for themselves."

In other words, Carnegie believed that an average man who got rich would just squander his money. But a man who was smart enough to earn enormous wealth was also smart enough to use that money for the good of mankind. So it was really much better for the country that some people were poor (because that meant they really didn't have the ability to spend money wisely anyway). The very rich would spend that money on their behalf!

Andrew Carnegie practiced what he preached. He gave away 350 million dollars for college scholarships, libraries, scientific research, and many other good causes. He made a name for himself as a *philanthropist* (a person who gives away money for the good of others).

But this did not make him popular with everyone. Many people objected to Andrew Carnegie's idea that the poor have less wisdom and ability than the rich. Others pointed out that Andrew Carnegie was rich only because he had spent years and years paying the men and women who worked in his steel factories a tiny salary—while he took most of the profit at the end of the year. Carnegie, they claimed, was no better than an outlaw. Like many wealthy stockholders, Andrew Carnegie had stolen the work of others and taken it for himself.

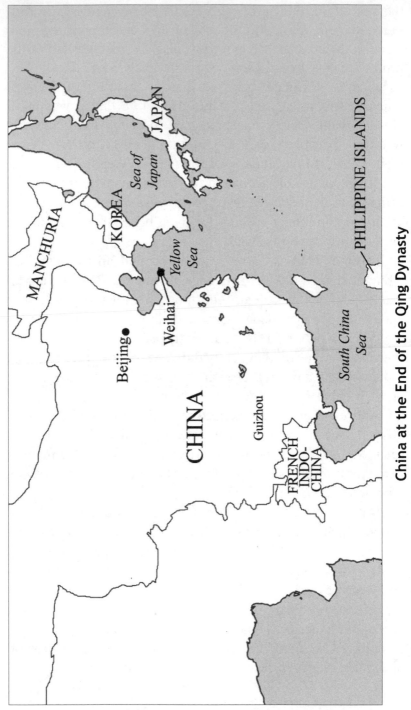

China at the End of the Qing Dynasty

Chapter Seventeen
China's Troubles

The Boxer Rebellion

As Americans were moving west into Native American land, another kind of invasion was taking place in the great country of China.

For many years, European countries, along with the United States, had been trying to creep into China. After the Opium Wars, China had been forced to open its ports to American and British ships—and whatever those ships brought with them. While Russia was trying to take land away from the Ottoman Turks, it was also trying to push down into the northern Chinese province called Manchuria. In the year 1897, the Germans had moved into the southern province of Guizhou and occupied it, stationing German soldiers throughout the whole area. And in 1898, the British seized control of Weihai, an important port city on the Yellow Sea.

To fight the invasions of the West, a small group of Chinese rebels formed a secret society. Like the secret societies of the Young Turks, the Young Bulgarians, and the Young Italians, this society was called "secret" because it wasn't officially recognized by the government. It was made up of men and women who were fiercely patriotic (loyal to their country), but who didn't think that their government was doing a very good job protecting the Chinese people. This Chinese secret society called itself "Yihhe Quai," or the "Society of Righteous and Harmonious Fists." But Westerners just called it "the Boxers," because the members were so good at martial arts.

The Boxers weren't just good at fighting. They also believed that they could become possessed by spirits who gave them strength and skill. When they got ready to fight, they went into a trance and started foaming at the mouth. They believed that this ritual made them invincible, and that swords and bullets would simply bounce off them! And they also claimed that thousands of "spirit soldiers" would rise from the dead and join them in their fight against Western occupation. As they went into battle, the Boxers chanted their slogan: "Destroy the foreigners! Destroy the foreigners!"

The Boxers planned to begin their war against foreigners by attacking both missionaries from the West and Chinese Christians. They believed that these Chinese Christians were traitors to their country, because they had converted to a "Western" religion. According to the Boxers, Christian missionaries brought Western ways into China, and helped to destroy the traditions of the Chinese.

The first attacks were made against German missionaries. Germany had sent hundreds of missionaries into the center of China, near the Yellow River. And these missionaries had been very unwise. Instead of simply preaching Christianity, the missionaries had gotten involved in the local government. They had promised the Chinese near them that, if they became Christians, the Germans would help them sue non-Christians in court—and win. This made them very unpopular with Chinese who already resented Western involvement in China's business.

German missionaries were attacked and killed. Chinese Christians who were friends of the missionaries were also killed. And Germany's ambassador to China was murdered by Boxers right in the middle of the street in the city of Beijing. He had been on his way to complain to the Chinese government about the Boxer violence against Germans in China!

The government of China had done very little to stop the Boxers. The emperor of China himself refused to approve of the Boxer attacks. But many of his court officials did—and so did his aunt, Cixi.

Cixi was the real ruler of China. Her actual title was "Empress Dowager." Her nephew, Guangxu, had inherited the throne and the title of "Emperor." But when Guangxu first became emperor, he made himself unpopular very quickly. In a hundred days, Guangxu made forty separate decrees, changing China's government, law, schools, money systems, army, and police so that China would be more modern. This was a lot of change, all at once—especially for a country that thought "more modern" meant "more like the Western countries that are trying to take us over."

When Cixi saw how nervous Guangxu's new decrees made the Chinese officials and the Chinese people, she rounded up the army, convinced them to fight for her, executed six of Guangxu's advisors, and put her nephew on an island in the middle of the palace lake. Now she held the real power in the capital city of Beijing. And she hated the foreigners who were pushing into China.

The Boxers roamed through the country, killing missionaries who could not get away from them, burning churches, and pulling up railway lines. Almost all of the railroads in China had been built by European merchants, with European money, in order to bring trains filled with European soldiers, European goods, and European customs into the center of China. Getting rid of the railroads was an important step in getting rid of European influence in China!

Governments from around the world sent messages to Cixi, ordering her to stop the rebels. Cixi agreed. She called up the army and put them on the alert—but she never actually told them to attack. She liked what the Boxers were doing. Although she might pretend to obey the Western countries telling her to stop them, she had no intention of actually doing so.

As the Boxer Rebellion grew larger, many foreigners in China fled to the city of Beijing. In Beijing, many different countries had offices called "embassies." These embassies were, by tradition, off-limits to Chinese officials. They were like little outposts of each country *in* China. And they were all located in a walled section of the city called the "legation compound."

The foreigners ran to their embassies and closed the gates of the legation compound. And not a moment too soon. The Boxers were already marching into Beijing, shouting, "Protect the country! Destroy the foreigners!"

Instead of stopping the Boxers with the imperial army, Cixi let them come in and surround the embassies. She declared that China was at war with the countries of the West.

Now the legation compound was under siege. There were almost five hundred foreign diplomats, journalists, and missionaries inside, along with about 450 soldiers from eight different countries. Three thousand Chinese Christians had also fled to the legation compound for safety. And the compound also had a stable inside it with 150 racehorses. When the besieged foreigners ran out of food, they ate the horses.

But news of the siege had reached the outside world. Soldiers from several different countries were preparing to march on Beijing to rescue the foreigners. The largest group of soldiers was from Russia (which was very happy for an excuse to send more armed Russians into China!). The second largest division of soldiers was from Japan. And the third largest was from the United States.

These soldiers were joined by British and French fighters. Nineteen thousand men landed on the shore of China and marched towards Beijing. Along the way, the army was attacked by Boxer raiders. But they pushed on towards Beijing. On August 14, 1900, two months after the siege of the legation compound had begun, the army of foreigners arrived in Beijing.

The Boxers, convinced that the special charms they wore and the words they recited would make them invincible, went out to meet them. But the Western soldiers shot the Boxers down. They broke down the gates of the Forbidden City, where the Chinese government had its headquarters, invaded the city, and burned the great Summer Palace—one of the greatest and most beautiful buildings in the world. Cixi barely escaped. She dressed herself as a peasant, grabbed her nephew from the island in the middle of the palace lake, got into a cart, and rattled out of the city.

The government officials who were left in Beijing had to face the victorious Western army! They promised that if the soldiers would go back home instead of staying in Beijing, the Boxers would be properly punished. They insisted that Cixi's declaration of war hadn't been an official *Chinese* declaration. Finally, they signed an agreement with eleven foreign countries, spelling out how the Boxers would be punished. The Chinese agreed to punish officials who had supported the Boxers, to build stronger walls around the legation compound, to repair the railroads, and to pay 333 million dollars in fines to the rest of the world.

Once again, Western countries had managed to take control of Chinese affairs. As a matter of fact, Great Britain assumed that it could do as it pleased with China. One British official wrote that the British had three options, after the Boxer Rebellion. Britain could divide China up, replace the Qing dynasty with another dynasty, or just try to patch things up with the existing Qing ruler.

The third option seemed to be the best. So Cixi was allowed to return to Beijing as Empress Dowager. But she had to agree that schools would now teach Western ideas. She had to agree to outlaw several traditional Chinese practices, such as footbinding (wrapping girls' feet in tight bandages so that they would stay small). She also had to agree to send Chinese officials abroad to study and learn from the constitutions and governments of other countries.

The Qing dynasty had survived the Boxer Rebellion. Seven years later, when Cixi died of a stroke, the three-year-old prince Puyi inherited the throne of China.

But China had already been conquered by Western ideas. And Puyi would be the last Qing emperor of China.

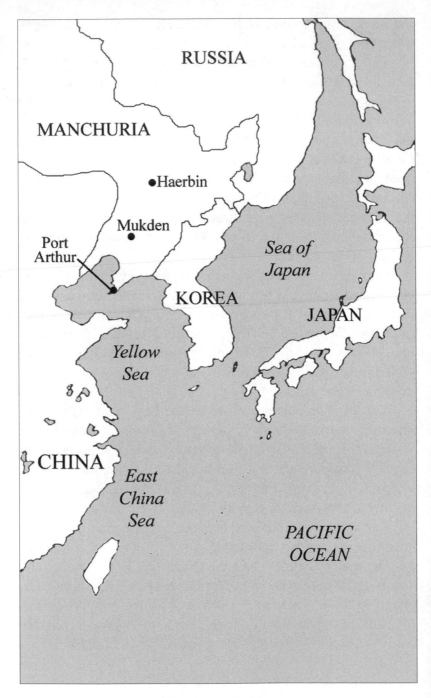

The Rise of Japan

The Czar and the Admiral

When those nineteen thousand soldiers landed on China's shores, ready to put the Boxer Rebellion down, Russian and Japanese soldiers had marched side by side. Together, they had fought against the Boxers, invaded Beijing, and set the besieged foreigners free.

But now that the Boxer Rebellion was over, Russia and Japan would no longer be allies. They would become enemies, because both countries wanted to grab part of China for themselves.

At the time of the Boxer Rebellion, the czar of Russia was Nicholas II, who had inherited the throne from his tyrannical father Alexander just six years earlier. Under Nicholas II's reign, Russia had started to build a new railroad in China. It would run from Haerbin, a large city in the northern province of Manchuria, all the way down to Port Arthur on the Yellow Sea. Russia had convinced China to rent Port Arthur to Russia for ninety-nine years. This meant that, for almost a century, Port Arthur would belong to Russia—in exchange for a large amount of money.

The Russians needed Port Arthur. The easiest way to move soldiers, food, tents, and other supplies quickly along the Russian coast was by sailing through the Pacific Ocean. And Russia only had one other port that lay on the Pacific. That port was so far north that it was completely frozen over every winter! Without Port Arthur, Russia had no way to move troops and supplies by sea.

The railroad was almost as important as Port Arthur. When the railroad was finished, Russian ships could land at Port Arthur, filled with soldiers. The soldiers could travel up the railroad into the center of Manchuria. For years, Russian soldiers had occupied Manchuria. Now, the railroad would allow Russia to build this small occupying force up into a huge army—that could invade and seize other parts of China.

Port Arthur and the railroad were both part of Russia's plan for taking over land in Asia. After the Boxer Rebellion ended, Nicholas II decided that Russia should begin by seizing the little country of Korea.

This wasn't the first time Russia had considered a takeover of Korea. A few chapters ago, we read about Queen Min of Korea, who doomed herself by sending Russia a message, asking the Russians to become her allies against Japan. When the Japanese found this out, they got rid of Queen Min. Japan didn't want Russia to ally itself with Korea—and Japan certainly didn't want to lose Korea to Nicholas II.

The Japanese tried to make this known through *diplomacy* (sending polite messages to another country by way of an ambassador). Japan sent its ambassadors to Moscow with a message to Nicholas II: "Japan would appreciate it if you would move your soldiers out of Port Arthur, and also out of Manchuria." What this respectful-sounding message *really* meant was: Don't even think about using those soldiers to invade Korea!

Nicholas II refused to remove the Russian soldiers in Port Arthur, so Japan called its ambassadors home and told them to take no more messages to the czar. This was called "breaking off diplomatic relations." When a country told all of its ambassadors to leave another country and come home, this was often an announcement that a declaration of war was coming!

The czar wasn't worried. After all, for centuries Japan had been an old-fashioned, isolated country without a modern army. During the Meiji Restoration, when the emperor was returned to the throne, Japan had started to make its army more modern. The traditional army of samurai had been replaced with a new, Western-style army—an army made up of paid soldiers who carried Western guns. But this new Japanese army had not been in existence for very long, and the Russians were not very afraid of it. Russian officers didn't even tell the battleships and troops at Port Arthur to keep a special watch. "If a shot is fired," Nicholas II remarked, "the Japanese, not the Russians will have to fire the first shot."

He only said this because he was sure that the Japanese would not dare to attack the Russian ships and soldiers in Port Arthur. After all, the Russians had the third largest navy in the world. Only France and Great Britain had more ships.

This was a mistake.

It was February 9, 1904, just after midnight. The Russian ships lay quietly at anchor at Port Arthur. On board, Russian sailors stood along the bridge, keeping watch. Off-duty sailors lay in their bunks, sleeping. Searchlights from the battleships swept over the dark surface of the water, showing nothing but the ripples of the waves.

In the dark of the ocean beyond the floodlights, Japanese destroyers were steaming silently towards the port. The commander of the Japanese navy, Admiral Togo, was a shrewd and fearless man. He had been given permission by the Japanese government to start a war—not by sending an official declaration of war to the Russian government, but by firing at the Russian fleet. The Japanese government had decided to follow a traditional piece of advice often given to samurai: "If your sword is too short, take one step forward." Since their army was not as strong as it could have been, the Japanese were attacking, without waiting for their enemy to move first.

Admiral Togo's spies had told him that the battleships and the forts at Port Arthur were expecting an attack. The spies were wrong. The Russians expected nothing. But Admiral Togo thought that the ships would all be waiting for him. So he told his captains to be as silent and secret as possible. They were to cover up the lights on deck, and keep any sparks from flying out of the steamship funnels.

At half-past midnight, the captain of the lead Japanese ship gave the signal to his men. A torpedo flew from the ship's torpedo tubes and slammed into the nearest Russian battleship. On the shores, the Russian officials heard explosions, and wondered why the battleships were doing target practice in the middle of the night. For hours, no one on shore realized that an attack was underway.

The Japanese fired sixteen torpedoes. Only three Russian ships were hit—but two of those ships were the most valuable battleships in the Russian fleet.

The attack at Port Arthur was just the first. Admiral Togo launched attack after attack on the larger Russian force, defeating the Russian ships again and again. Three months after the initial attack, the Japanese navy managed to destroy the *Petropavlovsk*, the flagship of the Russian navy. The admiral who commanded the whole Russian fleet was on board. The boat sank, and the admiral was never found—just his coat with his admiral's insignia on the shoulders floating on top of the water. Now Russia had lost its most experienced commander.

For 148 days, Japanese ships kept Port Arthur under siege. Finally, the Russian forces at Port Arthur had to surrender. Then the Japanese army marched against the Russian soldiers on land. In the Battle of Mukden, the largest land battle ever fought up to this time, the czar's army was defeated.

On May 27, 1905, the rest of the Russian fleet was destroyed by the Japanese fleet, still under the command of Admiral Togo. Huge Russian battleships turned upside down and sank. The men who leaped from them described how the setting sun flooded, blood-red, over the capsizing steel ships. The war was over, and Japan had won.

The president of the United States, Theodore Roosevelt, helped to arrange a peace treaty between the two countries. Russia was forced to give up all plans for ever invading Korea. Russia also had to give Japan part of Manchuria, all of Port Arthur, and several other pieces of land.

In August of 1905, the treaty between the two countries was signed in the United States—in the city of Portsmouth, New Hampshire. Four hundred thousand Russian soldiers and sailors had died, and the war had cost Russia the equivalent of millions of dollars.

Japan had stopped Russia's attempts to expand east, into China. For the first time, a European army had been defeated by an Asian country. And it had become clear to the whole world that Japan, not China, was now the master of the East.

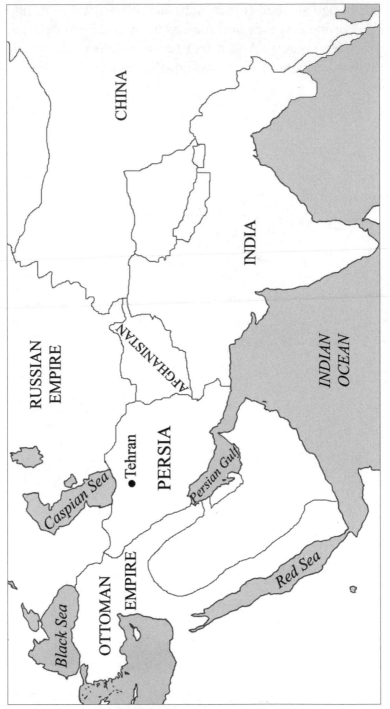

The Fight for Persia

Chapter Eighteen
Europe and the Countries Just East

Persia, Its Enemies, and Its "Friends"

Russia had failed to extend its power over China. But the czar and his army would have better luck a little further to the west.

Just below the Caspian Sea lay the ancient empire of Persia, now shrunk down to the size of a small country. In an earlier chapter, we read about Persia's attempts to invade Afghanistan. Persia and Russia made an alliance with each other, so that a Persian-Russian army could attack Afghanistan and bring it under Russian control. But when Great Britain threatened Persia, the Persian *shah* (king) decided that it would be wiser to withdraw and let the Russians and the British quarrel over Afghanistan.

Soon, the Russians and the British began to quarrel over Persia as well.

For years, the Russians had been trying to creep over Persia's northern border and take away Persian land. Although the Persians fought back, they were forced to give some of their land to Russia. Meanwhile, the British tried to gain power in Persia too—not by fighting, but by diplomacy. Remember those polite messages that one country sends to another by way of an ambassador? Diplomacy *looks* courteous and well mannered, but usually one country agrees to the polite messages of another country only because both countries know that a war will start if it doesn't.

Great Britain asked the shah, politely, to let British merchants sell and buy goods in Persia freely, and to let British citizens enter and leave Persia without any restrictions. The shah had to agree. He knew that British soldiers might invade unless Persia did as Great Britain asked, and Persia couldn't fight both the Russians and the British.

Persia was trapped between these two great powers, Russia and Great Britain: powers that distrusted each other and were likely to fight. Persia also had to keep an eye on the Ottoman Empire, which lay on its western border. To the east lay the country of Afghanistan, which still hated Persia because Persian rulers had claimed to rule over Afghanistan for so many years. Persia was surrounded by enemies!

In 1896, the shah of Persia died. His son, the crown prince, Mozaffar od-Din Shah, inherited the throne of Persia. Mozaffar od-Din Shah was thirty-five years old, but he had very little idea about how to rule Persia. All his life, he had hated his father—and had spent as much time away from him as possible. So his father had never taught him how to run his country. And when Mozaffar od-Din became shah, Persia was not only surrounded by enemies, but was deep in debt. His father had spent far, far too much money!

In order to raise money for Persia, Mozaffar od-Din Shah sold permission to develop an oil field to an Englishman named William Knox D'Arcy. This permission meant that, in exchange for a large sum of money, D'Arcy could drill holes in the ground almost anywhere in Persia, looking for oil. Oil, or *petroleum*, is a thick liquid that burns quickly. It lies in huge pools beneath the earth's surface, often under thick sheets of rock. Sometimes the pools are near the surface—but more often, they are hundreds of feet below the ground. To find oil, D'Arcy had to use a steel drill to dig down through the earth, hoping to find a pool (or *reservoir*) of oil. He might drill two hundred holes to find one reservoir. And if his drill finally went through rock into a pool of oil, the oil might explode out of the hole and spray into the air, like soda out of a soda bottle that's been shaken up.

Besides selling permits to D'Arcy, Mozaffar od-Din Shah raised money by borrowing it from Russia and from Great

Britain. He didn't use this borrowed money wisely. Instead, he took three expensive trips through Europe, spent huge sums on decorating his palace and on lavish parties, and bought very expensive clothes and jewels for himself and his family. Meanwhile, Persia sank more deeply into debt.

The Persian people rebelled.

Like the people of many other countries, the Persians demanded a constitution. This constitution would put limits on what the shah could do, so that he couldn't borrow or spend money without the approval of the Persian people. In the capital city of Persia, Tehran, armed rebels who wanted the shah to leave his throne set up their headquarters in a shrine. (Persian tradition said that the shah couldn't send his soldiers into a shrine to arrest anyone who had taken refuge there, because a shrine was a religious building.) Other Persians rioted in the streets. Workers went on strike. Tehran was in chaos. By December of 1906, Mozaffar od-Din Shah realized that he would have to give in to the demands of the people.

The shah agreed to give Persia a constitution. He also agreed that Persia would have an assembly, like Parliament in England or Congress in the United States. This assembly, called the National Consultative Assembly or the "Majles," would help rule the country. The constitution and the assembly would take much of the shah's power away. Mozaffar od-Din Shah had been in poor health for some time. Now, he became so upset by the changes in his country that he had a heart attack and died.

After Mozaffar od-Din Shah's death, both Russia and Great Britain claimed control over different parts of Persia. The British insisted that Great Britain had authority over the land along the Persian Gulf. The Russians announced that the northern part of Persia, close to the Russian border, was under their protection. And Russia also wanted to be able to send Russian ships to the Persian ports in the Caspian Sea. After all, Russia had lost Port Arthur, so its only port to the Pacific was still frozen every winter.

The new shah of Persia, Mohammad Ali Shah, had to figure out how to deal with these two empires who were quarrelling over his land. Unfortunately, Mohammad Ali Shah didn't have much power to fight back. Persia owed Russia and Great Britain so much money that British and Russian banks had the right to print and issue Persia's money. Even Persia's banknotes came from the foreigners Mohammad Ali Shah wanted to get rid of! Worse, many of the commanding officers in the Persian army weren't even Persian. They were British and Russian.

Mohammad Ali Shah thought that taking stronger control over his country might help him deal with the foreigners. So in 1908, he told his own personal band of bodyguards, the Persian Cossack Brigade, to dissolve the Majles. Mohammad Ali Shah intended to rule on his own.

But the Persian people were so angry over the shah's actions that they drove him out of the country. Mohammad Ali Shah had to escape. He ran to Russia!

Mohammad Ali Shah left his eleven-year-old son Ahmad behind him. The young boy became the next shah, but because he was so young a regent ruled for him—along with the Majles, which re-formed as soon as Mohammad Ali Shah fled to Russia.

While Mohammad Ali Shah was running away, William D'Arcy was finally discovering oil. He had just drilled down into an enormous oil reservoir in the southwest of Persia. As soon as he found the oil, he sold his company to the British government and retired. Now the British government owned an oil company that had the official right to pump oil out of Persia's land. This company, the Anglo-Persian Oil Company, could send this Persian oil back to Great Britain.

Why was oil so important to the British?

The British navy had two kinds of ships—ships with engines that burned coal, and ships with engines that burned oil. On a coal-burning ship, many of the sailors had to spend their time shoveling coal, which meant they couldn't fight. An oil-burning ship, on the other hand, only needed a few men to run the engines. The rest of the men could be manning guns. Ships that ran on oil also could go faster, and had to refuel less often.

Great Britain's ships were mostly coal-burning. But when the British government discovered that the Germans were building oil-burning ships, the British got worried. This new German navy would be stronger and faster than the British navy. Britain needed oil-burning ships too.

The future prime minister of England, Winston Churchill, knew that if Great Britain built oil-burning ships, the British Empire would have to find a good reliable source of oil. After all, Great Britain had "the finest supply of the best steam coal in the world, safe in our mines under our own land." But Great Britain had no oil. "We must carry it by sea," Churchill warned, "in peace or war from distant countries." Unless Great Britain could gain control of a country where oil was found, the British oil-burning ships might end up sitting at anchor, empty of fuel.

Now that oil had been discovered in Persia, Great Britain had two reasons to take control of Persia. If the British controlled Persia, it would keep Russia's power in the east from growing. And Great Britain would also be able to use Persian oil to fuel the British navy.

Meanwhile, the Majles (the Persian assembly) decided that it was time to ask for help from another country. It sent a message to the American president, William Taft, asking for the United States to lend Persia enough money to pay off both the British and the Russians. The president sent over a whole team of American bankers to figure out whether this could be done.

Great Britain wasn't happy about the American bankers in Persia, but Russia was furious. Russia sent the Majles a diplomatic message: "Send those Americans home right away!"

The Majles ignored the message. So Russian soldiers marched down from Russia, over the border into Persia, towards the city of Tehran. As the soldiers got closer and closer, the American bankers fled the country. The Majles dissolved, and its members left Tehran. Now the young shah of Persia would rule—under the supervision of the czar of Russia.

Persia would stay under Russian control for another decade. But the Russians allowed the Anglo-Persian Oil Company to keep on piping oil out of the ground and shipping it out of the country. Eventually, the Anglo-Persian Oil Company, which became known as British Petroleum, would become one of the largest oil companies in the entire world.

The Balkan Mess

If you look at a map of the Mediterranean Sea, you'll see the boot of Italy jutting down into the water. Just across a little stretch of sea, another peninsula also juts down into the Mediterranean, surrounded by little islands and laced through with rivers and inlets.

If you've studied ancient history, you know that the country of Greece sits on the south end of this peninsula. But the whole peninsula is not known as "Greece." Instead, it is called "the Balkan Peninsula." North of Greece lies a handful of other little countries called "the Balkans."

Until the year 1878, much of the Balkan Peninsula belonged to the Ottoman Empire. If you look at your map again, you'll see Macedonia (the homeland of Alexander the Great) just above Greece. The Ottoman Turks claimed Macedonia as theirs. Above Macedonia, Albania (also part of the Ottoman Empire) sits on the western side of the peninsula, with the tiny country of Montenegro just above it. For many years, Montenegro had managed to remain independent from Austria, the Ottomans, and the other powerful countries of Europe and the East.

Beside these two countries, in the middle of the peninsula, is the country of Serbia, which the Turks also ruled; and to the east, on the top of the peninsula, stretching overtop of the Aegean Sea, lies the country of Bulgaria. And just north of the peninsula, along the Adriatic Sea, are two more little countries: Bosnia and Croatia. Croatia had been folded into the eastern half of Austria, years before, but Bosnia belonged to the Turks. The Turks also ruled over the country of Romania, which lay above Bulgaria and just below the Russian border.

If you're confused, don't worry too much. Most people in Europe and the Americas didn't really have a good idea of who was ruling what on the Balkan Peninsula! This little patchwork of countries kept getting claimed by the larger countries around them. But the Ottoman Empire claimed more of the Balkans than any other country.

After the war between the Turks and the Russians in 1878, the Ottoman Turks had lost some of their land on the Balkan Peninsula. If you think back to Chapter Nine, you'll remember that the Russians marched down to attack the Ottomans in revenge for the sultan's cruelty to Bulgaria. When the Russians won, the Ottoman Empire had to give Romania and most of Asia Minor (called "Anatolia" at that time) to Russia. It also had to agree to give Bulgaria its freedom.

This arrangement made the rest of Europe nervous. It made Russia much larger, and it also turned Bulgaria into a big independent country that would always be a loyal ally of the Russians. Russia was getting far too powerful.

So the great powers of Europe—France, Germany, Great Britain, and Austria—told Russia that it could keep Romania, but it had to give Anatolia back to the Turks. They also decided that since Bulgaria would always fight on Russia's side in any war, Bulgaria would have to be smaller. So they forced the newly freed Bulgarians to give the whole southern part of their new country back to the Turks as well. The new, much smaller country of Bulgaria would be ruled by a Russian prince named Alexander of Battenberg, the nephew of the Russian czar.

The Balkan Mess

The Bulgarians in the south of country—the part that had been given back to the Turks—were furious. They didn't want to be part of the Ottoman Empire. They wanted to be free to join the north.

Together, the northern and southern parts of Bulgaria decided to reunite. The Ottoman Turks, worn out by war, didn't try to stop them. But Russia became angry over this decision, because Alexander of Battenberg and the northern Bulgarians hadn't asked Russia for permission. All Russian army officers in Bulgaria and all Russian diplomats were ordered to come home.

Now that Bulgaria was no longer friendly with Russia, the rest of Europe wasn't quite so worried about it. Bulgaria was allowed to stay one country.

Now the Balkan Peninsula had changed. Bulgaria was independent, and no longer an ally of Russia. The Ottoman Empire still controlled Anatolia (Asia Minor). Montenegro was still free. Serbia, which had been part of the Ottoman Empire, was set free as well. Austria took Bosnia for itself (so now Bosnia and Croatia were both part of Austria). The Ottomans got to keep Albania and Macedonia.

Just a couple of years later, Macedonia tried to break free from the Ottoman Turks. On August 2, 1903, Macedonian rebels joined together in the city of Krusevo and declared themselves independent of Turkish rule. This became known as the St. Elijah's Day Uprising.

Apparently the Turks hadn't learned anything from the Bulgarian rebellion. When the Bulgarians had revolted, the Turks had killed thousands—and had brought a devastating war down on themselves. But when the Macedonians revolted, the Turks did exactly the same thing. The sultan Abdulhamid ordered Turkish soldiers to march into Macedonia and kill the rebels.

This violence disgusted many Ottoman Turks—and gave the Young Turks a chance to finally get rid of the sultan. Remember, the Young Turks had already tried to start a rebellion against Abdulhamid. They had been forced to flee from their country, but they had gathered together in other cities, such as Geneva and Paris. In these cities, exiled Turks had been planning a takeover of their own country.

Now Abdulhamid had grown unpopular not just with his people, but with the Ottoman army. The Young Turks convinced the army to join them in demanding that Abdulhamid bring back the Turkish constitution. Faced with his own soldiers, Abdulhamid had to agree. He also had to reassemble the Turkish parliament. And then he left the country.

The Young Turks, now in power, issued a "Proclamation for the Ottoman Empire." The government, they announced, would now obey the "predominance of the national will." In other words, it would do what the people wanted. All Ottomans older than twenty would be allowed to vote. All Ottomans, whether Christians or Muslims, would have the same rights. And the Young Turks had even bigger plans for the Ottoman Empire. They wanted to get rid of the Islamic laws (laws based on the Muslim religion) that had always been part of the empire's government. Instead, they wanted to have *secular* laws (laws not based on any particular religion). They sent messengers to other European countries, asking for advice about how to make Turkish farms and factories more modern. They tried to force everyone in the empire to speak Turkish. They hoped that in this new "Ottoman nation," everyone—whether Christian or Muslim—would follow the same laws, speak the same language, and be loyal to the same government.

This didn't work very well.

Macedonia and Albania, where most of the people were Christians, still didn't want to be part of the Ottoman Empire, even if it claimed to be an "Ottoman nation" where Christians and Muslims were treated the same. But even though the Young Turks claimed that their government was ready to listen to the wishes of the people, when the people wanted to be independent, the Young Turks stopped listening. They were ready to send the Turkish army to keep the Ottoman nation together by force.

It became clear to the people of the Balkan Peninsula that the Young Turks were not going to allow them to leave the empire any more than the sultan had. So after only four years of Young Turk rule, the Balkan countries began to fight for their independence. Serbia, Bulgaria, Greece and Montenegro joined together, with the help of the Russian government, and tried to free Macedonia from Turkish rule. Together, the countries managed to put together an army of seven hundred and fifty thousand men to march against the Turks.

This "First Balkan War" began in 1912. In less than two months, the weak, disorganized Ottoman army realized that it would have to surrender the rest of its Balkan land.

Albania was finally independent. A prince descended from a good German family became the head of the Albanian government, and the countries of Europe agreed to recognize Albania as a free nation.

But Macedonia never did get its freedom. Instead, the "Second Balkan War" began between Serbia, Bulgaria, and Greece. These three countries, which had been allies against the Turks, started to argue with each other about how they would divide up Macedonia. In 1913, Bulgarian soldiers attacked their own allies, trying to take away a larger part of Macedonia by force.

The attack failed. Greece and Serbia divided Macedonia up between themselves. Bulgaria only got a tiny bit of land.

Now all of the Balkans were free of the Ottoman Turks. But the countries on the Balkan Peninsula were furious with each other. Bulgaria began to make an alliance with the country of Austria, in order to increase its own power. Serbia, which had been attacked by Bulgaria over the division of Macedonia, grew more and more hostile to Bulgaria—and to Austria, Bulgaria's new friend.

On June 28, 1914, a Serbian would show how much Serbia hated both Bulgaria and Austria. He would kill the heir to the throne of Austria. But this wouldn't begin a "Third Balkan War." Instead, it would start the first World War.

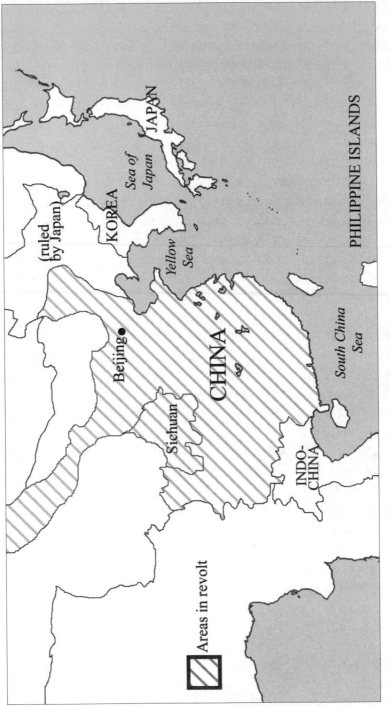

Rebellion in China

Chapter Nineteen
China, Vietnam—and France

The Last Emperor

China was filled with unhappiness. Its population had grown so quickly that the country couldn't raise enough food to feed itself. China's factories, farming machines, and weapons were all old-fashioned and shabby. China could no longer defend itself; instead, other countries fought wars over its cities. Forty million Chinese used the drug opium.

Worst of all, the Qing dynasty seemed to have no power at all. After the Boxer Rebellion, China had been forced to do whatever the British and French ordered. When Russia and Japan fought over Chinese land, the United States had to step in to make peace. One Chinese official exclaimed, "The Russians are spying on us from the north, the English are peeking at us from the west, the French are glaring at us from the south, and the Japanese stare at us from the east. We are in great danger!"

The last Qing emperor could do nothing to protect his country from this danger. He was only three years old.

The empress Cixi had died in 1908. Guangxu, the emperor that the Dragon Empress had removed from his throne, was still alive—but he died not long after. It was rumored in the palace that Cixi had left instructions for Guangxu to be poisoned, so that her chosen heir, the three-year-old Qing prince Puyi, would have no rival for his throne.

At three, Puyi couldn't rule China. Instead, he lived in his palace inside the Forbidden City. Walls thirty-five feet high separated him from the common people of China. The roof of his palace was gold, the royal color. His blankets, dishes, clothes, and everything else he owned was also the color of gold.

Until he was seven years old, Puyi never even saw another child. Scores of servants followed him everywhere, carrying extra clothing in case he got cold or wanted to change, and food in case he got hungry. At each meal, he was given twenty-five different kinds of food, laid out on six tables, to choose from. A doctor, carrying medicines, followed him around in case he sneezed or coughed.

Puyi was treated like a little god, but the real rulers of China were his regents. These Qing noblemen were supposed to run China for Puyi. The truth was that the regents, like the empress who had just died, had to do whatever Russia, Japan, and the United States told them to do.

In 1911, the people of China finally rebelled against this foreign control.

The revolt began in the Sichuan Province, near China's center. Officials in the Sichuan Province wanted to build their own railroad—a railroad that would belong to the Chinese, not to a foreign country like Russia. Many Sichuan merchants had contributed money to build the railroad. But they hadn't raised quite enough money to start laying down the railroad ties.

Then the Qing regents announced that the government would take over the project of building the railroad.

This meant that the Sichuan railroad would no longer belong to China. To finish the railroad, the Qing government meant to make a deal with French, German, and English bankers to get enough money. So the railroad would actually belong to French, German, and English banks.

The Sichuan officials refused to hand over the railroad project. They announced that they would no longer obey the Qing regents or the Qing government. Instead, they would set up a new Chinese government—a Chinese republic. The capital of this new Chinese republic would be the city of Nanjing, far south of Beijing. The president of the republic would be a doctor named Sun Yixian.

Sun Yixian (also called Sun Yat-sen) had tried to lead a rebellion against the Qing dynasty in 1895, sixteen years before.

When his plans to overthrow the Qing ruler were discovered, Sun Yixian had to run for his life. He went to Japan, and afterwards travelled in Europe. But now he had returned to China as the head of a group of revolutionaries who called themselves the "Kuomintang," or the "Nationalist Party."

The Sichuan rebellion spread all over China. The Qing regents knew that they could not fight against the will of the people, or against the armed members of the Nationalist Party. So in February of 1912, they announced that the little emperor would *abdicate* (leave his throne).

The Qing dynasty had ended. For the first time in thousands of years, China no longer had an emperor.

Now, Sun Yixian governed China. He told the Chinese people that, rather than following the rule of an emperor, they should live by the Three Principles of the People. The First Principle was "democracy": The Chinese should be able to vote for their leaders. The Second Principle was "livelihood": Everyone in China should be able to find a job and earn enough to buy food. And the Third Principle was "nationalism": The Chinese, not foreigners, should run the country of China.

The little prince, barely eight years old, was allowed to keep on living in his palace. A British official visited him to give him English lessons. Puyi liked his English lessons, and asked his tutor whether he could have an English name. The tutor gave him a list of English kings. From this list, Puyi chose the name Henry. From then on, he was known as Henry Puyi.

When he was twenty years old, Henry Puyi finally left the Forbidden City, and Beijing, and his country. He went to live in Japan. The Forbidden Palace, which for so long had been closed to the common people of China, was opened up so that anyone could come and see it.

When he was fifty-two years old, Henry Puyi visited his home again—for the first time in thirty-two years. Few people noticed him, or knew who he was. Just like a tourist, he wandered through the palace where, so many years before, he had been treated like a god.

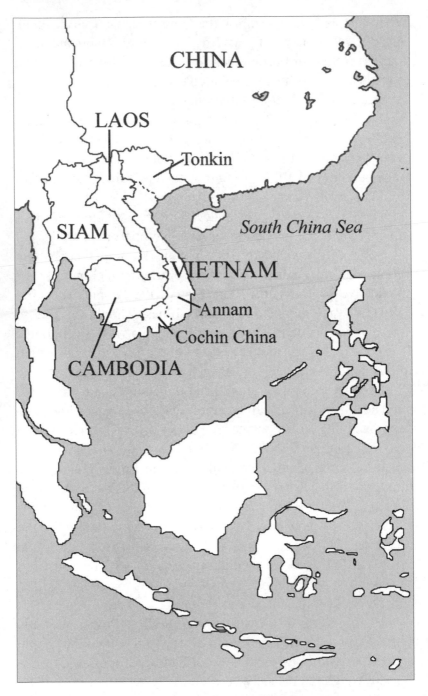

French Control of Indochina

The Vietnamese Restoration Society

If you were to travel south, down from China, you would find yourself on a large peninsula that juts down from the Chinese mainland into the ocean. The northern edge of this peninsula touches China; the southern end of it almost touches the Dutch East Indies. Travel west from the peninsula, and you would go across the Indian Ocean and find yourself on the eastern shore of India. Sail due east from this peninsula, towards the rising sun, and you would make your way through another cluster of islands. If you kept on sailing, after many days you would see the western coast of the United States in front of you.

Because this peninsula lies close to both China and India, it was known as "Indochina." Just as India had been taken over by Great Britain, and the East Indies by the Dutch, Indochina had been claimed by the French.

France, now ruled by the Third Republic, didn't have much of an empire left. Long before the Third Republic, France had settled in Canada—but it had been forced to surrender those colonies to Great Britain. France had built trading posts in India—but had been forced out of India by the British East India Company.

But in Indochina, France had managed to hang onto a little empire of its own.

The left side of the peninsula, the country of Siam (which today we call Thailand), belonged partly to France and partly to Great Britain. But France claimed to rule all of the right side of Indochina—the lands that today are Vietnam, Laos, and Cambodia.

Along the eastern coast—the country of Vietnam—the French divided their territory into three colonies. They called the northern colony Tonkin. The middle colony was called Annam. And the colony the furthest to the south was known as Cochin China.

For a hundred years, the Nguyen dynasty of emperors had ruled in Vietnam. The French allowed the Nguyen emperor to stay on his throne. But the French, not the Nguyen emperor, made all of the decisions about Vietnam's government. The French built railroads through the country and ports on its coast. The French owned rice plantations, groves of rubber trees, and coal mines. The Vietnamese worked in these plantations, groves, and mines—for very little pay. Almost all of the profit went to the French owners.

Under French rule, a very small group of rich Vietnamese who had allied themselves with the French overlords also made money from the plantations. But Vietnamese citizens, even wealthy ones, were not allowed to hold important jobs. It isn't surprising that the Vietnamese wanted the French out of their country.

The very first revolutionary group that tried to fight for Vietnamese independence was led by a Vietnamese patriot named Phan Boi Chau. Phan Boi Chau was born in 1867. As he grew up, he saw the French gaining more and more power over his country. He hated the French occupiers. Because his family was rich, Phan Boi Chau was allowed to go to school, and was even offered a job in the Vietnamese government.

But this meant that Phan Boi Chau would be working for the French. He refused.

Instead, in 1903 he formed a group called the Restoration Society—in Vietnamese, *Duy Tan Hoi*. He convinced a Vietnamese prince from the Nguyen family to join the Restoration Society. But all of this rebellious activity was noticed by the French. Phan Boi Chau, afraid of arrest by French police, fled to Japan.

From Japan, Phan Boi Chau—like many other patriots in exile—wrote articles about the evils of French rule. He asked other Vietnamese patriots to come and join him in exile. He hoped that, one day, this group of exiles could attack the French.

But the Japanese didn't want to anger France. So in 1908, they ordered Phan Boi Chau to leave Japan. Instead of returning to Vietnam, Phan Boi Chau went to China. He renamed his revolutionary group the "Vietnamese Restoration Society," or *Viet Nam Quang Phuc Hoi.*

From China, the Vietnamese Restoration Society tried to organize rebellions against the French. But it was difficult for Phan Boi Chau to start a revolt while he was living in another country. None of the rebellions succeeded.

The Chinese noticed what Phan Boi Chau was doing, though. Like the Japanese, they didn't want to anger the French. So in 1917, they arrested Phan Boi Chau and put him in jail. Before long, the Chinese agreed to set Phan Boi Chau free. But he had grown more and more discouraged by his long exile, and now by his imprisonment. He even wrote an article suggesting that, maybe, it would be better for the Vietnamese to try to get along with the French. He had begun to doubt that the Vietnamese would ever be able to get the French out of their country.

A few years later, Phan Boi Chau was in the Chinese city of Shanghai when French officials, visiting the city, recognized him. They ordered him to be arrested and taken back to Vietnam. There, Phan Boi Chau was tried for treason—and convicted. He was sentenced to spend the rest of his life in his house, guarded by French soldiers. He spent fifteen years under this "house arrest" before he died.

Phan Boi Chau had failed. But because of his work, other Vietnamese began to think more seriously about independence from France. Eventually, the seeds of revolution Phan Boi Chau planted would grow—and bloom. Because of this, Phan Boi Chau is remembered today as one of the greatest Vietnamese patriots.

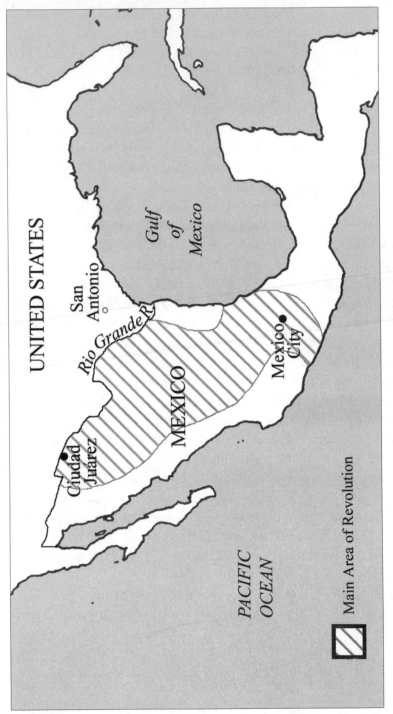

The Mexican Revolution

Chapter Twenty
Revolution In the Americas...
War In the World

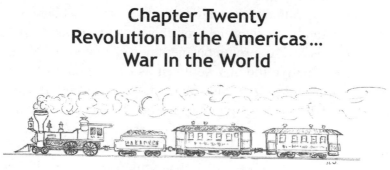

The Mexican Revolution

Around the year 1900, the president of Mexico was a man named Porfirio Díaz. He had been president for over thirty years. This was odd—because Mexico's constitution said that no one could be president for more than four.

Look between North and South America, and you'll see a bridge of land that connects them. On this land, which we call Central America, lies the country of Mexico.

Like South America, this land was home to native American tribes before Spanish *conquistadores* arrived and settled down. Spain claimed Central America for its own and gave it the name "New Spain." In 1821, "New Spain" declared its independence from Spain and became the country of Mexico, with its own constitution and its own elected president.

President Díaz had been elected again, and again, and again. He had been president for so long that his presidency had earned itself a name: "the Porfiriato." Porfirio Díaz claimed that no one in Mexico wanted to end his presidency by running against him. The truth was that his supporters paid visits to anyone who might be thinking about running for president against Díaz, and scared them out of the idea.

This had worked for thirty years. But now many Mexicans were growing discontented with Porfirio Díaz's government. Most of the decisions about how Mexico should be run were made by a small and powerful group of very rich men. Díaz had treated the native Central American tribes cruelly. He had ordered them rounded up and sent off to work as slaves on tobacco plantations; then, he took their land away and sold it to his friends and to foreign businessmen. The poor Mexicans who weren't native Indians were just as bad off. Even though they worked hard to farm their land, they couldn't sell the food they raised for enough money to feed themselves. When a dreadful famine swept across Mexico, thousands began to die of starvation.

Meanwhile, the powerful, wealthy men who owned large, modern farms were still watering their crops with artificial irrigation, raising healthy harvests—and then shipping the food out of the country for sale. People in other countries were ready to pay good money for their produce. Why should they waste it on starving peasants? These rich Mexicans didn't seem to care if the poor people of their own country died. In fact, to the common people of Mexico, they seemed less and less like Mexicans, and more and more like Europeans. Many of them had gone to school in Europe. They dressed like Europeans and talked like Europeans. Some had even begun to speak French instead of Spanish, the language of Mexico.

Groups of rebels—like the Young Turks, the Young Italians, and the groups that had formed all over Europe a few years earlier—started to band together and protest. They pointed out that for years and years, no one had dared to run against Porfirio Díaz. He had only been reelected again and again because he had no opponent! Mexico needed presidents who would only serve for one term. Mexico needed presidents who would see that all Mexicans got a decent education, proper food, and enough pay to live on.

In 1910, President Díaz allowed another presidential candidate to run against him. Francisco Madero was from a rich family, and had a huge fortune of his own. But even though he was a wealthy man who owned large farms, he treated his workers well. He made sure that they had decent houses, good food, and clean water. He sent his own doctor to take care of the sick laborers. He even used his own money to build schools for the children of the men and women who worked for him. Madero wanted Mexico to become a true democracy—not a dictatorship, run by a president who never left office.

Madero's kindness made him popular—and well loved. When Díaz saw that Madero might well beat him in an election, he had Francisco Madero arrested and thrown into jail. On the day of the election, Porfirio Díaz's officials announced that Mexicans had once again elected Díaz president.

The day after this fake election, Madero escaped from jail. He left Mexico by dressing himself as a railroad worker and catching a train that took him across the Mexican border into the United States. In San Antonio, Texas, he set up headquarters for a revolutionary group that would fight against President Díaz's government. He used his huge fortune to buy guns

Pancho Villa, Mexican guerilla fighter

and send them into Mexico, for the use of rebel soldiers who banded together to fight against the Mexican army.

One of the most famous of these rebel soldiers was a man named Doroteo Arango. Arango was a cattle thief from the north of Mexico, a bandit who had survived through stealing and hiding. But now he became a guerilla warrior and earned the nickname Pancho Villa. Pancho Villa raised an army of about three hundred men, stole enough food and supplies to keep them alive, and began to mount raids and attacks on government forces. Other revolutionary leaders joined him. All over Mexico, rebels were fighting against government forces, taking over villages, and driving away government officials. The Mexican Revolution was in full swing.

Soon, Porfirio Díaz realized that he would not be able to hold on to power very much longer. He was eighty years old, and suffering horribly from an abscessed tooth and other illnesses. He could barely get out of bed.

Late one May night, less than a year after the Mexican Revolution began, Porfirio Díaz hobbled slowly through the dark, surrounded by his advisors. He had agreed to meet a group of rebels outside of the city of Ciudad Juárez. Automobiles had been pulled into a circle, their headlights shining on a table where a treaty sat. By signing the treaty, Díaz would promise to give up his power. He bent over the paper and signed it slowly, with a shaking hand. His helpers supported him as he walked away. The next day, Porfirio Díaz left his country and went to France. He died in Paris four years later.

Madero marched into Mexico City to the cheers of the people. The wife of an American diplomat who watched the victory parade wrote, "People came from far and near, in all sorts of conveyances or on foot, just to see him, to hear his voice, even to touch his garments for help and healing. … It is a curious experience to see a people at the moment of what they are convinced is their salvation, to see the man they hail as 'Messiah' enter their Jerusalem. … The only thing they didn't shout was 'Hosanna.'"

The people of Mexico hoped that Madero would bring a true democracy, with peace and prosperity, to Mexico. Unfortunately, Madero found himself with a big problem. All of the rebel leaders who had helped fight for Díaz's removal had different ideas about how Mexico should be reformed. Some of them just wanted free elections. Others wanted the government to take the land owned by foreign businessmen away from them, and give it back to the people. And the rich men of Mexico, even those who had supported Madero's presidency, wanted as little change as possible.

For two years, Madero struggled to make all of these different powers work together—and failed. Once again, rebellion broke out. This time, it was against the very man that the rebels had hoped to put into power! Madero found himself sending out the Mexican army to fight against the revolutionaries who had once been his allies.

By February of 1913, the rebels had invaded Mexico City itself, and had set up their headquarters in the government armory (the place where weapons were stored). Madero's troops besieged them. For ten days, the two sides shot at each other. The shells set off fires all through the city, burning homes and stores. People who left their homes were likely to get caught in the crossfire. The people of Mexico City were too frightened to leave their homes. Some of them ended up cooking and eating their pet cats in order to stave off hunger!

These days became known as the Ten Tragic Days, or La Decena Trágica.

Finally, rebel forces charged into President Madero's office and dragged him out. They put him under guard, and took control of the city. The leader of the rebels, a general named Victoriano Huerta, was now in charge of Mexico City.

Huerta and the other rebels promised that they would keep Madero safe. But late one night, Madero was murdered by Huerta's officers. Huerta told the people of Mexico that the ex-president had been accidently killed while trying to escape.

Now, Mexico was under the rule of Huerta—who was as much of a dictator as Porfirio Díaz had ever been! But Huerta didn't keep power for long. The rebel leader Pancho Villa, who had fought against Díaz, continued to fight against Huerta. Less than a year later, Huerta himself fled.

For the next thirty years, civil war, assassinations, struggle and rebellion continued in Mexico. The Mexican Revolution had gotten rid of a tyrannical president—but it had not brought peace to Mexico.

World War I

While Mexico was struggling with its own people, a great war was about to spread across the other half of the world. This war became so huge that for years, people in Europe simply called it "The Great War." Today, we call it World War I.

World War I began in the Balkans. Remember how Bulgaria attacked Serbia, back when the Balkan Peninsula was fighting for independence from the Ottoman Turks? Bulgaria, Serbia and Greece had been planning to divide up Macedonia, but Bulgaria didn't think it was getting enough land. After the attack, Serbia and Bulgaria were enemies—and Bulgaria began to make an alliance with Austria (also called the "Austro-Hungarian Empire," since Austria was really the two countries of Austria and Hungary, united under one Austrian ruler).

If Austria was a friend of Bulgaria, Serbia would be Austria's enemy. The Serbs had another complaint against Austria as well. Austria had taken the little country of Bosnia and made it part of the Austro-Hungarian Empire. But the people who lived in Bosnia were from the same ancient race as the people who lived in Serbia. Both were "Slavic." Many Serbians thought that all Slavs should be united together—and that no Slavs should be ruled by Austrians.

On June 28, 1914, a nineteen-year-old Serbian assassin named Gavrilo Princip shot Archduke Franz Ferdinand, the heir to the Austrian throne.

The assassination was a disaster. To start with, it almost didn't work. Six teenagers, none of them older than nineteen, had planned to throw a bomb into the Archduke's car as it passed by. But the boy given the job of throwing the bomb missed! The explosion went off behind the Archduke's back fender. Immediately, police charged into the crowd and grabbed the bomb-thrower. He tried to swallow a capsule of cyanide to kill himself, but he couldn't get it into his mouth properly. He was arrested at once and dragged off to jail.

At this, the other five boys fled. Gavrilo Princip went into a coffeehouse nearby to calm himself down by drinking a cup of coffee. When he finished his coffee, he stepped out onto the side-walk and looked around. A car was coming towards him—the Archduke's car, leaving the scene of the bombing to take the Arch-duke to safety. Princip, hardly able to believe his luck, drew his gun and shot into the car ... killing both the Archduke and his wife.

The leaders of Austria insisted that the assassination attempt must have been planned by the Serbian government. Serb leaders denied it. But the denial did no good. On July 28th, the Austro-Hungarian Empire declared war on Serbia.

Two other countries immediately got involved. Russia, an ally of the Serbians, started to gather its troops together to attack Austria. So Germany, an ally of Austria, declared war on Russia. Two days later, Germany also declared war on France, and started to march towards the French border.

What did France have to do with the Balkans?

Not a lot. The truth was that most of the countries of Europe were ready to fight anyway. For decades, they had been arguing with each other about their borders, the size of their armies, and who got to control which colonies in Asia and Africa. Even though the bullet that killed the Archduke was often described as "the bullet that started World War I," the Archduke's assassination didn't really cause World War I.

Europe Before World War I

If you remember your ancient history, you know that the Trojan War started when a Trojan nobleman fell in love with the beautiful Helen and kidnapped her. The Greeks set out to take revenge on the Trojans—but the truth was that the Greeks and Trojans had hated each other for years, and were glad to find a reason for war. Helen was described as "the face that launched a thousand ships," but, like "the bullet that started World War I," Helen was a convenient excuse for a fight.

When the German army began to march towards France, it went through Belgium, which had already declared that the Belgians wouldn't get involved in the Austrian-Serbian quarrel. Now, Germany was ignoring a declaration of "neutrality" (refusing to join either side) and invading yet another country. At this, the British began to worry. Remember, Germany had been building new oil-powered ships for its navy, and Great Britain was already nervous about this growing fleet of battleships. If Germany was left alone, German soldiers might take over all of Europe.

On August 4, 1914, Great Britain declared war on Germany. The war had truly begun.

Before long, most of Europe was in on the fight. On one side were the "Central Powers"—the Austro-Hungarian Empire, Bulgaria, and Germany, soon joined by the Ottoman Turks. On the other side were the "Allied Forces"—Great Britain, France, Russia, China, Greece, Japan, Serbia, and a collection of other countries (including Belgium, which wasn't neutral any more).

No one believed this war would take very long. After all, the four countries of the Central Powers were defying the rest of the world. But it did. The fighting went on and on. Countries as far away as Australia and South Africa declared themselves ready to fight. Canadian soldiers marched off to fight in defense of Great Britain. The United States was one of the few powerful countries that refused to get involved.

Germany's new, powerful ships sailed along the British coastline, attacking British vessels and merchant ships. On

May 7, 1915, a German submarine fired a torpedo at a British ship called the *Lusitania*. The ship turned on end and sank, as the passengers scrambled frantically to get above decks. Almost twelve hundred people drowned.

The rest of the world was furious. The *Lusitania* wasn't carrying soldiers; it was a passenger ship, filled with civilians. This broke all the rules of war. German submarines could torpedo British warships, but they were supposed to leave civilian ships alone.

The United States government was particularly angry, because over a hundred of the drowned passengers were American citizens. For the first time, Americans began to think that perhaps the U.S. should get involved in the Great War.

By the winter of 1916, it seemed that the war might never end. So Great Britain passed a new and frightening law. It declared that the British government could now order young men to join the army and go fight—even if they didn't want to. This was called the *draft*. Never before had Great Britain forced its men to join in a war.

Young men bravely went when called. But the war was dangerous, exhausting, and brutal. At the *front* (the place where the fighting between enemies actually took place), British soldiers sang a song that went like this:

I don't want to go in the trenches no more,
Where whizzbangs and shrapnel they whistle and roar.
Oh my, I don't want to die, I want to go home.

The draft, of course, meant that even more men were away at war. Women had to begin working in factories and shops, driving trucks, and doing other "men's jobs." By 1918, almost a million women worked in British weapons factories. A seventeen-year-old girl named Lottie Wiggins, who drove a crane at one of the factories, described the long hours at her new job: "[We worked] twelve hours [a day] Monday to Saturday, then we changed to eighteen hours [a day], going on duty at 6 o'clock Saturday evening and working to 2 o'clock Sunday afternoon. ... [Then on] Monday at 6:00 a.m. ... we would resume normal twelve-hour shifts."

Meanwhile, young men from France and Great Britain travelled to the front, fought bravely—and died. In a five-month battle fought at Verdun, in France, three hundred thousand German soldiers and almost half a million French soldiers died. In another attack called the Somme Offensive, four hundred thousand British soldiers died, trying to push back the German army. In the Great War, Great Britain lost almost an entire generation of young men, killed in the fighting. Those who survived were often crippled by wounds, or by the sheer horror of their years of fighting.

But the Allies refused to yield.

Three years after the Great War began, Germany came up with an idea to bring it to an end. The Germans sent a secret telegram, in code, to the German Ambassador in Mexico, telling him to make a deal with the Mexican government. If Mexico would fight on the side of the Germans, and Germany won, Germany would reward Mexico. It would take the land that America had claimed during the Mexican War and give it back to Mexico. That land included New Mexico, Texas, Utah, Nevada, Arizona, California, and part of Colorado!

Before the Germans could actually make this deal, British *cryptographers* (professional code-breakers) managed to get a copy of the telegram and decoded it. American newspapers published the contents of the telegram, so that American citizens all across the United States could read it. Both the British and the Americans were outraged by this sneaky attempt to pull the United States into the war.

On April 6, 1917, the United States declared war on Germany. Now American soldiers would join the British, Canadian, and French soldiers, along with the soldiers of a dozen other nations, in fighting against Germany and its allies.

The Russian Revolution

Chapter Twenty-One
A Revolution Begins, and the Great War Ends

The Russian Revolution

In the same year that the United States joined the Allies, the Allied country of Russia went through a huge, world-changing revolution.

Even before the Great War began, the people of Russia were unhappy. Most Russians were peasants. They lived a difficult life: The noblemen of Russia had power to order them around, they didn't own the land they farmed, they had to labor for long hours, and they had just barely enough food to survive.

Meanwhile, the royal family of the Romanovs was leading a very different life. Nicholas II, his wife Alexandra, and their five children lived in a huge palace, surrounded by servants, with all the food they could eat. The palace had a Great Hall with golden marble columns, and a floor so smooth and polished that servants who went into it had to wear special shoes so that they wouldn't slip and fall. The children had warm bedrooms all to themselves, and a large playroom where shelves and boxes of toys waited to entertain them. Nicholas II had two different libraries all his own: the Great Library and the Small Library. Many of his books were covered in hand-made leather, and had gold or silver locks attached to fasten the covers shut. The books cost more money than an entire village of Russian peasants could earn in a year. The czar paid two librarians just to look after his book collection!

The wealth of the Romanovs, compared to the miserable, cold poverty of millions of their subjects, angered many Russians. The Romanov family had also grown unpopular with the Russian people for another reason. They spent too much time with a strange, mystical, unpopular monk named Rasputin.

The Romanovs had good reason for spending time with Rasputin. Nicholas and Alexandra's only son, Aleksei, had a disease called *hemophilia*. If you scratch or cut yourself, you'll bleed a little bit and then stop, because your blood clots and keeps any more blood from coming out. But Aleksei's blood wouldn't clot. If he scratched himself, he bled and bled and bled. He could die from the tiniest injury. Many of the men in the royal Russian family had inherited this horrible disease.

Nicholas and Alexandra were sick with worry for their son. And Rasputin claimed to have magical powers that could heal little Aleksei. So Aleksei's worried parents invited Rasputin to stay at the royal palace with their family.

Even though he was a monk, Rasputin drank too much, spent too much time at wild parties, and lived for pleasure and money. The Russian people hated and feared him. And because the czar and his wife had never told anyone outside of the family about Aleksei's illness, the Russians didn't understand why the royal family had welcomed this strange magician to the palace. Many whispered that Rasputin had put a spell on the czar!

Three Russian noblemen who also hated Rasputin finally decided to get rid of him. They invited him to dinner and gave him poisoned wine and poisoned candy. Oddly enough, the poison seemed to have no effect on him. So one of the three men shot Rasputin. That didn't kill him either. He got up and went outside. The noblemen followed him and shot him again! He still didn't die. Finally, they threw him into the river. This time, Rasputin sank and didn't come back up again.

But even with Rasputin gone, Nicholas was still unpopular. He only made things worse when World War I began. Nicholas immediately brought the Russian army into the war. It was a huge army; in 1914, it had six and a half million soldiers in it. But the army wasn't very well prepared. As a matter of fact, it had fewer than five million guns—which meant that almost two million Russian soldiers marched into battle with no weapons at all. They were supposed to grab guns that other Russian soldiers dropped when they died, and go on firing.

At first, the Russian army was commanded by the czar's cousin, the Grand Duke Nicolai. But in the first year of fighting, two million Russian soldiers were killed. Millions more were cold and hungry, because it was so difficult to carry food across the wide, cold plains of Russia to the battlefront.

After a year of this, Czar Nicholas II booted his cousin the Grand Duke out of his position, and took over command of the army himself. This was a big mistake. Nicholas didn't know how to command an army or how to plan strategy. As Commander in Chief of the Russian army, he made disastrous decisions, one after another. More and more Russian soldiers died on the battlefields of the Great War. With every death, Nicholas grew more hated. All of Russia blamed him for the deaths of the Russian soldiers.

At the same time, food had become scarcer and scarcer—not just at the front, but all across Russia. On March 8, 1917, a group of women and children waited all day in a line for bread. Finally, they reached the head of the line—and were told that the bread was all gone. The hungry peasants in line were furious. They began to chant, "We want bread!" and "Down with the czar!"

Like the peasants in line, more and more Russians began to demand that Nicholas II give up his throne. Finally, Nicholas II realized that he had lost the loyalty of his people forever. He gave up his throne and took his family to live in one of their favorite homes. In place of the czar, a "Provisional Government" (temporary government) took over running Russia.

The leader of this Provisional Government, a lawyer named Aleksandr Kerensky, knew how unpopular Nicholas II was. So he ordered the entire Romanov family taken far away, into Siberia, so that mobs would not attack and kill them in their home.

Aleksandr Kerensky began to try to change Russia's laws so that the country would be a better place to live. But he refused to pull the Russian army out of the Great War. As a matter of fact, he ordered the army to begin new battles against the Central Powers. The soldiers in the Russian army were exhausted and angry. Almost two million of them simply left the army and started home. Many of these ex-soldiers took their weapons, went back to the Russian countryside, murdered rich landowners and took over their land. Kerensky and the Provisional Government were helpless to stop the killing.

It was time for a new government to take control of Russia.

The group of leaders who seized control of Russia were called the Bolsheviks. The leader of the Bolsheviks was a man named Vladimir Ilich Lenin. Lenin believed that the peasants had the right to take over the land owned by the wealthy, because the wealthy had so often earned their money by forcing the poor to work hard for very little reward. He wanted the land in Russia to be used by the whole nation—the whole "community"—not just the rich.

Lenin's ideas were popular with the poor, and also with the millions of working people in Russia. Now, with the poor and working people discontent not only with their lives, but with the government's decision to stay in World War I, Lenin had the chance to get more and more Russians on his side.

On October 24, 1917, Lenin and his followers made their move. Over twenty-five thousand angry peasants, workers, and soldiers stormed through the city of St. Petersburg, where the government of Russia had its offices. The workers flooded through the Winter Palace and took control of the government offices. Kerensky's followers were arrested—but Kerensky himself ran fast enough to get away.

Now Lenin and the Bolsheviks were in charge. Lenin suggested renaming the Bolsheviks the "Communist Party"—the party working for the common good. The communists believed that Christianity was false and wrong, so they changed the names of the cities in Russia that were named after Christian saints. St. Petersburg became "Leningrad." And right away, Lenin and the communists signed a peace treaty with Germany.

Finally, Russia was out of the war.

There were two problems left. One was that the çzar, Nicholas and his family, were still alive and living in Russia. The second was that the people of Russia were still very poor.

Lenin dealt with the czar first. He ordered Nicholas II and his whole family imprisoned in a house in the city of Yekaterinburg, far to the west of Petrograd. Then he sent word to the czar's guards: Every member of the royal Romanov family had to die. Lenin didn't want any Romanovs left to claim that they had the right to rule over Russia.

On July 17, 1918, in the dark of night, guards ordered the Romanovs to get dressed and go to the basement. In the basement, twelve men shot the Romanovs to death. Then they took the bodies twelve miles away, into the heart of a dark forest, and buried them. The Romanov family, which had ruled Russia since 1613, was no more. Now Lenin and the Communist Party governed Russia.

Lenin tried to tackle the problem of Russian poverty in a new way. To make sure that the rich people of Russia didn't own all the land while the poor people had none, the Communist Party decided that all of the land in the whole country would belong to the government! The government would allow people to use the land equally. Instead of individual Russians building businesses, making money, and perhaps forcing other Russians to work for little pay, the government would own and run most of the businesses—not just the electric company and the water company, but hospitals, schools, grocery stores, bookstores, and even hot dog stands.

This new way of living, "communism," was supposed to make sure that the government, instead of a small group of powerful people, had control over Russia. But who was in the government? That's right—a small group of powerful people, Lenin and his followers!

The End of World War I

Russia had resigned from World War I. But the United States had just joined, on the side of Great Britain and the Allied forces.

The president of the United States, Woodrow Wilson, had once believed that the United States should stay neutral in the

Europe During World War I

Great War. But he had changed his mind. Now he was sure that the United States had a duty to fight against Germany. If Germany, ruled by a kaiser (emperor), took over Europe, the democratic countries of Europe would lose their right to elect their own leaders. Woodrow Wilson announced that America had to join the war so that "the world may be made safe for democracy."

American soldiers marched off to join the Allied troops in Europe. These American soldiers were nicknamed "doughboys." No one is quite sure where this name came from. It might refer to a type of food that soldiers ate, a doughy mixture of flour and rice, cooked over a campfire. Or it might come from the old expression "dough-head," which meant "stupid"!

But "doughboy" wasn't an insult when it referred to American soldiers. Americans were proud that their soldiers were going overseas to help Great Britain and France fight against the German threat. Just as in Great Britain, women jumped in to help at home and do the jobs that men left behind when they went off to war. American women also joined the Navy and Marine Corps. They weren't allowed to fight, but they served as nurses, clerks, telephone operators, electricians, and photographers. They also put together torpedoes and designed camouflage. Three Army nurses earned Distinguished Service Crosses, America's second highest military award.

Four months after America entered the war, American soldiers won their first battle against soldiers of the Central Powers. In May, June, and July, Allied soldiers triumphed in three more important battles. After the last, the Second Battle of the Marne, a French general named Charles Mangin paid tribute to the American soldiers who had fought so courageously. "Shoulder to shoulder with your French comrades, you threw yourselves into the counter-offensive," he told them. "You ran to it as if going to a feast. Your magnificent dash upset and surprised the enemy.... You have shown yourselves to be worthy sons of your great country and have gained the admiration of your brothers in arms. ... American comrades, I am grateful to you for the blood you generously spilled on the soil of my country. I am proud of having commanded you during such splendid days and to have fought with you for the deliverance of the world."

The new strength of the American soldiers, joining with the Allied forces that had fought for four long, weary years, finally tipped the balance of the war against the Central Powers. On November 11, 1918, Germany was forced to surrender. The power of the Second Reich was broken. All over the world, exhausted soldiers heard the great news: An *armistice* (an end to fighting) had been declared.

A few years later, an American soldier named Thomas Gowenlock, who had been on the front lines of World War I, described the soldiers' response when they learned that Germany had surrendered. "All over the world on November 11, 1918, people were celebrating, dancing in the streets, drinking champagne, hailing the armistice that meant the end of the war," he wrote. "But at the front there was no celebration.... The men ... were trying to reassure themselves that there were no enemy batteries spying on them from the next hill and no German bombing planes approaching to blast them out of existence. They talked in low tones. They were nervous. After the long months of intense strain, of keying themselves up to the daily mortal danger, of thinking always in terms of war and the enemy, the abrupt release from it all was ... agony. Some suffered a total nervous collapse. Some, of a steadier temperament, began to hope they would someday return to home and the embrace of loved ones. Some could think only of the crude little crosses that marked the graves of their comrades. ... What was to come next? They did not know—and hardly cared. Their minds were numbed by the shock of peace."

Although peace had finally arrived, as many as ten million soldiers and another ten million civilians had died, all around the world. In France, Great Britain, and Germany, almost every family had lost brothers, husbands, and fathers to the Great War.

But in England and America, the war helped to bring about at least one good thing. For the first time, women were allowed to vote.

For years, British and American women had been demanding the right to vote (also known as *suffrage*). Women who marched, protested, and spoke in public about their right to suffrage were called suffragettes. If you've ever seen the movie *Mary Poppins*, you might remember that Mrs. Banks is a suffragette. She wraps a banner around her, proclaiming that women should have the right to vote, and marches off singing:

We're clearly soldiers in petticoats
And dauntless crusaders for women's votes....
Our daughter's daughters will adore us
And they'll sing in grateful chorus
"Well done, sister suffragette!"

After World War I ended, it seemed obvious that women should be allowed to vote. After all, while the men had gone off to fight, women had done the men's jobs—and done them perfectly well. Why in the world shouldn't they be given the same right to vote as the men?

In 1918, Great Britain passed a new law called the Reform Act. Because women had worked so hard to help win the war, every woman over the age of thirty could vote. (In 1928, Britain changed the law so that women twenty-one and older could vote, too.)

For women in America to vote, an amendment to the Constitution had to be passed. In 1918, Congress agreed to begin the process of changing the Constitution so that women could gain suffrage. One representative to the Congress, Frederick Hicks of New York, was sitting by his dying wife when it came time to pass the amendment. She told him to leave her deathbed and go help pass the amendment—so he did!

On the day that Congress would take its final vote on passing the amendment, "suffragists" crowded into the Senate to hear the outcome. The *New York Times* reported that "deafening applause" broke out when a senator stood up to announce that the amendment had passed Congress. The Great War was finally over. Now, in America and Great Britain, women could help pass the laws that would shape the world after the war.

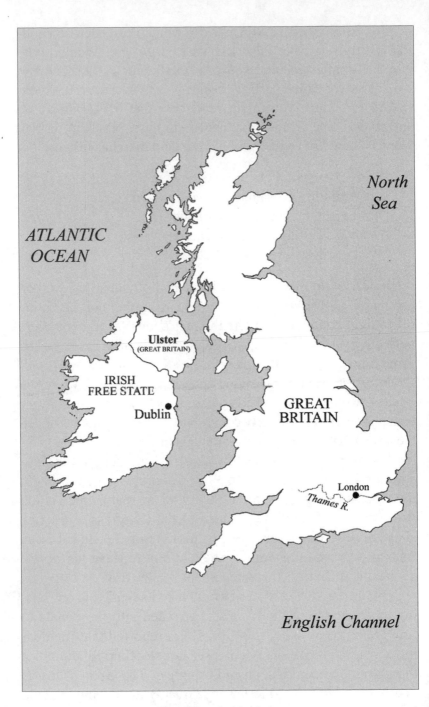

The Easter Uprising

Chapter Twenty-Two
National Uprisings

The Easter Uprising

Right in the middle of World War I, Great Britain had to deal with a battle at home.

The last time we visited the country of Ireland, just off England's western coast, the people of Ireland were fretting under British rule. Ireland had been part of the British Empire for more than three hundred years. For the last hundred years, Ireland had to send its representatives to the British Parliament and had no government of its own. The Irish had suffered from famine—and the English had done little to help. And when the prime minister, William Gladstone, had tried to convince Parliament to pass the "Home Rule" bill that would give the Irish the freedom to govern themselves, Parliament refused.

Gladstone had long been convinced that the way the English treated the Irish was not only wrong, but also stupid. The worse the English treated the Irish, the more the Irish would hate the English. He called the English rule of Ireland "seven centuries of misgovernment," and warned the English that this misgovernment was bound to bring trouble: a "cloud in the west, the coming storm." The Irish would remember being forced to pay "rent to absentee landlords" and being "forced [into] obedience to the laws" those landlords had made, "to the end of time."

William Gladstone's fiery speeches did convince Parliament to pass laws that gave Irish peasants the right to buy back some of the land they had lost to greedy English landlords. Parliament hoped that this would help to make Ireland a little more peaceful. William Gladstone also helped to pass a law that would give Protestants and Catholics equal rights in Ireland.

Meanwhile, the people of Ireland were beginning, more and more, to speak of themselves as Irish, rather than "British." The Irish poet William Butler Yeats wrote poems that celebrated Irish ideas and Irish words. The Gaelic League was founded; its members hoped that the Irish would be able to abandon speaking English, in favor of the ancient Irish language called Gaelic. An organization called the Gaelic Athletic Association taught Irish boys to play ancient Irish games like hurling. Resistance groups—like those that had grown up in countries all over the world—had formed. The group Young Ireland wanted to work towards freedom from England by changing the laws of Great Britain. The Irish Republican Brotherhood, also called the Fenians, wanted to fight for freedom. And the Irish Land League organized poor tenants against their landlords. The Land League taught poor Irishmen and women that they could resist the English by refusing to work for English employers and by not buying from English merchants. One of the English landlords who found that his Irish employees were no longer willing to work for him, or buy from him, was named Charles Boycott. From then on, this form of resistance was known as "the boycott."

But the most powerful of these resistance groups was organized in 1905. It was called Sinn Féin, which is Gaelic for "Us Alone." Sinn Féin wanted Ireland to remain under the British crown, but to get its own parliament and its own self-rule back again. Ireland would be a separate, independent country, but it would be loyal to the English monarch—just like Canada.

Many Catholics in Ireland liked Sinn Féin's ideas. But Protestants in the north of Ireland were afraid of what might happen if Ireland—which still had more Catholics than Protestants in it—got self-government back again. Under British rule, Protestants and Catholics were equal. But if Irish self-rule were restored, Catholics would be in the majority. What if Catholics then turned around and treated Protestants badly?

Most of the Protestants who didn't want Ireland to have home rule lived in the north of Ireland, in six counties called

"Ulster." Ulster was very different from the rest of the country. Because Scottish Presbyterians had settled there many years ago, many Ulster Irish were Presbyterians. The rest of Ireland was filled with farms, but Ulster was filled with factories and ship-building companies.

Almost half a million people in northern Ireland, most of them Protestants, joined together to sign a document called the Ulster Covenant. It read:

[We are] convinced in our conscience that home rule would be disastrous ... [that it would destroy] our civil and religious freedom ... our citizenship and ... the unity of the Empire. ... [We will use] all means which may be found necessary to defeat the present conspiracy to set up a Home Rule Parliament in Ireland.

"All means necessary" meant that, if the British government gave Ireland home rule, the northern Irish Protestants would fight back. A secret army called the Ulster Volunteer Force formed. It had a hundred thousand soldiers in it! The Ulster Volunteer Force was well-armed, because it bought hundreds of guns and many tons of ammunition from Germany. (Germany was happy to do anything that would cause the British trouble at home—and distract them from the war!)

Now there were two different sides in Ireland, one threatening to fight if Ireland wasn't given home rule—and the other threatening to fight if it was. Violence was inevitable. And it erupted on April 24, 1916, the Monday right after Easter Sunday.

A Fenian leader named Patrick Henry Pearse led about a thousand Irish rebels in taking control of the post office in the Irish city of Dublin. These rebels, who were fighting *for* Home Rule, also took control of government buildings. British troops marched in to put the rebellion down. After a week of fighting in the streets, the rebels were captured.

This short revolt caused dreadful problems for Great Britain. Almost four hundred people had died—and half of those had been innocent people shot by accident during the gun battles. Many had been killed by British soldiers. And after the "Easter Uprising" ended, the British ordered sixteen captured rebels put to death. One of them was so badly wounded that he had to be tied to a chair in front of the firing squad!

This made both the Irish and many English angry. More Irish than ever now wanted independence. Sinn Féin, the rebel organization, gained even more followers. The Irish poet William Butler Yeats wrote one of his most famous poems about the Easter Uprising, called "Easter 1916." "Too long a sacrifice," he wrote, "can make a stone of the heart." Now, the poem concludes, the times are "changed, changed utterly." Ireland and England could never go back to their old relationship. They would always be enemies.

Almost three years after the Easter Uprising, Sinn Féin set up its own government in Ireland, calling it the "Dáil Éireann," or "Irish Assembly." The Dáil Éireann announced that Ireland would now govern itself—no matter what the British thought. In order to protect their new government, a Sinn Féin leader named Michael Collins organized his own army, the "Irish Republican Army."

At once, Great Britain sent over soldiers to defeat the Irish Republican Army, or "IRA." Fighting raged over the island. Houses were burned. Innocent people were killed. More and more British began to think that Ireland should simply be allowed to govern itself. In the United States, where so many Irish now lived, plenty of Irish-Americans agreed with the Fenian movement and began to call for Home Rule too.

When World War I ended, Great Britain and Sinn Féin began to talk about independence. Months and months later, in 1921, Sinn Féin and the British government signed a treaty. This treaty would make most of Ireland into a country called the Irish Free State. Like Canada, the Irish Free State would still be loyal to the British monarch, but it would rule itself, have its own parliament, and make its own laws. William Butler Yeats was invited to become a member of the brand-new Irish parliament.

But Ulster, the six counties in the north of Ireland where so many Protestants lived, would not be part of the Irish Free State. Ulster would remain part of Great Britain.

Not everyone in Ireland was happy with this treaty. Some of the Irish objected to losing Ulster. Others wanted Ireland to be completely independent, without even formal allegiance to Great Britain. Michael Collins himself was assassinated by Irish rebels who believed that Collins had betrayed Ireland by agreeing to be loyal to Britain's monarch.

Sinn Féin itself didn't like the idea of Ulster remaining part of Great Britain. But the treaty seemed to be the only way to end fighting between the two countries.

By 1923, the Irish Free State was governing itself. Fourteen years later, Great Britain would agree to allow the Irish Free State to become a completely independent country called "Éire," or "the Republic of Ireland." But Ulster, or "Northern Ireland," remained part of the British Empire—an unhappy and trouble-filled part, where Catholics were too often harassed, robbed, and even beaten by their neighbors.

Indian Nationalism

While the Irish were battling for independence, so were the people of India.

When we last left India, the British had put India under the rule of an official called the Viceroy of India. The Viceroy, or "vice-regent," ruled India in the name of Queen Victoria of England. The British called India the "Raj" (the Indian name for kingdom), because India was now firmly part of the British Empire. The new capital of this Raj was now Delhi, not the old capital city of Calcutta.

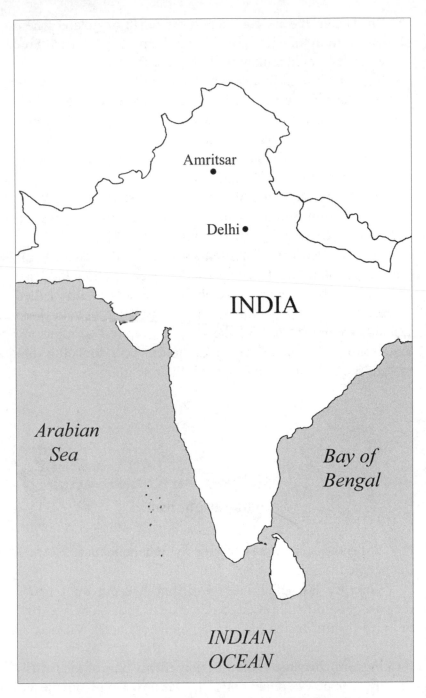

India During the Time of Mohandas Gandhi

With the rebellion over, the British tried to improve India for their subjects. They built railroads and roads, laid telegraph lines, and improved India's harbors so that more ships could trade in Indian ports. The British in India thought that they had a duty to bring English customs and ways to India, because they believed that English customs were much better than Indian ways. The writer Rudyard Kipling called this duty the "white man's burden."

But Indians wished that the British would set down this "burden." No matter how much the British talked about doing good for India, the Indians could see clearly that the British had more privileges, more wealth, and a better life. British citizens lived in separate neighborhoods, where the only Indians were servants. Most British in India had plenty of Indian servants, nursemaids, cooks, and nannies. The Indians called the white men *sahibs*, and the white women *memsahibs*—Indian words that meant "master" and "mistress."

The Indians didn't want masters and mistresses. The British knew this; as a matter of fact, before World War I, the British had begun to agree that they might try to treat India in the same way that they had treated Canada and Australia, by giving the Indians self-rule.

After World War I, the British no longer paid attention to this promise. They were too occupied with trying to recover from the dreadful fighting that had killed so many Englishmen. But the Indians had also suffered from World War I. Over a hundred thousand Indian soldiers had also died, fighting in British regiments and in defense of Great Britain. At the very least, India should be rewarded with freedom!

The loudest group of Indians calling for independence was called the Congress Party. By the time World War I ended, the Congress Party was led by a lawyer named Mohandas Karamchand Gandhi. He had grown up in a Hindu family, studied law in England, and then travelled to South Africa. There, he spent years working to improve the lives of Indian immigrants. In South Africa, Indians were treated as badly as blacks, because their skin was dark.

Gandhi stayed away from India for twenty-one years. When he returned to his home country, he felt like a stranger. But news of his work for Indians in South Africa had spread back to India. Gandhi already had a reputation as a man ready to work for justice and independence.

In the first year after he came back to India, Gandhi decided to travel around his country by train and see the villages and cities that he had not visited for over two decades. What he found was an India in which there was poverty, dirt, disease, and misery. So he joined the Congress Party, and tried to get Indians from every small village in India to join it. The Congress Party swelled to include millions of people!

In 1919, demonstrators from the Congress Party met in the holy city of Amritsar, to protest against British rule. Amritsar, in the north of India, was the most sacred city on earth for the Sikhs (followers of the Sikh religion) who lived in India. Like Muslims, Sikhs believed that there was only one god. In ancient times, Sikhs had been warrior princes; in more recent times, they had served as the royal bodyguard for the emperor of India.

Amritsar was a sacred city because the Golden Temple stood in it. This Golden Temple was at the center of a wide, still pool of water, whose waters were said to give eternal life to those who wash in them. A white stone bridge led to the Golden Temple, so that Sikh worshipers could walk across the water into the Temple and see the Granth Sahib, the holy books that were kept inside it.

The demonstrators gathered in a garden, near the pool and the golden temple, called Jallianwala Bagh. Even though they were unarmed and not causing any trouble, this gathering was illegal. The British had passed laws against large public demonstrations.

The British officer in charge of Amritsar's soldiers came out to the grassy garden with his troops. But instead of telling the unarmed demonstrators to go away, the soldiers began to fire at them without any warning. Over three hundred unarmed people died. Over a thousand were wounded. Today, if you visit Amritsar, you can still walk in the garden of Jallianwala Bagh and see the bullet holes in the brick archways that surround it.

The whole country was outraged. This seemed like the perfect time to begin a war for independence.

But Gandhi refused to allow his followers to pick up weapons. He told the members of the Congress Party that an armed man could be a coward—but that an unarmed man must be courageous. Real independence had to be won with *satyagraha*—the nonviolent fight for freedom and justice.

Instead of fighting with weapons, Gandhi and the Congress Party began to use other methods of resisting the British. They

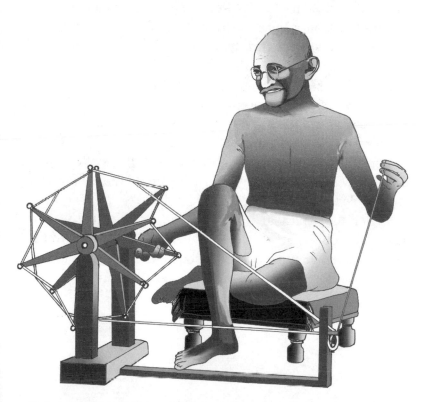

Mohandas Gandhi taught noncooperation and *satyagraha*— the nonviolent fight for freedom and justice.

taught the Indians to resist with "noncooperation"—meaning that Indians simply refused to pay taxes to the British government. They encouraged Indians to "boycott" British goods (refuse to buy anything made in Great Britain). Gandhi told his followers to make their own handmade cloth for their clothes, rather than buying British cotton. When the British put a tax on salt, Gandhi led his followers on a march of 240 miles to go collect salt from the sea, rather than buying the taxed salt. He started with seventy-eight people. By the end of the march, thousands of people were following him.

Gandhi told Indians to take their children out of British schools. He asked them to give up privileges given to them by the British. He himself sent back a medal that the British government had given him for his work in South Africa. When a factory refused to give its workers enough money to live on, Gandhi went on a hunger strike. He refused to eat until the factory owners agreed to the raise. It took three days for the factory owners to give in and agree. They didn't want to be responsible for Gandhi starving to death!

The British put Gandhi in jail again and again. But the resistance in India, called a "nationalist movement," continued to grow. It wasn't always peaceful. Sometimes, Gandhi's nonviolent protests inspired other rebels to fight with weapons. Between violent and nonviolent resistance, India had grown impossible to govern.

After the Amritsar Massacre, the British finally agreed that they would start to change the way India was governed, so that the country could slowly become independent. But it would take thirty years for that promise to be fully kept.

Europe in 1919, After the Peace of Versailles

Chapter Twenty-Three
"Peace" and a Man of War

The Peace of Versailles

World War I was over. Every country in Europe had suffered. Among the Allies, Great Britain had lost nearly a million men. Another million and a half had been wounded, hundreds of thousands so badly that they would never again have a normal life. France had suffered even more; almost a million and a half French soldiers had died, with millions more wounded. Russia had lost nearly two million men, Italy over half a million. Among the Central Powers, nearly two million German soldiers, over a million Austrian men, and half a million Turkish and Bulgarian fighters had died. The war had shattered much of the countryside. Houses were in ruins. Roads had been blown up. Coal mines had been destroyed.

Now it was time to decide how these countries would recover from the war.

In 1919, the leaders of the victorious countries gathered together at the immense, glittering palace built by Louis XIV at Versailles, not far from Paris. Here, they would try to decide what penalties Germany, Austria, and their allies would have to pay.

The three most powerful leaders at the conference were Woodrow Wilson, the president of the United States; David Lloyd George, the prime minister of Great Britain and Georges Clemenceau, the French prime minister. All three of these men had different ideas about what the peace treaty should do.

Of the Allies, France had suffered the most from the war. Clemenceau, the prime minister of France, had seen much of his country destroyed. He wanted Germany punished!

England too had suffered. The people of England shouted, "Make Germany pay!" at the British prime minister, Lloyd George, whenever he went out in public. But Lloyd George was also afraid that, if Germany were treated too harshly, its people would turn to communism and make another alliance with Russia. He didn't want the Germans to feel so desperate that they were willing to become a communist country. Great Britain had always been a little bit afraid of Russia. It was huge and well armed, and it always seemed to be getting bigger. Now that Russia was communist, Great Britain was even more worried about it. What if the Communist Party decided to spread communism through force, by conquering other countries in Europe? If Germany and Russia allied together, they might make an unbeatable enemy.

Woodrow Wilson of the United States had a third set of ideas. He too agreed that Germany should be punished. But he thought the most important job of the meeting in Versailles was to figure out how to keep such a war from happening again. He believed that the countries of the world should join together to work out an agreement that all countries would honor. This agreement, he thought, should have fourteen different points. But three of the points were the most important.

1. All countries should try to make their armies and their collections of weapons smaller.
2. Every nation should be able to govern itself, independently.
3. And every country should belong to an organization called the League of Nations.

The League of Nations would act like the parents of a big, argumentative family. If two countries argued about something, they wouldn't start a war over it—any more than two siblings should settle an argument by a fist-fight. Instead, the countries would bring the problem to the League of Nations. The countries in the League would discuss the problem, decide what should be done, and tell the hostile countries to do it. Wilson thought that a League of Nations might stop a world war from ever happening again.

When the three leaders and representatives of the other countries that had fought in World War I all got together at Versailles, they agreed on three important points. First, the other leaders agreed that Wilson's idea about the League of Nations was a good one. The Versailles Peace Settlement, a document that both the winners and the losers of the Great War signed, formed this League of Nations.

Second, they agreed that the Versailles Peace Settlement would rearrange the whole map!

When World War I began, the large country of Austria—land that had once belonged to the Holy Roman Emperor of the Middle Ages—lay just east of Germany. Remember, Austria was also known as the "Austro-Hungarian Empire" because the people in the eastern half of it had insisted that, although they would pay allegiance to the Austrian emperor, they wanted their part of the empire to have its own name (Hungary) and its own, separate constitution—even though both countries were ruled by the emperor and the same army. The countries of Croatia and Bosnia lay within the borders of the Austro-Hungarian Empire. Just south lay the independent countries of Serbia and Montenegro, and to the east Bulgaria, with the Russian territory of Romania above it. Greece, on the south of the peninsula, and Albania, just above it, were independent countries.

The Peace of Versailles changed almost all of this. First of all, Austria would be divided into two parts. From now on, the empire would be two separate countries—Austria to the west, and Hungary to the east. A big slice of land across the top of both was taken away and made into a brand new country called Czechoslovakia. On the bottom half of the Austro-Hungarian Empire, Croatia and Bosnia were taken away from Austro-Hungary, put together with Serbia, and made into yet another brand new country, called Yugoslavia. Montenegro was also folded into Yugoslavia. Only Albania and Greece got to keep their own land.

Bulgaria, which had sided with Germany, would also be punished by losing some of its territory. Land in western

Bulgaria would be pulled into the new country of Yugoslavia as well. So this new country would have people from five different old countries in it.

And what about the Turkish Empire, which had also sided with Germany? The only part of the Turkish Empire left to the Turks was Asia Minor—the land that today we know as the modern nation of Turkey. France and Britain divided up the Turkish land south of Asia Minor. The land along the eastern coast of the Mediterranean Sea went to France; Britain claimed the land north of the Arabian Peninsula, all the way over to the border of Persia. (Ten years later, in 1929, Britain would divide part of this land that once belonged to the Turks off, and name it "Iraq.") The empire of the Ottoman Turks, an empire that had governed in the east for centuries, was no more. It would become the Turkish Republic instead.

Rearranging the whole eastern part of Europe was the second task of the Peace of Versailles. The third was the punishment of Germany.

Germany had to give up huge amounts of its empire. The northern part of the empire was divided up. Some of the land went to Poland, which lay on Germany's eastern border, between Germany and Russia. Some went to Russia itself. Other parts of Germany were given their freedom and became the independent nations of Lithuania, Latvia, and Estonia.

Germany would lose all of its colonies. It could never have an army larger than one hundred thousand soldiers. Its navy could only have six battleships. Germany wasn't allowed to have any air force or submarine fleet. Most damaging of all, the Germans had to agree to sign a part of the treaty called "Article 231," or the "War Guilt Clause." This clause said, "Germany accepts the responsibility for all the loss and damage that the Allies suffered during the war, since the war was caused by Germany and her allies." This meant that Germany was solely responsible for the war—and had to pay over thirty-two billion dollars in losses and damages to other countries.

The German representatives were furious over this clause. Germany too had suffered during the war. If Germany had to pay all of this money, the country would never be able to recover. And why was Germany being blamed for the entire war, when it had actually started over on the Balkan Peninsula?

But the Allies refused to budge. Each one of the leaders had gotten what he wanted. Wilson of the U.S. got his League of Nations. Clemenceau of France saw Germany punished. Lloyd George of Great Britain was happy, because all of the new countries formed by the Peace of Versailles would act like a barrier between Great Britain and Communist Russia.

Unfortunately, the Peace of Versailles led to a lot of trouble.

When Woodrow Wilson returned home, he wasn't able to convince the United States Congress to join the League of Nations. Congress didn't want the United States too involved with European politics! Instead, it thought that Americans should focus only on what was good for America. So the League, which had been thought up by an American president, went on without America.

Most of the countries formed by the Peace eventually fell apart. After all, their boundaries had been drawn by people who didn't live in them. Different groups of people, who didn't share the same history or the same culture, had been shoved together and told that they were now citizens of the same countries. In some of these new countries, people who had hated each other for centuries were now trapped inside the same borders.

And the debt imposed on Germany made it poorer and poorer, and its people more and more miserable. In a few years, the German people would be ready to listen to anyone who offered to revenge the wrongs done to Germany, and who promised to make their country great again.

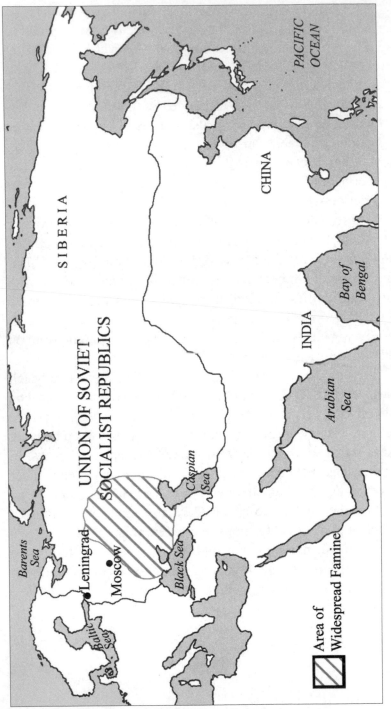

Russia Under the Rule of Stalin

The Rise of Joseph Stalin

After Nicholas II and his family were killed, civil war broke out in Russia.

Russians loyal to the czar formed an army called the White Army to avenge the czar's death. In return, the communists organized their own army, the Red Army. For three years, civil war raged between the White Army and the Red Army.

By 1922, the Red Army had won. A million and half Russians who had supported the czar and the White Army, called "White Russians," were forced to leave their country. Those who didn't leave were arrested, jailed, or executed.

Now Russia was a *totalitarian state* (a country with only one political party). Most countries have at least two political parties (the United States has Republicans and Democrats). In a country with more than one political party, the two parties argue with each other about how the country should be run. Usually, the two sides have very different ideas. The people of the country listen to the arguments and decide which side has a better chance of making the country work. This way, all of the candidates get a chance to air their ideas. Perhaps the arguments even change some people's minds.

But in a totalitarian state, no one gets to disagree with the one political party that runs the country. Lenin and the Communist Party exiled, jailed, or executed the Russians who disagreed with the communist takeover, or who wanted Russia ruled in some other way.

Lenin didn't get to govern his totalitarian state for very long. Almost as soon as the war between White Russians and Red Russians was over, Lenin had a stroke (an illness that caused his brain to stop working properly). He remained "leader" for two more years—but during those two years, the real leader of Russia was Joseph Stalin.

When he was born, Joseph Stalin's name was Ioseb Dzhugashvili. He changed his name to "Stalin" when he joined the Communist Party at the age of 24. "Stalin" came from the Russian word for "steel." Joseph Stalin, the steel ruler of Russia, was as hard as metal—and as cruel as a steel sword.

When Lenin died, Joseph Stalin became Russia's undisputed leader. He ordered the city of Petrograd (once St. Petersburg) to be renamed Leningrad, in honor of Lenin. Stalin also ordered Lenin's body put in a glass coffin, so that Russians could come and look at him. Scientists took out Lenin's brain so that they could study it to find out why he was such a political genius. Then, other scientists soaked the body in chemicals to preserve it. Today, Lenin's body is still in its glass coffin, in the Moscow town square known as "Red Square." Anyone who visits the square can see it. A fifteen-member committee has taken care of the body for the last eighty years. Every week, they check the body to make sure that it isn't beginning to disintegrate, and put more chemicals on it. Every once in a while, they change Lenin's clothes.

Under Joseph Stalin, two things happened to Communist Russia.

The first was that Russia became the Union of Soviet Socialist Republics, or the "USSR." Threatening war if they didn't join, Joseph Stalin told the countries that lay just at the western border of Russia, between Russia and Poland, that they had to become part of a new communist empire. Over the next twenty years, the USSR, or "Soviet Union," would spread eastward and swallow five little countries in the center of Asia. It would also reach over to the Baltic and gulp up Estonia, Latvia, and Lithuania, countries that had been given their freedom after World War I by the Peace of Versailles. That freedom didn't last for long!

The second thing that happened during the rule of Joseph Stalin is that millions of Russians died. Many were executed by Stalin. And many more starved to death.

Stalin had his own ideas about how Russia should become great. Most of Russia was farmland, where peasants grew crops. But Stalin wanted Russia to have factories and mines, like the wealthy western nations. He wanted steelworks that would make new rails for railroads that would go across Russia, and parts for electrical generators that would light up Russia's homes and streets. He ordered these new industries built—many of them in the icy wasteland of Siberia. And then he forced thousands and thousands of Russians to work in these factories, steelworks, and mines. If they didn't produce a certain amount of metal and goods, they were punished.

He also ordered the peasants who still worked on farms to produce more food by working harder and planting more. They had to join together into huge "collective farms," where hundreds of farmers worked on the same fields. Almost all of the food grown in these fields went into a "common stockpile." In other words, most of it went to the government! The communist government was supposed to then hand it back out evenly to the people of Russia.

The peasants and farmers of Russia hated these new arrangements. Many didn't want to leave their land and work in factories. Those who were still allowed to work on their farms now couldn't own their own fields, or decide how to care for their own crops. And after all that hard work, they had to turn most of the food over to the government.

The new "collectives" were so unpopular that many farmers simply refused to work on them. But Stalin knew how to deal with disobedient Soviet citizens. Anyone who resisted Stalin was arrested and shot, or sent to "work camps." The work camps, scattered all through Siberia and far to the east, were freezing cold. The prisoners who lived there labored for days, or weeks, or months, with very little to eat. These labor camps, scattered through the open wasteland of Siberia, were nicknamed "the Gulag Archipelago," because they were spread out and isolated, just like a string of islands. Most people sent to the Gulag died there.

Then a drought spread across Russia. Crops began to wither. The harvests grew poorer and poorer; the peasants grew hungry. But instead of offering help, Stalin ordered them to keep on sending the same amount of grain to Leningrad.

The peasants began to die of hunger. In the end, six million Russians starved during the famine. Joseph Stalin didn't care. He was determined to make Russia powerful. If people died, that was just part of the process.

Anyone who muttered about Stalin's methods or his cruelty could expect to be shot or sent to Siberia. Stalin became infamous for his "purges." To "purify" Russia of dissent, Stalin ordered his critics, called "dissidents," to be arrested and sent to the Gulag. During Stalin's power, fifteen million Russians went to the Gulag! Almost nine million were arrested and shot. One of the most famous Russian dissidents, Alexander Solzhenitsyn, spent eleven years imprisoned by the Soviets, many of those in a labor camp in the Gulag. He wrote that Russians could expect to be arrested at any time of the day or night, by Russian police in disguise. Often, the prisoners weren't even told what their crime was. "They take you aside in a factory corridor after you have had your pass checked—and you're arrested," he wrote. "You are arrested by a religious pilgrim whom you have put up for the night 'for the sake of Christ.' You are arrested by a meterman who has come to read your electric meter. You are arrested by a bicyclist who has run into you on the street, by a railway conductor, a taxi driver, a savings bank teller." Once arrested, you could expect to be sent to a camp without trial—or a chance to clear your name.

Solzhenitsyn wrote that revolution can never get rid of the evil inside human beings. It can only get rid of particular governments. Even when the evil of those governments is destroyed, the evil inside human beings remains.

Solzhenitsyn was right. The communist government had been formed to get rid of tyranny. But Joseph Stalin, the leader of Communist Russia, was as cruel, as tyrannical, and as evil as any Russian czar had ever been.

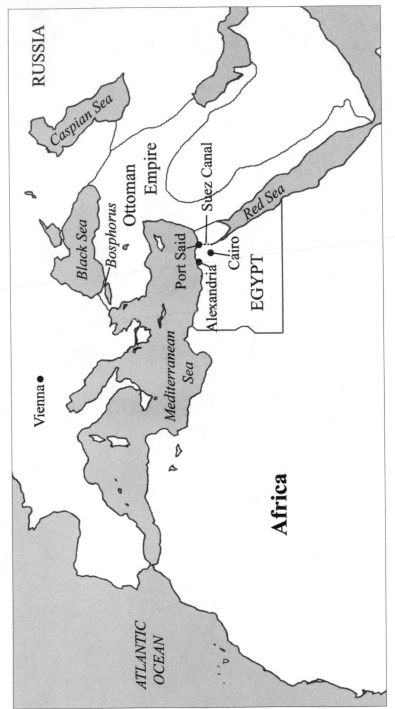

Egypt Under a King

Chapter Twenty-Four
The King and Il Duce

The First King of Egypt

In 1922, the year that the communist government finally gained control over all of Russia, the country of Egypt also changed its government. For the first time in centuries, Egypt got its own king.

In ancient times, of course, Egypt was ruled by a pharaoh. But by the time of the 1800s, Egypt had become part of the Ottoman Empire. And by 1900, Egypt had been occupied by British soldiers. The leader of Egypt, the *khedive*, ruled under the guidance of a British "consul general." Great Britain wanted to keep Egypt under its control because the Suez Canal, which connected the Mediterranean Sea to the Red Sea, was in Egypt. As long as British ships could sail through the canal, the trip to Japan would be six thousand miles shorter!

Just before World War I broke out, the khedive of Egypt was 'Abbas II. 'Abbas II had become khedive twenty years earlier, at the age of seventeen. He had only been a little boy when the British marched into Cairo and took it over. He had never known an Egypt without British soldiers.

Although he was young, 'Abbas resisted following the orders of the British. Under his rule, Egyptian patriots began to talk and write about an Egypt ruled only by the khedive, without a British consul general or British soldiers occupying it.

At the beginning of World War I, Great Britain announced that Egypt would no longer have any relationship with the Ottoman Empire, its old ruler. The Ottoman Turks had joined the Central Powers, along with Germany, and Great Britain wanted Egypt to be on the side of the allies. The Egyptians weren't given any choice. To make sure that Egypt stayed loyal, the British also declared that Egypt was now under "martial law." This meant that the army, filled with British soldiers, had the final say in running Egypt—not 'Abbas II and the rest of the Egyptian government.

When this declaration was made, 'Abbas II wasn't even in the capital city of Cairo, where the Egyptian government had its offices. A few weeks before, an Egyptian student had tried to assassinate him in the street. The assassin had shot at the khedive, wounding him in the cheek and in the arm—and then had been killed by 'Abbas's bodyguard as he ran away.

'Abbas wasn't in danger of dying from his injuries, but he was in pain. So he left Cairo for a few days and went to his summer palace on the shores of the Bosphorus to recuperate. The Bosphorus beach, cooler than the hot city of Cairo, was a good place for a sick man to rest.

When martial law was declared, 'Abbas realized that it would be dangerous for him to return to Cairo. He didn't want Egypt to declare itself the enemy of the Ottoman Empire. Most Egyptians were Muslims, like the Ottoman Turks, and still felt loyalty towards the Turks. But he couldn't go back to Cairo and tell the British that he would prefer to be an ally of the Central Powers. He'd be surrounded by British soldiers, all of them enemies of Germany and of the Turks.

The British seized on 'Abbas II's absence as an excuse to remove him from power. The official in charge of Egypt announced that the British had "ample evidence" that 'Abbas was already an ally of the Ottoman Turks. This made him an enemy of Great Britain. He had "forfeited" his right to the throne. Now, Egypt would become a protectorate of Great Britain—an extension of Britain's empire.

'Abbas II fled to Vienna, in Austria, and watched from a distance as his country was changed. Instead of a khedive, Egypt would now have its own sultan—a Muslim ruler who didn't have any loyalty to the Turkish sultan. This position would be filled by 'Abbas's own uncle, Ahmad Fu'ad.

Even while World War I raged all around them, the Egyptians continued to hope that they might gain freedom from British rule. Just three days after World War I came to an end, three Egyptian patriots visited the British consul general and asked for permission to travel to London, in a formal diplomatic visit called a *wafd*. There, they hoped to present their request for Egypt's independence to Parliament. They promised that their visit would be peaceful, and that the British could keep control of the Suez Canal.

Instead of allowing them to go to London, the consul general had the leaders imprisoned!

In protest over this unwise act, riots broke out in Cairo. Students refused to go to class. Office workers stayed home. Railroad engineers and bus drivers refused to go to work. Taxis wouldn't carry anyone. Lawyers announced that they wouldn't go to court. The Irish technique of "boycotting" had spread to Egypt. The failure of the wafd turned into a national movement for independence—one that took the name Wafd to identify itself.

On March 15, 1919, fighting erupted between armed Egyptians and British soldiers. Ten thousand Egyptian men and women joined in—the first time that women had ever taken part in modern Egyptian politics! The battles went on for eight months. More than eight hundred Egyptians were killed.

Once again, the British began to realize that they could not keep hold of a country if its people were determined to win their freedom. On February 28, 1922, Great Britain formally granted Egypt its freedom. The sultan, Ahmad Fu'ad, would become King Fu'ad I—the first king of an independent Egypt. The Egyptians also drew up their own constitution, and began planning to elect an Egyptian parliament. Egypt would become a constitutional monarchy, a country with a king whose powers were limited by a constitution and by an elected assembly.

On March 16, Fu'ad I was publicly declared King. He sent out a letter to the whole country that said, "God has graciously permitted the independence of Egypt to be attained by our hands.... We have taken for ourself the title His Majesty, King of Egypt, in order to insure the country's dignity.... We hope this day will inaugurate an era which will restore Egypt's grandeur." Throughout Egypt, this letter was read aloud to gathered crowds. A salute of 101 guns was fired in Cairo, Alexandria, and Port Said.

Egypt was free.

But a three-way struggle for power had begun. In Parliament, the Wafd had won most of the seats—and wanted to keep as much power out of King Fu'ad's hands as possible. Fu'ad I didn't always agree with the Wafd, so he tried to bring Egyptians who weren't members of the Wafd into positions of power. And the British still hadn't left Egypt. British soldiers were still assigned to stay in military camps throughout the country, and British officers still held jobs in Egypt's police force and army. The prime minister of Great Britain was afraid that, if the British left Egypt altogether, other countries might seize control of the Suez Canal. He warned the rest of the world, "We will consider any aggression against the territory of Egypt as an act to be repelled with all the means at our command."

For the next few years, the king, the Wafd, and the British would all push and shove at each other, trying to increase their power in Egypt.

Fascism in Italy

In 1923, the year after Egypt was declared independent, a great upheaval began in Italy. It happened because nine thousand square miles of land wasn't enough.

Italy had joined World War I on the side of the Allies in 1915, the year after the war began. Over half a million Italian soldiers had died fighting against the Central Powers. When the prime minister of Italy, Vittorio Orlando, arrived in Versailles for the peace talks after the armistice, he expected that he would join with the other victorious leaders in writing out the treaty.

But this didn't happen. David Lloyd George, the British prime minister, and Georges Clemenceau, the French prime minister, refused to allow Orlando to have much of a say about the treaty's terms.

Why? Because they didn't trust Italy. Before the war began, Italy, Germany, and Austria had signed a treaty called the Triple Alliance. According to this treaty, if any one of the three countries went to war, the other two would join it.

When the war began, Italy broke the Triple Alliance and didn't join with Germany. But Italy didn't immediately join the Allies either. Instead, Italy's government remained out of the war for a year. During this year, thousands of French and British soldiers died. Now that the war was over, Italy's leader was still treated with suspicion, because Italy had once been Germany's friend, and hadn't immediately joined with Germany's enemies.

The British, French, and American leaders took credit for the Allied victory in World War I. As a matter of fact, the French and British viewed Woodrow Wilson of the United States as the savior of the Allied forces, even though the U.S. had entered the war so late. When David Lloyd George of Britain was asked how he had fared, at the Peace of Versailles, he answered, "Not bad, considering that I was seated between Jesus Christ and Napoleon"—by which he meant Woodrow Wilson of the United States and the French leader, Clemenceau.

So at Versailles, the three powerful countries set the terms of the peace treaty, while Vittorio Orlando watched. Orlando had hoped that, at the very least, Italy would get some of the land that lay along the Adriatic Sea. But Woodrow Wilson thought that it would be much better to create new, independent countries, so he refused to agree. The land along the Adriatic became part of the new country of Yugoslavia.

Mussolini's March to Rome

Italy did get some of the land that had once belonged to Austria, including the city of Trieste and the land surrounding it. It got nine thousand square miles—an area just a little bit bigger than the state of Massachusetts. But that didn't seem like nearly enough to the Italians. After all, Great Britain had claimed more than two hundred thousand square miles of Turkish land—an area almost as big as the state of Texas. And Italy had another complaint. When Italy had joined the war in 1915, it had signed a secret treaty with Great Britain. In return for Italy's help in the war, Great Britain had promised to give Italy huge amounts of land, all down the Adriatic Sea. Now, the British were ignoring the secret treaty.

When Vittorio Orlando returned home, he discovered that he had become very unpopular. The Italian people were angry that their country hadn't gained more land from the treaty. Italy had lost half a million men in the war, and almost another million had been wounded—a quarter of them crippled for life. Italy had spent as much money fighting World War I as it had spent in the fifty years before! Italy deserved more—and Orlando hadn't managed to get it.

Just days after the end of the Versailles conference, Vittorio Orlando resigned his position. This was the opportunity for a young politician named Benito Mussolini to move into power.

In the year of the Versailles peace conference, Mussolini was twenty-six years old. He came from a poor family, and had worked as a blacksmith alongside his father. He had fought in World War I, but in 1917 he was wounded and sent home. Like many Italians, Mussolini believed that Italy should have gotten more land in return for helping the Allies.

He also believed that Italy needed a new kind of government. If you remember, the Italian states were all united under King Victor Emmanuel II in 1861. Italy was a constitutional monarchy, which meant that a prime minister and an elected assembly had power, as well as the King. But even at that time, many people still thought that the nation of Italy should be a republic, not a monarchy.

In the fifty years since then, the king had not exactly been the most popular man in Italy. Victor Emmanuel II had passed the throne on to Umberto I—who had signed the Triple Alliance with Germany and Austria. During Umberto's rule, Italy grew poorer because it fought with its neighbors and also fought in Africa to protect its colonies. The people grew so restless and unhappy that they began to riot. Umberto announced that the country would be put under martial law. This made him so hated that he was assassinated! The throne went to his son, Victor Emmanuel III.

Victor Emmanuel III allowed Vittorio Orlando, his prime minister, to help him make his decisions. When Orlando resigned, Victor Emmanuel III could not find a strong prime minister to replace him. Italy had four different prime ministers in three years!

In the middle of all this chaos, Mussolini began to write and talk about his new political philosophy. He made speeches, and put out a newspaper called *Il Popolo d'Italia*, or "The People of Italy." In this newspaper, Mussolini explained that the most important thing for any country was that its government be strong. The government, and the nation itself, were more important than individual people. Individuals shouldn't demand rights if those rights would be bad for the country as a whole. Instead, each person should find fulfillment in serving the state. Mussolini also believed that a strong Italian leader could make the state of Italy as glorious as it had once been in the days of the Roman Empire. And because the state was so important, everyone should pay unquestioning, absolute loyalty to the leader of the state.

This might not sound like a very appealing idea to you. But Italy was poor, unhappy, and had no leader at all. For many Italians, the idea that a strong leader might take control, fix all of Italy's problems, and return Italy to a glorious place as the strongest nation in Europe was very wonderful indeed!

Mussolini's followers joined together in an organization that he called the *Fasci di Combattimento*, or the "Band of

Fighters." The word *fasci*, or "band," actually referred to the *fasces*, the bundle of tightly joined-together sticks with an axe in its center that had been a symbol of the ancient Roman government. Mussolini believed that individuals should be bound together so tightly that they formed a single united state, and that this state could never be broken apart.

Soon his followers were nicknamed "Fascists." And because they wore black shirts as part of their uniform, they also were given the name "Blackshirts." They saluted their leader by holding out their right arms at a stiff angle. They claimed that this salute was the same as the one the ancient Romans used—but this was a myth. The stiff-arm salute isn't found in one single painting or statue. It had been used in different countries for many years. No one knew for certain where it came from—but in movies made in the early 1900s that were set in ancient Rome, movie directors told the actors playing Romans to use this salute. So the "ancient Roman salute" probably came from the movies!

Mussolini planned to gather Fascists from all over Italy and march into Rome. Some of his followers would seize the government buildings. Others would wait outside the city, carrying guns. If the Italian government refused to give Mussolini the power to run Italy, the Fascist army waiting outside would march in and begin a war.

Mussolini collected his Fascist followers and marched towards Rome. But he never really had to occupy the city. Victor Emmanuel III was too afraid of starting a civil war.

If Victor Emmanuel had called out the army and declared martial law—as his advisors begged him to do—the army could have driven off the Fascists. There were many, many more Italian army soldiers than there were fighters in the Fascist army. Many of the Fascists hadn't actually managed to get hold of guns. They carried hoes and pitchforks instead.

But Victor Emmanuel didn't call out the army. Perhaps he remembered what had happened to his father, Umberto I, after he declared martial law! He didn't even wait for Mussolini's

Fascists to arrive in Rome. Instead, he summoned Mussolini to meet him and agreed to make him prime minister.

By 1923, Italy was firmly under control of the Fascists. Mussolini, the prime minister, was nicknamed *Il Duce*—"The Leader." He would remain prime minister of Italy for the next twenty-one years.

Although he held the title prime minister, Mussolini was actually a military dictator. He wanted to build a new Roman Empire by recapturing land all around the Mediterranean Sea. He knew that Romulus, the legendary founder of Rome, was supposed to have taken a plow and plowed out the borders of his new city. So, imitating Romulus, Mussolini got on a tractor and drove around the borders of new cities that he hoped to build in his "new Roman Empire."

If Italy had to go to war to build this new empire, Mussolini would declare war.

Japan, China, and the Area of Manchuria

Chapter Twenty-Five
Armies In China

Japan, China, and a Pretend Emperor

Across the Pacific Ocean, Japan was also trying to build an empire.

Around the time of World War I, Japan's empire-building got mixed up with China's ex-emperor. When the young Qing emperor Henry Puyi left the Forbidden Palace, he went first to Japan. He lived in Japan for several years, hoping that the Japanese might one day help him to get his throne back.

Over in China, Sun Yixian was forced to hand over power to a warlord named Yuan Shikai. Sun Yixian fled to the city of Canton, while Yuan Shikai took over the new Chinese government and ruled as a military dictator.

To keep his power, Yuan Shikai had to fight off other warleaders. While all this fighting was going on, Japan ordered Yuan Shikai to hand over not only Manchuria, but also the nearby provinces of Shantung and Inner Mongolia. Yuan had no choice. He couldn't resist Japan *and* fight against other warlords to keep his power in China. He agreed.

A year later, Yuan died. Now competing warlords and their bands of soldiers battled to rule the parts of China that hadn't been given over to the Japanese.

Sun Yixian, still in Canton, hadn't abandoned the hope of a united, peaceful China. He had organized a group of followers into a political party called the Nationalist Party, or the Kuomintang. The members of the Nationalist Party hoped to get rid of the warlords and unite China again, into a republic.

Sun Yixian and another Chinese revolutionary, Chiang Kai-shek, asked Russia to send help so that the Nationalist Party could fight against the warlords. When Russia agreed, Chiang Kai-shek went to the Soviet Union to see how the Red Army worked. With the help of Soviet advisors and Soviet weapons, the Nationalist Party started its own military academy to train its own soldiers. Soviet officers came to China to help prepare the new National Revolutionary Army for battle. Chiang Kai-shek, now the commander in chief of the National Revolutionary Army, began to plan a campaign against the warlords of the north.

In 1925, Sun Yixian died. But his plan to unify China lived on. A year later, the National Revolutionary Army began to march north. One by one, the army defeated the warlords that lay between Canton and Beijing. By 1928, the Nationalist Party had taken control of the city of Beijing, and of China's government.

But further away from the capital city, in the most distant provinces of China, warlords still reigned supreme.

In Japan, meanwhile, a new emperor had just ascended the throne. Hirohito was twenty-five years old. For the last five years, he had been the regent for his father, the emperor Yoshihito. Yoshihito had grown so old that he had begun to lose his wits. When Hirohito was twenty, Yoshihito went to a solemn meeting of Japan's government leaders. The meeting was long and dull, so the old man rolled up the papers on which his royal speech was written, and amused himself by peering at all of the important men through it, like a telescope.

At this, the leaders decided that Yoshihito was now too old to rule the country. Hirohito would take control of Japan and rule in his father's name. Five years later, in 1926, Yoshihito died and Hirohito became emperor in his own name. He was the 124th emperor of Japan, and he would rule Japan longer than any other emperor.

Hirohito governed a Japan that was torn by disagreement about who was really in charge. Like many other nations, Japan now had a constitution, and an elected assembly that made and passed laws. The emperor was only supposed to make decisions after his "cabinet" (a group of advisors) told him what the people wanted.

Hirohito was an energetic, well-educated young man. Before he became emperor, he had travelled in Europe, gone fly-fishing in Scotland, and visited with the king of England. He didn't want to be a figurehead; he wanted to be a real emperor. And all of his life, Hirohito had been taught that, like all emperors of Japan, he was part divine—a descendant of the sun goddess Amaterasu. Hirohito would not be content to simply sit and do as his advisors told him.

Hirohito wasn't the only man who wanted to rule Japan. Japan's large army had become less and less willing to do as the government ordered. The Japanese army had already taken land away from China, occupied Korea, and seized Manchuria. It was a powerful, well-organized force, and many Japanese military officers didn't like the attitude of the Japanese assembly towards the armed forces. After the war with Russia, the assembly had reduced the size of the army. The officers resented this. Some wanted Japan's constitution thrown out, so that Japan could be led by military officers who would expand the Japanese Empire all across Asia.

In 1931, five years after Hirohito ascended the throne, the Japanese soldiers posted in Manchuria took matters into their own hands.

These soldiers were alarmed when the Nationalist Party took control of Beijing. If China grew strong and unified again, it might manage to reclaim Manchuria. So the soldiers in Manchuria accused Chinese soldiers of trying to bomb a train with Japanese soldiers on it.

Was there really an explosion near the train? No one knows—but the train certainly arrived safely at its station. Still, Japanese soldiers started to invade and capture Chinese towns all over Manchuria, in revenge. Other Japanese soldiers marched up from Korea to help. Back in Japan, the government knew nothing about this military action. When the Japanese assembly did find out that the Japanese soldiers had begun a small war in Manchuria, they were powerless to stop it. The army simply ignored all of the instructions coming out of Tokyo, Japan's capital city.

Next, the army found Henry Puyi and offered to smuggle him into Manchuria. There, he could become the emperor of a Japanese Empire in China, called Manchukuo. Puyi accepted the offer at once. So the officers put him on a ship that would take him to Manchuria.

Puyi didn't know it—but the Japanese had no intention of allowing him to fall back into Chinese hands. The boat was booby-trapped. If it were attacked by the Chinese, it would explode—and Puyi would die. Fortunately, the boat reached Manchuria safely. The Japanese army immediately announced that Puyi would be the Chief Executive of the new country Manchukuo.

No one was particularly happy about this. The Chinese said that Manchukuo was an unreal country, a fairy tale, and that Puyi was a traitor. Puyi was indignant, because he had thought he would be made emperor. "Chief Executive" was not nearly as interesting a job. The Japanese government in Tokyo was unhappy with the army's actions—but was afraid of too much resistance. Hirohito could make an imperial decree removing the army from Manchuria, but what if the army simply refused to go? Then it would be obvious to everyone that the Japanese assembly and the emperor were helpless. So Hirohito and the Japanese government agreed to recognize Manchukuo as a legitimate country.

China appealed to the League of Nations. The League of Nations, after hearing the whole story of the founding of Manchukuo, announced that Japan was at fault, and should withdraw from China. Instead, Japan simply left the League of Nations.

But both Italy and Germany (neither of which was very fond of the League of Nations) agreed to recognize the new country of Manchukuo as a real nation. The Japanese army, to keep Puyi happy, agreed to give him the title of emperor. They gave him money, a palace—and no power. They made all of his decisions for him.

Manchukuo would remain under Japanese power for many years. In time, Japan would use Manchukuo as a place to build naval and army bases—and the Japanese military would grow stronger yet.

The Long March

Chiang Kai-shek, the commander in chief of the National Revolutionary Army, had led his army into Beijing and captured it. But he still had a civil war to fight. The National Party, or Kuomintang, controlled part of China, but elsewhere powerful warlords with bands of soldiers claimed to rule over the distant provinces of China.

Chiang Kai-shek still had to defeat them. And soon he would have a falling out with his own allies.

Chiang Kai-shek and his army had grown stronger with the help of Soviet advisors and Soviet allies. Many Chinese, seeing the devastation of their country caused by the weakness of the Qing emperor, and the struggle for power between warlords that followed, believed that the Soviet Union was a good model for a new China. Representatives of the Russian Communist Party travelled to China, to help the Chinese learn more about communism. They even drew up a "manifesto," or statement of beliefs, that the Chinese communists could use, and brought it to Shanghai. There, people who were interested in seeing China become communist gathered to read the manifesto, talk about it, and argue about it.

After a week of discussion, these "delegates" formed the Chinese Communist Party. One of the first members of the Chinese Communist Party, or CCP, was a young teacher named Mao Zedong (also spelled Tse-tung).

At first there were only about seventy Chinese communists in all of China. But these first Chinese communists left Shanghai and went back to their hometowns, ready to convince other Chinese to become communists. Mao Zedong went to his home in Hunan, quit his job as a teacher, and started to hold classes to teach the Chinese more about communism.

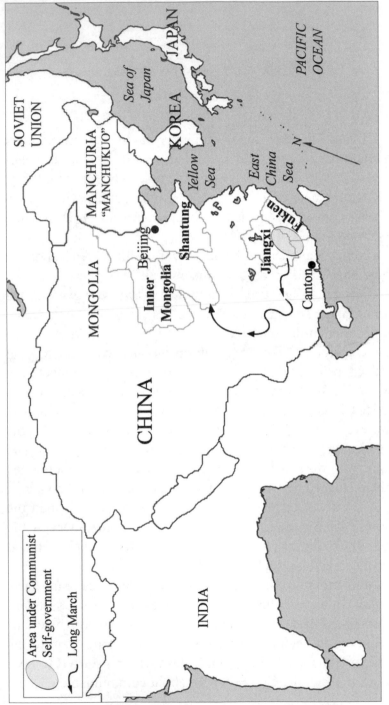

The Long March

As the CCP grew bigger, some of its members thought that the CCP should try to take over and drive the Kuomintang and the National Revolutionary Army out of power. But the Soviets in Russia thought that it would be better for the CCP and the Kuomintang to be allies. So the CCP, which now had its own army, agreed to help the National Revolutionary Army defeat the rest of the warlords.

But when the CCP and the Kuomintang tried to agree on policies by which China would be governed, trouble began. Many Kuomintang members and National Revolutionary Army officers began to suggest that the CCP was more Russian than Chinese. They accused the Chinese Communist Party of helping foreigners, once again, gain control over China.

Chiang Kai-shek agreed that the Russians had too much power in the CCP. So he ordered all CCP members, including Mao Zedong, to be fired from their jobs. He had all of the Soviets in China he could find, and many Chinese communists as well, arrested. He ordered some of them to be executed. The CCP and the Kuomintang would no longer be allies; now they were deadly enemies.

Mao Zedong and three thousand soldiers, peasants, and laborers gathered in Hunan and tried to attack the Kuomintang back. But this small rebellion was at once scattered by the National Revolutionary Army. Other Chinese Communist Party members who tried to fight back were defeated as well. By the time fighting had ended, scores of Chinese communists were dead.

Now that Chiang Kai-shek had driven off the CCP, he settled down to fight against the warlords that still ruled over the western provinces of China. For years, the National Revolutionary Army fought against and defeated them, one by one. And although the goal of the Kuomintang was supposed to be to make China into a republic, with a constitution and assemblies, the truth was that Chiang Kai-shek and the army really held all of the power in China.

At first, Chiang Kai-shek was too busy worrying about the Japanese in Manchuria and the warlords in China to pay any more attention to the CCP. But by 1930, he decided that it was time to worry about the Chinese communists once more.

The Chinese communists had retreated to wild, distant places, setting up camps in the mountains. Mao and his remaining followers had gone east, into the Jinggang Mountains on the edge of the province of Jiangxi. Over the years, other CCP members came to join them. One of them, an army officer named Zhu De, brought a whole troop of soldiers with him.

In the mountain retreat where they had settled, Mao and Zhu De took the land away from the rich landlords who owned it and gave it instead to the peasants. This made all of the peasants very happy to join with the Chinese communists! Mao and his followers announced that this new community was actually a new nation, the Chinese Soviet Republic (or the Kiangsi Soviet), and that Mao was its chairman.

In 1930, Chiang Kai-shek ordered a hundred thousand National Revolutionary Army soldiers to surround the Kiangsi Soviet. The CCP fought back. Even though they were outnumbered more than two to one, they managed to drive Chiang's men back.

Chiang sent another force—this time, with two hundred thousand men. The same thing happened. Twice more, the Kiangsi Soviet drove back the invaders. Four attacks had been unsuccessful.

But the fifth was a different story.

In 1934, Chiang Kai-shek sent four hundred thousand men against the Kiangsi Soviet settlement. This time, Mao realized, the army was too large to defeat. The Chinese Soviet Republic would fall—and its people would have to flee.

The members of the Kiangsi Soviet began to retreat away from the approaching army, towards the outer, western edges of China. On October 15, 1934, a hundred thousand men, women, and children began to march west.

They would march for over a year. They crossed rivers by building rafts, attaching baskets filled with stones to the rafts by ropes, and then poling the rafts into place, end to end, and dropping the baskets. This formed a narrow wooden bridge! As they marched, they passed Nationalist Army outposts and were fired on. Some were killed. Some drowned while building the raft bridges. Women who had babies while marching gave them to families in villages that they passed, because it was too hard to care for a little baby while marching. When they reached the high mountains at the border of the province, Mao told them that they could only cross if they kept walking. If they sat down, in the high mountain passes, they would freeze! The marchers made up a song to remind themselves of this:

> The mountain is high, so high,
> We cannot stop.
> Wrap your feet up! Rub them well!
> Don't rest at the top!

As they marched through the mountains, sleet storms lashed at them. Some of the marchers collapsed from cold. No one had the energy to rescue them. Others lay down at the very top, where the air was thin and there was not very much oxygen, because they felt sleepy. They never woke up.

On the other side of the mountains, they had to cross the Grasslands—a wide, dry waste with few villages and little food. The grain they carried with them began to run out. They started to eat grass and plant roots. They boiled their leather shoes and belts with leaves of nearby plants and made soup out of it. They called it the "Soup of the Three Delicacies" to make it taste better!

When the Kiangsi Soviet arrived in the town of Wuqi, in Shaanxi province, one year and four days later, only five thousand remained. Their journey became known as the Long March.

With the Long March over, Mao had become the best-known, the most respected, and the most powerful of the Chinese communists. He was now acknowledged as the leader of the CCP. Meanwhile, many Chinese who were not communists were beginning to wonder why Chiang Kai-shek was spending so much energy fighting the CCP, when the Japanese were trying to take away more and more of Manchuria. Rather than fighting other Chinese, why didn't the Nationalist army put all its energy into fighting Japan?

The CCP wanted these Chinese on their side. They began to use as their slogan, "Chinese don't fight Chinese." Many of the Chinese soldiers in the Nationalist Army agreed—and didn't want to fight against the CCP any more.

Chiang Kai-shek had to make a journey north, to tell the commanding officer of the National Army soldiers stationed there that he needed to fight against the Chinese communists with more fervor. When he arrived, the commanding officer took Chiang prisoner for two weeks! The officer realized that keeping Chiang in jail would cause a big problem, so he released Chiang Kai-shek.

But Chiang had gotten the message. Continuing the fight against the CCP would make his authority weaker. The Kuomintang and the Chinese Communist Party would have to become friends. It was time for the long civil war to end.

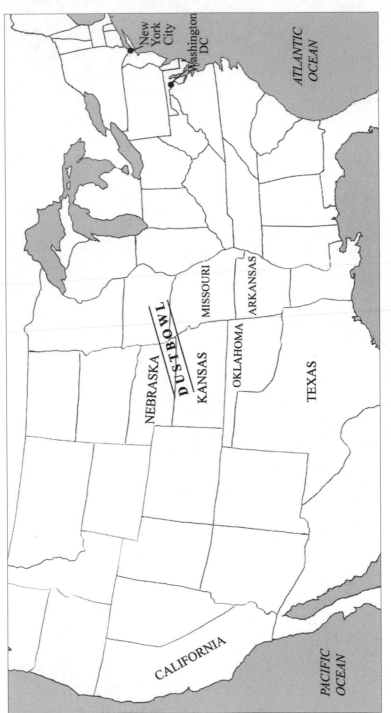

The United States and the Dustbowl

Chapter Twenty-Six
The Great Crash, and What Came of It

Black Tuesday and a New Deal

In the United States, after World War I, life just seemed to get better and better. The doughboys had come home victorious, the stores were full of food, and everyone seemed to have plenty of money. Architects were designing triumphant new buildings called skyscrapers that rose up high above the roofs of America's cities. Schools were packed with students. For the first time in American history, almost everyone could read, and authors like William Faulkner (*The Sound and the Fury*) and Hendrik Willem van Loon (*The Story of Mankind*) were publishing books that made them famous. Almost three hundred plays were performed in New York City alone. Musicians sang silly, light-hearted songs like "Yes, We Have No Bananas" and "I Wish That I Could Shimmy Like My Sister Kate." Dance marathons—all-night contests, where the contestants had to keep moving without once stopping or falling asleep—were held all over the country.

Everywhere, new things were happening. The first Miss America pageant was held. (A sixteen-year-old girl from Washington DC, Margaret Gorman, won!) The first Oscar awards for the movies were handed out. In his little plane *The Spirit of St. Louis*, Charles Lindbergh became the first person to fly alone, without stopping, across the Atlantic Ocean. Nothing seemed impossible. Life in America seemed like a beautiful dream.

In 1929, the dream ended.

During the 1920s, hundreds of thousands of people were spending money on something called the "stock market." A market is a place where people go to buy and sell. Many cities have a "farmer's market," where people with gardens come with their extra vegetables and sell them to others who don't have gardens. The "stock market" is a place where people buy "stock," and stock is a small portion of a company.

We read about stocks in Chapter Sixteen. When the chocolate factory owner took money from his friends to improve his factory, and promised them that in return they would get some of the profits at the end of the year, he was selling them "stock." Each friend now "owned" part of the company, and would get part of the money that the company made. They had become "stockholders."

If the chocolate factory did well, each stockholder would make money at the end of the year. But if the chocolate factory didn't make any profit, the money that each stockholder gave to the factory owner would be gone. As a matter of fact, if the factory was *really* doing poorly, the stockholders might even have to chip in some more money to help pay salaries and keep the factory open.

In the United States, people who wanted to sell parts of their companies, and people who wanted to buy those "stocks" because they hoped to share in the year-end profits, all met together in an area of New York City called Wall Street. (The name comes from a real wall that was built along the street in the seventeenth century, to protect the original Dutch settlers of the city from the attacks of Native Americans and hostile Englishmen.) In the early 1800s, a group of businessmen decided to open a "stock exchange" on Wall Street. There, company owners and company buyers could come to buy and sell stocks. This place of business was called the New York Stock Exchange.

In the 1920s, after the end of World War I, factories and companies were making wagonloads of money. People who bought stock in those companies were making lots of money too, sharing in the company profits. If they spent $100, they got $1,000 back; if they spent $25,000, they might get a hundred thousand dollars in profit. Buying stock seemed like the easiest way in the world to earn money. People were so excited about this easy money that they spent hundreds of thousands of dollars on stocks. Sometimes, they even borrowed money to buy stocks. After all, they were sure they would make enough profit to pay back the loan.

But when factories and companies are raking in money, more factories get built and more companies get started. More sellers compete for the same buyers. The buying starts to slow down. Money gets a little tighter, and a little scarcer.

In 1929, the stock market didn't just slow down. It came to a crashing halt, all within a week.

On October 24, 1929, people began to sell off their stock. As they sold their stock, others began to think that it might be a good idea to sell as well. With so many people selling, and not too many people wanting to buy, the prices of the stocks had to go down, and down, and down. (Think of it this way: if twenty people want a candy bar, and one person has five candy bars to sell, the person with the candy bars can probably charge $2 per candy bar, and at least five of the twenty people will be willing to pay it. But if twenty people have candy bars that they really want to sell, and only one person wants to buy a candy bar, all twenty people will charge as little as possible for their candy bars, hoping that the hungry person will pick *their* five-cent candy bar instead of another seller's fifteen-cent bar.)

The prices of stocks kept going down, and down, and down. More people sold their stock, hoping to get some money back for it before the prices dropped even more. The value of the stocks went down even more. A man who owned $50,000 worth of stock on the morning of October 24 found, at the end of the day, that his stock was worth less than a hundred dollars.

This selling went on for a week. It was known as the Wall Street Crash. The worst day of the whole Crash was Tuesday, October 29, 1929. On that day, which became known as Black Tuesday, fourteen billion dollars worth of stock lost so much of its value that it was worth almost nothing.

Stockholders who had put most of their money into buying stocks now had no money at all. Many owed loans to banks that they couldn't possibly pay. The banks couldn't get their money back—so the banks themselves had to close. Some businessmen were plunged so deeply into great debt that they killed themselves. Buyers and sellers lost so much money that for the next ten years, most Americans had very little to spend. They didn't buy new clothes, they didn't buy new cars, they didn't buy a lot of food, and they certainly didn't buy Christmas presents. If you got an orange for Christmas, you were a very lucky child.

This time, the 1930s, was called the "Great Depression." To make matters worse, the weather turned bad. Tremendous droughts killed off hundreds of thousands of acres of crops. The Great Plains of the United States had so little rain that winds picked up the dust and blew it back and forth in huge dust storms. During a dust storm, people locked themselves in their houses, put towels under the doors and around the windows—and still found an inch of dirt all over their floors, beds, and furniture at the end of the storm. The middle of America became known as the Dust Bowl. Unable to make a living on their dry farms, thousands of Americans left the Dust Bowl states and headed to California. These emigrants were called "Okies," because although many hailed from Arkansas, Missouri, and Texas, one out of every five came from Oklahoma.

When the Great Depression began, a man named Herbert Hoover was president. Hoover knew that he would have to do something to help the thousands of poor, hungry, and homeless Americans. In 1932, President Hoover and the United States Congress set up something called the "Reconstruction Finance Corporation." The RFC was like a bank that would lend money to banks, businesses, and farms, so that they could keep going until times got a little better.

The RFC was a good start, but it wasn't enough. Another American leader, a New Yorker named Franklin Delano Roosevelt, promised Americans that if he were elected president instead of Herbert Hoover, he would give America a "New Deal" that would reverse the Great Depression.

Roosevelt, nicknamed FDR, had suffered from a disease called polio as a child. He was in a wheelchair, because he couldn't walk. But even from his wheelchair, he seemed more energetic and more full of ideas than Herbert Hoover. And Americans were desperate for an answer to their poverty. On Election Day, FDR beat Hoover by millions and millions of votes.

Now that he was president, FDR wanted to get immediate help to people who were homeless and hungry. He wanted to provide jobs for people who were out of work. And he wanted to change the stock market and the banks so that a Great Crash could never happen again.

Along with Congress, FDR created new "companies" that would give Americans jobs and salaries. The Civilian Conservation Corps, nicknamed the CCC, hired men to plant forests, fight fires, and control floods. The Works Progress Administration, or WPA, hired even more men to build roads and bridges. The Agricultural Adjustment Administration, or AAA, helped farmers rebuild their herds and get their fields back. FDR created so many programs with abbreviations like

President Franklin Delano Roosevelt delivering a radio address

CCC, WPA, and AAA, that Americans said, "FDR is making alphabet soup for the USA!"

FDR's alphabet soup put real soup into the bellies of millions of hungry Americans. And his "New Deal" would slowly bring the United States out of the Great Depression.

Hitler's Rise to Power

The Great Depression of the United States didn't just affect America. It affected the whole world. All during the 1920s, Americans bought expensive things, from cars to coffeemakers, from European businesses. Americans travelled to Europe and spent millions of dollars on hotels and food. American money poured into Europe.

When Americans began to lose their money, they stopped buying fancy European goods. They quit travelling to Europe. European factories and businesses suddenly had much less money. Hotels and restaurants started to fire waiters, bellboys, and maids. Like America, Europe became poorer. The Great Depression spread across the countries of Europe.

One of the countries hardest hit by the Depression was Germany.

Germany was poor and unhappy even before Black Tuesday, the day the stock market crashed in New York. When Germany was forced to sign the Peace of Versailles, after World War I, the German government had to agree to pay France and England *reparations*—huge sums of money to make up for all the money France and England had spent beating Germany in World War I.

Germany, which had already lost almost two million young men to war and had spent enormous amounts of money fighting, began to try to pay the reparations. But the government simply didn't have the money to pay. So Germany borrowed the money for reparations from American and British banks—and then paid it back to the French and British governments.

When the stock market crashed, the American banks that had lent money to Germany demanded that Germany repay the loans. Germany didn't have the money—not unless it could borrow from yet another country. But all the countries of Europe became poorer during the Depression. No one had money to lend. Now, Germany couldn't afford to pay off its loans *or* the reparations.

People began to lose their jobs in Germany. Every week, more German businesses folded and disappeared. Prices began to rise higher and higher. Soon, a German housewife needed an entire wheelbarrowful of cash to buy a loaf of bread.

A young Austrian named Adolf Hitler thought that he had the answer to Germany's problems.

Although Adolf Hitler was born in Austria, he considered himself German. Many Austrians did think of themselves as German—which is one reason why Germany and Austria fought together in World War I. Hitler studied German art and listened to German music, especially to the operas of composer Richard Wagner.

When World War I began, Hitler joined the German army. He believed that Germany was the strongest, worthiest country in the world, and that German culture was the most beautiful. If Germany conquered Europe, German ways would spread across the land—and that could only be good. If Germany wanted to add other countries to the German Empire by force, those countries were *lucky* to become German.

Hitler was surprised to find out that many Germans didn't support the war. After a few years of fighting, thousands of German citizens just wanted life to go back to normal. They wanted the war to end, even if Germany had to give up some of its land and its power.

Hitler was appalled. How could his fellow Germans be so unpatriotic? Some evil force must be spreading discontent throughout Germany, keeping Germans from recognizing the importance of German victory.

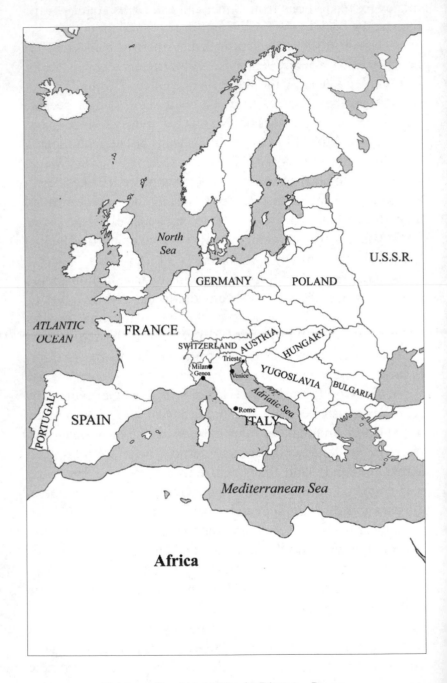

Europe During Hitler's Rise to Power

Hitler decided that the evil people who were spreading this discontent must be the Jews.

Since the Middle Ages, Europeans had been suspicious of Jews. Christians who knew almost nothing about Jewish culture and the Jewish religion thought that the Jews had strange, illegal rituals. They accused Jews of being proud and boastful, and caring about nothing but money. None of these things were true, but hatred of Jews, called *anti-Semitism*, was so widespread that, in many European countries, Jews couldn't even own land until the 1700s.

In the twentieth century, thousands of people still hated and feared the Jewish people. When Hitler began to make speeches about how the Jews were responsible for Germany's troubles, he found many Germans who were willing to listen.

After World War I, Hitler became part of a political group that became known as the National Socialist German Workers' Party. Like the communists, the National Socialists believed that the poor and working people of Germany should have more of a say in how the country was run. Like the Fascists, the National Socialists believed that they needed a strong leader who could make Germany a great and wealthy nation again. And like many Europeans, the National Socialists were anti-Semitic.

Hitler made speeches at the National Socialist meetings. He turned out to be a mesmerizing public speaker. When he talked about the greatness of the German people, his listeners were almost hypnotized. After he spoke, the audience would stand up, cheering for Hitler's ideas. Before long, Hitler had become the leader, or *führer*, of the National Socialists.

When the Great Depression hit America and Europe, Hitler's audiences grew even larger. The German people had already been poor and discouraged. Now they were poorer, and hungrier, and more desperate. They were willing to listen to anyone who could promise them a better future.

Hitler travelled through Germany, promising that if Germans would vote the National Socialists (nicknamed the

"Nazis" for short) into office, Germany would change. He would bring order, wealth, and greatness to Germany. He would cancel the terms of the Peace of Versailles, so that Germany would be free of its crushing war debt. And he promised that the Nazi party would get rid of all of the menacing Jews who were helping to cause Germany's difficulties.

By 1932, over a third of the German voters supported the Nazis. The Nazis had become the most popular political party in Germany. When elections were held, the führer of the Nazi party, Adolf Hitler, won the job of German chancellor.

He was now the most powerful man in Germany.

Spain Under the Rule of Franco

Chapter Twenty-Seven
Civil War and Invasion

Red Spain, Black Spain, a King, and a General

The country of Spain hadn't taken part in World War I. It hadn't fought against Russia or Great Britain or Japan. It hadn't been divided up during the Peace of Versailles, or lost thousands of soldiers in the battles of the Great War. Despite that, Spain was no more peaceful than any other part of the world.

The king of Spain, Alfonso XIII, had inherited the throne even before his birth. His father had died when his mother was still pregnant—so the unborn Alfonso became king! Alfonso's mother ruled for him as regent until 1902. In that year, the sixteen-year-old Alfonso was *coronated* (crowned) in the great cathedral in Seville. He was the youngest crowned king in the world at that time.

While Alfonso XIII was being coronated—in an elaborate ceremony that lasted for hours—a little boy named Francisco Franco Bahamonde was sitting on the doorstep of his house, tossing rocks into a puddle and wondering what he would be when he grew up. Francisco's father had left their family, years before. His mother struggled to feed her family and raise her children. Francisco didn't want to spend the rest of his life struggling to survive. He decided that the life of a soldier was a good one for him.

When he grew old enough, Francisco Franco entered the Spanish army and became an officer. He fought well, and always obeyed orders. He won medals for bravery and was promoted again and again. He even came to the attention of King Alfonso XIII. When Franco was only twenty-eight, Alfonso put him in charge of the Spanish Foreign Legion—a Spanish fighting force commanded by Spanish officers, but mostly made up of soldiers from other countries.

When World War I began, Spain remained neutral. Instead of fighting, Spain made a lot of money by selling steel, machines, and engines to the countries who *were* fighting. But when the war ended, so did the sales. Spanish factories closed. Ships sat idle. Many Spanish workers lost their jobs.

Three years after the Great War ended, Spain had to fight a smaller war. A Spanish territory called Morocco, a small strip of Northern Africa just across the Mediterranean Sea from Spain, rebelled. Spain sent its army across the Straits of Gibraltar (the small neck of the Mediterranean Sea between Spain and North Africa) to stop the revolt. Over ten thousand Spanish soldiers were killed by the much smaller army of Moroccan rebels.

The slaughter humiliated Spain and angered the Spanish people. Spain was poorer than ever, and unhappy over the loss of its men. As in so many countries, hard times gave revolutionaries a chance to call for change.

These revolutionaries were known as "Red Spain." For many years, Spanish rebels had been insisting that Spain needed to get rid of its king and to become a republic, with a constitution, like so many other countries in Europe. These "Red Spanish" wanted to see the end of the monarchy and the beginning of rule by the common people. As a matter of fact, "Red Spain" had tried more than once to get rid of the king. Alfonso XIII had almost been assassinated on his wedding day!

Wealthy, aristocratic Spaniards who wanted Spain to stay a monarchy were called citizens of "Black Spain." In this traditional Spain, the king and his noblemen had most of the power. The army, which had many Spanish noblemen as officers, tended to be on the side of "Black Spain."

In the five years after the Moroccan War, "Red Spain" and "Black Spain" quarrelled with each other—and threatened violence. Alfonso XIII became less and less popular. He was blamed for the Spanish losses in the Moroccan war, for ignoring the needs of his people, and for having too much power. By 1931, Alfonso XIII could see that, if he kept holding onto his power as king, Spain would break apart into civil war between Reds and Blacks.

So he composed a public statement, to be read to the Spanish people. "[It is clear that] I no longer enjoy the love of my people," he wrote. "I could very easily find means to support my royal powers against all comers, but I am determined to have nothing to do with setting one of my countrymen against another in a fratricidal civil war." Then Alfonso XIII left Spain, and went to Rome.

While he was gone, Spain held an election for an assembly—a Spanish Parliament. Spanish voters elected a president. The assembly wrote out a constitution. Spain had become a republic, and it looked as though "Red Spain" had triumphed over "Black Spain" for good.

But although Alfonso XIII had told his people that he didn't want civil war, he also refused to give up his throne. Even in exile, he claimed to be the rightful ruler of Spain. And the new Republican government wasn't supported by all of Spain. Some Spaniards wanted Alfonso XIII to come back to his country. Others wanted the Roman Catholic Church to have more power than it was allowed under the new constitution of Spain. One area of Spain, called Catalonia, started to insist that Catalonia should be a free country in its own right, independent of Spain.

In 1936, open war broke out in Spain. Monarchists, Republicans, and independence fighters took up weapons and started battles in the streets. Spain was full of political groups, each wanting something slightly different. Leaders of each group were assassinated by others. Down in Morocco, Spanish soldiers who were supposed to be keeping order in this restless Spanish territory declared that they would no longer obey the republican government of Spain. They were soon joined by army soldiers in Spain itself.

By now, Franco had become a general in the Spanish army. He was the youngest general in Europe—just as Alfonso had been Europe's youngest king. The Spanish army, calling itself the "Nationalist" party of Spain, made Franco their leader.

After the army rebelled, the fighting in Spain settled down into two opposing sides.

The Nationalists (the army), under Francisco Franco, didn't want Alfonso XIII back. But they did believe that Spain needed a strong, decisive leader—like Mussolini of Italy. The other side, called the "Popular Front," were the Spaniards who wanted Spain to keep its constitution. The Spanish Civil War, between the Nationalists (who had adopted Fascist ideas about the need for a strong leader) and the Popular Front (who wanted Spain to be a republic) went on for three years.

Many Spanish were killed in the battles between the Popular Front and the Nationalists. The rest of the world got involved. Fascist Italy and Nazi Germany were on the side of the Nationalists. Communist Russia, on the other hand, sent money and weapons to the Popular Front, because the Soviets thought that the Popular Front might be sympathetic to communism.

So the United States decided to support the fascist Nationalists and General Franco, so that the Communist Party wouldn't have the chance to gain more power. The Nationalists slowly won the upper hand. Nationalist soldiers took over the west of the country, and began to march north and east.

The two largest cities of Spain, Barcelona and Madrid, remained under the control of the Popular Front. But after months and months of fighting, the Soviet Union saw that the Popular Front cause was doomed—and stopped sending help. Now, the Popular Front had lost its steady supply of weapons and supplies.

Nationalists took over Barcelona and then surrounded Madrid. A siege began and went on for months. "Madrid is a hungry city," wrote an American reporter who was in Madrid, describing the war for the *New York Times*. "Rice cooked in rancid olive oil, a thin slice of beef ... and oranges—just that and nothing more, day after day, week after week. ... Winter is nasty in Madrid ... the cold is particularly penetrating. ... [In] the districts of Madrid that have been most heavily bombed, it is a common sight to see men, women and children foraging among the ruins of houses for parts of beams, pieces of flooring, broken furniture—anything so long as it is wood and will burn."

Finally, the Popular Front was forced to give up the last city that they still controlled. On March 1, 1939, Madrid surrendered.

Francisco Franco and his army now controlled Spain. Another *New York Times* reporter described his experiences, driving through Spain and seeing peasants and schoolchildren everywhere giving the straight-armed Fascist salute. The country, he wrote, was "orderly, subdued if not unified. ... There are no books on sale ... but there are newspapers, cigarettes, large loaves of bread, coffee and wine. In the train soldiers fill the compartments and aisles, sit or lie on the platforms, overflow into the vestibules."

Those soldiers would help Franco keep control of his new power. General Franco would now rule as a military dictator over Spain! Like Mussolini, he would control his country with his army.

Franco earned a reputation as a ruthless, intolerant dictator. Those who opposed him were taken prisoner—and often died of starvation, if they weren't put to death. Later, historians estimated that as many as two hundred thousand Spaniards died because of Franco's rule.

Two years after the surrender of Madrid, Alfonso XIII died in Rome, on the last day of February 1941. He left the throne of Spain to his son Prince Juan Carlos, who had been born in Rome just three years before. But Juan Carlos would not rule over Spain until Francisco Franco died—forty years later!

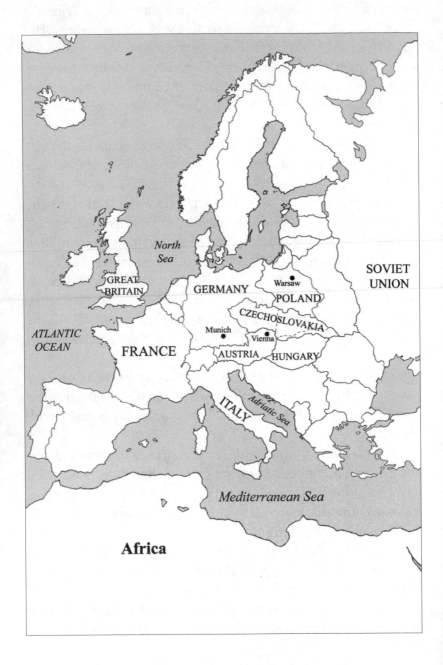

Europe During Hitler's Rule

Rebuilding the "Fatherland"

Adolf Hitler had now been the chancellor of Germany for five years. For five years, he had preached to the German people that their nation was the best in the world. Anyone who was born German had a natural right to rule. Everyone else, in his own words, was "eternally fated to serve and obey" the German people. "We must rule Europe!" Hitler declared.

Hitler intended to claim Europe for Germany a little bit at a time. First, he intended to "reunite" Germany by taking over all of the countries where German-speaking people of German descent lived. Hitler explained to the German people that he wouldn't be conquering a new German Empire; he would just be *re*creating the "Fatherland," a Germany that had existed in older times and had been destroyed.

The way that the Peace of Versailles had created new countries made this quest simpler for Hitler. To start with, the treaty had divided the Austro-Hungarian Empire into two separate—and weaker—countries: Austria and Hungary. Hitler wasn't very interested in Hungary. But for decades, Hitler had believed that Austria, whose people spoke German, should be part of Germany. He thought that Austria's separation from Germany made both nations weaker. And since Austria was his own home country, he wanted to enfold it into his new, restored Germany.

In March of 1938, Germany claimed Austria for its own. Hitler led a triumph parade into Vienna. Many Austrians supported him; Austria had been humiliated and made weaker by World War I, and German-speaking Austrians thought that Hitler might lead Austria back into a glorious time of victory. During the German takeover of Austria, called the *Anschluss*, these Austrians lined the streets of Vienna and shouted, "Sieg Heil! Sieg Heil!" In German, this meant, "Hail, Victory!"

But this was only the beginning. Just before claiming Austria, Hitler had made a speech to the *Reichstag*, the German parliament, in which he said, "There are more than ten million Germans in states adjoining Germany which before 1866 were joined to the bulk of the German nation. ... Against their own free will they were prevented by peace treaties from uniting with the Reich. ... To ... the German Reich belongs also the protection of those German peoples!"

Great Britain and France grew nervous. Just how big would this "reunited" Germany grow? Germany had already signed an alliance with Italy, so Mussolini's soldiers would support Hitler's army in whatever Hitler commanded them to do. Hitler's army itself had grown enormously. For years, Hitler had been secretly breaking the Treaty of Versailles by training thousands and thousands of soldiers. Remember, according to the Treaty, the German army was supposed to be smaller than one hundred thousand men. But by 1938, Germany's army had close to a million soldiers in it.

Of course, it wasn't possible to keep an army with a million soldiers in it secret for long. Most of the powerful countries in the world knew Hitler was making his army larger. But the United States, which had refused to join the League of Nations, had decided not to interfere in Europe. The U.S. was still recovering from the Depression. It had its own problems! And France and Great Britain, the other two countries that had helped to write out the treaty, were more afraid of communism than of the Nazi party. At least if Hitler had a large army, the Soviet Union wouldn't be able to claim Germany as a communist country.

No one knew just how determined to rule the world Adolf Hitler was. And no one realized that, in 1938, Hitler was a much bigger problem than communism.

But then Hitler announced that he would now add Czechoslovakia to the German "Fatherland." Czechoslovakia had millions of German-speaking citizens in it who needed to be reunited with their own people. At this, France and Great Britain were worried enough to send their prime ministers to the German city of Munich to talk to Hitler.

It became clear that Hitler was determined to have Czechoslovakia, and would fight for it if necessary. Disastrously, both countries decided not to oppose Hitler. Neville Chamberlain, the prime minister of Great Britain, worked out a careful agreement with Hitler that would let Hitler have the western half of Czechoslovakia—the part called the "Sudetenland." When he went back home, Neville Chamberlain made a famous speech to the British people. By giving Hitler what he wanted, he told them, he had assured that there would be "peace in our time."

Here are Neville Chamberlain's exact words.

"Last Wednesday. ... a war more stark and terrible than had ever taken place before seemed to be staring us in the face. ... [Now] our anxiety has been lifted from our hearts. ... Hard things have been said about the German Chancellor. ... [but I hope to] extend a little further the personal contact which I had established with Herr Hitler, which I believed to be essential to modern diplomacy. ... We regard the agreement signed. ... as symbolic of the desire of our two peoples never to go to war with one another again. Does any one doubt that this is the desire of the people? ... I believe that there is sincerity and goodwill on both sides. ... The path that leads to peace is a long one and bristles with obstacles. This question of Czechoslovakia is the latest and perhaps the most dangerous. Now that we have got past it I feel that it may be possible to make further progress along the road to sanity."

The British politician Winston Churchill retorted that Chamberlain's speech was cowardly and short sighted. England had been given the choice between war and shame. Chamberlain had chosen shame. And now war would come as well.

Churchill was right. Hitler, perhaps thinking that he would not be opposed at all, didn't stop at the Sudetenland. He marched into the rest of Czechoslovakia and claimed it as well. Just months later, he made a deal with Joseph Stalin, the Soviet leader. Hitler wanted to claim Poland too. If the Soviets would help Germany conquer Poland, Germany and Russia would divide Poland between them. Russia also agreed to a "pact of nonaggression," meaning that Russian soldiers would not join in any resistance to Germany.

Far from serving as a protection against communism, Hitler had made an alliance with the Soviets—so that Germany could claim Europe.

On September 1, 1939, the German troops marched into Poland from three different directions. Later, the beginning of the war that sprang from this invasion—World War II—was put at 4:45 a.m. on September 1. A German soldier who belonged to one of the invading divisions, Erich Hoppe, later wrote, "We were at war, but there was no sound of conflict, except for a low rumble which could have been thunder but wasn't. It was gunfire, but very distant. ... That first morning of the war was a warm, bright, quiet and peaceful one."

By 6 a.m., German bombers were swooping over Warsaw, the capital city of Poland. German bombs destroyed Polish fighters before the planes could even lift off from the ground. The Polish army, ill equipped, had to line up on horseback to face approaching German tanks.

This invasion showed both Great Britain and France that there would be no peace. Just two days later, on September 3, Great Britain and France declared war on Hitler. Before long, Canada, Australia, New Zealand, and India joined Great Britain and France. The armies fighting against Hitler became known as the Allied Powers. Germany, Italy, and their allies were known as the Axis powers.

The Polish army resisted for a single month. But on September 28, Warsaw could no longer resist. Thousands of Polish soldiers had died. The city had to surrender.

It would be the first surrender of many.

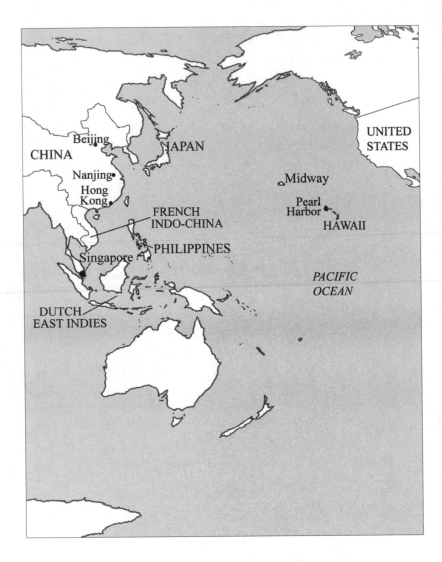

The Second Sino-Japanese War

Chapter Twenty-Eight
The Second World War

The Three-War War

The League of Nations and the Peace of Versailles hadn't prevented another great war from spreading across Europe. Soon, like World War I, the war would spread across the whole world. It would become known as World War II.

The Allies (France, Great Britain, and Britain's allies) were fighting against Germany and Italy, called the Axis powers. Before long, Germany and Italy were joined by another powerful country: Japan.

Two years before Hitler's invasion of Poland, the hatred between Japan and China had erupted into out-and-out war. In 1937, Chiang Kai-shek of China had agreed to make an alliance between his Kuomintang government and the Chinese Communist Party because he knew he could not fight both the CCP and the Japanese. Almost at once, the new allies found themselves fighting the Japanese army, which had marched from Manchuria down towards the Chinese city of Beijing.

On July 7, 1937, the Japanese army had attacked the Marco Polo Bridge outside of Beijing. The bridge, a beautiful marble span with eleven different arches, was controlled by the Kuomintang army in the east—and the Japanese army in the west. Early in the morning, the Japanese demanded permission from the Kuomintang to cross the bridge, over to the Kuomintang side, and search the houses nearby. The Japanese said that their officers needed to search for a deserting Japanese soldier who might be hiding there. But the Chinese thought that this was just a pretense to get across the bridge.

When they refused to let the Japanese officers pass, the Japanese began to march across the bridge—with tanks!

The Kuomintang army managed to drive them back. But the Japanese reorganized themselves and attacked again. After two weeks of fighting, the Japanese finally made it across the bridge and seized hold of the Chinese side.

This was the beginning of the Second Sino-Japanese War.

The Chinese had a different name for this war. They called it the Chinese People's Anti-Japanese War of Resistance. China lost land to the Japanese all along the north of China, and in the middle of the country as well. One of the most horrible events in modern history took place in China, when Japan marched into the southern city of Nanjing, in the province of Jiangxi. Japanese soldiers killed two hundred thousand unarmed Chinese citizens who had nothing to do with the war.

Still, China refused to surrender.

This war had been going on for two years by the time that World War II began over in Europe. When Great Britain and France declared war on Germany, Japan saw a chance to expand its own empire. Great Britain, France, and the Netherlands (which also joined the Allies) all had colonies in southeast Asia: the British ruled Hong Kong, the French still had control over Vietnam, and the Dutch governed the East Indies. Those European countries were so busy fighting against Hitler that none of them had the time or the soldiers to defend their Asian colonies. Japan could swoop in and take those colonies for itself.

In 1940, Japan declared itself to be an Axis power, along with Germany and Italy. Now, Japan had the perfect excuse to attack the colonies held by the Allies.

Japan did have one country standing in the way of its conquest of Asia: the United States.

The United States wasn't fighting in World War II, so Japan wasn't at war with them. In 1940, more than three-quarters of American citizens didn't want the United States getting involved in Europe's troubles. The president of the United States, Franklin Delano Roosevelt, knew that his people didn't want to fight. The United States had agreed to send oil, guns, and other necessary supplies to Great Britain, even if Britain couldn't pay, but that was as far as most Americans wanted to go.

But even though the United States wasn't one of the Allies, Japan knew that the U.S. wouldn't sit quietly and watch Japan take over the colonies in Asia, one by one. A whole fleet of American battleships lay in the South Pacific, anchored at Pearl Harbor in Hawaii. If Japan moved against the Allied colonies, the U.S. battleships at Pearl Harbor would set out to block Japan's ambitions.

Years before, Japan had beaten one of the world's strongest navies by torpedoing Russian battleships first—and then declaring war afterwards. In December of 1941, the Japanese commander, General Hideki Tojo, decided to follow the same strategy. Tojo wasn't just an army general; he had also become the prime minister of Japan, the man who advised Emperor Hirohito. He told the emperor that unless Japan stood up to the United States, Japan would never be a great country. Hirohito agreed that the time had come to attack the U.S.

On a quiet Sunday morning, December 7, 1941, U.S. servicemen who were scrubbing the decks, eating their breakfasts, and going through the morning routine heard the sound of airplanes. Some scrambled up on deck. Others didn't bother to look. No one in Pearl Harbor expected an attack.

Over the horizon swept wave after wave of Japanese fighter planes—almost two hundred. Bombs began to fall. The Americans, taken off guard, were almost helpless. Some of the ships caught on fire and burned. Others capsized, trapping sailors inside them. A marine named E. C. Nightingale later described how he was finishing breakfast when he heard warning sirens go off. He didn't pay much attention to the sirens until he began to hear explosions. He ran up to his battle station, seeing that men all over the ship had already manned their guns and begun to fire. But then the ship began to shake. It had been hit by a bomb. The entire front of the ship was burning. Many of his friends had been killed already.

Before Nightingale could escape, another bomb hit the ship. The jolt threw him over the side, into the water! He was about to go under when an officer swimming by grabbed his shirt and hauled him towards the beach.

The attack was over in less than two hours. But twenty-one American ships and 188 American fighter planes had been destroyed. A high school student on the shore wrote in her diary that when the attack ended, the barracks where the soldiers lived was burning and the warehouse where supplies were kept was on fire. Houses all along the harbor had been blown up. The water of the harbor couldn't even be seen. A solid wall of smoke blocked it from view.

Pearl Harbor brought an end to American neutrality. Almost three thousand American soldiers were killed. Thirteen hundred men had died on one battleship, the *Arizona*, alone—the ship that E. C. Nightingale had escaped. News photographs published in American newspapers showed American ships burning and sinking and U.S. servicemen dying. December 7, said President Roosevelt, was a "date which will live in infamy."

The American people could no longer ignore the disaster sweeping over the rest of the world. Roosevelt asked Congress to declare war on Japan and all its allies, meaning Germany and Italy.

While the Americans were trying to recover from the destruction of the fleet at Pearl Harbor, the Japanese swept down over Hong Kong and the islands south of the Asian mainland. Japanese troops took over the Philippine Islands and Malaya too. British soldiers who occupied all three of these places had to flee to Singapore. Soon they were forced out of Singapore as well. Japan was extending its empire all over Asia. Within a year, the Japanese would claim the Dutch East Indies for themselves.

The Americans fought back. Recruits poured into the American navy, anxious to avenge Pearl Harbor. Half a year after Pearl Harbor, in the spring of 1942, the Americans launched an attack against the Japanese fleet near the island of Midway. In the Battle of Midway, four huge Japanese aircraft carriers (ships that carried fighter planes that could take off, attack targets, and return to the ship for refueling, so that planes could fight much further away from land) were destroyed by a much smaller American force.

The war between Japan and the Allies in the east had its own name: the War of the Pacific. When Allied soldiers went to China to help the Chinese fight back against Japanese invasion, the War of the Pacific mingled with the Sino-Japanese War. And now that the Allies and the Axis powers were fighting in both Europe and in the East, the three wars had all blended together. The Sino-Japanese War, the War of the Pacific, and World War II had become one huge, world-swallowing disaster.

The Holocaust

When Hitler came to power in Germany, before the beginning of World War II, he promised the German people that he would get rid of the Jews. During World War II, he did his best to fulfill this promise.

This is a very difficult story to tell, because it is so horrible. All during World War II, Hitler was sending his soldiers to fight against the Allies. But this was only part of his scheme for a German takeover of Europe. Because Hitler believed that Germans were better than any other race, he also wanted to wipe out people who were "inferior."

Hitler's ideas about "inferior people" were based on very bad science. He believed that people with "Aryan" (German) blood were smarter, stronger, and better than other people. Scientists working for the Nazis believed that they could measure the length of someone's nose, the size of his skull, look at the

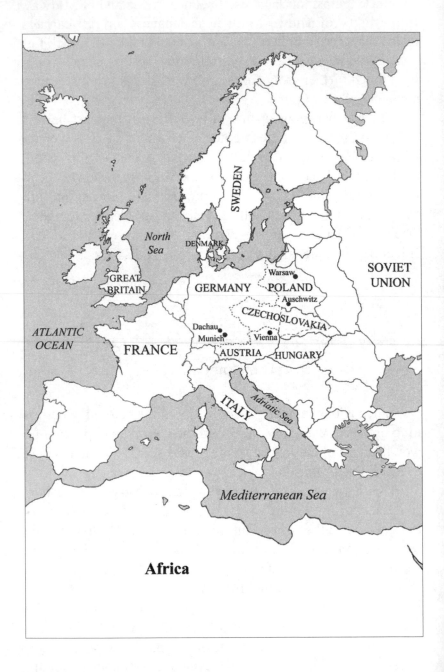

Germany During the Holocaust

color of his eyes, and tell whether or not he was "Aryan." In other words, the length of your nose and the color of your eyes could tell how intelligent you were.

For Hitler and his followers, Roma (often called "Gypsies"), Africans, and other races were all inferior to Aryans. But the most "inferior" people of all were the Jews.

German attacks against Jews had begun even before Austria was claimed. In 1935, German laws were changed so that no Jew could be a German citizen, marry a German, or vote.

In 1936, the Olympics were held in Berlin. No Jews from Germany were allowed to compete. The Germans took down many of the signs that said "No Jews Allowed" in Berlin, because they did not want to make the rest of the world angry. But they made sure that every German athlete was blond, blue-eyed, and tall—like perfect Aryans were supposed to be. Even though the anti-Semitic signs were missing, it became very clear what Hitler thought of non-Aryans during the Games. An African-American athlete named Jesse Owens won four gold medals and beat the most famous German athlete in the long jump. The German athlete, Lutz Long, congratulated Jesse Owens on his victory, in full view of all the Nazi officials. But Hitler refused to acknowledge that Owens had won the competition.

Just before the beginning of the war, Germans launched a night of attacks against Jews. All over Germany, German mobs broke the windows of houses and shops owned by Jews. Many of them were burned. This night, November 9, 1938, became known as *Kristallnacht*, or "Night of the Broken Glass."

In every territory that the Germans claimed, Jews were forced to wear yellow six-pointed stars on their clothing so that everyone would know they were Jews. This six-pointed star was called a "Star of David," after the great Hebrew king in the Bible.

It was bad enough to live with a yellow star on your clothing. Often shops and restaurants would not serve Jews wearing the Star of David. Sometimes Jews were attacked and beaten on the street. Their businesses were broken into and destroyed, and the police refused to do anything about it. Jewish children were expelled from all public schools and were not allowed to go to museums or playgrounds. In many cities, Jews were forced to all move to the same part of the city. This neighborhood, or "ghetto," was surrounded with barbed wire and guarded by armed Nazis.

But soon, the Jews with yellow stars were rounded up into groups, put on trains, and taken to concentration camps—camps like those that the British had put Boers in, forty years before.

The concentration camps were not the end of their journey. Hitler was not content only to keep the Jews in camps. He wanted to kill them.

In 1942, Hitler's advisors agreed with him that Germany needed to find a "final solution" for the "problem" of the Jews in Europe. The concentration camps were turned into death camps. Jews were killed in hundreds of camps all through Germany and German-held territory. The most horrible, and most well known, of these death camps were at Dachau and Auschwitz.

By 1945, six million Jews had been put to death by Hitler. This systematic killing of an entire nation, or *genocide*, had never been carried out before. The six million Jews weren't Hitler's only victims. Other "inferior" people like Catholics, handicapped people, gypsies, and many Russians, Poles, and Serbs were also killed in the death camps.

Even before the end of the war, the Allies heard about the death camps. Many people didn't believe the stories, or thought that the stories had been exaggerated.

But after the surrender, Allied soldiers came to the camps and opened the gates. They found bones, heaps of shoes, and piles of hats and jewelry taken from Jewish prisoners. They found thousands of graves—and thousands of bodies that the Nazis had not yet buried.

Hitler's "final solution" became known as the Holocaust. "Holocaust" is a Greek word for a sacrifice that is completely burned up by fire. Hitler tried to completely wipe out the Jewish nation—along with five million other people.

Adolf Hitler, führer of the Nazi party

Many Europeans in the occupied countries stood by and watched as Jews and other "inferior" peoples were taken to death camps. The only country to act officially in protection of its Jews was Denmark, which rounded up all of the Danish Jews and helped them get across to Sweden, where they would be safe.

A few brave people fought back. In France, clergymen helped Jewish children hide and escape to Switzerland. Dutch families like the ten Booms, whose story is told in a famous book called *The Hiding Place*, hid Jews in their basements and helped them escape. In Poland, the director of the Warsaw Zoo hid Jewish children in the cages, beneath the straw, so that Nazi soldiers couldn't find them.

In the United States, Franklin Roosevelt organized a War Refugee Board that helped rescue Jewish refugees from countries where Nazis were in charge. The War Refugee Board was formed in 1944, and helped to rescue over two hundred thousand Jews.

But United States government officials had known that Jews were being murdered at least two years before, and had done nothing. The same was true of officials in France and in many other places. The Holocaust was a horrible shame to the German people, but the shame was shared by many other people who knew that Jews were being put to death—and yet made no protest.

Europe at the End of World War II

Chapter Twenty-Nine
The End of World War II

The War that Stretched Across the World

By the time the United States entered World War II, in 1941, Hitler's Germany had already claimed Austria, Czechoslovakia, and part of Poland. The Soviet Union had taken the rest of Poland, and had also taken over Estonia, Latvia, and Lithuania (countries that had been given their independence after World War I). Soviet soldiers had also invaded Finland, on the eastern side of the Scandinavian peninsula.

What else had happened, in the months before the United States entered the war?

The war had gone badly for the Allies. German soldiers had invaded Denmark, a Scandinavian country that lay not on the Scandinavian peninsula, but instead jutted off the mainland of Europe, just north of Germany. Then, German forces began what was called a "Lightning War," or *Blitzkrieg*, by sweeping down the coast of Europe, through the Netherlands and Belgium, and invading France.

France had already lost thousands and thousands of men in the fighting that had already taken place. The approaching German soldiers overwhelmed the French defenders and the Allied soldiers who fought with them. The Allied troops in France were forced to retreat to the port of Dunkirk, where they hoped they could sail across to England, and safety. Over three hundred Allied ships began to ferry the soldiers across to England, as the Germans showered down bombs and torpedoes on them. The German gunners had been told to aim especially for hospital ships, which were marked with large crosses to show that they carried wounded men.

The "Dunkirk evacuation" was a defeat for the Allies. But Winston Churchill, who had now become the prime minister of Great Britain, told the British people that, no matter what happened, Great Britain would never give in to the Nazis. On June 4, 1940, just after the Dunkirk evacuation, he told the House of Commons:

Even though large tracts of Europe and many old and famous states have fallen or may fall into the grip of the Gestapo [the Nazi police] and all the odious apparatus of Nazi rule, we shall not flag or fail. We shall go on to the end, we shall fight in France, we shall fight on the seas and oceans, we shall fight with growing confidence and growing strength in the air, we shall defend our island, whatever the cost may be. We shall fight on the beaches, we shall fight on the landing grounds, we shall fight in the fields and in the streets, we shall fight in the hills; we shall never surrender. And even if, which I do not for a moment believe, this island or a large part of it were sub-jugated and starving, then our Empire beyond the seas, armed and guarded by the British Fleet, would carry on the struggle, until, in God's good time, the New World, with all its power and might, steps forth to the rescue and the liberation of the old.

After Dunkirk, in 1940, France was forced to sign a peace with Germany. The Germans took control of the northern beaches of France, the ones that faced Great Britain, and seized Paris. The northern part of France refused to cooperate with the Nazis at all, so Nazi soldiers occupied it, and Nazi officials governed it.

In the south of France, some of the French agreed to live at uneasy peace with the Nazis. A French official named Henri-Philippe Pétain swore allegiance to the Nazis, and in exchange was given the right to govern the south. Now the south of France was the only official "France" in existence, with the city of Vichy as its "capital." The Allies called this southern France "Vichy France" and despised it for agreeing to cooperate with the Germans. But even in Vichy France, many loyal French men and women worked secretly to defeat the Nazi forces. Outside of France itself, French soldiers continued to fight in Allied troops against the Axis powers. They called themselves the "Free French" to distinguish themselves from the French who were cooperating with Hitler.

Now that the Germans controlled France, Hitler turned his forces towards Great Britain.

Like Napoleon's forces so many years before, Hitler hoped to sail troops across the English Channel and land them on the shores of England. But first, he planned to weaken Great Britain by starving it. Hitler told his naval commanders to sink every ship headed for England. That way, the British would begin to run short on weapons, ammunition, oil, clothing—and food. The most dangerous ships in Hitler's navy were the "U-boats," or submarines. German U-boats prowled along underneath the water in groups called "Wolf Packs." Germany built almost a thousand U-boats, and they sank more than two thousand ships headed for Great Britain. Winston Churchill, the prime minister of England, called the U-boats the "worst evil" faced by the British forces.

Before an invasion could succeed, the Germans also had to destroy the British air force, called the Royal Air Force, or RAF. The German air force, the *Luftwaffe*, began to attack the RAF in the air. The fight between the two air forces, which became known as the Battle of Britain, went on for two whole months.

The RAF managed to keep the Luftwaffe at bay. Finally, Hitler decided to postpone the invasion of Great Britain. Instead, he turned around to attack his allies, the Soviet Union! German troops took Estonia, Latvia, Lithuania, and other territories away from the Russian troops and began to drive them back into Russia. German soldiers marched so far into Russia that they reached the edges of the city of Moscow.

It was at this point that the United States entered the war. And not only did the American soldiers flood over to help the

Allies—so did the Soviet troops. The Russians changed sides, rejecting their alliance with Germany and instead fighting for the Allies.

The war now covered the world. In the east, British and American forces fought with the Chinese against the Japanese. All across Russia and Europe, Soviet, British, and American soldiers fought against the German occupiers. Down in North Africa, British soldiers were battling with Italian and German soldiers for control of Egypt.

But Germany was about to lose another ally.

The Italians, tired of the war, had begun to protest against Mussolini's determination to keep Italy on Germany's side. The Italian soldiers were exhausted and wanted to come home. In 1943, Italian troops in North Africa surrendered. Not long after, Allied troops invaded the island of Sicily and occupied it.

At this, the Fascist Grand Council that ruled Italy gathered together, under orders from King Victor Emmanuel III, and told Mussolini that he would no longer be Italy's prime minister. Mussolini ignored this decree—so the Council arrested him and locked him in a hotel, high in the Italian mountains. German soldiers flew gliders up to the hotel, rescued Mussolini, and helped him set up a new government in the north of Italy. But from this point on, Italy was divided. Mussolini's northern government was still allied with the Germans (as a matter of fact, the German government was actually running it, not Mussolini). The rest of Italy declared war on Germany. For the remainder of the war, Fascist and Nazi supporters in Italy fought a civil war against Italians who wanted nothing more to do with either Fascism or Nazi Germany. These anti-Nazi Italians were called *partisans*.

Now Japan and Germany were the remaining Axis forces, arrayed against almost the rest of the world. Japanese soldiers held their own in the east. But in Europe, the Soviet army began to push the German forces out of Russia. By 1944, after a year of fighting, the Germans had been driven back into the center of Europe.

The Allies planned one huge attack that might finally break the German army. The Allies would land on the beaches of France and try to take them away from Germany. If this could be done, Allied soldiers could fight their way, on land, through France and attack Germany's western borders. At the same time, the Soviets would be pushing over from the east. The Germans would have to fight on two fronts at once.

The attempt to capture the beaches of France was known by the nickname "D-Day." It would be the largest assault ever made on German forces. The plan was to land as many men on the beaches as possible, in as short a time as possible, even though German troops would be firing on the men as they landed. Over five thousand ships and ten thousand airplanes were lined up. Five different groups of soldiers would land along a northern stretch of France. The Americans would land at two beaches in Normandy that were given the code names Omaha and Utah. Soldiers from England and Canada would land on three other beaches, nicknamed Gold, Juno, and Sword.

On June 6, 1944, Allied soldiers landed on the beach at Normandy. Airplanes dumped paratroopers (soldiers using parachutes) and dummies dressed like paratroopers down on the Germans to confuse them. But the Germans could see that the attack was coming from the water. German gunners, firing machine guns and cannons, killed thousands of Allied soldiers as they charged ashore.

By the end of the day, at least five thousand men were dead. But the Allied troops, under the command of the American General Dwight Eisenhower, had managed to capture the beach. Now, Allied troops could land safely and begin the job of recapturing France—and then march through France against Germany itself.

Months of fighting followed. American and British forces began to advance forward, taking mile after mile of French land away from German control. They were joined by Free French soldiers, commanded by the French general Charles de Gaulle. As they got close to Paris, long occupied by Nazi soldiers, American and French troops raced each other to be the first soldiers into the city!

On August 25, 1944, the Allies marched into Paris. The long Nazi occupation was over. That night, the street lights of Paris were turned on for the first time since September 1, 1939.

Then Allied forces began to move into Germany. Meanwhile, Soviet troops marched in from the east, towards Berlin. German surrender seemed inevitable—but Hitler planned one last effort to drive the Allies back. On December 16, 1944, the German army launched the biggest attack the American soldiers had ever seen.

This battle, fought in the Ardennes Forest in Belgium, became known as the Battle of the Bulge, because the German attack pushed the Allied lines so that they bulged backward, like a capital "C" on the map. The Allies were overwhelmed by the power of the German attack, but the Allied soldiers dug themselves down into trenches in the ground and kept on shooting. Finally, the Germans were forced to retreat one more time.

It was the last German offensive of the war. By April 1945, Soviet troops were marching into Germany's capital city of Berlin. The power of the Nazis was broken.

Over in Italy, anti-Nazi partisans killed Mussolini and dumped his body on an Italian street, where a mob spat on it. In Berlin, Hitler was hiding underground, in a reinforced room called a bunker. On April 30, 1945, Hitler shot himself. A little more than a week later, Germany officially surrendered. May 8, 1945, became known as V-E Day—"Victory in Europe" day.

In Europe, the fighting was over. But hundreds of thousands of men had died. The ancient cities of London, Coventry, Brussels, Dresden, and Berlin had been bombed, their great buildings destroyed. Europe lay in ruins.

The Atom Bomb

In the United States, August 6, 1945, just seemed like another hot summer day. In the cool of the evening, families all over America turned on their radios to catch the evening's news.

They heard the voice of the president of the United States, telling the world that the United States had just dropped an atomic bomb on the Japanese city of Hiroshima.

In Europe, World War II had ended on May 8. But although Germany surrendered, Japan refused to do the same. Fighting in the East went on for three more months. At the end of July, the president of the United States, Harry Truman, met together with Winston Churchill of Great Britain and Joseph Stalin, the leader of the Soviet Union. The three leaders decided together that they would give Japan a choice: Surrender and sign a peace treaty, or be invaded by Allied forces.

The Japanese considered the offer, and rejected it. They would not surrender.

Now the Allies had to form a plan. Invading Japan might mean more years of war, with more soldiers dying every day, and no assurance of victory against the fearless Japanese fighters.

There was another option: to use a new kind of bomb, developed by the United States, against Japan.

Let's go back a few years, to the 1930s. The German scientist Albert Einstein had been studying how atoms (the smallest building blocks of matter) worked. He was making discoveries that would astound the world. But because Einstein was Jewish, Hitler believed that his discoveries must be wrong. He sent thugs to terrorize Einstein. They trashed his home, burned his papers, and even stole his violin.

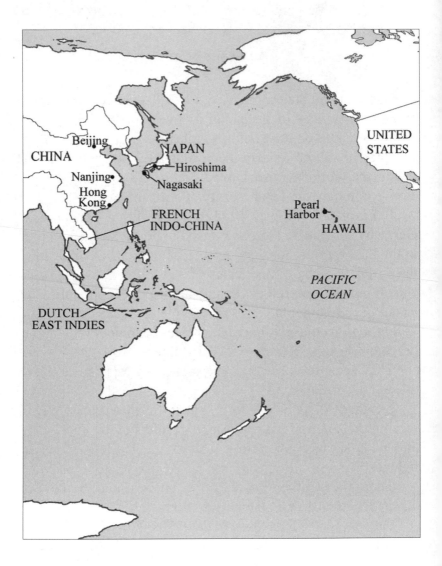

The End of World War II

So Albert Einstein left Germany and came to the United States. He told the president of the United States at that time, President Roosevelt, that he had a great fear. He was afraid that the German army was developing an atomic bomb.

An atomic bomb was the most destructive kind of bomb that could be built. It split atoms apart, so that the energy at the heart of the atoms created a huge explosion. A country that had atomic bombs could rule the world in a very short time.

On December 6, 1941—one day before Pearl Harbor was attacked— President Roosevelt ordered government scientists to begin figuring out how to build an atomic bomb for the United States. This research was top secret. It was known by the code name "the Manhattan Project" (although the work was done in Washington, New Mexico, and Tennessee). Two famous scientists, an Italian named Enrico Fermi and an American named J. Robert Oppenheimer, led the research. On December 2, 1942, Enrico Fermi managed to create the kind of reaction (in his laboratory) that the bomb would need in order to work properly. The scientists were eager to tell President Roosevelt the good news, but because the project was top secret, they had to communicate with FDR in code. The message the scientists sent to Roosevelt read: "The Italian navigator has landed in the new world."

It took three more years to make the reaction into a bomb. In July of 1945, two months after the German surrender, the United States was finally ready to test its first atomic, or nuclear, bomb. The test bomb was exploded in secret on July 19, at 5:30 in the morning, at Alamogordo, New Mexico. A scientist named Kenneth Greisen who got to watch the test later said, "I felt heat on the side of my head toward the tower [where the bomb had exploded], opened my eyes and saw a brilliant yellow-white light all around. The heat and light were as though the sun had just come out with unusual brilliance. ... A tremendous cloud of smoke was pouring upwards, some parts having brilliant red and yellow colors, like clouds at sunset. These parts kept folding over and over like dough in a mixing bowl." Germany had never actually managed to develop an atomic bomb, but now the United States could use them—if the president approved.

By now, Truman was president of the United States. He decided to use atomic weapons on Japan so that World War II would finally end. On August 6, a U.S. Air Force colonel named Paul Tibbets flew his plane, the *Enola Gay* (named for his mother, Enola Gay Tibbets) over the Japanese city of Hiroshima. He dropped one atomic bomb, nicknamed "Little Boy," on the city beneath him.

Eighty thousand people died in a moment. The Japanese did not know what had hit them—literally. The Japanese Broadcasting System noticed that Hiroshima could no longer be reached by radio. Army officials tried to call the military headquarters in Hiroshima, but couldn't get through. The entire city had been obliterated.

Three days later, on August 9, another American plane dropped a second bomb, nicknamed "Fat Man" (in honor of the portly Winston Churchill), on the Japanese city of Nagasaki. Seventy-five thousand people were killed at once. "A warm wind began to blow," one survivor said "Here and there in the distance I saw many small fires … smoldering. Nagasaki had been completely destroyed."

Today, not only Americans but people from many countries still argue about President Truman's decision to drop the bomb. Some say that the killing of so many Japanese men, women, and children who were not soldiers, and were not involved in the fighting, can never be justified. Along with the thousands who died when the bombs exploded, hundreds of thousands more died later on because the "nuclear fallout" (the poison spread by the bomb) caused them to develop cancer and other diseases. Others say that by dropping the bomb, the United States prevented many more years of war, in which many more people would have died—because the Japanese had no intention of ever surrendering.

But one historical fact is certain: The atomic bomb spelled the end of World War II. On August 10, the day after Nagasaki burned, Japan offered to surrender. The Japanese could see that there was no purpose in fighting against a country that had atomic bombs.

On August 14, 1945, World War II officially ended all over the world.

After the end of the war, the nations of the world made another attempt to prevent a world war from happening again. Do you remember the League of Nations, which formed after World War I? After World War II, a new organization of "peace-loving nations," called the United Nations, was formed. The United Nations, or UN, still exists. You can visit their headquarters in New York City, or you can just visit them online at http://www.un.org/.

The countries of the United Nations are supposed to join together to defend freedom and democracy. Like the League of Nations, the UN is also supposed to try to prevent war, by helping countries settle their differences. But right after World War II, the most pressing job of the UN was to prevent any more atomic bombs from being dropped. At the very first meeting of the UN General Assembly, in 1946, the UN formed a committee to try to convince the nations of the world to stop developing atomic weapons—and to disarm (take apart) the weapons they already had.

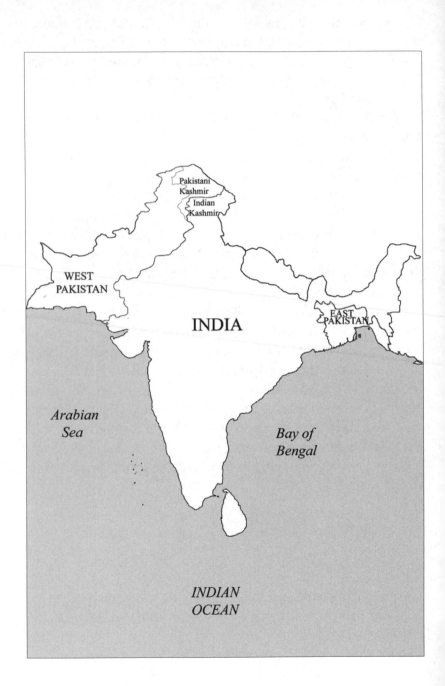

India Partitioned

Chapter Thirty
Partitioned Countries

Muslims and Hindus in India

In the 1920s, well before the start of World War II, Great Britain had promised to give the country of India the right to govern itself. The nonviolent protests led by Gandhi, and the violent protests of Indian revolutionaries who wanted British soldiers out of their land, had made India impossible to govern.

But India was not declared free and independent until August 15, 1947—because it took more than twenty years for Indian Muslims, Indian Hindus, and British officials to agree on how the new country would be governed.

Between the Amritsar Massacre in 1919 and the declaration of independence in 1947, Muslims and Hindus in India argued over how the two different religions could live together in the same country. Most people in India were Hindu. The Hindu religion is very old; it goes back to at least 2000 BC (or BCE). Hindus practice spiritual disciplines called "yogas." One of the most important yogas is karma-yoga, selfless service to others.

The Muslims of India, who were a much smaller group, didn't object to selfless service; this was part of their religion as well. But they disliked the Hindu belief in many different gods. Muslims believe in one God, Allah. Instead of "yogas," Muslims practice five "pillars" of their religion, including the giving of money to the poor and the practice of fasting.

During the British occupation, both Muslims and Hindus were governed by British officials—who were Christians. When Indian Hindus began to demand the right to govern themselves, Muslims in India also began to dream about a country in which they would not be governed by people of another faith. They didn't want to live in a country run by Hindus, any more than the Hindus wanted to live in a country run by Christians.

One of the most outspoken Indian Muslims was a man named Muhammad Iqbal. He was a lawyer, a poet, and a scholar of Islam. And he believed Muslims from India should have their own country, where they could govern themselves.

Another outspoken Muslim, Mohammed Ali Jinnah, agreed with Muhammad Iqbal. Jinnah was also a lawyer. His nickname was Qaid-e-Azam, which meant "Great Leader," and he became the leader of a powerful group of Indian Muslims called the Muslim League. Jinnah suggested that, since Muslims and Hindus were two separate peoples, they should be separated into two different Indian nations—instead of being forced into one country. Jinnah wanted India *partitioned*.

A partition is a wall or divider that you place in a room to break the room in half. You might have partitions at your local public library—tall, rolling boards that can be wheeled in to divide one giant room into, say, four smaller rooms.

Jinnah did not want a real wall to be built down the middle of India. But he did want some of India to be "partitioned," or set aside, to be a new, Muslim country. In 1940, Jinnah announced that the Muslim League had a demand. The League didn't believe that Gandhi's Congress Party, now known as the Indian National Congress, would treat Muslims fairly once it had power over India. When India achieved independence, the British and the Hindus had to agree to separate off part of the country for Muslims to rule. This part would be called Pakistan.

When World War II swept across the world, Indians had to put off their wish for independence. But once the war was over, the British promised to give India its freedom just as soon as the Muslim League and the Indian National Congress could decide how India should be governed.

Gandhi, still the leader of the Indian National Congress, was firmly against partition. Muslims and Hindus, he insisted, could learn to live together in peace. He tried to convince Jinnah to give up the idea of partition, but Jinnah could not be budged. He threatened to use violence to create Pakistan, if necessary.

After more than a year of arguments and riots, the Muslim League and the Indian National Congress still had not managed to come to an agreement. So the British decided that partition would have to be put into place. Only this would bring an end to the hostility— and the violence—between India's Hindus and Muslims.

On August 14 and 15, 1947, India was declared independent—and the country of Pakistan was born. The new Islamic Republic of Pakistan was divided into two parts, East Pakistan and West Pakistan, separated by India in the middle.

Partition caused horrible chaos in India. Hindus who lived in the lands that had suddenly become Pakistan were terrified of staying, afraid that Muslim mobs would attack them. They collected their belongings and their children and piled onto trains headed south, hoping to get into India safely. Muslims in India were doing the same thing and going north into Pakistan. The trains filled with panicked Indians, all fleeing to the country where they would be in the majority instead of the minority, often passed each other, headed in opposite directions. Thousands of men, women, and children died in riots where Muslims killed Hindus and Hindus killed Muslims. In all, fifteen million Indians left their homes.

Independence and partition didn't end the violence between Hindus and Muslims. For years, Pakistan and India argued and sometimes fought over a piece of land called Kashmir, just north of India. Both countries wanted to claim it. Finally, they agreed to divide it (although the two countries still argue about where the boundary line between Pakistani Kashmir and Indian Kashmir should lie). In both India and Pakistan, Indians were still killed in riots because of their religion.

Gandhi had agreed to partition, with great reluctance, but he was deeply saddened by it. He had hoped that all Indians, whatever their religion, could live together in India. The bloody riots in India and Pakistan disturbed him so much that he went on a fast that lasted for days. When Indians across India learned of Gandhi's fast, the riots began to die down; both Hindus and Muslims were afraid that Gandhi might die if they didn't stop fighting.

Not all Hindus had such respect for Gandhi. A small group of Hindu Indians was furious with Gandhi because he had allowed the partition to take place. They believed that all of India should have remained under Hindu rule.

One member of this fanatical group was a young man named Nathuram Vinayak Godse. Less than a year after partition, Godse put a pistol in his belt, under his shirt, and went to a prayer meeting where Gandhi would be speaking. Gandhi had just finished another fast, and he was too weak to stand alone. He was leaning on a friend's arm, speaking to the Hindus who had come to the meeting, when Godse leaped out of the crowd and shot Gandhi to death.

The Partitioning of Palestine

The Hindus in India and the Muslims in Pakistan were not the only people who wanted to be ruled by a government of their own faith. Jews from around the world wanted their own country, too.

The Jewish people had not lived all together in Israel since the year AD 70 (or 70 CE), when the Romans drove the Jewish people out of Jerusalem and out of their country. But Jews had always thought of the land of Judea, on the eastern edge of the Mediterranean Sea, as their homeland. Their sacred scripture told them that God had chosen that land for the Jewish people and that one day they would return to it.

In the nineteenth century, some of the Jews in Europe began to think that the time had come for Jews to have their own country. Why should Jews live scattered all over the world—a few in Russia, a few in Germany, a few in England, a few in America? There should be one land where all the Jews could come and live. This idea that there should be a Jewish country is called *Zionism*, because one of the scriptural names for the city of Jerusalem is Zion.

There were a handful of Zionists in the nineteenth century. But Zionism did not really gain a big following from thousands and thousands of Jews until after World War II.

After the horrible killings in Hitler's death camps, both Jews and non-Jews became more interested in the idea of a Jewish homeland. Many Europeans had grown up knowing that their neighbors, and sometimes their own parents and aunts and uncles, disliked Jews. But few had imagined that a government might build death camps and try to kill *all* the Jews.

World War II made many Jewish people feel that they must have their own country. They believed Jews would never be safe living in a nation governed by non-Jews, a country that might secretly—or not so secretly—dislike Jews and Judaism. Many non-Jews around the world, sickened by the events of the Holocaust, understood why the Jews wanted and needed their own country.

Where would this new Jewish country be? Some Zionist leaders said it didn't really matter—it could be anywhere, as long as it was a Jewish country governed by Jews. Some suggested a Jewish state could be squeezed into the continent of Africa!

But most Zionist leaders said that the Jews should return to the land that God had promised their ancestors. They should go back to the ancient land of Israel.

At the beginning of the twentieth century, that land was called Palestine. For the last thousand years, Arabs had been living in Palestine. The Jews believed that Palestine was their

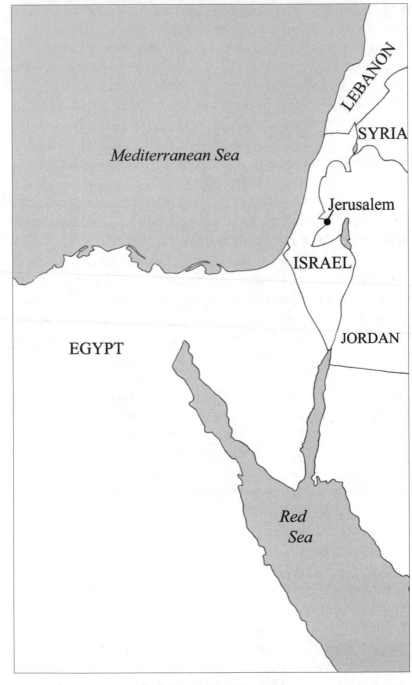

Palestine Partitioned

homeland, because their ancestors had lived there for centuries and their sacred scriptures promised it to them. But the Palestinian Arabs had lived there for a millennium. It was their homeland too.

How could one homeland become two countries? Through partition. In 1947, the United Nations voted to partition Palestine into two countries—an Arab country and a Jewish country.

Zionists around the world cheered! The Jewish people would have their own country again, after living scattered through all nations (the "scattering" of the Jews or *diaspora*) for almost two thousand years. In New York City, Jewish families partied in the streets for joy.

Not everyone was pleased with the UN decision. Imagine that, when your mother was a child, she grew up in the house you live in now. Her grandmother grew up there. So did her great-grandmother, and her great-great-grandmother, all the way back for a thousand years. Then, one day, a family you never met knocks on your door and says, "We lived in this house two thousand years ago, and it was taken away from us. So we'd like to move back in now."

How would you feel? Of course it was wrong for the family to lose their house two thousand years ago. But, after all, it has been yours for as long as anyone can remember. You'd probably be surprised, confused, saddened, and outraged—like the Palestinian Arabs felt when the UN announced that the Jews could have part of Palestine back again.

On May 14, 1948, the Jewish state of Israel was born. May 14 is Independence Day in Israel. In Hebrew, the term for the day is *Yom Ha'atz'ma'ut*.

Fighting between Jews and Arabs broke out almost at once. The Arabs who had lost their land were angry at the UN, and at the Jews. So were the Arabs who lived in the nearby countries of Syria, Lebanon, and Egypt.

Let's go back to our illustration about the house. You'd be upset if you had to give your house back to a family that owned it two thousand years ago—but so would your relatives and neighbors who live nearby. Your neighbors have gotten used to living near *you*. They like *you* and *your family*. They don't want new neighbors. That's not too different from the reaction that the Arabs near Palestine had. They didn't want to see their friends and neighbors kicked off the land where they had lived for hundreds of years.

Arabs from the neighboring countries decided they would fight Israel. They would try to destroy the new Jewish state before it was even a year old. On the very day that independence was declared, troops from five different Arab countries— Egypt, Lebanon, Iraq, Jordan, and Syria—invaded Israel. The new Jewish country knew it would have to act quickly if it was going to win this war. They recruited thousands of Israeli soldiers, both men and women. Volunteers from other countries came to help the fledgling Israeli army.

Six thousand Israeli soldiers, one out of every hundred Israeli citizens, died in the fighting. But to everyone's amazement, the Israeli army managed to win the war! In 1949, the attacking countries (except for Iraq, which refused) agreed to sign peace agreements with Israel.

The victory made the Israelis proud of themselves, and of their country. Nations around the world now knew that Israel was a strong nation that would protect itself. But this would not be the last conflict between Israelis and Arabs. In fact, it was only the beginning.

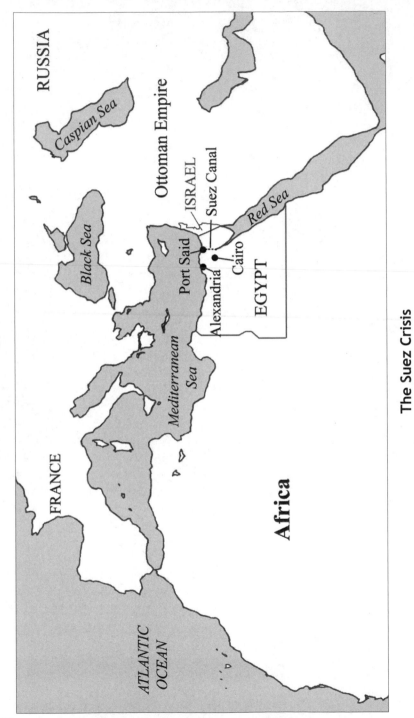

The Suez Crisis

Chapter Thirty-One
Western Bullies and American Money

The Suez Crisis

When Egypt helped invade the new country of Israel, it did so under the rule of King Faruk, Egypt's second king.

The first king of Egypt, King Fu'ad I, had died a few years earlier. His son Faruk, only sixteen years old, inherited the throne in his father's place. Egyptians hoped that Faruk would manage to bring some agreement between the three powers jostling each other for control of Egypt—the king, the Wafd, and the British.

But Faruk wasn't a skilled ruler—or even a moral one. He spent a lot of money travelling to Europe, where he gambled away still more money and went to parties at disreputable clubs. He also kept getting Egypt involved on the losing side of wars. When World War II broke out, Faruk tried to keep Egypt neutral. This was foolish, since Egypt had actually signed a treaty to fight on Britain's side in any war. It also annoyed the British, who forced Faruk to change his mind. Then, when Egypt lost the 1948 war with Israel, Faruk's people blamed him.

In 1952, an Egyptian military officer named Gamal Abdel Nasser threw Faruk off his throne.

Nasser grew up in a household that was respectable, but not rich. His father was a postal clerk. Nasser was able to go away to school, as poorer boys couldn't—but he said, later in life, that he often came home from school to discover that there was nothing to eat at home!

Nasser was a reckless boy, full of fight. He got into more than one street brawl, where Egyptian boys did their best to punch each other out. So it isn't surprising that Nasser decided as a young man to join the army. When the 1948 war with Israel began, Nasser was an army officer of thirty, tough and experienced.

During the war, Nasser learned a lesson that stayed with him for the rest of his life. One evening, he was sitting beside one of his friends, a man named Kamal. Kamal was telling Nasser about another officer, a colonel they had both known, who had just died. "Do you know what the Colonel said to me, before he died?" Kamal said to Nasser. When Nasser remained silent, Kamal went on, "He said that *the real battlefield is Egypt.*"

Nasser thought about this—and took it to heart. As an Egyptian, his future would not be spent fighting wars in other countries. He would put his energy into defending and shaping his own homeland.

Four years after the war ended, ninety army officers, led by Nasser, took over the Egyptian government. The officers, like most of Egypt, were fed up with Faruk's weak, useless leadership. They seized control of the government offices (almost no one tried to stop them), ordered Faruk to leave the country, and set up an eleven-man council to run Egypt.

The rest of the world watched carefully to see what Nasser would do with the Suez Canal. Remember, the Suez Canal made it cheaper and much quicker to travel from Europe to India and the east. No one wanted Nasser to close the canal, or to put restrictions on who might be able to use it.

During World War II, both the Italians and the Germans had tried to invade Egypt and take over the canal. But when Nasser came to power in 1952, the canal was still under Egyptian control—which meant that it was also under the control of the British, who still had soldiers stationed in Egypt.

Nasser wanted all of the Arabs in the world to unify into a powerful country that would, he hoped, become known as the United Arab Republic. Above all, he wanted Egypt to be free and independent of any European influence.

Still, Nasser knew that it would be very bad for Egypt if he were to challenge the British over control of the Suez Canal.

The canal made a lot of money for Egypt. Ships that used the canal had to pay a fee, and in the 1950s, 122 million tons of cargo (over half of which was oil) were ferried through the canal each year.

But in 1956, Nasser got angry enough to close the canal. This became known as the "Suez Crisis."

The crisis began when Nasser tried to borrow enough money from the United States to build a dam across the Nile River. The dam would be huge—365 feet high, and 3 miles across. It would catch the Nile waters, and allow the Egyptians both to irrigate their fields and to generate electricity from the power of the running water.

But the president of the United States, Dwight Eisenhower, didn't trust Nasser. He thought that Nasser was too friendly with the Soviet Union. Even though the Soviets and the Americans had ended up on the same side by the end of World War II, Americans feared the growing power of the USSR. So Eisenhower refused to give Nasser a loan.

Nasser was furious. On July 26, 1956, he gave a rousing speech to a gathering of Egyptians. In this speech, Nasser said that the history of the Arabs had been, for a hundred years, the history of a struggle to get out from under the thumb of Western countries like the United States. He declared that from now on, Egypt would show its independence by taking full control of the Suez Canal. Egypt had the right to decide who could use the canal, and who couldn't. And the first country that would be banned from using the canal was Israel.

Actually, Egypt still owed France and Great Britain a great deal of money that Said Pasha and Ismail Pasha had borrowed in order to build the canal in the first place. Technically speaking, the canal belonged, in part, to French and British banks. But Nasser didn't let this bother him. He claimed control over the canal anyway.

The prime minister of France and the prime minister of England worried that Nasser was a dictator in the making. They knew Nasser wanted to unite all the Arabs together.

Didn't that sound a little bit like Hitler's plan to make Europe into one German Empire? What if Nasser tried to take over the whole Middle East? The European countries should stop him before he grew more powerful.

The leaders of Israel were willing to help out. They believed that Israel needed to show that Arab countries couldn't bully the Israelis. If they reacted to Nasser's closing the canal to Israeli ships with force, other Arab states would be more likely to leave Israel in peace.

Officials from Israel, Britain, and France held a secret meeting in a suburb of Paris. Huddled in a tile-roofed villa, the officials hatched a plan called "Operation Musketeer"—all for one and one for all! Afterwards, they toasted each other with champagne.

The plan was a little bit complicated, but here's what Operation Musketeer (*Operation Mousquetaire* in French) involved:

First, Israel would invade Egypt.

Then, France and Britain would step in and offer to help. They would tell Nasser, "Turn the control of the Suez Canal over to the French and British, and we'll tell Israel to leave you alone."

Then, after Nasser agreed, the Israelis (who never really intended to conquer Egypt at all) would retreat. France and Britain would get the canal, Israel would be able to use it, and Israel's invasion of Egypt would show that the Israeli army was strong and ready to fight.

Although Israeli officials didn't realize it, France and Britain actually hoped that Nasser would turn down their offer to help. That way, French and British soldiers would have a good excuse to invade Egypt and take the Suez Canal over by force—permanently.

The plan went into action on October 29, 1956. The Israeli army began to march into Egyptian territory. British and French officials at once sent a message to Nasser, offering to help. If Egypt would just let England and France supervise the Canal for a little while, they would convince Israel to back out of Egypt.

Nasser laughed at this offer, and refused. So British and French soldiers joined the invasion. Fighting began between Israeli and Egyptian soldiers. Several thousand Egyptians were killed. When French and British soldiers arrived at the Egyptian city of Port Said, another battle began. Almost three thousand more Egyptians died.

The fighting ended only because the United States decided to get involved. American officials objected that France and Great Britain were breaking one of the rules that all of the countries in the United Nations had agreed to: Every country has the right to control its own territory. The French and the British were trying to take this right away from Egypt.

The United Nations agreed, and ordered Great Britain and France to leave the Egyptians alone.

This was terribly embarrassing for both countries. The French and British had been accused, in front of the whole world, of acting like bullies. Both governments ordered their troops out, with as much dignity as possible, and tried to act as though they had never really intended to take over the canal by force. The British prime minister was so humiliated that he resigned just a few months later.

The Suez Crisis had two other results. In the United States, President Eisenhower asked the U.S. Congress to pass a new law called the "Eisenhower Doctrine." This new law said that U.S. soldiers could go and fight on the side of any Middle Eastern country that asked the United States for help against an attacking army. Congress agreed to pass the law.

And in the Middle East, Nasser became a hero. He had defied the orders of European countries—and particularly Great Britain, which had so long ordered Egypt around. Arab leaders all around the world cheered for Nasser, who had shown himself to be strong, decisive, and ready to stand up to bullies.

Germany Divided

The Marshall Plan

In the same year that the United States refused to lend Nasser money for his dam, millions of American dollars went to the war-destroyed countries of Europe.

Imagine that you were born in London, in the year 1930. When you are four, Adolf Hitler becomes the leader of Germany. Maybe you notice that your parents frown and furrow their brows when they read about this in the newspaper. They don't know much about Hitler, but what they know, they don't like. But for the most part, you don't pay much attention. You're four years old, after all.

By the time your ninth birthday rolls around, though, you are more and more aware that things happening in the far away country of Germany *do* matter to you in England. Just after your birthday, England declares war on Germany. The very next day a German ship sinks a British ship with 1,418 people on it. Most of the people are saved—but the event is terrifying anyway. Your parents say that you won't be travelling anywhere on a ship, not until the war is over.

In 1940, the year you turn ten, the government declares that most English sugar, butter, and meat needs to go to the army, to feed soldiers. Your family is issued a *ration book*, which has coupons in it for each of the scarce items. You have to turn over a coupon every time you want to buy sugar, butter, or meat. When the coupons are gone, you can't buy any more of those foods. There's not enough sugar to make you a birthday cake, so you get "war cake"—cake made without eggs, butter, or sugar in it.

It doesn't taste much like cake, and it doesn't feel much like a birthday.

Next, clothes are rationed. Then soap. Your mother learns to make casserole out of chicken bones. The German air force starts to bomb London. When you walk to school, you see that houses nearby have been flattened during the night. Everyone in them was killed.

Soon the government announces that all children must leave London, because it is too dangerous for them. Your parents put you on a train that takes you out to Wales, a country place where distant cousins of your mother have a farm. You live in their spare bedroom, learn to milk cows, and help in the garden. You miss your mother, you're sick of bone casserole, and you want to go home.

Finally in 1945, when you are fifteen, the war ends. Everyone in England is ecstatic. There are even parties in the streets! No more bone casserole, no more ration books, and no more bombs. You can go home! Your parents greet you at the train station with big smiles. Now, they say, everyone can go back to normal.

But, after six years of war, what is normal?

The Allied Powers—especially England and France—had made huge sacrifices to fight, and win, World War II. Many English and French citizens were dead. People were tired. Businesses and banks were out of money. Many buildings, from churches to schools, had been bombed and needed to be repaired or rebuilt.

America had made sacrifices to win the war too. American soldiers had died. But the closest place to America that had been attacked was Pearl Harbor, and that was in Hawaii—still far away. No battles had been fought on American soil. American schools didn't need to be rebuilt. After 1945, life could get back to "normal" in America pretty quickly.

America knew it needed to help its allies in Western Europe get back on their feet. The job fell to the secretary of state, a man named George Marshall.

The secretary of state is an advisor to the president. His job is to help America keep its friendship with other countries around the world. On June 5, 1947, Secretary of State Marshall made a speech at Harvard University, explaining that America had an obligation to help Europe recover from the war. He said, "I need not tell you, gentlemen, that the world situation is very serious.... It is logical that the United States should do whatever it is able to do to assist in the return of normal economic health in the world, without which there can be no political stability and no assured peace."

The United States very much wanted stability and peace! George Marshall had a plan to bring this stability and peace. In his speech at Harvard, he went on to explain what the plan was. The United States would give twenty billion dollars to the countries of Europe so that they could rebuild. This plan became known as the Marshall Plan.

The United States offered some of this money to Joseph Stalin, the leader of the Soviet Union. Stalin refused to take the money. He had been willing to fight on the side of the United States during the war, but if he took money from the U.S., America might one day ask him for a favor. He was sure he didn't want to do whatever the United States might ask, so he decided that the Soviets would do without the American money.

The other countries in Europe accepted the help. Now, George Marshall had to convince the people of the United States that Europe *needed* twenty billion dollars of American money. So, as the money began to go out to the countries of western Europe, the government made a series of movies about the Marshall Plan. These movies helped persuade Americans that the Marshall Plan was a good idea.

One movie, made in 1950, was called *The Home We Love*. It was about a real town in southern France called Mazamet. Mazamet was shattered by the war—but because of the Marshall Plan money, life in Mazamet was finally getting better. The movie showed the people of Mazamet buying food, going back to school, and working in the factories that had been reopened with the help of American dollars.

Another movie, called *The Extraordinary Adventures of a Quart of Milk*, was made in 1951. The hero of this film was a container of milk that made its way from a farm in Normandy to a factory that transformed the liquid milk into a can of powdered milk. What did the adventures of this quart of milk have to do with the Marshall Plan? Without American aid to France, the roads would not have been good enough to get the milk from farm to factory—and, indeed, there might not have been any factory at all! Thanks to the Marshall Plan, the French people had roads, factories, and milk—liquid *and* powdered.

The Marshall Plan even gave money to Germany.

After World War I, Germany had been forced to pay huge amounts of money to the rest of the world. The Allies weren't going to repeat this mistake after World War II. Instead of saddling Germany with a huge debt, America, France, England, and the Soviet Union wanted to help Germany rebuild its government.

But while America, France, and England wanted Germany to become a democracy, the Soviet Union wanted to turn it into a communist country. The four countries couldn't come to an agreement about Germany's government—so they divided Germany in half. England, America, and France got to re-organize the western half of Germany. They helped set up a new German democracy, and used Marshall Plan money to rebuild Germany's roads and buildings.

Meanwhile, the Soviets turned the eastern half of Germany into a communist country. They decreed that the other Allies could have nothing to do with East Germany. No shipments could go back and forth between communist East Germany and democratic West Germany.

For several years, people could travel back and forth between East Germany and West Germany. People went across the border to visit relatives or friends. Shops in West Germany were often better stocked, so East Germans crossed the border to buy everything from food to pantyhose!

Often, they didn't come back. Life in West Germany was easier and freer than life under the communist government of

East Germany. Over two million East Germans went west and never returned. The East German government realized that it was losing too many scientists, university professors, doctors, and lawyers to the west.

So in the middle of the night on August 12, 1961, East German soldiers put up a fence right through the middle of the city of Berlin, and also along the border between the two Germanies. People got up in the morning to discover that barbed wire and cinder blocks now cut them off from the other half of Berlin. People visiting relatives were caught and couldn't go back home. Families were divided. No one was allowed to cross the fence without government permission.

Over the next few years, concrete walls fifteen feet high, lined with electric wire, topped with guard towers, and surrounded by guns and land mines, were built to replace the fence. It was illegal to sneak across this wall, which became known as the Berlin Wall. Almost two hundred people were killed by East German guards or by land mines, trying to get from one side of the Berlin Wall to the other. The Wall would stay up, dividing East from West, for almost thirty years.

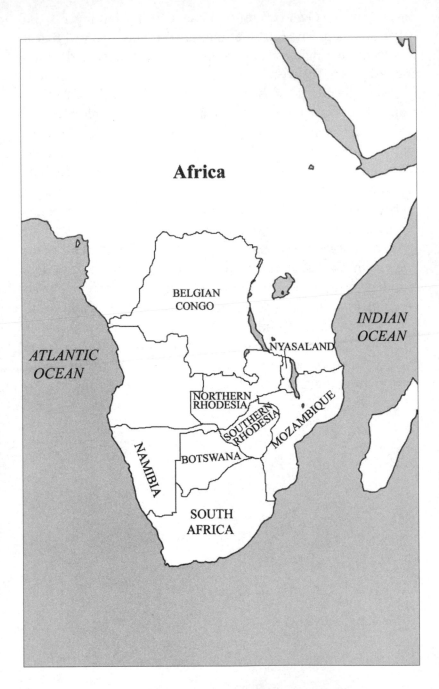

South Africa Under the National Party

Chapter Thirty-Two
Africa and China After World War II

One Country, Two Different Worlds

During World War II, South Africa fought on the side of the Allies. But in 1948, after Germany's defeat and Hitler's death, a political party that *liked* Hitler's ideas gained power in South Africa.

To understand how this happened, let's look back at South Africa's history for a moment. When we last visited the southern part of the African continent, a war between white British in South Africa and white Afrikaners, descended from Dutch settlers, had just ended. The south of Africa had been made into a country called the Union of South Africa.

In 1931, the Union of South Africa became independent from Great Britain. It would now govern itself—under a constitution that gave almost all of the power in the country to the whites who lived there.

Just north of the Union of South Africa lay other white-controlled African countries. Mozambique, on the eastern coast, was governed by Portugal. The country next to that, Rhodesia, and the country beside Rhodesia, Botswana, still belonged to Great Britain. The country on the western coast, Namibia, had once been a German colony. But after World War I, the League of Nations had given Namibia to the Union of South Africa.

This meant that the entire south of Africa was under the oversight of whites—not the Africans who had lived there for thousands of years.

Black Africans had gathered together into a group called the African National Congress, to gain more rights for blacks in South Africa. The African National Congress, or ANC, believed that Africa should be governed by the people who were native to Africa. "In the land of their birth," one ANC leader told his followers, "Africans are treated as hewers of wood and drawers of water. The white people of this country have formed what is known as the Union of South Africa—a union in which we have no voice in the making of the laws and no part in their administration."

In South Africa, blacks couldn't even vote for other blacks. They did have the right to elect three representatives and four senators—but all seven elected officials had to be white. Whites earned ten to twelve times more than blacks for doing the same jobs. All of the best work was reserved for whites. There were no government schools for black children. They could only go to schools run by Christian missionaries.

During World War II, South Africa fought on the side of the Allies. As the war dragged on, a political party called the National Party began to gain more and more followers. The National Party wanted the power in South Africa to belong to whites, but not to whites of British descent—only to Afrikaners, who were white South Africans of Dutch descent. Even though Germany was defeated in World War II, the National Party agreed with Hitler's views about how superior white civilization was to any other culture.

Many of the whites in South Africa were of Dutch descent. They liked the idea that the National Party would put Afrikaners, not British whites, into power. Many Afrikaners resented Great Britain's efforts to help run South Africa. (And after all, South Africa had been forced to fight in World War II because of its alliance with Great Britain.)

In 1948, white South Africans voted to put the National Party into power.

The National Party began at once to pass laws that would make blacks even less free. Party leaders claimed that, unless whites kept control of South Africa, the black descendents of South Africa's native tribes would spend all of their time fighting tribal wars with each other. (It was convenient for the National Party to forget that the white people of Europe had just spent six years fighting the most devastating war in history.)

In a 1948 statement, the National Party told South Africans:

[Our] aim is the maintenance and protection of the ... pure White race, the maintenance and protection of the indigenous [native] racial groups as separate communities. ... We can act in only one of two directions. Either we must follow the course of equality, which must eventually mean national suicide for the White race, or we must take the course of separation, through which the character and the future of every race will be protected ... The party therefore undertakes to protect the White race properly and effectively against any policy, doctrine or attack which might undermine or threaten its continued existence. At the same time the party rejects any policy of oppression and exploitation of the non-Europeans by the Europeans as being in conflict with the Christian basis of our national life and irreconcilable with our policy.

But despite this "rejection" of oppression, every law passed by the National Party over the next ten years did nothing but oppress the nonwhites of South Africa.

National Party laws, called *acts*, gave every bit of power in South Africa to whites. To keep whites "pure," the acts also separated whites from the rest of South Africa, so that they could lead totally separate lives.

The Population Registration Act identified every single South African as belonging to one of four groups: white, African, colored (people of mixed white and African descent), and Asian. Only whites had full privileges. The Immorality Act said that whites could not marry anyone from one of the other three groups. The Group Areas Act made many areas in cities off-limits to blacks, coloreds, and Asians. The Separate

Amenities Act said that blacks, coloreds, and Asians had to use separate buses, separate taxis, separate movies theatres, separate restaurants, and separate hotels. They had to sit on special non-white park benches, swim at non-white beaches, and even climb up and down non-white staircases. They even had to use separate funeral homes, with black-only hearses to carry the coffins. The Bantu Education Act said that the Christian missions could no longer educate black children. Instead, blacks would be taught in government schools. These schools only got one-tenth of the money spent on white schools. All of the textbooks in the black schools explained how good the separation of the races was for South Africa.

This separation was called "apartheid," a word from the Afrikaner language meaning "apartness."

"Apartness" wasn't the only goal of the National Party acts. The acts also kept black South Africans from having the freedom that whites had. Black South Africans couldn't vote. They had to carry identification cards at all times. Blacks (but not whites) had to observe a curfew—after a certain time of night, they had to stay in or near their homes.

Nonwhites in South Africa called these acts the "Unjust Laws." But blacks could do little to resist the unjust laws. The South African government also passed decrees, saying that the police could arrest any black South African without having to give a reason. Any black South African could be put in jail and kept there, without ever having been tried or sentenced. No black South African had the right to see a lawyer.

How could the African National Congress resist such injustice?

For many years, the ANC followed the ideas of Mohandas Gandhi and taught black South Africans to use nonviolent resistance. Members of the ANC simply refused to carry their identification cards, just as Indians had refused to hand over their taxes. When police arrested them, they didn't resist.

The government reacted even more harshly than ever. ANC members were thrown into jail. Anyone suspected of joining the

ANC could expect to be followed, spied on, and reported to the authorities. Newspapers couldn't write about any protests that the ANC organized—so even if blacks demonstrated against their white government, no one would ever hear about it.

Desperately, the ANC went on resisting and protesting. But for years and years, blacks in South Africa lived under the Unjust Laws, without seeing any change for the better.

Two Republics of China

In China, after the end of World War II, Chiang Kai-shek had to figure out how to deal with the victorious Soviets—and with his own allies.

Chiang had decided, reluctantly, that his Kuomintang government needed the help of the Chinese Communist Party to fight off the Japanese invaders. When Japan declared itself to be an Axis power during World War II, the united army of the Kuomintang and the Chinese communists got a little more help. British and American soldiers came to China to fight against the Japanese.

But Chiang Kai-shek had never trusted the communists of China, even when he most needed their alliance. "The Japanese are a plague on our skin," he once remarked, "but the communists will infect our hearts." He meant that although the Japanese might bother and torment the Chinese, communism was more dangerous because it might change how the Chinese people thought, and who the Chinese people *were*.

When Japan surrendered, Chiang Kai-shek no longer needed his alliance with the Chinese communists. Also, he didn't like the idea that the Chinese communists were such good friends with the Soviets. Now that World War II was over, he could see that the power of Communist Russia was growing.

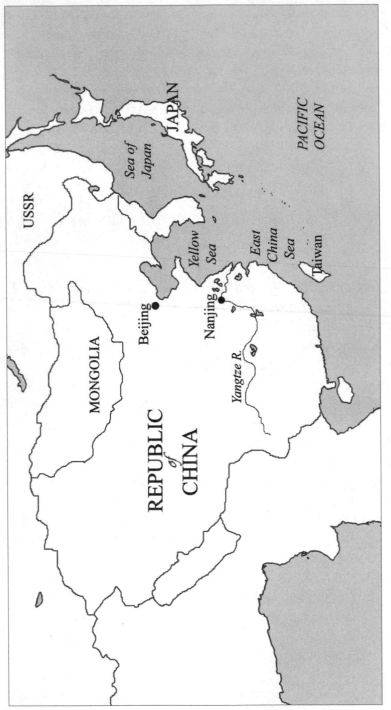

Republic of China

He was afraid that the CCP and the Soviet Union might ally themselves together, and make China a communist country by force.

Actually, Joseph Stalin didn't want to make an enemy of Chiang Kai-shek and the Kuomintang. A few years before, he *had* hoped that China could be brought into the Communist Party. (And he had remarked about Chiang Kai-shek, "We'll squeeze him like a lemon, and then we'll get rid of him." So Chiang Kai-shek was wise to be worried!)

But now the Kuomintang army had grown to more than three million soldiers, well-armed and well-trained. The Soviet army, on the other hand, had lost hundreds of thousands of men pushing the Germans back out of Russia. Stalin wasn't anxious to take on those millions of Chinese soldiers.

So Stalin told the CCP that they should try to keep the alliance with the Kuomintang together. After all, Mao's communist army had less than half a million men. And only a hundred and fifty thousand or so even had weapons!

Mao and the CCP refused. They didn't like Chiang Kai-shek any more than he liked them, and they no longer wanted to ally themselves with the Kuomintang. As soon as Japan surrendered, the CCP and the Kuomintang began to fight between themselves for control of China's government.

The Nationalist troops had soldiers, weapons, and control of China's largest cities. But Mao and the CCP had the peasants and poor people of China on their side. Millions and millions of poor Chinese knew that a communist government would take land away from the rich and redistribute it to the poor. During World War II and the struggle against the Japanese, millions of Chinese had lost their jobs, along with any hope of making enough money to buy food and clothing. Chinese currency was so useless that one American dollar was worth ninety-three thousand *Yuan* (units of Chinese money)!

Peasants and poor workers flooded into the Chinese Communist Party. Communist bases began to grow up all across the country. The Kuomintang began to realize that they were outnumbered. Kuomintang soldiers began to switch sides. Many were glad to change armies, because the Kuomintang army had run out of money and hadn't paid its soldiers for months. As a matter of fact, many Kuomintang soldiers had been earning money to buy food by selling their guns to Mao's unarmed communist soldiers.

Chiang Kai-shek's army was shrinking as the communist army grew. Whenever the CCP soldiers (also called the "Red Army") captured land, the generals would take the huge tracts

Chairman Mao

of land owned by the rich and give them away to the poor in the area. Not surprisingly, more and more poor people became loyal to the communists!

By 1949, the communist army was ready to attack the capital city of the Kuomintang government: Nanjing. They boarded a fleet of tiny fishing boats, sailed across the Yangtze River, and invaded the city. The Kuomintang soldiers were forced to flee. Over the next six months, they ran further and further south, with the CCP army behind them taking city after city.

At last Chiang and his remaining men left China and crossed over to the island of Taiwan. Here on Taiwan, Chiang Kai-shek announced, he would re-establish the true Republic of China, a democracy that would have free elections and that would truly preserve the culture and traditions of China—in exile.

But in China itself, the Chinese Communist Party announced, on October 1, 1949, that *they* governed the true Republic of China—the People's Republic of China, a communist nation, with Mao as its chairman. In this new Communist China, all people would have equal access to land, to food, and to goods. Chairman Mao made an appearance in Tiananmen Square, in the ancient city of Beijing. The Chinese people cheered wildly. Mao had become the hero of the People's Republic of China. Parades were held in his honor, with huge posters of him carried before enthusiastic crowds. Young Chinese boys and girls carried collections of his writings, known as Mao's "Little Red Book." Mao himself liked to be worshipped by his people. He even thought of himself as the sun, and told his people to sing a hymn to him that went, "From the Red East, a sun rises; Mao has appeared in China!"

Under Mao, China began to grow more prosperous. Peasants who owned their own land worked harder than they had in the days when all their profits were taken away by landlords. But although he was a hero to many, Mao also led a communist party that was harsh and repressive. As soon as the communists were in power, Mao's government executed over a million people who still supported the Kuomintang. Twenty million people were sent to concentration camps and prisons. Some of these were supporters of the Kuomintang. But others were simply rich, or had been to European universities and so were considered "Westernized."

Mao would remain popular for years. But before long, the prosperity he brought to China would begin to disintegrate, and China would sink once more into fighting, unhappiness, and violence.

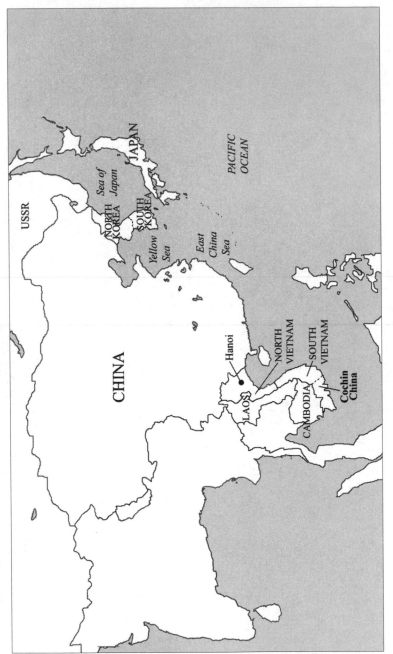

Vietnam and Korea, Divided

Chapter Thirty-Three
Communism in Asia

Ho Chi Minh and the Viet Minh

By the time World War II ended, France had lost all of its Asian colonies.

Remember, the French had built a little empire in "French Indochina"—the land that today is held by the countries of Vietnam, Laos, and Cambodia. In French Indochina, French landowners and a few wealthy Vietnamese held most of the power and money, while most Vietnamese worked for them for very low wages. The Vietnamese patriot Phan Boi Chau had tried to drive the French out, but he had failed.

World War II changed French Indochina. When Germany moved into France and occupied it, Germany's ally, Japan, moved into French Indochina. Beginning in 1940, French Indochina was under Japanese rule. The Japanese let the French officials stay in power, but—as in Vichy France—the officials had to obey Japanese orders.

To the Vietnamese, this seemed like a good chance to make another bid for independence.

The rebellion that rose up against both the Japanese and the French who obeyed them was led by a man named Nguyen Ai Quoc. He was probably born around 1890, although no one knows for sure. He used fifteen different names for himself. But the name that he made famous in Vietnam was Ho Chi Minh, "He Who Enlightens."

Even when he was a child, Ho Chi Minh hated the French occupiers. He could see that, in their own country, the Vietnamese had almost no power. They worked as servants and field hands. The French treated them with scorn. Before he was ten, Ho Chi Minh was working for the resistance movement in Vietnam, carrying messages from one anti-French fighter to another. His family also resented and worked against the French. His father refused to learn to speak the French language. His sister stole weapons for Vietnamese freedom fighters. And his brother joined a resistance movement.

When he was twenty-one, Ho Chi Minh decided to leave his country. He took a job as a ship's cook and sailed away from Vietnam.

He would not return for thirty years. In those years, he visited countries all over the world, as his ship moved from port to port. He lived for a little while in London, and then in Paris, and then in New York. He began his own newspaper, writing articles that called for every country in the world to be free from foreign occupiers. He visited Russia, read the writings of Lenin, and joined the Communist Party. He organized the Vietnamese living in China into a resistance group called the Revolutionary Youth Organization, and started the Indochinese Communist Party. He became more and more convinced that if Vietnam were ever to be free from France, it would have to fight for its independence.

In 1941, when Germany occupied France, Ho Chi Minh saw his chance. Surely the French occupiers would now be at a disadvantage! He returned to Vietnam and proposed that the different revolutionary groups—working secretly against the French—all unite together. Ho Chi Minh and the Indochinese Communist Party would lead all the other patriotic groups in resisting the French and the Japanese.

The other Vietnamese agreed. The new rebel army, called the "Viet Minh," was commanded by Ho Chi Minh. Over ten thousand Vietnamese joined the Viet Minh. They spent the years of World War II fighting a guerilla war against the Japanese, appearing from the brush of the jungles, attacking, and then melting back into the wilds.

Between 1940 and 1945, not only war but also famine turned Vietnam into a place of death. Crops failed. Nearly two million people starved to death. And for part of this time, Ho Chi Minh's Viet Minh had to fight without him. He had gone to China to ask Chiang Kai-shek to help him fight against the Japanese. But Chiang Kai-shek, who was busy fighting the Japanese himself, didn't trust Ho Chi Minh because Minh was a member of the Communist Party. He threw Ho Chi Minh in jail for eighteen months.

Meanwhile, the Viet Minh had begun to spy for the Allied forces, giving the Allies news about the plans and movements of the Japanese in Asia. Being on the side of the Allies—even though the French, their original occupiers, were Allies too—seemed like the best way to get the Japanese out of Indochina.

Finally, Chiang Kai-shek agreed to release Ho Chi Minh. By the time Ho Chi Minh got back to Vietnam, World War II had begun to turn against Germany. In Vietnam, the Japanese decided to change the way Vietnam was governed. Since the Allied troops had driven Germany out of France, the nation of France was no longer under German control. French officials could no longer be trusted to cooperate with an Axis power like Japan. So all of the French officials in Vietnam were arrested and removed from their positions. The Japanese decreed that Vietnam would be ruled by a puppet emperor, Bao Dai—but the country was really under Japanese control.

This "puppet monarchy" would only last for five months, because Japan was close to surrender. When Japan surrendered to the Allies in August 1945, after the bombing of Hiroshima, the Japanese had to give up their control of Vietnam. Bao Dai, Japan's chosen emperor, had to give up his throne.

On September 2, 1945, Ho Chi Minh announced to a huge gathering of Vietnamese in the capital city of Hanoi that Vietnam was now a free country, called the Democratic Republic of Vietnam. The new Vietnamese Declaration of Independence was based on the American Declaration. It began, "All men are born equal. The Creator has given us inviolable rights to life, liberty, and happiness!"

Just a few months after the surrender of Japan, the French moved back into Vietnam. They wanted to try to rebuild the empire they had lost during World War II. Although they didn't immediately attack the Democratic Republic of Vietnam, they announced that they were reclaiming the southern part of Vietnam. It would no longer belong to the Democratic Republic; instead, the south would be a separate, French-controlled colony known as Cochin China.

Ho Chi Minh didn't think that Vietnam could win an out-and-out war with the French. He offered to allow the French to put military bases in the Democratic Republic of Vietnam, as long as they promised to leave the Democratic Republic alone to rule itself as a sovereign country.

But the Vietnamese didn't trust the French, and the French didn't trust the Vietnamese. In 1946, France and the Democratic Republic of Vietnam declared war on each other. Ho Chi Minh called to his followers, "Let him who has a rifle use his rifle. Let him who has a sword use his sword. And let those who have no sword pick up axes and sticks to fight."

The "French Indochina War" would go on for eight years. In the south, the French put Bao Dai back on a throne, announcing that he would rule over a southern Vietnamese (and French) country. The Vietnamese refused to recognize him, and went on fighting. French troops grew weary of fighting against Vietnamese guerillas who could slip easily through the brush and jungles.

Finally, in 1954, the French agreed to give up their claim to Vietnam.

But they would only surrender under certain conditions. They insisted that Ho Chi Minh divide the country in half. The northern part would still be the Democratic Republic of Vietnam, under Ho Chi Minh as president. The south wouldn't belong to France, but it wouldn't belong to the Democratic Republic either. Instead, it would be a separate country, with its own elections and a different president.

Ho Chi Minh agreed to these terms. Vietnam was finally free of both France and Japan.

But the decision to divide the country in two would turn out to be a disaster. Struggles between the north and south of Vietnam would continue for another twenty-one years, and would lead to yet another foreign country—the United States—fighting a war in Vietnam.

The Korean War

In the years after World War II, the Soviet Union did its best to draw other countries into communism, while the United States grew more and more worried about this spreading change.

During World War II, the United States had not been nearly as worried about the USSR. The possibility that Nazis might take control of Europe and that Japanese soldiers might seize all of Asia had seemed much more threatening than the chance that the Soviets might convince other countries to become communist.

But now Germany and Japan were defeated. The Soviet Union was claiming other countries for itself. The enormous country of China was communist. So was the northern half of Vietnam, and the eastern half of Germany.

The country of Korea would become the next place where communism and democracy collided.

When Japan surrendered in 1945, the Japanese were forced to give up the land that they had seized during World War II. But what about Korea? Korea wasn't part of the original land of Japan. On the other hand it *had* been part of the Japanese Empire since 1910—well before World War I. Korea had been ruled by Japan for so long that it had no Korean government left that could step up and run the country once the Japanese were gone. Korean officials would have to learn how to govern their own land. And hundreds of thousands of Japanese, many of whom had lived in Korea for twenty years or more, had to be moved back to Japan.

The United States and the Soviet Union decided to divide up the responsibility for slowly giving Korea back its independence. For convenience, they agreed to split the country in two. They drew an imaginary line right at the "38th Parallel" (the line of latitude that ran roughly across the middle of the country). North of the 38th Parallel, Japanese troops would surrender to the Soviets. South of the 38th Parallel, they would surrender to American troops.

If this sounds arbitrary, it was. There wasn't anything particularly distinctive about the 38th Parallel. In the United States, you can find the 38th Parallel on a map if you draw a line from Charlottesville, Virginia, on the East Coast, straight across to Stockton, California, on the West Coast. This division was as arbitrary as saying that everyone above that line would speak one language, and everyone below it another. No one had yet figured out that partitioning off countries into smaller pieces didn't work very well.

And the Americans and the Soviets began to distrust each other very soon. The division of Korea was supposed to be temporary. But by 1948, neither the U.S. nor the Soviet Union was willing to move out of Korea. Each was sure that the other country would immediately grab power.

So instead of helping Korea return to independence, the Soviet Union set up a communist government in the north of Korea: the People's Republic of North Korea. It was led by a Korean soldier named Kim Il-sung, who had served in the Soviet army.

Down in the south of Korea, a different country formed. The president of the United States, Harry S. Truman, appealed to the United Nations for help. Even though American soldiers were occupying the country, the United Nations agreed to give South Korea a hand in holding its own elections. In August of 1948, the southern Republic of Korea had its first elections. A Korean politician named Syngman Rhee became president. Rhee was friendly to the United States. As a matter of fact, he had lived in America, and had even earned a PhD at Princeton University, in New Jersey.

But North and South Korea were both a mess. The president of the south hadn't exactly been appointed in a free and fair election; Syngman Rhee had been very willing to look the other way while his supporters assassinated the politicians who might run against him. And in the north, the Soviet-led People's Republic of Korea was sending soldiers to silence anyone who objected to a communist government.

Refugees from North Korea were flooding into South Korea. At the same time, South Koreans who sympathized with communism were trying to fight their way into North Korea.

In June of 1950, ninety thousand North Korean soldiers, given all the most recent and powerful weapons by the Soviets, marched past the 38th Parallel and into South Korea. They brought with them 150 huge, powerful, Russian tanks. The South Koreans were completely surprised. It was a Saturday night, and many South Korean soldiers had gone to Japan for the weekend. Others had left their posts and had gone home. Those who were still guarding the border didn't have any weapons powerful enough to fight off the enormous Soviet tanks.

The North Korean soldiers trooped on southwards. When the United Nations learned of this invasion, its members agreed that soldiers should be sent into South Korea to help the South Koreans push the Soviet-trained North Koreans back.

So British Commonwealth soldiers and American soldiers, under the command of the American General MacArthur, were sent back into Korea. They were given the job not just of driving the North Koreans out of South Korea—but of capturing North Korea and forcing it to rejoin the south.

The British and American soldiers managed to push the communist forces back past the 38th Parallel, and then kept marching. They managed to march so far north that they were almost up to the Chinese-Korean border. At this, the Chinese grew worried about being invaded themselves! Two hundred thousand Chinese soldiers marched south into Korea to push the UN forces back.

Now, instead of helping Korea recover from occupation, four different countries—the U.S., Great Britain, the Soviet Union, and China—were fighting on Korean land. The Chinese pushed the South Korean and UN forces back across the 38th Parallel again. Then the UN sent in more troops and pushed back up to the 38th Parallel once more.

Back and forth, back and forth! A North Korean soldier named Chung Dong-kyu described an old woman who lived in a farmhouse near the 38th Parallel, who cooked meals for the soldiers who came to her door. She seemed entirely unworried by the explosions and battles going on nearby. "Living so close to the 38th Parallel had caused her to see northern and southern soldiers take and retake her village many times," he wrote. "She showed neither surprise nor fear over the fact of the latest changeover."

By 1953, more than three million people had died in this pointless fight. Half of them were civilians who had not even been armed. Finally, after the death of Joseph Stalin, everyone involved agreed to a truce so that the Korean War would end. Korea would remain divided into two. The north would stay the People's Republic of Korea, and would be a communist nation. The south would still be the Republic of Korea, with an elected president. And the border between the two countries would be exactly where it had been placed at the end of World War II, almost ten years before—right along the 38th Parallel.

Argentina During the Time of Perón

Chapter Thirty-Four
Dictators in South America and Africa

Argentina's President and His Wife

In the ten years between the end of World War II and 1955, the South American country of Argentina put a new president into power and then threw him off again.

When World War II began, Argentinians were divided about what side Argentina should join. The people of Argentina were descended from at least four different kinds of people: the original Native American inhabitants, Spanish settlers who had come to South America in the seventeenth century, and Italian and German settlers who had arrived in Argentina during the 1800s. The Argentinians with Italian and German backgrounds hoped that their country would join with the Axis powers. Other Argentinians wanted to join the Allies.

The president of Argentina, Ramón Castillo, decreed that the country would remain neutral during World War II. But although Argentina didn't fight on either side, it was friendly towards the Axis powers of Italy and Germany. During the war, Argentina even sent a few of its army officers over to Europe to learn new strategies from Axis commanders.

One of those officers was a captain named Juan Perón. Right at the beginning of the war, Perón went to Italy to study the best ways to fight in mountain territories. He spent two years in Italy, watching the Fascist army fight in World War II, learning techniques from the Italian officers—and observing Mussolini. Perón liked Mussolini's ideas about how to run a country. He agreed that a country should obey its leader without debate in order to be strong. Even though Italy was at war,

Perón thought that Mussolini's Fascism had made the country purposeful, organized, and efficient.

In 1943, four years into World War II, Juan Perón joined a group of military officers who wanted to take over the government. He had returned to Argentina to find that its president, Ramón Castillo, had become weaker and more unpopular than ever. The poor people of Argentina believed that Castillo only cared about rich landlords and factory owners, not about the hungry workers who were struggling to survive. Rumors had also begun to spread about the coming presidential election. Ramón Castillo was up for reelection. But now, everyone was whispering that Castillo had already picked a rich plantation owner to be the next president—and that his government was ready to tamper with the votes, in order to make sure that Castillo's chosen candidate was elected.

In the uproar, the military officers marched soldiers to the Casa Rosada, the president's house in Buenos Aires, and suggested that Castillo resign. Faced with all those armed and hostile officers, Castillo had no choice. He left the Casa Rosada and his position as president. The officers then set up a *junta*—a military government—to rule Argentina.

A military government doesn't seem any more fair than a president who had been elected by fraud. But Argentinians seemed willing to give the junta a chance.

In this new government, Juan Perón was put in charge of taking care of working people. Perón wanted to make sure that working people were paid a fair wage and had money to live on when they were too old to work. He introduced laws to bring these reforms about—and this made him very popular with the working poor.

But Perón became more and more unpopular with his own government. The other officers didn't like the idea that Perón had so much popular support. And they also were worried about Perón's admiration of Mussolini.

In 1945, when the junta had been in charge of Argentina for two years, the Axis powers surrendered to the Allies. It was a good time to point out that Perón had supported the Fascists—who were on the losing side! On October 9, 1945, Pcrón was arrested by his own government and put on a small but very comfortable island where he couldn't command his supporters to rise up and free him.

Anti-Fascists rejoiced. But soon, the working people who loved Perón demanded his release.

Juan Perón was engaged to be married to a young woman named Maria Eva Duarte, an actress he had met several years before. When Eva heard that her fiancé had been thrown into jail, she encouraged the working people of Argentina to demand an explanation. What had happened to their champion?

These workers, nicknamed *descamisados*, or "shirtless ones" because they worked without shirts in the hot sun of South America, gathered in the streets in the thousands, demanding Perón's release. The other officers could see that Perón would have to be set free.

He was. On October 17, 1945, Perón was set free. He went out to speak to his supporters. A huge mob cheered when he appeared, and waved torches in celebration. The next day, the workers all stayed home from work and took a vacation day in celebration of Perón's release. They called this day, jokingly, the "Feast of Saint Perón"!

By arresting their champion, the officers of the junta had lost the confidence of the working people. The junta couldn't hold onto its power. Its members agreed to hold an election for a new president.

Juan Domingo Perón won the election.

As president, Perón went on trying to improve the lives of the poor. He also did his best to get the important businesses of Argentina back under Argentinian control. Like China, Argentina was filled with foreign businessmen who controlled factories, trains, and ports. Great Britain owned most of the railroads. The United States owned almost all of the car factories. Perón brought these businesses back to the people of Argentina—by seizing them in the name of the government.

Although Perón worked for the people of Argentina, he also used the methods of the Fascists to make sure that he kept his power. If a newspaper criticized him, Perón ordered it shut down so that it could never print another issue. If a schoolteacher told his students that Perón's policies might not be good for the country, he lost his job. Anyone who objected too loudly to Perón's reforms and laws was likely to disappear, mysteriously. Perón called this way of running a country *justicialismo*. He believed that the poor people should have power—but the way to give them power was for the government to tell everyone how they could use their land and their money.

Argentina *did* have a constitution that gave the citizens the rights to certain freedoms—such as the right to be tried in a court if they were accused of a crime. So how did Perón get away with "disappearing" Argentinians who disagreed with him (and violating all sorts of other rights that the people were supposed to have)? There was one clause in the constitution that gave the president of Argentina the power to act like a dictator if the country was in the middle of a national emergency. So Perón simply declared that Argentina was suffering from an emergency! Argentinians put up with Perón's dictatorship for nine years. In part, Perón was able to keep his position because his wife Eva was so popular. Eva was beautiful, charming, and soft-hearted. As wife of the president, she started an organization called the Eva Perón Foundation that gave money to the poor, helped working people visit doctors, and paid for children to get an education. The poor people of Argentina called her "Evita," a nickname showing their love for her. She was even nicknamed "the Madonna of America" for her mercy.

In 1952, Evita died. She was only thirty-three years old. At her funeral, thousands of Argentinians lined the streets and wept out loud as her coffin was carried past.

After Eva died, Juan Perón grew more cruel. More and more Argentinians "disappeared" and were never seen again. The people of his country began to mutter (very quietly) about Perón's tyranny. Meanwhile, Argentina was growing poorer and poorer. Perón had spent huge amounts of the government's money on education and health care for the poor. This was good for the poor—but now the government was out of money.

Perón, faced with a rapidly emptying treasury, announced that for two years, no one in Argentina would get a pay raise. He suggested that Argentinians eat less meat and more bread, so that the meat could be sold to other countries for money. Argentinians weren't too happy at the prospect of a meatless diet!

Then Perón made himself even less popular by starting to criticize the Roman Catholic Church. He accused Catholic priests of preaching against him in their sermons, and sent two of the most well-known priests back to Rome, accusing them of treason. He declared that several church holidays—days when Argentinians were accustomed to staying home—would now be regular workdays. The devout Catholics of Argentina resented all of these actions.

Perón had begun to lose the loyalty of his people.

On June 16, 1955, the armed forces suddenly rebelled against Perón. Military planes flew over the Casa Rosada and dropped bombs on it. The rebellion only lasted a day. But Perón reacted by announcing that he would wage war on anyone who opposed him. He also ordered his supporters to attack anyone who criticized him.

Even Perón's supporters were shocked by this. Perón was encouraging Argentinians to beat each other up! The army again tried to revolt. This time, soldiers managed to capture several large Argentinian cities. They began to call for Perón to resign, and for Argentina to hold new elections for another president.

Perón left his country and went first to Paraguay and then to Madrid, in Spain. Back in Argentina, his own people knocked his statues over and smashed them, and chipped his name out of all of the engravings in public squares.

Over the next eighteen years, Argentina had nine different leaders. In 1973, eighteen years after his flight, Juan Perón even returned to Argentina and became president again—for a single year. Then, at the age of seventy-nine, Juan Perón died.

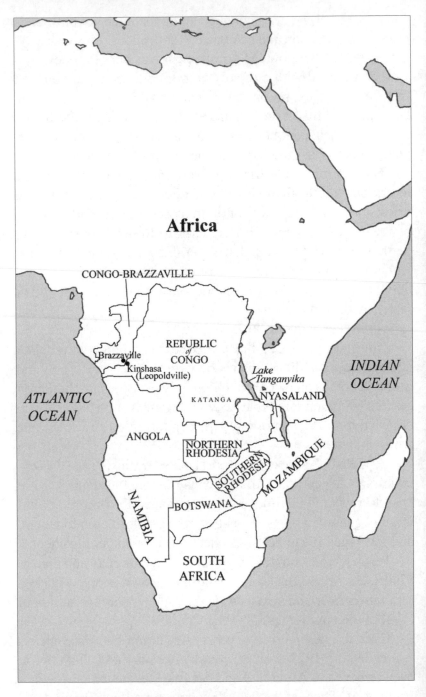

The Congo Under the Rule of Lumumba

Freedom in the Belgian Congo

Across the Atlantic from South America, the countries of Africa were struggling to establish their own governments. One by one, the countries that Europeans had created were throwing off European rule.

One of these struggles for freedom took place in the Congo, at the center of Africa. Almost a hundred years before, King Leopold II of Belgium had claimed the Congo as his own personal property. He called his land in Africa the "Congo Free State" and named one of its cities after himself: Leopoldville.

The Congo Free State stretched from the Atlantic Ocean, on the western coast of Africa, all the way to Lake Tanganyika. It went from just below the Sudan in the north down into the south of Africa. The Congo Free State was huge. Its land was fertile, and many different African tribes lived in it.

King Leopold treated the many tribes in his colony badly. He forced them to pay high taxes. To earn enough money to meet the king's demands, Africans had to work long hours making rubber or go on dangerous elephant hunts so that they could sell the elephants' ivory tusks. Leopold allowed slave traders to raid the Congo, taking Africans to sell in Europe as slaves. Every village in the Congo had to send four people every year to work as slaves for Leopold—like sacrifices to a dragon. He even made a notorious slave trader the governor of part of the Congo.

By the time the Congo had been in Leopold's possession for twenty-five years, half of its people had died. By 1908, many people both in Belgium and in the rest of the world were so indignant about the way that the Congo had been treated that the officials in the Belgian government appointed a new governor of the Congo and forced King Leopold to give up his personal claim to the land.

Life got to be a little better for the Africans of the Congo. They were no longer taxed quite so heavily or made to serve as slaves—but they weren't free. Like the blacks of South Africa, the African peoples of the Congo had to live separately from the whites. They couldn't study to be doctors, lawyers, or even tradesmen, and they weren't allowed to leave their country to find a better life elsewhere.

In 1956, an African patriot named Patrice Lumumba wrote a petition to the Belgian government, asking for more freedom for his country. Lumumba was from a small tribe known as the Batetela. He didn't have much political experience; he had worked in a post office and then taken a job as a salesman for a company that made beer. But he had always been active in speaking and writing about the Congo's need for independence.

In 1958, Lumumba formed a group called the MNC or the "Mouvement National Congolais." Lumumba told his followers, "Independence isn't a gift that can be given by Belgium. It is the right of the Congolese people."

The MNC led demonstrations and riots, trying to claim this right for themselves. At first, the Belgian government arrested some of the MNC leaders, hoping that the movement for independence would die down.

Instead, it grew more powerful, thanks to an action taken by the country of France. The French prime minister, Charles de Gaulle, allowed the French colony just northwest of the Belgian Congo to declare itself free. This area, known as Congo-Brazzaville, was only separated from the Belgian Congo by a river. As a matter of fact, the capital city of Congo-Brazzaville, Brazzaville, was right across the river from the capital city of the Belgian Congo, Leopoldville. Now the people of Leopoldville could look across the water and see free Africans.

Again, Congolese leaders sent messages to Belgium, asking for independence. When the Belgian government refused, riots broke out in Leopoldville. Belgian soldiers couldn't bring the mobs under control, even when more troops were sent from Belgium.

When the Belgian government realized that the Congo was out of control, it agreed to give the Congo its independence. In 1960, the first Congolese election was held. It had been arranged so quickly that the people of the Congo hadn't been able to form political parties, or find out much about different candidates.

Patrice Lumumba, the most well-known Congolese leader, was elected prime minister of the newly independent Congo. In his speech to his people, he delivered the Congo's Independence Day address. "I salute you in the name of the Congolese Government!" he announced. "[A] noble and just struggle ... was needed to bring to an end the humiliating slavery imposed upon us by force. ... We have experienced contempt, insults and blows, morning, noon and night, because we were 'blacks.' ... We have known that the law was never the same for a white man as it was for a black. ... All this has meant the most profound suffering. But all this ... is now ended. The Republic of the Congo has been proclaimed, and our land is now in the hands of her own children. ... Long live the independence and unity of Africa! Long live the sovereign and independent Congo!"

To celebrate independence, the people of Leopoldville pulled down and broke up the statue of Leopold II that stood in their capital city. They changed the name of the city to Kinshasa.

Not every African who lived in the Congo was pleased with independence. Under Patrice Lumumba, the Congo become one big country called the Republic of the Congo. But before the Europeans had settled in Africa, the area of the Congo had been divided into many small territories, each the home of a different tribe. Now, many Africans thought that the Congo should go back to being many small, independent states, each governed by its native tribe.

Just six days after the election, the eastern part of the Congo declared itself independent from the big Republic of Congo. Patrice Lumumba didn't want the eastern area, known as the Katanga, to leave the Republic. His new government needed money to run the country properly, and the copper mines that provided the Congo with most of its wealth lay in Katanga.

Lumumba's government demanded that Katanga rejoin the Republic. Katanga asked Belgium for soldiers to protect its new independence. Civil war broke out. Less than a year after becoming prime minister, Patrice Lumumba was captured by Katanga rebels and murdered.

A Congolese general named Joseph Mobutu announced that the Congo would now be ruled by a "caretaker government"—in other words, by military officers who had seized control of the country. (No one tried to organize another election.) Four years later, Mobutu gave himself the title "president." (Still no election!)

Under Mobutu, the Congo was a totalitarian state. Mobutu's own political party, the "Popular Movement of the Revolution," was the only party allowed to take part in the government. He kept control of the country with his army. And he got some of the money he needed to run the Congo from the United States. Mobutu had promised the U.S. that, if America helped him out, he would keep the Congo from becoming a communist country.

Mobutu ordered the Belgian names of the Congo and its cities changed to African names. Today, the Congo is known by the African name "Zaire." And during Mobutu's rule, Zaire was controlled by Africans, not by Europeans.

But Mobutu, like many rulers, managed to keep his power by threatening his opponents. He arrested those who disagreed with him, accused his enemies of treason, and sent out spies to find out whether anyone was criticizing him. He even had a squad of special police called "The Owls" who went out at night to drag people from their homes if Mobutu thought they were a threat to his power. The people of Zaire were afraid to even say his name—in case someone might be listening. They called him "Uncle Mo" instead. Under Mobutu, government officials took bribes to do their jobs. Policemen threatened to arrest innocent people unless they were given money. The Congo was free from European rule, but it still wasn't free from tyranny and corruption.

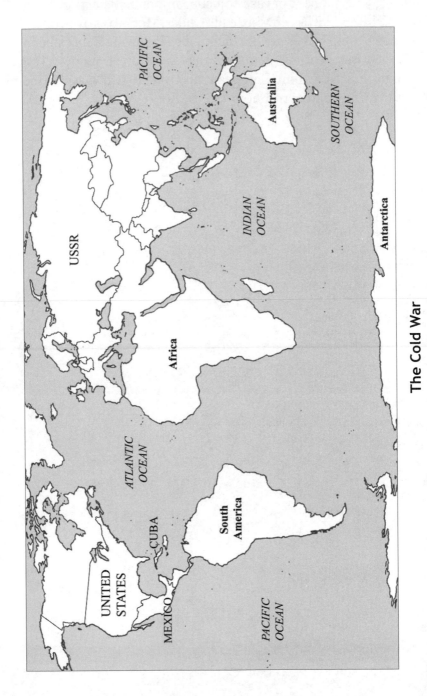

The Cold War

Chapter Thirty-Five
The Cold War

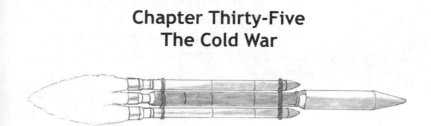

The Space Race

On the night of October 4, 1957, a glittering shape rose from the ground, a flame shooting from its tail. On the ground below, people began to cheer, "She's off! Our baby is off!"

They were actually cheering in Russian, because the Soviet Union had just launched a satellite, called *Sputnik*, into space. *Sputnik* (a Russian word that means "fellow traveler" or "companion") would circle around the Earth once every hour and a half, beeping constantly and sending radio waves back to Earth. It was the first man-made satellite to ever be launched into space, and the first to *orbit* (circle) around the Earth.

A month later, the Soviets launched a second satellite into orbit. This time the satellite, *Sputnik II*, had a passenger, a dog named Laika. The Soviets wanted to see whether living creatures could survive in space; one day, they hoped to send a human being into space.

Over in the United States, the news that the Soviet Union had managed to send two satellites into space—one with a living creature on board!—caused Americans to react with awe and fear. American and Soviet scientists had both been working for several years to design a satellite that could go into space. Both countries wanted to be the first to launch a satellite. The Americans thought that they were well ahead of the Soviets in this "race to space." When they realized that the Soviets had better and more powerful space technology, they were frightened.

By the middle of the 1950s, the United States and the Soviet Union were firm enemies. After World War II, both countries had wanted to spread their own form of government through Western Europe and Asia. The struggles over the divisions of Germany and Korea showed that the two countries had begun to hate and fear each other.

This hatred never erupted into open war. Instead, Americans and Soviets fought a battle without weapons. They tried to steal each other's allies. They refused to cooperate on anything. The United States called the Soviet Union repressive, tyrannical, and evil. The Soviet Union called the United States greedy, overbearing, and obsessed with money. Both countries were sure that the other was trying to figure out a way to attack.

This conflict became known as the "Cold War." When *Sputnik* flew into space, the Cold War was at its height. The United States at once began to worry that, if the Soviets could invent satellites that could make it to outer space, they could also use those rockets to carry powerful weapons over to the United States. In fact, on November 5, 1957, two days after Laika the dog went into space, a *New York Times* reporter wondered if the Soviets were planning to explode a nuclear weapon on the moon. (They weren't.)

Even though the United States managed to launch its own satellite two months later, the U.S. rockets were less powerful, and its satellites were smaller. The Soviets were winning the "Space Race," and the Americans needed to catch up. As soon as *Sputnik* launched, American engineering schools were flooded with students who wanted to learn to build rockets. Congress created a new government agency, the National Aeronautics and Space Administration (NASA) to oversee a program that would get Americans into space as soon as possible. That same year, Congress passed the National Defense Education Act, which gave schools more money to spend on teaching science. If Americans were going to win the Space Race, young scientists needed to be trained!

Americans hadn't been so determined to triumph over an enemy since the Japanese had attacked Pearl Harbor. In fact, that's what the launching of *Sputnik* felt like to many Americans: an attack. The Space Race wasn't just a race. It was a war, and America was losing.

The Soviet Union managed to stay in the lead for several years. They became the first country to put a human being into space. On April 12, 1961, Yuri Gagarin orbited the earth in a rocket called *Vostok 1*. His flight lasted 108 minutes. He later said that as he passed over the Atlantic Ocean, he found himself thinking about his mother, and how she would feel when she learned about his space trip. He hadn't told her that he was flying into space, and she didn't know about his trip until she saw it on the news. Yuri Gagarin landed in a field in Siberia. A few cows and a few peasants were there to watch him land.

The news that a Soviet "astronaut" had been to outer space made Americans determined to work even harder at their space program. The president of the United States, John F. Kennedy, challenged the Soviet government to a competition: Who could get a man to the moon first?

Six weeks after Yuri Gagarin's flight, President Kennedy asked Congress to find enough money for NASA to send men to the moon within eight years. Kennedy knew that this would be almost impossible. It would take an enormous amount of money, discipline, and hard work. But he believed Americans could pull it off. To the people of the United States, President Kennedy said, "The exploration of space will go ahead whether we join in it or not. ... We choose to go to the moon in this decade, and do all the other things, not because they are easy, but because they are hard."

Kennedy's wish came true. The United States did get a man on the moon in the 1960s. On July 16, 1969, the *Apollo 11* spaceship was launched from the Kennedy Space Center in Florida—NASA's headquarters, named after the president. The *Apollo 11* mission had one goal: Land on the moon, step out, and then come back.

Four days later, astronauts Neil Armstrong and Buzz Aldrin climbed into a smaller vehicle called the *Eagle*. It was designed to separate from *Apollo 11* and land on the moon. The two men piloted it to the moon's surface and touched down on a low, even plain called the Sea of Tranquility. Armstrong sent a message back to Earth: "The *Eagle* has landed."

Then Armstrong and Aldrin climbed out of the *Eagle*. Americans across the country watched them on television as they descended the ladder, down to the surface of the moon. Neil Armstrong was the first astronaut to put his foot on the moon's surface. As he took his first step, he said, "That's one small step for a man, one giant leap for mankind."

U.S. astronaut Neil Armstrong,
the first human to walk on the moon

The astronauts walked around the moon for almost twenty-one hours, wearing special suits that kept them warm and supplied them with oxygen to breathe. There was very little gravity on the moon, so the astronauts could jump high and take huge steps. They performed scientific experiments, and collected soil to take back to Earth. Before they left, they planted an American flag on the moon—a sign that although the Soviets had launched the first satellite, the Americans had won the Space Race. But they also left a plaque on the moon that said, "We came in peace for all mankind"—as a reminder that something greater than a simple political victory had been accomplished. For the first time, man had left the surface of the earth where he lived.

Thirteen Days in October

For thirteen days in October of 1962, it seemed that the world was about to end. The Cold War grew so hot that the United States and the Soviet Union almost declared war.

The conflict boiled up on the island of Cuba, just south of Florida. After the Spanish-American War, Cuba had been given the right to govern itself. It became the "Republic of Cuba." But in fact, the United States claimed to have certain powers over Cuba. According to U.S. law, the United States government could interfere in Cuban politics whenever it seemed that the government of Cuba might not be respecting "independence.... life, property, and individual liberty." And the U.S. could also keep naval bases in Cuba.

The people of Cuba disliked this law. This meant that the United States could interfere in Cuban affairs whenever it pleased. But the United States had insisted that this law be written into the Cuban constitution.

For the next forty years, American soldiers were stationed in Cuba. If the United States approved of the Cuban president, American troops would help him stay in power. Americans ran many of Cuba's biggest businesses—including the telephone company and the sugar plantations.

This was exactly the sort of interference in another country's affairs that the United States had objected to during the Suez Crisis! Finally, the United States agreed to repeal the law that allowed America so much say in Cuba's government. In 1940, just after the beginning of World War II, Cubans voted on a new constitution, without the hated provision that gave the U.S. its power. Elections were held again, this time without American help. Cuba had actually become a real democracy.

But not for long. In 1952, an army general named Fulgencio Batista led a military revolt against the president of Cuba. He and his men drove the president out of office and announced that the constitution was no longer in effect.

Cubans were no happier about Batista than they had been about the influence of the United States. A young lawyer named Fidel Castro led a group of Cuban citizens in an armed attack on Batista's men. But the attack was a disaster. Most of the Cuban citizens were killed. The rest were put on trial for treason.

Castro, then twenty-six years old, was convicted in just four hours. But at his trial, he spoke for two of those four hours against Batista's government. He called Batista's government "a single illegitimate power which has usurped and concentrated in its hands the legislative and executive powers of the nation." He demanded the return of the Cuban constitution, and an end to military government over Cuba. "I know that I shall be silenced for many years!" he shouted. "I know that there will be conspiracy to force me into oblivion. But my voice will never be drowned. … Condemn me, it does not matter! History will absolve me!"

And then he was thrown into prison, sentenced to fifteen years.

If he had served all fifteen years, the history of Cuba might have been entirely different. But after only two years, Batista felt confident enough in his power and in his control over the country to agree to set his political prisoners free. If he set them free, he would be able to demand favors and power from those who opposed him, because he would be doing them a favor.

Castro and the others were released. Fidel Castro left Cuba for Mexico—along with other revolutionaries who were determined to overthrow Batista's unjust, illegal dictatorship. Castro wrote, before he left, "I am convinced more than ever of the dictatorship's intention to remain in power. ... I believe the hour has come to take rights and not to beg for them, to fight instead of pleading for them."

Twenty-five thousand copies of this message were spread around Cuba. Meanwhile, in Mexico, Castro and a small group of rebels in exile were preparing to fight for Cuba's rights. They practiced shooting, climbing mountains, swimming across rivers, surviving in the wilderness on what food they could find, and other guerilla tactics. Castro and his allies—including a rebel named Che Guevara, an expert on guerilla warfare—knew that when they returned to Cuba, they would have to launch a guerilla war, fighting from hiding against Batista's regular army.

After a year of training, Castro, Che Guevara, and eighty other Cuban rebels got on a tiny wooden boat, set sail across the Gulf of Mexico, and headed for Cuba. Eighty-two people wasn't much to start a war with. But back in Cuba, others gathered to join them. Fighting broke out between Batista's army and the revolutionaries who wanted Cuba's constitution restored. Batista's soldiers killed more than twenty-five thousand rebels. But the revolutionaries kept on fighting. They cut telephone lines to keep army units from talking to each other. They burned fields of sugar cane and sugar mills that were owned by foreigners. They launched surprise attacks on army outposts and stole weapons. Che Guevara directed the attacks.

"Never stay in the same place," he told his warriors. "Never spend two nights in the same spot. Distrust your friends, your informers, your guides, your contacts, your own shadows. Never sleep under a roof. Never sleep in a house that can be surrounded."

Using these techniques, Castro's little army held its own against Batista's—which was twenty times as big. The United States, watching in dismay, decided that Batista's government had become far too tyrannical to survive. The U.S. could no longer legally interfere in Cuban affairs. But the U.S. had long sent weapons to the Cuban army. Now, it announced that Batista could buy no more weapons or ammunition for its troops from the United States.

Batista's soldiers began to leave him and join the rebels. On January 1, 1959, Batista fled from Cuba. Now Castro and his allies—men who had been insisting that Cuba should be ruled by its constitution—were in charge.

Do you think they restored Cuba's constitution?

They didn't. Instead of holding elections and bringing the constitution back, Fidel Castro and his allies took control of the country. Castro ordered hundreds of Cubans who had supported Batista killed. He asked the Soviet Union for money to help Cuba recover from the war, and the Soviets agreed. Now Castro began to turn Cuba into a communist country. He took large companies away from their owners and made them the property of the state. He took large farms away from wealthy landowners, divided them up, and parcelled them out to the poorest Cubans. The state took over schools. Eventually, Castro made almost every business in Cuba government-owned.

As had happened in so many other countries, the man who drove out a tyrant became one. Fidel Castro had his own "secret police"—groups called "Committees for the Defense of the Revolution." The committee members were supposed to spy on their neighbors and tell the government if they heard anything critical of Castro's ideas. Anyone who opposed Castro risked arrest, exile, and execution. Castro's takeover of businesses meant that thousands and thousands of small business owners—owners of corner stores, little dress shops, and even hot dog vendors—lost their businesses.

Castro had not been in power long before thousands—and then tens of thousands—of Cubans began to leave the island. They left because they had lost their businesses, or because they were afraid of arrest, or because they could no longer say freely what they thought. Most of these went to the United States. Many of them settled down in Florida, where Cuban Spanish, Cuban food, and Cuban music soon became part of America.

The United States didn't like what it saw of Cuba's government. Cuba's friendly relationship with the Soviets was even more troubling, because Cuba was so close to the United States. So the U.S. government, led by President Kennedy, began to plan an invasion of Cuba.

The invasion was planned for April of 1961. The soldiers who actually invaded Cuba were all Cubans who had fled from Cuba to the United States—because the United States couldn't legally interfere with Cuba's affairs by invading with American soldiers. But the Cubans were trained by United States military officials and given weapons by the United States. They were to land at a horseshoe-shaped beach called the Bay of Pigs, set up a junta (military government), and try to convince Cubans to join them against Castro.

But the invasion was a disaster. Word leaked out ahead of time, so that when the invasion force arrived, Castro's soldiers were waiting. His planes sailed overhead, sinking the boats that brought the invaders to the shore. Tanks rolled in, firing. Every Cuban in the invasion force was either killed or taken prisoner.

Castro knew that the United States had sponsored the invasion. So he turned to the Soviet Union, America's enemy, and bought more weapons to protect Cuba. The Soviet leader, Nikita Khrushchev, wrote the president of the United States an angry letter about the invasion of Cuba. He warned that if the

U.S. tried to interfere with Cuba again, the Soviet Union would "reply in full measure." Kennedy wrote back an equally testy letter, insisting that the United States had the right to protect its own hemisphere against Soviet influence.

In other words, the real fight was between the U.S. and the Soviet Union—not just between Fidel Castro and America.

Only six years earlier, in 1956, Nikita Khrushchev had lost his temper at the U.S. representative during a meeting of the United Nations. The British prime minister was making a speech when Khrushchev grew so angry that he pulled his shoe off, banged it on the desk, and shouted "We will bury you!" at the American statesman.

When he heard the noise, the prime minister turned around, looked at Khrushchev's banging shoe, and remarked, "I will have to have that translated!" His joke made the meeting end without any more shouting, but Khrushchev had made his position clear. America was his enemy.

In October of 1962, American spy planes, flying over Cuba, took pictures of weapons that had apparently just arrived in Cuba from the Soviet Union. The photos showed nuclear missiles, enough to destroy cities all through the United States.

Nuclear weapons in Cuba were a terrifying prospect for the United States. Cuba was so close to America that missiles could easily be fired at Washington DC, wiping out the whole city. Worst of all, although the missiles were in Cuba, the controls—the "red buttons" that would launch them—were over in the Soviet Union.

Immediately, John F. Kennedy sent U.S. ships to surround Cuba and keep any more weapons from coming in. He warned the Soviet Union and the people of the United States that if a nuclear weapon were dropped on the United States, the United States would launch a "full retaliatory attack on the Soviet Union." The Soviet Union prepared its own troops and announced that it would fight back.

For thirteen days, the Soviet Union and the United States were at a stand-off over the missiles. Nuclear war seemed inevitable. This was what the whole world had dreaded ever since the first atomic bomb had exploded over Hiroshima. Nuclear weapons were so powerful, and so deadly, that if the United States and the Soviet Union attacked each other, the entire world could be poisoned and destroyed. People prayed, hoped, and held their breath. Men driving to work wondered whether they would drive home that night. Families eating breakfast didn't know whether their world would still exist at dinnertime.

Later, an American politician would remark that the United States and the Soviet Union were standing toe to toe, having a staring contest—and that the Soviet Union blinked first. On October 29, the Soviet Union offered to take its nuclear missiles back, as long as the United States would promise not to invade Cuba. The United States agreed.

The "Cuban Missile Crisis" was over, but the Cold War still raged on.

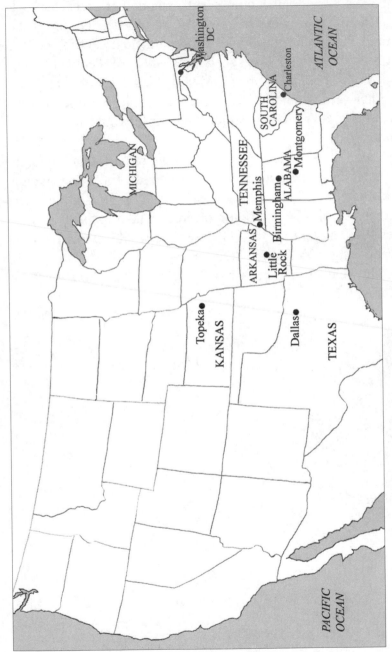

Struggles and Assassinations in the United States

Chapter Thirty-Six
Struggles and Assassinations

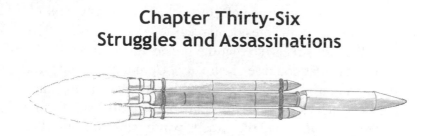

The Death of John F. Kennedy

John F. Kennedy, the president of the United States during the Space Race and the Cuban Missile Crisis, was one of the most popular presidents in American history. Kennedy was handsome and well-spoken, a graduate of the famous American university Harvard. He was married to a beautiful, charming wife, Jacqueline Bouvier Kennedy. He was a war hero who had served in the Navy during World War II; when his boat was attacked and sunk by the Japanese, Kennedy, although badly wounded, managed to get his men to safety. On top of all that, President Kennedy had also written two famous books. One, called *Why England Slept*, suggested that England should have gone to war against Germany much sooner. The other book, *Profiles in Courage*, described the lives of eight American heroes, and won the 1957 Pulitzer Prize.

Surely such a popular president would be reelected? Kennedy thought he would be. As he got close to the end of his first four-year term as president, he started to campaign for a second term.

A president who wants to be reelected has to travel all around the country, making speeches, meeting Americans face to face, and convincing them to vote for him. In November of 1963, President and Mrs. Kennedy took a short trip to Texas, to campaign for votes there.

On November 22, 1963, they travelled to Dallas. The sun shone, but the weatherman had predicted it would be cool, so Jackie Kennedy wore a pink wool suit. She and the president were due to have lunch in downtown Dallas with local business leaders. The governor of Texas, John Connally, had offered to arrange for the presidential car to take a winding drive through the city streets, so that the president could see Dallas (and so that Dallas could see Kennedy). Connally, his wife, the president, and Mrs. Kennedy all got into an open car together, with Secret Service agents (official bodyguards) all around them. Huge crowds lined the streets, waving and smiling. The president waved back. Nellie Connally, the governor's wife, said "Mr. Kennedy, you can't say Dallas doesn't love you!"

John F. Kennedy, 35th president of the United States

At 12:30 p.m., the president's car passed a tall building called the Texas School Book Depository. Shots rang out. President Kennedy was hit twice, once in the neck and once in the head. Governor Connally was shot in the back.

The driver sped away, towards a nearby hospital. But it was too late. When the car arrived at Parkland Hospital, Governor Connally was still alive, but the president of the United States was dead.

At the hospital, two priests came to pray over the president's dead body. A nurse asked Mrs. Kennedy, whose suit was spattered with blood, if she wanted to change her clothes. Mrs. Kennedy refused. "No," she said, "I want them to see what they've done." Every picture taken of Jackie Kennedy that afternoon shows her in her pink suit with blood staining the skirt and jacket.

Since the president was dead, his vice president, Lyndon Baines Johnson, was now the acting president of the United States. Secret Service officials were afraid that the mysterious assassin would try to kill Johnson next. They begged him to go back to Washington as soon as possible, but he refused to leave Dallas without President Kennedy's body.

Around 2:30 in the afternoon, only two hours after the assassination, President Kennedy's body was put in a casket and taken onboard Air Force One, the presidential airplane. The president's aides had already sent for a judge named Sarah Hughes. She boarded the airplane as well. On the airplane, she administered the oath of office to Lyndon Johnson, while Jackie Kennedy stood beside him. The new First Lady of the United States, Mrs. Johnson, later wrote in her diary that Jackie Kennedy's dress somehow made the horror of the whole day even worse: "I looked at her. Mrs. Kennedy's dress was stained with blood. One leg was almost entirely covered with it. ... Somehow that was one of the most poignant sights—that immaculate woman exquisitely dressed, and caked in blood."

Then the plane took off and carried the new president and the body of John Fitzgerald Kennedy back to Washington DC.

Kennedy was not the first president in American history to be assassinated. You might remember that John Wilkes Booth shot Abraham Lincoln while the president watched a play in Ford's Theatre. In 1881, a man named Charles Guiteau had shot and killed President Garfield as the president walked through a railroad waiting room in Washington DC. Guiteau was angry because Garfield hadn't given him a job. And in 1901, President McKinley was shot while he was shaking hands with a crowd in Buffalo, New York. He died eight days later.

But somehow, this assassination was different.

After President Kennedy died, people began to compare his presidency to Camelot, the mythical kingdom ruled by King Arthur and Queen Guinevere. (One of President Kennedy's favorite plays was a musical called *Camelot*. In an interview a few days after President Kennedy's death, Mrs. Kennedy quoted some of the lyrics: "Don't let it be forgot, that once there was a spot, for one brief shining moment, that was known as Camelot.")

Looking back, it seems that America really did change after Kennedy died. From the end of World War II until 1963, America was prosperous, excited about the future, and filled with energy. In the 1950s, Americans built more houses than ever before. Magazines and TV shows painted a picture of an America where those houses were filled with happy families eating dinner together, playing with hula hoops, and going to drive-in movies. In this America, every man had a good job, and every woman had a beautiful and immaculate house.

But in the 1950s, there were plenty of worries under the surface. The Cold War had grown more frightening. Immigrants who came to America from other countries often lived in poverty, surrounded by dirt and disease. Especially in the South, African-Americans were denied the right to live peacefully, to vote, and to do all of the things that white Americans took for granted.

These problems had been there all along—but after Kennedy's assassination, they seemed to rise to the surface. They became easier to see. Life in America seemed a little less glittering and a little less wonderful. Americans were forced to face up to the troubles in their own country. You'll read more about some of those troubles in the next few chapters.

People still debate who killed President Kennedy, and why. But most people believe a man named Lee Harvey Oswald shot the president. Oswald was an ex-Marine who knew how to handle a rifle. He had lived for a while in Russia and had come to believe in the glories of communism. And Oswald worked at the Texas School Book Depository, the building from which the shots had been fired.

On the afternoon of the assassination, police began looking for Oswald. A police officer named John D. Tippitt spotted Oswald walking around the streets of Dallas. Tippitt rolled down the window of his car and spoke to Oswald for a few minutes. Then he got out of his car. Oswald drew a gun and shot him; Tippitt died immediately.

After this, Oswald ran. But police caught up with him, handcuffed him, and took him off to the police station. He insisted that he had nothing to do with Kennedy's death, but the police didn't believe him. They were sure that they had arrested the assassin.

Two days later, the police got ready to take Oswald to the county jail, where he would wait until his trial could be arranged. They walked him through the basement of the police offices, towards an outside door that led to the street where a car that was waiting for him. TV cameras were recording Oswald's journey, while people all across the United States watched, live. As Oswald walked towards the door, a Texas night club owner who had sneaked into the basement ran at him, shouting, "You killed the president, you rat!" The night club owner, Jack Ruby, pulled out a gun and shot Lee Harvey Oswald. Millions of people saw the shooting on live television.

Oswald died two days later in Parkland Hospital. He was buried with no funeral service and no mourners; reporters who came to cover the funeral carried his coffin. Jack Ruby died from a blood clot before he could be finally convicted of shooting Oswald.

President Kennedy was buried at Arlington National Cemetery, near Washington DC, on November 25, 1963. His tombstone says, in part:

AND SO MY FELLOW AMERICANS
ASK NOT WHAT YOUR COUNTRY CAN DO FOR YOU
ASK WHAT YOU CAN DO FOR YOUR COUNTRY
MY FELLOW CITIZENS OF THE WORLD
ASK NOT WHAT AMERICA WILL DO FOR YOU
BUT WHAT TOGETHER WE CAN DO FOR THE FREEDOM OF MAN

Civil Rights

In the United States during the 1960s, not all men were free.

Slavery had ended a hundred years earlier. But the lives of African-Americans who lived in the South were still hard and unfair. After slavery was abolished, white Southerners passed new laws, designed to keep the black people poor. Black Southerners couldn't vote or marry whites. Like blacks in South Africa, American blacks couldn't eat in the same restaurants as white people. They had to go to separate black schools, different beauty parlors, and all-black barber shops. They drank from black-only water fountains, sat in the black-only sections of public buses (the back seats), and were even buried in black-only graveyards. In the American South, this separation was called *segregation*.

The segregation laws of the American South were nicknamed "Jim Crow laws." They took this name from an old, nineteenth-century song called "Jump Jim Crow." The song had forty-four verses, but the first goes like this:

> Come listen all you galls and boys
> I's jist from Tucky-hoe.
> I'm goin to sing a little song,
> My name's Jim Crow.
> Weel about and turn about and do jis so,
> Eb'ry time I weel about and jump Jim Crow.

The spelling in "Jump Jim Crow" is a white person's idea of how a black Southerner might talk.

Most of the Jim Crow laws had been passed by 1900. From the very beginning, black Southerners protested these laws as unfair. By the 1950s, these protests were becoming louder. Blacks became more outspoken about the injustice of the Jim Crow laws. All over the world, other people were gaining their freedom—and here at home, in the country that was supposed to stand for freedom and democracy, people with dark skin were not allowed to be free.

African-Americans wanted the same civil rights as other Americans. They wanted to be able to vote, and to live and work where they pleased. Their protests against the Jim Crow laws became known as the "Civil Rights Movement."

The Civil Rights movement began in Clarendon County, South Carolina. About thirty-two thousand people lived in this county. Most of them were black. But white people owned most of the land, and black people had to work for the whites for very little pay. Many black families earned less than a thousand dollars for an entire year's work. And the schools for blacks were shabby old buildings, with no electricity or water. The white students, on the other hand, went to school in a lovely brick building that was almost a mansion.

On May 28, 1951, three lawyers brought a case before federal judges in Charleston, South Carolina. ("Federal" means that the judges were appointed by the U.S. government, not by the state of South Carolina. All three judges were white, of course.) The lawyers argued that racially segregated schools—separate schools for whites and blacks—violated the United States Constitution, which said that all U.S. citizens should be treated equally. One of the judges was persuaded by the lawyers' arguments. Two of them were not, and the lawyers lost the case.

But that case was just the beginning. The next case about school segregation would be more successful.

It was filed in Topeka, Kansas. Once more, lawyers protested that black-only schools were against the Constitution. This time, the case, called *Brown v. Board of Education*, was heard by the U.S. Supreme Court (the highest court in the land—meaning that no other judges could disagree with its decisions). In 1954, the Supreme Court agreed: Racially segregated schools violated the Constitution.

In 1955, December 1 became another landmark day for the civil rights movement. On that day, Rosa Parks, a black seamstress, boarded a bus in her hometown of Montgomery, Alabama. She sat down in a seat reserved for blacks only, with three other black bus riders. But as the bus filled up, all of the white-only seats were taken. One white man was left standing in the aisle.

The bus driver asked all four black riders in Rosa's row of seats to move. The white man couldn't sit with them, because it was against the law for whites and blacks to sit in the same row of seats. The other three moved, but Rosa Parks refused to budge. Police arrived and arrested her for breaking the law.

Rosa's arrest gave the blacks of Montgomery a chance to protest segregation. They gathered together and agreed to boycott the buses. They wouldn't ride buses again until the buses were "desegregated," so that blacks could sit wherever they wanted.

The Montgomery boycotters asked a minister who lived in Montgomery to head up the boycott. He was new to town, but he had already become known as a powerful, moving public speaker. His name was Martin Luther King, Jr.

The bus boycott lasted longer than anyone expected it to. It dragged on for weeks, and then for months. Whites in Montgomery tried to frighten blacks into giving up the boycott. Someone even set off a bomb at King's home.

The boycott wasn't the only tactic the Montgomery blacks used. They also took the bus company to court and accused it of violating the Constitution. After all, the Supreme Court had declared that separate schools were unconstitutional. Weren't separate bus seats just as unequal?

The great civil rights leader, Martin Luther King, Jr.

The U.S. Supreme Court agreed once more. It issued an order, forcing the bus company and the bus drivers to allow blacks to sit wherever they wanted.

After the boycott, Rosa Parks went on to work in the government. She joined the staff that worked for John Conyers, a U.S. congressman from Michigan. Martin Luther King, Jr., went on to speak for civil rights all over the South, and then all over the United States. Like Gandhi, whom he admired, he wanted change without violence. Like Gandhi, he led marches and peaceful protests all over the South. He spoke at public gatherings all over the country, trying to convince his listeners that segregation was wrong.

All over the South, black people followed Parks, King, and the other civil rights activists. They demanded equality, not segregation. Some white people agreed that segregation was wrong and supported the Civil Rights Movement. But others tried to fight back. After the Supreme Court ordered the Montgomery buses desegregated, some whites actually shot at the buses. Others set off more bombs at the homes of black leaders.

And others tried to keep the schools from changing. Even though the Supreme Court had ruled, in 1954, that segregation in the schools was illegal, many public schools were still segregated well into the 1960s. The Supreme Court had ordered that all schools be open to blacks and whites equally. But this order simply said that the schools should be integrated "with all deliberate speed." No particular deadline was given.

Imagine that you've checked your favorite book out of the library. If the library gives you a due date, and threatens to charge you a big fine if you don't return the book by then, you'll probably get the book back on time. But if the library says, "Return it as soon as you can, if that's convenient" (which is not so different than "with all deliberate speed"), you might not return the book for months. In fact, you might never actually bring the book back to the library, because you want to read it just one more time.

The public schools of the South were in this same position. Many white school principals, and many white parents, did not want the schools to integrate. Since the Supreme Court hadn't given them a date on which segregation *had* to end, many schools never got around to admitting black students.

In some towns in Virginia, local communities simply closed all of their public schools when they were told to integrate. This was called "massive resistance." Parents in these towns so hated the idea of sending their children to school with black children that they preferred for their children to go to expensive, all-white private schools—or, in some cases, not to go to school at all.

In 1957, in Little Rock, Arkansas, the desegregation of a public school was finally carried out by force. On September 4, 1957, a black teenager named Elizabeth Eckford and eight of her friends got ready to go to the local school—a school that had never admitted a black student. The law of the United States of America said that Elizabeth and her friends could attend Little Rock Central High School, but the governor of the state of Arkansas, Orval Faubus, didn't intend to obey the Supreme Court order. He sent National Guard troops—Arkansas soldiers who are supposed to protect the state in case of invasion or disaster—to keep the nine teenagers from walking up the school steps. Later, Elizabeth told a newspaper reporter, "I walked up to the guard who had let the white students in. When I tried to squeeze past him, he raised his bayonet and then the other guards closed in and they raised their bayonets. They glared at me with a mean look and I was very frightened and didn't know what to do. I turned around and the crowd came toward me. Someone started yelling, 'Lynch her!'"

When the president of the United States learned about the governor's actions, he ordered Governor Faubus to allow Elizabeth into the school. The governor refused. So the president ordered federal troops—United States soldiers—to travel down to Arkansas and walk beside Elizabeth, so that she could enter the school.

Imagine how much courage it took for Elizabeth to walk up the steps of the school a second time. But she and the other eight students went back to school—even though some of the white students and parents shouted filthy names at them and threatened to hurt them.

It took years for the schools of America to become fully integrated. The courage of boys and girls like Elizabeth Eckford, and of men and women like Rosa Parks and Martin Luther King, Jr., helped to bring about full civil rights for American blacks. The civil rights movement was also helped by the power of the United States government, which often told the states that they had no choice but to follow the orders of the Supreme Court—or else.

In 1964, the United States Congress passed the Civil Rights Act. This law said that restaurants and other establishments would no longer be allowed to discriminate on the basis of skin color. They would have to serve both whites and blacks. There would be no more separation. In 1965, Congress passed the Voting Rights Act, which guaranteed black people the right to vote.

Three years afterwards, on April 4, 1968, the great civil rights leader Martin Luther King, Jr., was staying in a hotel in Memphis, Tennessee. He was preparing to lead a march that aimed to help local black workers get better pay. As he stood on the balcony of his hotel room, an assassin shot at him—and killed him at once. Even after Congress had passed laws guaranteeing equal rights for blacks, hostility between blacks and whites remained very much alive in America.

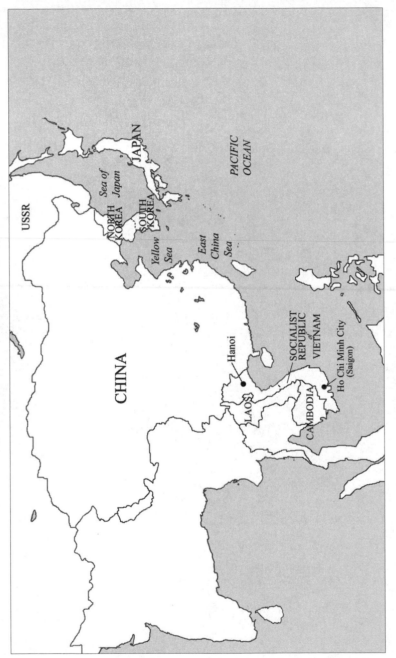

Communist Vietnam

Chapter Thirty-Seven
Two Short Wars and One Long One

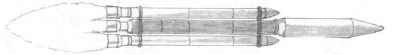

The Vietnam War

When we last visited Vietnam, the country had been split in two. Ho Chi Minh governed the Democratic Republic of Vietnam, a communist country in Vietnam's north. In the south, President Ngo Dinh Diem governed a different country—the Republic of Vietnam, which was *not* communist.

Now that you know about the Cold War and the American fear of communism, you can guess how the United States felt about the communist government of North Vietnam. The American government was afraid that North Vietnam would invade the south and take it over. If that happened, the whole country would be communist. And if one South Asian country became communist, all the others might follow—like a "row of dominoes," in the words of one American official.

So the United States sent advisors and military officers to the south of Vietnam. These American "helpers" were supposed to make sure that the communist north didn't take over South Vietnam as well.

The United States was right about one thing: the communist north *did* want to take over the south. Members of Ho Chi Minh's revolutionary group, the Viet Minh, were still down in the south. In 1959, Ho Chi Minh ordered the Viet Minh to begin a guerilla war against the South Vietnamese government. He intended for this guerilla war to go on until South Vietnam surrendered to the north.

President Diem, who was supposed to be ruling over a republic, started to use his army to control South Vietnam and to fight back against the rebels, who were known in the south as Viet Cong. By 1962, he had declared South Vietnam under martial law.

A year later, the South Vietnamese army seized the government offices and murdered President Diem. Now the army would both fight the Viet Cong *and* try to govern the country.

The fighting grew fiercer and more widespread. Then, the civil war turned into an international war.

China and the Soviet Union sent guns, ammunition, and supplies to the Viet Cong, so that they would have a better chance of overcoming the South. This was exactly what the United States feared. So, in 1965, President Lyndon B. Johnson ordered U.S. Marines to go into South Vietnam.

This was the beginning of the longest war the United States had ever fought. It would drag on for eight long years. In 1969, at the height of the war, over half a million American soldiers were in the tiny country of Vietnam. American soldiers fought against the Viet Cong in the south, while American fighter planes bombed North Vietnamese military bases and cities.

The U.S. wasn't the only country that sent soldiers to help the South Vietnamese fight against communist takeover. Soldiers from South Korea, Thailand, Australia, New Zealand, and the Philippines also fought with the South Vietnamese. But America sent more soldiers into Vietnam than any other foreign country. Between 1965 and 1973, American soldiers poured into Vietnam. In all, almost three million Americans fought in the Vietnam War.

Because so many soldiers were needed, young American men were *drafted*—forced to join the military. A country decides to use a draft (also called *conscription*) when it needs more soldiers than those who volunteer to join. The United States had used a draft during the Civil War, and also in both World Wars. When the Vietnam War began, the United States government decided that it was once again time to build a larger army. So during the Vietnam War, young men between 18 and 25 were given a "draft number." If your number was called, you had to report to your nearest military office for a physical examination. If you passed it, you were sent off to train for war. And after you were trained, you might get sent to the jungles of Vietnam to fight against the Viet Cong, whether you wanted to or not.

Today, the American military is an "all-volunteer force." To be in the Army, Navy, Air Force, or Marines, a young man or woman has to go to a recruiting office and ask to join. Young men in the United States still have to register with a government agency called Selective Service when they turn eighteen. That way, Selective Service knows how many men could be drafted, if the U.S. ever needed a larger army. But before anyone could be drafted, Congress would have to pass a law authorizing a draft—and because so many people in the United States oppose the idea of a draft, this will probably never happen. (The last time the Congress voted on a draft law, it was defeated, 402 votes to 2. Even the representative who introduced the law voted against it.)

Despite the thousands of Americans drafted, and despite year after year of fighting, nothing much seemed to be changing in Vietnam. The Viet Cong and the North Vietnamese showed no signs of giving up. The North Vietnamese government kept on sending more men, armed with Russian and Chinese weapons, to fight in the south.

Back in the United States, Americans were saying (with louder and louder voices) that the Vietnam War was a mistake. Thousands of young men were dying in Vietnam. Hundreds of thousands of protestors gathered together to shout, sing, and burn their draft cards (the cards that told young men when they would have to report for military duty).

In 1968, Lyndon B. Johnson announced that he wouldn't try to be reelected. He was too unpopular—mostly because of the Vietnam War. Instead, Richard Nixon became president. As soon as Nixon took office, he announced that he would start pulling American soldiers out of Vietnam. In 1969, American troops began to leave Vietnam, a few at a time.

By 1972, the United States had agreed to meet with the North Vietnamese to talk about peace terms. Right at the beginning of 1973, the United States signed a treaty with the Viet Cong and both Vietnamese nations. The treaty said that every American soldier would leave Vietnam. South Vietnam would keep its independence—but North Vietnam would be allowed to leave over a hundred thousand soldiers in the south.

This wasn't a very good treaty for the south. And almost as soon as the American soldiers left, the north resumed its attacks. In 1975, the communist armies of North Vietnam invaded the south, captured the southern capital city, Saigon, and took over the South Vietnamese government. Less than a year later, Vietnam had been reunited into one country, under communist rule: the Socialist Republic of Vietnam. Saigon was renamed Ho Chi Minh City.

The fighting had ended. But the country was in ruins. Almost a million North Vietnamese had died, as had over a million South Vietnamese. South Vietnamese who had opposed the communist takeover were sent to concentration camps. The Vietnamese government called these camps "reeducation camps," and claimed that the camps would help southerners adjust to life in a communist nation. But many people in the camps died. Vietnamese who were afraid for their lives left their country, trying to sail across the South China Sea to other countries in southeast Asia. So many sailed away from Vietnam that they earned a nickname: the "boat people."

In the United States, Americans mourned the loss of almost sixty thousand men. Hundreds of American soldiers captured by the Vietnamese, called POWs (prisoners of war) had been released. But hundreds more were missing. Many never came home. They remained "missing in action" (MIA). Their families never knew what happened to them.

Almost three million Americans had fought in the Vietnam War. Thousands came back wounded, or so disturbed by their years of fighting that they had trouble leading normal lives. And because the war had been so unpopular, soldiers who came back from Vietnam weren't treated as heroes. After World War II, soldiers coming back home were cheered, honored, and thanked. Soldiers returning from the Vietnam War were just as likely to be jeered at, or criticized in public by those who had opposed the war.

Not until 1982, ten years after the withdrawal from Vietnam, did the United States build a memorial to the American soldiers who were killed in the war. Today, you can see the memorial, called the Vietnam Veterans Memorial, in Washington DC. The memorial is made of black marble, and is engraved all over with the names of those who died. It rises up out of the ground, like a huge scar that never healed. The memorial preserves the names of those who died in the war—and also shows that the Vietnam War wounded the American people.

Trouble in the Middle East

In the Middle East, two more wars were about to erupt around the new state of Israel.

When we last visited Israel, it had declared its independence and fought against invading nations, all in the same day. In 1967, after Israel had been a country for almost twenty years, another war began. We call it the Six-Day War. It lasted for six days.

Once again, Israel and the Arab states of Syria, Egypt, and Jordan went to war. Only now, Israel had the help of its brand-new and very skilled air force. This time, Israel didn't just defend itself. At the end of the war, Israel took land away from all three of the defeated countries. These territories—the Gaza Strip, the Sinai Peninsula, the West Bank of the Jordan

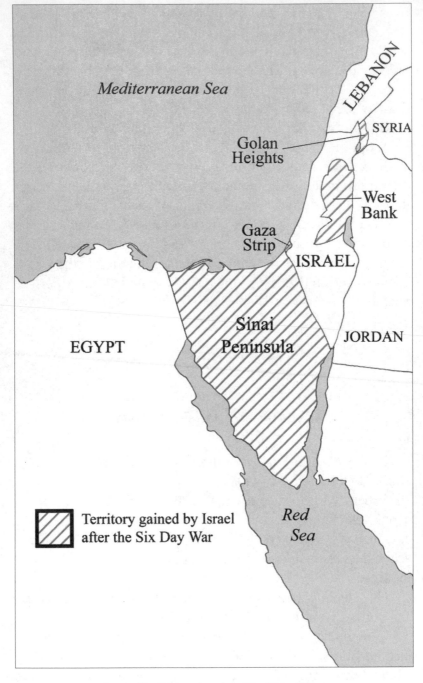

Israel's Gains in the Six-Day War

River, and the Golan Heights —quadrupled Israel's size. Suddenly, almost a million Arabs who had been living under Arab governments were instead controlled by Israel. Now, they were governed by a Jewish state.

Jews and Arabs were not good friends, and this new development didn't make the Middle East any more peaceful.

For six years, Israel governed the unhappy Arabs in its new territories. In 1973, another war broke out. Once again, Egypt and Syria attacked Israel, hoping to get back some of the land lost in the Six-Day War. This third war between Israel and her Arab neighbors is called the Yom Kippur War, because Egypt and Syria launched their attack on Yom Kippur, the Day of Atonement—the most sacred day of the Jewish year.

The Yom Kippur War lasted longer than the Six-Day War, but not a lot longer. This time, the fighting went on for three weeks. At first, it seemed that Egypt and Syria might win this time around. Israel had been caught off guard by the first attack, and Egypt managed to shoot down many of Israel's planes; this made Israel's air force much less dangerous. And the Egyptian and Syrian attack was so violent that Israel quickly began to run out of ammunition.

Israel appealed to the United States for help. At first, America (which had just scolded Great Britain for getting involved in Egypt) refused to send aid. But then the Soviet Union decided to send weapons to Egypt and Syria. At once, President Nixon announced that the U.S. had changed its mind. New weapons were on the way!

At this, Israel's soldiers took heart and began to fight with new energy. But after three weeks of fighting, the U.S. was afraid that the Soviet Union was getting ready to come into the war with soldiers—and nuclear missiles. American diplomats managed to convince all three countries to sign a cease fire. Israel claimed to be victorious, because all of the territories won in the Six-Day War were still under Israeli control. Egypt and Syria declared that they had won, because they had managed to destroy part of the Israeli air force and army.

Actually, not too much had changed in the Middle East. But the Yom Kippur War did have an immediate effect on the United States: It caused the U.S. to run out of gas.

The United States was filled with cars, buses, trucks, and other machines and vehicles that run on gasoline. That gasoline came from oil. The U.S. had some oil of its own beneath American ground—much of it in the state of Texas. But most of the oil used in the United States and in the world came from the Middle East. And most of this oil lay in Arab countries.

In 1960, five of the most powerful oil-producing Arab countries had formed an organization called the "Organization of the Petroleum Exporting Countries"—OPEC, for short. And as soon as the Yom Kippur War ended, the five countries in OPEC decided to stop selling oil to countries that had helped Israel in the Yom Kippur War.

That, of course, included the United States. From October 1973 to March 1974, OPEC refused to sell any oil to America. This was called an "oil embargo."

The United States suddenly realized how much it depended on foreign—and sometimes unfriendly—nations for oil. Once OPEC stopped selling oil to the U.S., there just wasn't enough gasoline to go around. Gas stations started to run out of gas. They had to put up signs for the cars driving by: "SORRY! NO GAS TODAY!" Some gas station owners wouldn't even sell gas to people they didn't recognize as regular customers.

The U.S. government announced that gas would be rationed. If the last number of your license plate was an odd number, you could only buy gas on odd-numbered days. If the last number on your license plate was even, you could buy gas only on even-numbered days. Since car engines use more gas when cars drive fast, the government also announced a new national speed limit. From now on, no state could have a speed limit higher than 55 miles per hour. (Until this time, some roads—long straight ones out in the desert—didn't have speed limits at all; you could drive as fast as you wanted!)

Even with rationing and a lower speed limit, people waited in line for two or three hours to buy gas. In just a few weeks, the price of gas went up from twenty-five cents to over a dollar per gallon.

The OPEC embargo ended in March. Rationing ended too. Now, drivers could buy gasoline whenever they wanted—although gas prices never did go back down to the original twenty-five cents per gallon. Right after the embargo, scientists in America started to do research on other kinds of fuel and other kinds of energy, like solar power, so that America could never again be brought to a standstill by an oil shortage. But as time went on, Americans grew less worried about another embargo. Less time and money was spent on finding new sources of energy. Today, Americans use more oil than any other country—and the relationship between America and the countries of the Middle East is still affected by America's need for Middle Eastern oil.

Five years after the Yom Kippur War and the embargo, the new president of the United States, Jimmy Carter, helped to bring a measure of peace between Egypt and Israel. The president of Egypt, Anwar el-Sadat, had led Egypt into the Yom Kippur War. Israel had a new prime minister, Menachem Begin.

Anwar el-Sadat had begun to hope for peace with Israel. In 1977, he became the first Arab leader to ever visit Israel. He even spoke to the Knesset, the Israeli Parliament. "I come to you today on solid ground to shape a new life and to establish peace," Sadat told the members of the Knesset. "We all love this land, the land of God. We all, Muslims, Christians and Jews, all worship God."

Anwar el-Sadat's visit to Israel made other Arab leaders furious. They still hoped that the Jewish state of Israel could be wiped out, and that the Arabs of Palestine could get their land back. But Sadat refused to give up his plans for peace.

President Carter of the United States wanted peace, too. In September 1977, he invited the two leaders to meet with him at Camp David. Camp David is a presidential retreat spot in the mountains of Maryland, about an hour from Washington DC. Camp David was where FDR and Winston Churchill met to plan their war against Germany. And at Camp David, Menachem Begin, Anwar el-Sadat, and Jimmy Carter sat down to discuss peace in the Middle East.

The talks weren't easy. Sadat and Begin didn't even really want to talk to each other. Many hours passed with President Carter talking to one man, then going into another room to talk to the other, and then bringing back the second man's remarks to the first. For twelve days, Carter persuaded the two men to stay at Camp David, listening to each other's ideas. It was probably the most important act of Carter's presidency.

Finally the two leaders worked out an agreement known as the Camp David Accords. The Accords stated that, from now on, Israel and Egypt would try to act in harmony with each other. Israel agreed to withdraw from the Sinai Peninsula and give it back to Egypt; and Egypt promised to be at peace with Israel.

In 1978, Begin and Sadat won the Nobel Peace Prize for their work at Camp David. But not everyone was thrilled. Many Arab leaders were outraged because Sadat had signed a treaty with Israel—which meant that he was recognizing Israel's right to claim part of Palestine. Others thought that he should have asked for more land; why hadn't he insisted that Israel return all of the territories it had won in the Six-Day War?

On October 6, 1981, President Sadat was watching a parade in Cairo when a handful of men, armed with guns and grenades, ran out of the parade towards the place where the president sat. They were members of the Egyptian Islamic Jihad, a group that wanted Muslim rule in all of the Middle East. They threw grenades and fired at Sadat. He was killed at once.

But although Sadat died, the assassins did not succeed in their plans. After Sadat's death, his successor, Hosni Mubarak, honored the treaty with Israel.

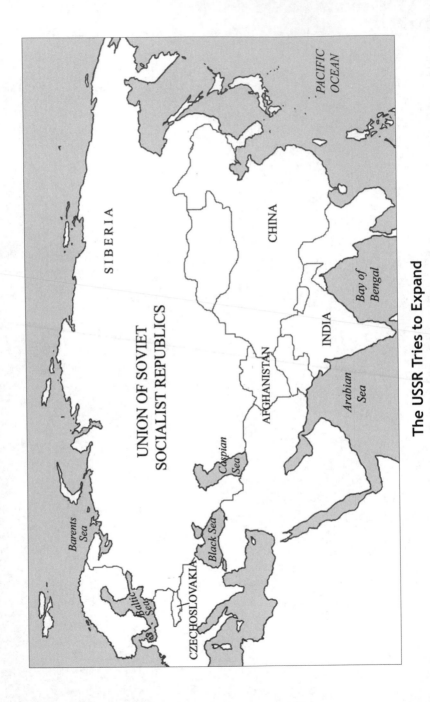

The USSR Tries to Expand

Chapter Thirty-Eight
Two Ways of Fighting

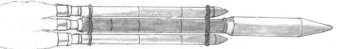

Soviet Invasions

Two years after the Cuban Missile Crisis, Nikita Khrushchev, the Russian leader who had threatened to "bury" the United States, had been forced out of his position. The new leader, or *premier*, of the Soviet Union was Leonid Brezhnev.

Brezhnev kept just as tight a watch on his people as Khrushchev had. The KGB, the Russian secret police, guarded the borders of the Soviet Union so that the Soviet people could not get out. Almost no one was given permission to leave the Soviet Union. Some Soviets did manage to escape and get to Western Europe or the United States. There, these "defectors" asked for permission to stay, called "asylum."

Why would people want to leave the Soviet Union? Because life under communism, for many people, was not as good as they had hoped it would be. It was difficult for people to buy the things that they needed; they had to stand in line for many hours for food, clothing, and other necessities. If you got married and wanted a house of your own, you couldn't just go and buy one. You had to ask the government to help you get a place to live. That might take a few weeks, or a few years.

When Brezhnev became premier, some parts of life in Russia improved. It became a little bit easier to get food, clothes, and work. More Russians were able to go to school. But like Stalin and Khrushchev, Brezhnev didn't let Russians speak their minds about communism. Anyone who said, or wrote, or published anything critical of the Soviet government might be arrested by the KGB.

The real name of the KGB was the *Komitet Gosudarstvennoy Bezopasnosti*, which was Russian for the "Committee for State Security." The KGB's job was to stamp out any opposition to Brezhnev's government. If you were arrested by the KGB, you might go to jail. Or you might be sent to Siberia, the huge, cold, northern wastelands of Russia, where in winter the temperature drops to more than a hundred degrees below zero—and in summer, never even gets above freezing. You might go to a labor camp—a concentration camp where you spend your days working at difficult tasks. You might even be executed.

The Soviet Union had not given up its hopes of spreading communism around more of the world. By 1968, Russia had drawn the small countries all around its western border into the Union of Soviet Socialist Republics, the USSR. Soviet soldiers had invaded Poland and Hungary and added those countries to the Soviet Empire as well.

In 1968 and 1979, the Soviet Union made two more bids to increase its territory. But the two invasions were very different.

The first bid took place during peace time. It was summer in Czechoslovakia, warm and peaceful: August 20, 1968. Many Czech citizens were on vacation. Some were on holiday in other parts of Europe. Others were lazing around, enjoying the cool of the mountains or simply the quiet of the summer night.

At eleven at night, when many Czechs were already asleep, Soviet tanks rolled across the Czechoslovakian border at four different places. Behind them marched thousands of soldiers. Jet fighters roared overhead; paratroopers jumped from airplanes and landed in the center of Czechoslovakian cities, armed and ready to fight. Prague, the capital of Czechoslovakia, was filled with Soviet soldiers in just hours. By the time the sun rose, the two most powerful men in the Czech government, Premier Cernik and Secretary Dubcek, had been arrested, put on a plane, and taken to Moscow.

The Czechs were so unprepared for the invasion that no one had any weapons. As tanks rolled in, young Czechs pulled up cobblestones from the streets to throw at the huge Soviet tanks. Others tried to set tanks on fire. In a desperate attempt to slow the invasion, Czechs with paint buckets and brushes painted over as many road signs as possible and relabelled them, so that almost all of the signs read, "To Moscow."

But the Czech resistance to the surprise invasion of their country failed. The Soviets forced both Premier Cernik and Secretary Dubcek to resign. In their place, the Soviets appointed a leader who would govern Czechoslovakia for the Soviet Union, and do as the Soviet government ordered.

The second bid for territory was much bloodier.

In 1979, the USSR invaded Afghanistan. Do you remember reading about Afghanistan? It lies south of Russia and north of India—and for a hundred years, Russian diplomats and Russian generals had tried to add Afghanistan to Russia's empire. Afghanistan survived, free of Russia, only because the British in India also wanted Afghanistan. Because both countries wanted it, neither country got it. Both Russia and Great Britain knew that claiming Afghanistan once and for all might start a war with the other powerful empire.

After World War I, Afghanistan had managed to become completely independent. Since 1919, Afghanistan had been ruled by Afghan kings who governed under a constitution.

But Afghanistan knew that its huge, powerful, neighbor to the north remained a threat. The Soviet Union wanted Afghanistan as much as the Russian Empire had. After World War II, the Soviets sent money to Afghanistan to help the country build schools, roads, and factories.

But so did the United States—hoping to keep Afghanistan from becoming a communist country. Once again, Afghanistan lay balanced between two huge and hostile countries.

In 1978, a rebel group sympathetic to Soviet ideas rose up and killed the king of Afghanistan. They took over the government and announced that Afghanistan would now be governed by ideas very much like communist ideas. Many Afghans saw this as the first step towards losing independence. They didn't want Soviet influence in their country! And they knew that communism's hatred of Christianity extended to all religious faiths. If Afghanistan slowly became communist, Islam—the religion followed by most Afghans—might be outlawed.

A civil war broke out between the new rebel government, and Afghans—who called themselves "righteous warriors"—Muslims fighting to preserve their faith. The Arabic word for them was *Mujaheddin*.

At this, the Soviet Union decided it was time to invade. Thousands of Soviet soldiers marched south, across the border, into Afghanistan.

But Afghanistan wasn't an easy country to conquer. The Mujaheddin knew how to stage guerilla warfare, attacking from the rough wild mountains of their country and then disappearing again. Instead of making Afghanistan part of the Soviet Union, the USSR had to treat it as an occupied country, filled with hostile rebels.

The takeover of Czechoslovakia had been simple and quick. But in Afghanistan, war between the Soviet army and the Mujaheddin would go on, for years and years.

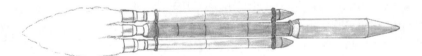

Terrorism

Just before sunrise, the city of Munich, West Germany lay almost asleep. The 1972 Olympics had been going on for ten days already. American swimmer Mark Spitz had won seven gold medals. Seventeen-year-old Olga Korbut, the Russian gymnast, had fallen off the uneven bars—but then had earned two golds and a silver in her other competitions. Now, on the morning of September 5, there were only four days of competition left.

Inside the Olympic Village, where the athletes lived for the two weeks of the Summer Games, a few athletes were up, stretching, eating, worrying about the day's events. Security guards around the outside of the Village saw a small group of men in sweatshirts, carrying gym bags, climbing over the fence. But for the last ten days, athletes who didn't want their coaches to know that they'd been out late at night had been climbing over the fence at all hours of the night. The guards ignored them.

Less than half an hour later, the sound of shots, fired from automatic weapons, broke the dawn quiet. The guards ran into the village, drawing their weapons. But it was too late. The men climbing the fence had broken into the rooms where the Israeli Olympic team slept. Two Israelis had already been killed. Nine more were being held hostage.

The men weren't athletes at all. They belonged to a group called Black September—a new kind of revolutionary group. These men were *terrorists*. Instead of fighting directly against their enemies, like most of the revolutionary groups we've read about, they fought against civilians. They carried out random, violent acts against people who weren't involved in governments or armies. Terrorists set out to get what they wanted, not by defeating an enemy army, but by creating so much terror among the people of a country that the people would force their government to do what the terrorists wanted.

Black September was a group that had broken off from yet another terrorist group, the Palestine Liberation Organization, or PLO. Both groups wanted the same thing: Israel should get out of the land that had once belonged to Arabs.

There were eight Black September terrorists in the Munich Olympic Village. They threatened to kill their nine Israeli hostages unless two hundred Arab guerilla fighters, taken prisoner by the Israeli army, were released from Israeli prison. But the Israeli government would not even listen to the terrorist demands. The German government, desperate to end this Olympic nightmare, asked other Arab countries if they would talk to the terrorists.

They all refused.

Terrorism in Europe and the Middle East

Finally, the Germans offered to fly the Black September terrorists and the Israeli hostages out of Munich, to anywhere the terrorists wanted. The terrorists agreed. But when they stepped out to walk to the airplane that the Germans had provided, German police opened fire on them.

By the time the shooting was over, five Black September terrorists and all nine Israeli hostages were dead.

Terrorism was in the world to stay. Over the next thirty years, different terrorists, hoping for different kinds of change, would launch many campaigns of terror.

The most well-known terrorist groups in the world came from the Middle East. In 1964, the Palestine Liberation Organization was formed in the Arab state of Jordan. At first, the PLO was a political organization. It wanted to form a new homeland for the Palestinian Arabs who had been forced to leave their homes in Palestine when their land was claimed by Israel.

After the Six-Day War, when Israel took land away from three other Arab nations, the PLO realized that Israel would never give up any land to form a country for Palestinian Arabs. Israel seemed much more likely to claim as much land as possible, and to keep it for Israelis.

So members of the PLO formed other groups—terrorist groups. Their goal was to attack crowds of Israelis; not just crowds of soldiers, but also civilian men, women, and children. If enough Israelis died, perhaps the Israeli people would force the Israeli government to give land to the Arabs.

These terrorist groups also wanted the rest of the world to know what they were doing. They hoped that other countries would recognize their demands and help pressure the Israelis into giving up land. So the terrorists didn't just make attacks. They called international newspapers and explained who had carried out the attack, and what they wanted—something called "claiming responsibility." If the terrorists could get their demands in newspapers and on television, people all over the world might see, understand, and sympathize.

The Black September attack at the Olympics was an attempt ᴑ get international attention. The Olympics was one of the most famous events in the world. Camera crews, newspaper reporters, TV anchors, and thousands of other news-gatherers attended the Games. When the Black September attack was broadcast on television, half a *billion* people watched it. Afterwards, a spokesman for the PLO-related group called the Popular Front for the Liberation of Palestine told a reporter, "The choice of the Olympics. ... was like painting the name of Palestine on a mountain that can be seen from the four corners of the earth."

Another group that gave birth to terrorism was the IRA— the Irish Republican Army. You may remember that the Irish Republican Army was organized by the Irish nationalist group Sinn Féin to fight for an Ireland independent of Great Britain.

When most of Ireland was made into the Republic of Ireland, Northern Ireland remained part of the British Empire. Hoping to reunite Northern Ireland with the rest of the Irish Republic, the IRA turned from being an army to being a terrorist group. Instead of attacking or challenging the British government alone, the IRA planted bombs in England to terrify the English into *wanting* to get rid of Northern Ireland.

By 1969, the IRA had begun to reject terrorism. But some of its members thought that terrorism was the only way to ever get Northern Ireland back for the Irish Republic. They split off and formed a new organization, called the Provisional Irish Republican Army. The PIRA attacked the English in Northern Ireland. But it also planted bombs in English pubs and businesses, along London streets, and in subways. The bombs killed innocent men, women, and teenagers.

In 1979, the PIRA managed to put a bomb on a fishing boat that belonged to Lord Mountbatten, the cousin of Queen Elizabeth. Lord Mountbatten was nearly eighty years old. He had fought in both World War I and World War II, and he had even been the Viceroy of India, back when India was still British. When the bomb blew up the boat, Lord Mountbatten, his grandson, and two other people were killed.

Irish and Palestinian terrorist groups planned many of the terrorist attacks of the 1970s. But every country in the world has had its terrorists. Before 1948, Jewish terrorists killed British civilians in Palestine, to try to scare Britain out of occupying Palestine. Terrorists in Spain have tried to get the Spanish government to declare a territory in the north, where a people called the Basque live, free of Spanish rule. Greek terrorists, Italian terrorists, Indian terrorists, and American terrorists have all killed and set off bombs to try to get their way.

Invasion of another country begins one kind of war. After invasions, armies and leaders clash with each other, trying to decide who will finally have power. But terrorism is another kind of war—one that changes forever the lives of those who have nothing to do with politics.

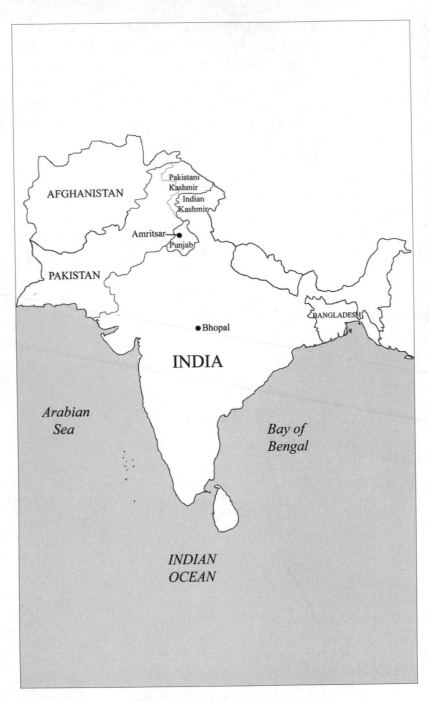

India Under Indira Gandhi

Chapter Thirty-Nine
The 1980s in the East and the Mideast

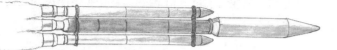

India After Partition

Once India and Pakistan had been partitioned, India held its first elections.

Gandhi—who had led the fight for freedom for so many years—was dead. In India's first elections, Gandhi's friend and ally Jawaharlal Nehru became the prime minister.

Under Nehru, India ripped off the very last rags of European power. France, which still held territories in India, agreed to give this land back. Portugal, which also claimed Indian land, refused. But in 1961, soldiers from the Indian army marched into the Portuguese territories and took them back by force. Not long after, Prime Minister Nehru died. He had served as the first prime minister of an independent India for thirteen years.

Two years later, Nehru's daughter, Indira, became prime minister in his place.

Indira had married a man whose last name was Gandhi, so she went by the name "Indira Gandhi." But she was no relation to Mohandas Gandhi. Gandhi is a common name in India, a little bit like "Baker" or "Johnson" in some parts of the United States. Between 1966 and 1980, Indira Gandhi battled to keep her position as the first female prime minister of India. In one of her addresses to the Indian government, she quoted a popular Indian song: "We are the women of India. Don't imagine that we are flower-maidens. No, we are the sparks in the fire!"

Indira Gandhi needed the energy of a spark to govern India. After independence, India went through difficult times. People lost their jobs; many were hungry. Indira tried to make

India's farms more productive. She convinced the United States to help India out with money and with exports of grain to feed the hungry of India.

In 1971, when she had been prime minister for five years, Indira had to deal with Pakistan.

Indira Gandhi, prime minister of India

At the time of partition, in 1947, Pakistan had been divided into two parts, East Pakistan and West Pakistan. But it was never a very good arrangement, because the two halves of this one country lay on either side of India—separated from each other by thousands of miles. The government offices and the army headquarters were in West Pakistan. As time went on, East Pakistan became poorer and poorer, while West Pakistan prospered.

In 1970, East Pakistan announced that it wanted to be free from West Pakistan.

West Pakistani troops marched east, ready to occupy East Pakistan. In the fighting that followed, millions of civilians from East Pakistan, afraid of being caught in the war, left their country and crossed over into India. West Pakistan was afraid that India might sympathize with these refugees, and join with East Pakistan against West Pakistan. So West Pakistani planes dropped bombs on eight Indian airports. Now Indian military planes couldn't use those airports to launch attacks on West Pakistan.

Instead of stopping India, the bombing made India angry—angry enough to join in the war. Under Indira Gandhi's direction, Indian troops allied themselves with East Pakistan and drove the West Pakistani soldiers out.

Now, East Pakistan could declare itself independent from West Pakistan. It changed its name to Bangladesh. West Pakistan became known, simply, as Pakistan.

The people of India gave Indira Gandhi most of the credit for success in the Pakistani war. She became more and more popular.

But then two catastrophes struck India.

The first came in 1984. For several years, Sikhs in India had been asking for their own independent country. Hindus governed India; the Muslims had gotten Pakistan. Now the Sikhs, who were neither Muslim nor Hindu, wanted to control *their* own part of India, an area called the Punjab.

Sikhs, who believed in one God and followed five holy rules of life, had once been warrior princes. For many centuries, they had served as the royal bodyguard for India's emperor because of their skill at fighting. When India became an independent country with a prime minister, Sikhs kept their traditional job. They now acted as the prime minister's bodyguard.

When the Sikhs in the Punjab began to ask for control of their own land, Indira agreed to make Punjabi, the language Sikhs spoke among themselves, the official language of the Punjab. But this made the Hindus who also lived in the Punjab angry. So Indira divided off a separate area in the Punjab, just for Hindus to live in.

This angered the Sikhs! They wanted all of the Punjab for themselves. They began to fight with the Hindus—not just in the Punjab, but all through India.

One group of warlike Sikhs went to the Golden Temple, in the holy city of Amritsar, and made it their headquarters. By tradition, the Golden Temple was off limits to Indian police because it was a religious shrine. The Sikhs who were using the Golden Temple as their headquarters started to make terrorist attacks on Indians, and then retreated to the Golden Temple—sure that the police would not come after them.

Indira ordered the Golden Temple invaded. On June 5, 1984, Indian army soldiers stormed into the Golden Temple to fight against the terrorists hiding there. Nearly a thousand Sikhs were killed.

Indira's advisors suggested that she might want to get rid of her Sikh bodyguard, since they might be angry with her over her treatment of other Sikhs. Indira refused. She insisted that her bodyguard was trustworthy.

She was wrong. On October 31, 1984, two of the Sikh guards killed the prime minister as they walked with her to her office.

A month later, a second catastrophe hit the country.

An American company called the Union Carbide Corporation had built a factory in the center of India, at a city called Bhopal. At its factory, Union Carbide made pesticides—chemicals to kill insects on crops and grasses. Just after midnight on December 3, 1984, poisonous gases began to leak out of the storage tanks at the Union Carbide factory.

No one in Bhopal knew what was happening. At first, some people thought the Sikhs were to blame again!

But what was to blame was a faulty tank at Union Carbide. Twenty-seven tons of a poison called *methyl isocyanate* escaped from the tank. According to Union Carbide, at least three thousand people died that night from the poisonous gases. People from Bhopal say that the number was much greater—that as many as fifteen thousand died.

No one knows exactly how many people died later, from sicknesses caused by the gasses. But at least another 150 thousand people, and maybe over half a million, were made horribly sick by the gases. Thousands never recovered. The Bhopal gas leak was the worst "industrial disaster" (a disaster caused by factories or manufacturing) in all of history, before or since. Even now, over twenty years later, the ground and water at Bhopal are still full of poison. Union Carbide never cleaned the mess up.

Indian investigators blamed the gas leak on sloppy safety procedures, and said that Union Carbide had not made sure that the storage tanks were secure because it would have cost too much money. None of the warning systems or safety systems at the plant were actually working at the time of the leak! Union Carbide, which is now part of an even bigger American company called Dow Chemical, insisted (and still insists) that the Bhopal tragedy had been caused by sabotage. Someone had deliberately arranged for the gas leak.

The highest court of Bhopal demanded that the American CEO come to Bhopal and take part in a court hearing. He refused. He is still considered a fugitive by Indian law, even today. And even today, twenty years later, many groups of protestors still campaign for justice for Bhopal.

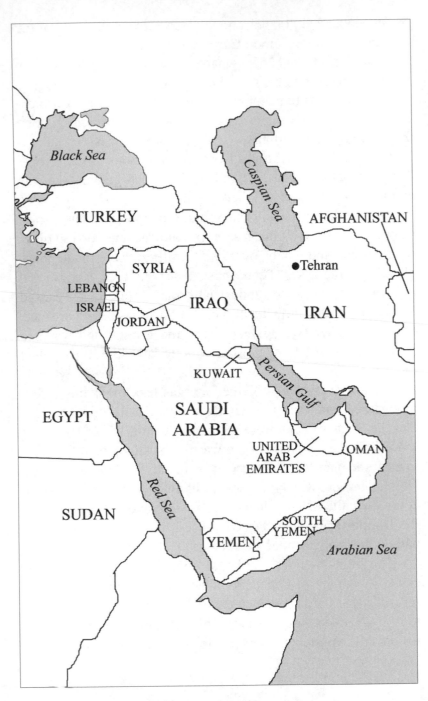

Iran and Iraq

Iran and Iraq

We've read about Israel and Egypt, their wars, and their attempts at peace. Now we come to two other Middle Eastern countries that were often at odds with each other: Iran and Iraq.

In Chapter Eighteen, we read about the country of Persia, which fell under Russian control before World War I. In the twentieth century, Persia became widely known by its other name: Iran.

After the two World Wars, Iran had become an independent country, ruled by a shah (king) along with the help of an elected assembly, the Majles, and a prime minister. In 1953, the shah of Iran was named Mohammad Reza Shah Pahlavi. His prime minister was also named Mohammad—Mohammad Mosaddeq.

Mohammad Mosaddeq was a strange but powerful man. Sometimes he wore pajamas to official state gatherings. He tended to burst into tears, in public, for no apparent reason. Once, when he had to give a speech to the Majles, he ordered his bed carried into the room where the Majles met, and gave his speech lying down.

Mosaddeq thought that Iranians, not foreigners (like the Anglo-Persian Oil Company, owned by the British) should control the oil that was being pumped out of Iran's ground. The Majles agreed. So Mosaddeq seized control of the oil fields in Iran.

The British, who had spent a lot of money pumping this oil out, protested—but could not change Mosaddeq's mind. So the British refused to buy any oil from Iran. At the same time, other countries started pumping more oil than ever. All of a sudden, there was too much oil in the Middle East, and too few buyers in the rest of the world. Since Iran couldn't sell its oil to Great Britain, it was having trouble selling oil at all. One of Iran's biggest sources of wealth was no longer producing any money for the country.

As you can imagine, this made Mosaddeq very unpopular. The shah tried to dismiss Mosaddeq as prime minister. Mosaddeq refused to go! His supporters rioted in the streets—until the shah, afraid for his safety, fled from the city.

Mosaddeq had held onto his power. But not for long.

Together, the United States and Great Britain plotted to get rid of Mosaddeq and bring the shah back to Iran. Mohammad Reza Shah Pahlavi was willing to keep on good terms with Great Britain and the U.S. He hadn't wanted to take the oil industry away from the British. Mosaddeq, on the other hand, was too independent, and too determined to keep Iran's oil under the control of Iran. (The United States also suspected that Mosaddeq might be a little too friendly with the Soviet Union, which was another good reason to get rid of him.)

The plan to get rid of Mosaddeq was called "Operation Ajax." The Americans and British trained Iranian soldiers to take over the government and sent these soldiers into Iran along with American and British "helpers." Mosaddeq was arrested, accused of treason, and put into jail. The shah returned triumphantly to the capital city of Tehran, with American and British forces ready to put down any opposition to him. (You might wonder what happened to the American worry about interfering in the affairs of other countries!)

Although the shah had the power of two large countries behind him, he knew that his rule over Iran was shaky. Many Iranians disliked the shah because he was so rich. During the 1960s, the shah kept on getting richer and richer from the oil that Iran sold to the world, while the common people of Iran didn't prosper all that much. And the conservative Muslims of Iran hoped that the shah would pass strict laws, making Muslim regulations against drinking and gambling part of Iran's legal code.

Instead, the shah worked on making Iran more modern—more "Western." He gave women in Iran the right to vote. He tried to improve schools and give more Iranians the chance to get an education. Instead of making religious laws, the shah tried to make religion *less* powerful in Iran. He changed Iran's calendar, so that it no longer followed the traditional Muslim calendar, and told religious newspapers and magazines to stop criticizing the government.

All of these changes became known as the "White Revolution." The White Revolution was supposed to make Iran stronger—but it made the shah even less popular with the religious Muslims of Iran. The shah was also growing unpopular with some of the educated men and women of Iran, because of his tyrannous power. His secret police, called the SAVAK, was infamous for its cruelty. SAVAK members had complete power to arrest, torture, and kill anyone who opposed the shah. Even Iranians who were caught reading forbidden books were likely to be tortured and imprisoned.

Those forbidden books included writings authored by Ruhollah Khomeini. He was an *ayatollah*, an Islamic religious leader. Ayatollah Khomeini's followers hated the shah's White Revolution because it went against Muslim religious practices. They believed that Khomeini could make Iran into a truly Muslim country—a country free of corrupt Western ideas and foreign influences.

The shah had always been afraid of Khomeini's power to gather loyal disciples around him. As a matter of fact, he had ordered Khomeini arrested and exiled several years before. Khomeini had gone to the neighboring country of Iraq—until the leader of Iraq, Saddam Hussein, also told him to leave. So Khomeini went to France. There, he made speeches onto tapes and sent them into Iran, encouraging Iranians to reject the shah's anti-Muslim White Revolution.

By 1978, Khomeini had managed to convince Iranians to riot against the shah. Mohammad Reza Shah Pahlavi tried to send his soldiers to put down the riots, but it was too late.

Millions of people took to the streets, shouting for the shah to leave. In January of 1979, the shah fled his country and went to Panama. The "Iranian Revolution" had driven out Iran's shah.

Ayatollah Khomeini arrived in Iran two weeks later. His followers welcomed him. Now, they hoped, Iran would become a truly Muslim country. Before too long, Khomeini had managed to get his followers to declare him leader of Iran—for life. He set about making Iran into a *theocracy*, a state ruled according to strict religious law. Women could no longer hold certain jobs reserved for men. Everyone had to dress according to Muslim law—covering their ankles and elbows. Women also had to cover their hair whenever they went outside. Drinking alcohol and gambling were illegal throughout Iran.

As soon as he took power, Khomeini had to fight a war—against his neighbor, the country of Iraq.

Until 1919, there was no country called Iraq. As part of the Peace of Versailles, the Allied nations created Iraq on the land that had been taken away from the Ottoman Turks. Great Britain was given the right to control Iraq until it was able to govern itself.

Britain chose a king for Iraq. This king and his relatives ruled the new country until the 1950s—when a group of revolutionaries decided that the time had come for Iraq to become a republic. They led a revolt, murdered the king of Iraq, and announced that Iraq would now be a republic. In 1963, the Iraqi republic was taken over by a political party called the Ba'th Party, which wanted all Arab countries to rule themselves without any help from the West. One of the Ba'th Party members was a young man named Saddam Hussein.

For many years, Iran and Iraq had argued over the control of a river called the Shatt Al-Arab, or the "Stream of the Arabs." The Shatt Al-Arab is formed by the meeting place of the Tigris and the Euphrates River. Boats sailing on the Shatt can go straight into the Persian Gulf.

Both Iran and Iraq wanted to use the Shatt. In 1975, the shah of Iran had signed a treaty with Saddam Hussein—who had now been elected vice president of Iraq. The treaty agreed that the Shatt Al-Arab would be controlled by Iran, not by Iraq.

By the time that the shah fled from Iran and Ayatollah Khomeini took over, Saddam Hussein had become president of Iraq. When Hussein saw how much chaos Iran was in, he thought that Iraq might be able to reclaim control over the Shatt.

On September 22, 1980, Iraq invaded Iran. The Iraqis hoped for a short war. Their army had almost two hundred thousand soldiers in it. They were well armed with Soviet weapons and tanks, and with guns from China, Germany, France, and England. Even the United States had agreed to support Iraq's attack against Iran and Khomeini. (The United States still wanted the shah back in Iran!)

Even though the Iranians were taken by surprise, they fought back—ferociously! Instead of ending quickly, the Iran-Iraq war dragged on for eight years. Saddam Hussein's planes bombed Iran's oil wells. Khomeini's planes bombed *Iraq's* oil wells. No one knows for sure, but perhaps as many as one and a half million people died during the eight years of fighting. And the oil wells and pipelines in both countries were so badly damaged that it took years after the war ended to rebuild them.

In 1988, Iran and Iraq agreed to stop fighting. Neither country had won. And who now controlled the Shatt Al-Arab?

The Iranians controlled it—just as they had in 1975, when the treaty was signed, and before any of the fighting began.

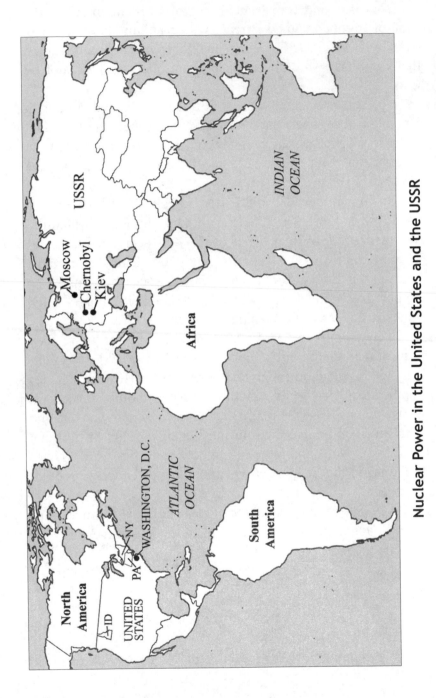

Nuclear Power in the United States and the USSR

Chapter Forty
The 1980s in the USSR

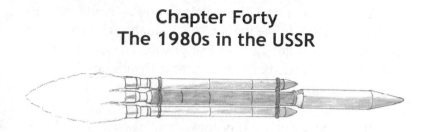

Chernobyl and Nuclear Power

On April 26, 1986, at 1:30 in the morning, an explosion shook the Russian town of Chernobyl, just eighty miles north of the city of Kiev. A power plant had exploded. The fireball from the explosion killed thirty people.

This might not seem like such a bad accident. But in fact, one hundred and thirty-five thousand people were in danger as soon as the explosion occurred. Another four hundred thousand were told that the accident might damage their health, permanently. The Chernobyl power plant was a nuclear plant—and the explosion in its fourth reactor was the worst nuclear disaster in history.

To understand the Chernobyl disaster, we need to go all the way back to the 1940s and the American scientists who worked so hard to make an atomic bomb before Germany could build one. These scientists had discovered that a tremendous amount of energy could be released when an atom was split apart. At first, all of the research that the Americans (and the Soviets) did on *atomic fission* (splitting atoms to produce energy) was intended to make better weapons. Scientists wanted to make atomic bombs and nuclear missiles more powerful, and to build military submarines that would run on nuclear power.

But then scientists began to think about the other ways nuclear power could be used.

Could nuclear power, for instance, produce electricity? Could cars, lights, refrigerators, and televisions be run by nuclear power? If so, countries that could use nuclear power wouldn't have to rely quite so much on gasoline and oil.

Scientists discovered that nuclear power *could* produce electricity. In 1951, in the town of Arco, Idaho, scientists managed to run a generator with nuclear power. The generator produced enough electricity to light up four light bulbs!

Scientists and government officials were very excited about those four light bulbs. They began to dream that nuclear power might be a wonderfully inexpensive source of electricity—and they began to work on building larger and better *reactors* (large, tube-like devices where atoms were split to produce energy).

Three years later, in 1954, the first commercial nuclear power plant (a power plant that would produce electricity, using nuclear power, and then sell the electricity) opened. The plant didn't actually produce power for three more years, until December 1957. When it did, the nuclear power helped produce electricity for the city of Pittsburgh.

And in 1955, Arco, Idaho—the hometown of those first four light bulbs—became the very first town to be powered *entirely* by nuclear power.

But nuclear power was very controversial. Some scientists and government officials thought it was a marvelous discovery. Nuclear power is cheap; and since, one day, people will use up all the oil in the ground, nuclear power seemed like a good alternative.

Others could not imagine that the splitting of atoms would ever produce anything good. Nuclear experiments had produced the atomic bomb, the most destructive weapon in history. How could such devastating power be controlled?

The president of the United States, Dwight Eisenhower, knew that Americans were worried about scientific experiments with atomic power. In December 1953, he gave a speech called "Atoms for Peace." He wanted to assure his listeners that atomic energy was good for much more than the making of bombs. He had decided to give the speech at the United Nations headquarters in New York, where people from all over the world could hear it. He was so concerned that the speech be exactly right that he kept working on it until the very last minute—even on the airplane ride to New York. As he made changes on each page, his secretary retyped his talk. But she didn't have enough time to finish typing, so President Eisenhower ordered his pilot to stay in the air, flying in circles, for an extra thirty minutes. That gave his secretary just enough time to finish typing.

When the plane landed, Eisenhower rushed to the UN to give the speech. Thirty-five hundred people had come to hear him. He began by reminding the audience how very dangerous nuclear weapons could be. But, he said, atomic energy could be used to improve medicine and farming. It could supply electricity to people in poor countries, where oil and coal were scarce.

Eisenhower's speech told all the good things that could happen if nuclear power plants were built. But nuclear power does have one big danger, even if it isn't being made into bombs. It produces *radioactivity*.

Radioactivity changes the way that atoms work, so that they no longer behave normally. A very small bit of radioactivity isn't dangerous. If you've ever had an x-ray, you'll remember that, before the doctors put you under the x-ray machine, they covered your body with heavy lead pads. This is because x-ray machines, too, are slightly radioactive—and the lead pads protect you. The lead pads ensure that you will only be exposed to a tiny amount of radioactivity, which won't hurt you at all.

But people who are very close to a large atomic explosion are soaked in radioactivity. Their bodies no longer work properly. In Hiroshima and Nagasaki, many people who weren't killed by the atomic explosions died several years later. The radioactivity from the explosions had caused them to get cancer and other diseases.

People worried that nuclear power plants might also leak radioactivity. They worried that working at these plants, or living near them, would make people sick. When nuclear power plants work properly, they are safe and effective.

But when accidents do happen, nuclear plants can be dangerous.

On March 28, 1979, an accident happened at the nuclear power plant Three Mile Island, in Pennsylvania. Very early in the morning, the plant's equipment began to fail. A pump that carried coolant, to keep the reactors from getting too hot, stopped working.

Over the next five hours, more parts of the reactors stopped working properly. Scientists realized that the plant was beginning to give off radioactive gases. At 9:15 a.m., officials called the White House to tell the president that Three Mile Island was in trouble. By 11 a.m., all the plant's workers had been told to leave Three Mile Island to get away from the radioactivity.

Two days later, scientists discovered that more radiation was coming from another part of the plant. The governor of Pennsylvania ordered all small children and pregnant women within five miles of the plant to leave—in case the radiation made them sick.

No one knew exactly how much radioactivity Three Mile Island had produced. Finally, scientists were able to figure out that most people nearby were only exposed to a tiny amount of radiation; one "millirem," less than what a patient would get during an X-ray. No one died or got sick from the accident at Three Mile Island.

But the accident frightened and angered the people nearby—and people who lived near other nuclear plants too. They were worried because the plant operators hadn't been able to figure out how to stop the radiation from escaping. They were frightened because it had taken scientists so long to measure the radiation that escaped. No one had been hurt this time—but what if a larger accident happened?

That larger accident happened at Chernobyl. The Russian power plant didn't just leak a little bit. One of its four reactors, where atoms were split, blew up—and radioactive gases spewed out of the explosion.

The gases drifted all over the Russian countryside. This time, the radiation was so heavy that six hundred thousand people were exposed to dangerous levels of radioactivity. They could develop cancer years and years later, because of the radiation. Animals nearby gave birth to deformed offspring. A Moscow reporter described one: "I was shown a suckling pig whose head looked like that of a frog. Instead of eyes there were large tissue growths, with no cornea or pupil. These animals usually die soon after birth, but this one survived."

People and animals near Chernobyl weren't the only ones in danger. Wind blew radioactive particles all over Europe. As far away as Poland, milk was tainted by the radiation, and no one was allowed to drink it. As far away as Sweden, reindeer and sheep were made sick by the radiation. "For the first time," the leader of the Soviet Union said, "we confront the real force of nuclear energy, out of control."

The land around the Chernobyl reactor that exploded is still radioactive. For thousands of years, it will be unsafe for anyone to use. Scientists decided to put a huge metal and concrete shell down over the ruined reactor, so that the radioactivity would be locked in forever.

The Chernobyl accident didn't stop the use of nuclear power. All over the world, nuclear power plants still produce electricity. Today, almost one-fifth of the world's electricity comes from nuclear energy. Meanwhile, scientists try to make sure that the power plants in their countries are safe, and that an accident like Chernobyl never happens again.

The End of the Cold War

The Cold War between America and the Soviet Union affected almost everything that both countries did, in the years following World War II. It shaped events from the Space Race to the Vietnam War.

Finally, in the 1980s, the Cold War was coming to an end. Politicians said that the relationship between the U.S. and the USSR was finally "thawing."

The two central characters in this story are the president of the United States during the 1980s, Ronald Reagan, and the general secretary of the Communist Party, Mikhail Gorbachev. Both men had odd quirks. Reagan had a strange nickname: "the Gipper." Before he became president, Reagan had been a Hollywood actor. One of his most well-known roles was a football hero named George Gipp. Even after he became president, Reagan was still called the Gipper after this movie character.

Gorbachev didn't have a nickname; he had a strange-looking birthmark, a large purple splotch right across his bald head. In newspaper cartoons from the 1980s, Gorbachev always looks as though someone has been painting on the top of his head!

These two men are remembered for their work in "melting" the Cold War.

The thaw began in Russia. In 1985, Gorbachev, who had become the leader of the Soviet Union, introduced a plan called *perestroika*. This is Russian for "economic restructuring"—in simpler words, changing the way that the government runs the banks and owns land. Since the Russian Revolution, most of the businesses and banks in the Soviet Union were owned, run, and controlled by the government. Under perestroika, ordinary people were allowed to have more control of Russian businesses—and even to own their own businesses once more.

Then, Gorbachev introduced a second plan, called *glasnost*, which is Russian for "openness." Under glasnost, people in the Soviet Union were given greater freedom of speech. Glasnost meant that it would no longer be a crime for newspapers to publish criticism of the Soviet government.

President Reagan believed that, since the Soviet Union was changing, perhaps America could become the USSR's friend rather than its enemy. But the two countries had been enemies for more than forty years. Both countries still had nuclear weapons, ready to launch at each other. It was difficult to believe that the threat of war between American and the Soviets could ever completely go away.

President Reagan believed that the key to ending—and winning—the Cold War lay in the way that both countries would deal with their weapons.

Reagan and Gorbachev wanted to avoid another World War. Atomic weapons had gotten even more powerful and more dangerous since the first generation of atomic bombs, the bombs America dropped on Japan at the end of World War II. However, both countries were too scared of each other to simply get rid of all their weapons. Reagan could just imagine: The Soviet Union might promise to destroy all of its weapons, as long as America would do the same. The U.S. would get rid of its atomic bombs. And then it might discover that the USSR had lied—and had kept some weapons back. Then the U.S. would be helpless.

The Americans and the Soviets were like two boys with water pistols facing each other. Neither one wants to get drenched with water. But both are sure that, if he puts *his* down first, the other guy will pull the trigger.

Reagan decided to solve this problem, not by getting rid of all of America's atomic bombs—but by inventing new, bigger, more powerful weapons. He believed that, if the Soviet Union knew America had weapons stronger than anything belonging to the Soviets, the Soviets would be too afraid to attack. This strategy was called "Peace Through Strength." America could ensure peace by being stronger than any other country.

And at the same time that Reagan was building up America's deadliest weapons so that America could achieve "Peace Through Strength," Reagan and Gorbachev were also entering into an agreement to reduce other kinds of weapons. This agreement was called the Intermediate-Range Nuclear Forces Treaty, or the INF Treaty for short. The two leaders signed this treaty on December 8, 1987. The treaty declared that both countries would get rid of weapons that were "short-range"— weapons that could travel only three hundred to thirty-four hundred miles. Reagan's new "Peace Through Strength" weapons didn't count, because they were designed to travel longer distances.

Although this may seem like a strange way to bring peace, it seemed to work. America still had strong weapons that it could use for self-defense—but it had also promised not to use other weapons to attack Russia. Glasnost, perestroika, and the INF Treaty spelled the end of the Cold War.

The Russian people celebrated. They wrote plays, poems, novels, and songs about the end of the Cold War. One Russian singer named Boris Grebenshikov wrote a song called "Radio Silence" about glasnost. In the song, he tries to describe how wonderful it is for Russians to be able to tell the truth about communism, and to speak freely to people around the world:

> It's strange I don't feel like I'm a stranger
> I feel like I belong here
> I feel like I've been waiting for a long time
> And now I can tell you some stories.

Americans sang about the end of the Cold War, too. In 1987, an American singer named Billy Joel visited the Soviet Union and gave concerts in Leningrad and Moscow. When he came back from his tour, he wrote a song called "Leningrad." The song ends:

> We never knew what friends we had
> Until we came to Leningrad.

After forty years of Cold War, the hatred between Americans and Russians had finally begun to change into friendship.

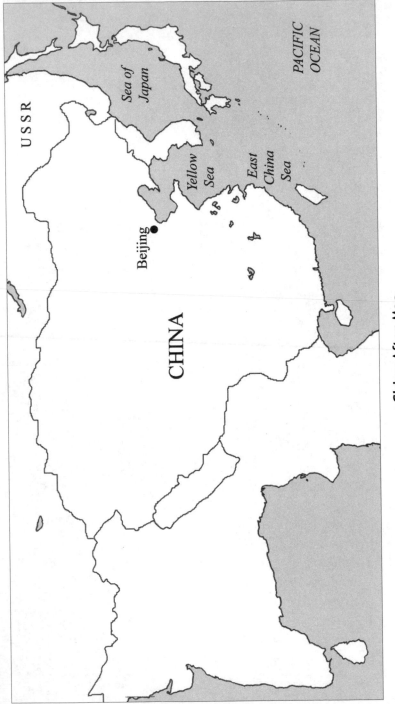

China After Mao

Chapter Forty-One
Communism Crumbles—but Survives

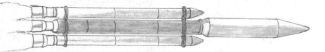

Democracy in China?

When we were last in China, the communist government of Chairman Mao was in power. Under communist rule, China expanded its territory. It took the island of Hainan Dao, south of the mainland, and then invaded and claimed the western nation of Tibet as its own.

Mao intended to make China the largest, most powerful, and wealthiest nation in the world. He thought that the best way to do this was to copy the Soviet Union. So Mao's government told farmers that they had to combine their farms into collectives, just as the Soviets had. These collectives were huge. Some had twenty-five thousand people in them, all farming one huge piece of land! No one in the collectives owned their own land, their own homes, their own animals, or even their own tools. It all belonged to the collective. And like the Soviet government, Mao's government also forced many of the peasants to stop farming and instead work at making steel.

As in Russia, this was disastrous. Harvests plummeted. Grain grew scarce. The collectives didn't yield as much food as the individual farms had, because the farmers hated working on land that didn't belong to them. The peasants now working in the steel mills weren't raising any food at all—and they had so little experience making steel that it was very poor quality. A famine swept over China. Thirty million people died.

The other members of the Chinese Communist Party decided that it was time for Mao to share some of his power. His attempt to make China a world power had failed. Mao had "lost face," and his time as leader of China seemed doomed to end soon. The general secretary of the CCP, a little man (less than five feet tall!) named Deng Xiaoping, seemed like a good choice to replace Mao.

Deng and the other CCP leaders may have thought that it was time for Mao to fade from the political scene, but Mao had a plan. He and his supporters began to accuse those who opposed him of being against communism, and of wanting to return China to the days of emperors. They started a rumor that Mao's opponents were planning to assassinate him. Mao used this rumor as an excuse to bring part of the Chinese army into Beijing to protect him. The part that he brought had over thirty thousand soldiers in it. That was the biggest bodyguard in history!

Now Mao was safe from arrest or assassination—and he had control of a large army. Mao's supporters wrote and preached that the Chinese must stay loyal to Mao. Loyalty to Mao meant loyalty to the Chinese Communist Party. China had been through a difficult time. But if the Chinese would join with Mao and support his policies, China would enter into a new time—a revolutionary and wonderful time.

This *propaganda* (words meant to persuade people of something that isn't necessarily true) worked. Huge numbers of Chinese citizens agreed, and supported Mao against his opponents. With the might of the army behind him, Mao had many of his enemies arrested and sentenced to death. Deng Xiaoping was spared death because he was an old friend of Mao's. But Mao had him marched through the streets with a dunce cap on his head. After that, Deng was sent to work in a factory, sandpapering the edges of unfinished screws.

The time between 1966 and Mao's death in 1976 became known as the Cultural Revolution. Every part of Chinese culture—newspapers, public gatherings, theaters, operas, and novels—had to praise Mao and Mao's policies. Children were encouraged to join the "Red Guard," a youth military that swore loyalty to Mao. Every house in China had a picture of Mao in it. (It was dangerous not to!)

After Mao died in 1976, Deng Xiaoping left his screw-factory and came back to Beijing. He claimed his old position as general secretary of the Communist Party, and—eventually—leader of China. Deng Xiaoping could finally make a few much-needed changes in China. Deng returned some of the farms to their owners. He let the factories give up making bad steel. He told peasants that, if they raised extra food, they could sell it and make a profit, instead of giving it to the government.

Under Deng, China grew more prosperous. People had more to eat, better clothes to wear, and a chance of earning enough money to live well.

But one thing in China didn't change. The Chinese were still not allowed to express their ideas openly—either in print or in speech.

The Chinese people began to protest this. They wanted not only freedom of speech, but also the right to take part in China's government. Deng's China was more prosperous than Mao's, but it was still run by a very small number of people—and many of those powerful people were corrupt, giving favors to those they liked and ignoring those they didn't.

The biggest protest began to gather itself on April 15th, 1989. Thousands of students joined together in Tiananmen Square, in Beijing. They demanded that the leadership of China change. They wanted to be given a chance to take part in China's government. They wanted something closer to democracy, where they could elect their own leaders.

Communist officials went to the square to talk to them and to ask them to go home. But the students were convinced that, if they left, China would simply stay the same. Over six weeks, over one hundred and fifty thousand students came to Tiananmen Square.

It became clear that the students would not leave Tiananmen Square unless China granted them democracy—or drove them away. But the Communist Party, like the monarchs of long ago, weren't willing to give up power simply because the people asked for it.

They chose to use force instead.

On June 2, 1989, the Chinese army warned the crowd to disperse. No one moved. The next day, June 3, tanks and soldiers closed in on the square. Tear gas grenades were thrown into the crowds of students. But the students refused to move. As a matter of fact, people from around the square who saw what was happening ran to join them.

So on June 4, the Chinese army attacked before the protest could spread over the entire city. They fired machine guns at the unarmed students. When the students linked their arms together and turned to face the army, the soldiers drove tanks towards them.

Over a thousand protestors were killed in the square. In the streets around the square, soldiers killed thousands more. "The army used tanks and machine guns on anyone who even threw a rock or shouted a slogan," one student who survived the attack wrote, after escaping. "We kept telling the crowds that ours was a peaceful demonstration.... We felt that the patriotic democratic movement... would fail if the students tried arming themselves."

Now that you have read the history of the twentieth century, you know that armies have often attacked their own people. But the June 4 Massacre in Tiananmen Square was different— because it took place on television. The Chinese army tried to put up canvas tents around the bodies of students, and wash the blood off Tiananmen Square. But it was too late. All over the world, millions of people had already watched in horror as the Chinese army shot at unarmed protestors. In one of the most famous pictures from that day, a single weaponless man stood in the middle of a street, shouting at tanks as they bore down on him. The tanks stopped—but the man was arrested and taken away.

The rest of the world protested the violence of the June 4 Massacre. But when it was over, the Communist Party still controlled China.

Communism Crumbles

The Chinese Communist Party was holding onto China. But the Communist Party in the Soviet Union was beginning to change. Glasnost and perestroika were causing ripples that ran through all of the other communist countries in Eastern Europe.

The most dramatic ripples were felt in Germany.

You'll remember that after World War II, Germany was divided into two countries. West Germany had a democratic government, and East Germany had a communist government.

Life in East Germany was hard. Under communism, people suffered. There were few jobs and not enough food. And the East Germans couldn't leave their country and go west, because a wall trapped them in their half of the country.

In the years that Germany was divided, about ten thousand East Germans tried to escape to West Germany. Some of them made it. Two families floated over the wall in a hot air balloon! In 1964, one group of Berliners dug a 164-foot tunnel from a bakery in West Berlin to an outhouse in East Berlin. The digging took six months, but hundreds of people crossed through it to freedom before East German officials found out about the tunnel and shut it down.

In September 1989, East Germans began to take glasnost (freedom of speech) seriously. They began to hold large, loud protests and rallies. They insisted that the communist government of East Germany allow them to travel—to West Germany, or to anywhere else in the world.

After a month of protests, the East German government could no longer resist. On November 9, 1989, the gates in the

Germany Reunited

Berlin Wall were thrown open. East Germans poured through them. For the first time in many years, Germans could travel freely between the two Germanies.

Germans began to tear at the wall. They hammered at it, broke it down with shovels and tools and iron bars, and took chunks of it away. A man named Andreas Ramos who went to the wall that weekend wrote,

> "The East German border was always a serious place. Armed guards kept you in your car, watching for attempts at escapes. Tonight was a different country. Over 20,000 East and West Germans were gathered there in a huge party. ... Everyone had their radios on and everywhere was music. People had climbed up into trees, signs, buildings, everything, to wave and shout. ... On both sides the guard towers were empty and the barbed wire was shoved aside in great piles. ... From the East German side we could hear the sound of heavy machines. With a giant drill, they were punching holes in the wall. Every time a drill poked through, everyone cheered. ... Many were using hammers to chip away at the wall. There were countless holes. At one place, a crowd of East German soldiers looked through a narrow hole. We reached through and shook hands."

By November 11, it was clear that more than the Wall was coming down. The communist rule over East Germany was falling too. In 1990, East and West Germany were reunited into one country.

In the USSR, more changes were on the way. Gorbachev was trying to change his country.

Remember, the USSR was made up of Russia plus a number of smaller communist countries. Gorbachev himself was the leader of the whole USSR. A Russian leader named Boris Yeltsin, thought that Gorbachev's reforms were happening too slowly. He believed that it was time to move towards a democracy much more quickly—and he had plenty of followers.

But another group of powerful communist leaders were resisting all of Gorbachev's changes. They didn't want the Soviet Union to become more open, or more free.

In August 1991, eight of these determined communists planned a takeover of the Soviet Union. They surrounded Gorbachev's house, locked his doors, and cut his telephone lines so that he couldn't contact anyone on the outside. Then they ordered him to resign. Gorbachev refused. So the eight conspirators announced, in public, that he was too sick to run the country, and that one of them would begin to act as Soviet leader in Gorbachev's place.

When Boris Yeltsin heard what was happening, he called to all of his followers in Russia to gather behind him. Not only did thousands of Russians who wanted democracy come to join Yeltsin—so did the tanks and soldiers that the conspirators sent to arrest Yeltsin and get him out of the way! None of the army would follow the conspirators.

The Communist Party had lost its power to control the Russian people. And Russia was the largest country in the USSR.

The conspirators gave up. One of them killed himself! Gorbachev, once he had gotten out of his house, joined with Boris Yeltsin to decide what to do next. He banned all Communist Party meetings, and ordered every Communist Party office in the country locked up. Over the next few months, the countries that had been brought into the Soviet Union declared their independence one by one: Ukraine, Lithuania, Latvia, Armenia, and all of the rest. When it was over, Gorbachev resigned. He had no more Soviet Union to govern! Boris Yeltsin would serve as the head of the ancient country of Russia—no longer communist, and no longer part of the USSR.

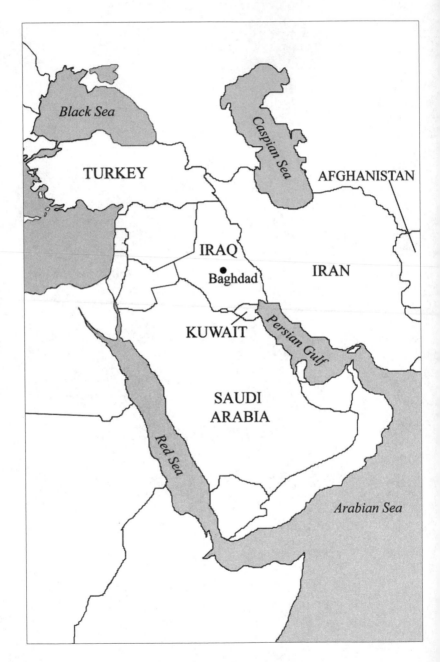

War in Kuwait

Chapter Forty-Two
The End of the Twentieth Century

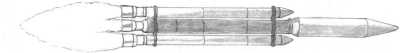

The First Persian Gulf War

In 1991, America went to war with Iraq, in a war we now call the First Persian Gulf War. That war might not have happened if the Iran-Iraq War (the pointless war fought between 1980-1988) had not occurred.

Here's how the story unfolded. During the war with Iran, Iraq borrowed money from several different countries so that it could buy weapons and pay its soldiers. After the Iran-Iraq war ended, Iraq was in debt to these countries—and didn't have extra money to pay off those debts.

One of the countries that had lent money to Iraq was a little country called Kuwait. Kuwait, which lies between Iraq and Saudi Arabia, looks like a triangle with two wobbly edges. The long base of the triangle lies along the Persian Gulf.

Although Kuwait is a little country, just a little bit smaller than the state of New Jersey, it is a rich one—because one-tenth of all the known oil in the world lies beneath its desert sands. Kuwaiti citizens get free education, free care from doctors and hospitals, and don't pay any income tax.

In August 1990, Iraqi soldiers obeyed Saddam Hussein's orders to march into Kuwait and seize it. Hussein had several reasons for invading Kuwait. For one thing, Kuwait had insisted that Iraq pay its war debts—and Hussein couldn't afford to. Hussein also claimed that Kuwait was taking oil from a patch of land on the Iraq-Kuwait border. He said that half of that oil should belong to Iraq! Furthermore, Hussein said that Kuwait was producing more oil than OPEC allowed, and that this was making the price of oil too low, which was like taking money away from the other countries that produced oil. And finally, Hussein said, Kuwait was actually part of Iraq anyway, and he was just reclaiming what belonged to him.

Those are a lot of different reasons.

Many of the soldiers marching into Kuwait had also fought in the Iran-Iraq war. They were experienced and tough, and Iraq had many more soldiers than Kuwait. They took over the small country easily. Less than a day after the Iraqi army had marched across Kuwait's borders, Iraqi soldiers controlled almost all of Kuwait.

Immediately the United Nations sent Iraq a message: "You had no reason to invade Kuwait!" The UN announced that Saddam Hussein's claim that Kuwait was part of Iraq was false, and that Iraq should withdraw from Kuwait by January 15, 1991.

January 15 came and went. Iraqi forces stayed in Kuwait.

Many nations in the UN, including the United States, worried that if Hussein stayed in Kuwait, he would not only control the oil that Western nations needed, but that he might next invade Saudi Arabia—and control even more oil.

So two days later, a group of soldiers from around the world attacked Iraq from the air. The attack was led by American soldiers, but Saudi Arabia, Afghanistan, Great Britain, and Egypt sent soldiers as well. In all, almost seven hundred thousand soldiers from twenty-eight countries joined in the war.

Factories and military bases all over Iraq were bombed. The city of Baghdad, Saddam Hussein's capital, was bombed first. So were roads, so that troops couldn't travel across the country. So were places where troops might get food and water.

The UN also announced that no country in the world could send anything to Iraq, except for food and medical supplies. No one was to buy from Iraq. Almost every country agreed to observe this embargo. As long as Iraqi soldiers were in Kuwait, Iraq would not be able to sell or buy anything from abroad.

But despite the bombing and the embargo, Hussein refused to withdraw his soldiers from Kuwait. So after five weeks, the UN agreed that soldiers should invade Kuwait by ground to drive the Iraqis out. By the end of February, soldiers from the different countries in the UN had managed to push the Iraqi solders back out of Kuwait. Iraq agreed to stop the fighting. On April 11, Iraq was forced to withdraw entirely from Kuwait and to destroy some of its weapons. Iraq's leader, Saddam Hussein, also had to promise that he would never try to build nuclear weapons for his army.

Iraqi President Saddam Hussein

The war was won. But despite the victory and the agreement, Kuwait was shattered. As they retreated, Iraqi soldiers had set the oil wells of Kuwait on fire. These oil wells pumped oil out of the ground in a steady black stream. When a stream of oil was lit, it burned like the wick of a kerosene lantern. The wells were turned into huge torches, hundreds of feet tall, that burned for weeks and weeks. More than seven hundred oil wells were set on fire in Kuwait. Around them, the sand grew so hot that it turned into glass.

It took nine months to put all of the fires out. And in the meantime, as the oil wells burned, poisonous smoke drifted over Kuwait, causing lung problems. All over Kuwait, people suffered from coughing, shortness of breath, and dizziness. The smoke turned day into night. Burning oil went up into the air, evaporated, and came back down as black rain. Pools of oil lay all over the ground. Some of the oil ponds were six feet deep. An oil fog drifted over leaves and grass. Sheep ate the grass and died. Oil clogged up fresh water wells. Oil fogs and black rain drifted as far north as Turkey, and as far east as Afghanistan.

Iraqi soldiers had also dumped eleven million barrels of oil into the Persian Gulf. A foot of oil lay on top of the water. All along the coast of Kuwait, birds and fish were dying from the oil in the water. Eventually, it would cost seven hundred million dollars to clean up the oil—and most of the oil still remained in the water.

The bombing in Iraq had done damage as well. By bombing roads and food and water supplies, the UN forces had put many civilians in danger of starving to death or dying from drinking dirty water. And many, many Iraqi people who had not taken part in the war did indeed die.

Some members of the UN wanted to press on further. They wanted to get rid of Saddam Hussein. They argued that Hussein was obviously going to keep on starting wars, no matter what. But many of the countries in the coalition, especially other Arab countries, wanted to end the war, now that Kuwait was free.

And so Saddam Hussein was left in power—for a little while.

Africa, Independent

Between 1960 and 1975, one by one, African nations freed themselves from the last bits of colonial rule. We've already learned about the Union of South Africa, and about the Congo (Zaire) and Brazzaville becoming free from Belgium and France. If we told the story of every single African country that declared itself free from the colonial masters who once ruled it, we would need a whole different book. But if you look at a map of Africa, here's what you will see: Between 1960 and 1964, almost every country in Africa became officially independent. The last countries to become free were Angola, on the western coast of Africa, and Mozambique on the east coast, which did not finally escape from Portugal's control until 1975.

So instead of telling all of these stories, we will tell two short ones—one sad, and one hopeful. Both show the ways in which Africa was changed forever by its occupiers.

There have been many sad stories in the twentieth century, but this first story is one of the saddest. A few chapters ago, we read about the Belgian Congo, and its attempts to be independent. Just east of the Belgian Congo, now renamed Zaire, was a little Belgian colony called Ruanda-Urundi. In this mountainous area lived two different tribes. The first tribe, called the Batutsi, are tall and lighter-skinned. They make up only fifteen percent of the population. The second tribe, called the Bahutu, make up eighty-five percent of the population. They are much shorter, and darker skinned.

Even though there are so many more Bahutu, the Batutsi, or "Tutsi," became rulers of the area for at least six hundred years. The Tutsi were the lords of the area; the Bahutu, or "Hutu," served them, herded their cattle, and grew their food.

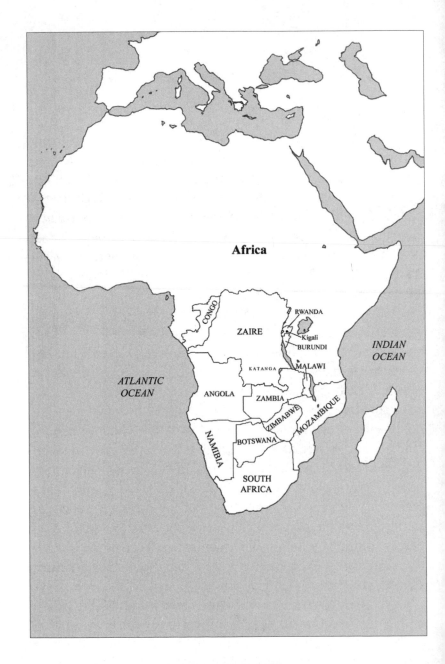

Africa

CONGO

ZAIRE

RWANDA

Kigali

BURUNDI

INDIAN OCEAN

KATANGA

MALAWI

ATLANTIC OCEAN

ANGOLA

ZAMBIA

ZIMBABWE

MOZAMBIQUE

NAMIBIA

BOTSWANA

SOUTH AFRICA

Independent Africa

When the different countries of Africa began to ask for independence, Ruanda-Urundi also asked for independence from Belgium. The Belgians said that the country could only be independent if it organized a democratic government for itself and held elections.

So the Hutus, who were the majority, put together a political party, held elections, and claimed the right to govern their own country. And then they turned and attacked the Tutsis. For centuries, the Hutus had resented their Tutsi rulers. During Belgian rule, this hatred had grown stronger. Because the Belgians were white, they tended to give all the important jobs and political positions to the lighter-skinned Tutsis. This meant that the traditional Tutsi rule had grown even more oppressive.

Now that the Belgians were gone, all of that hatred came out. Hutus began to kill Tutsis. Many Tutsi fled into the south of Ruanda-Urundi. (Others ran to surrounding countries.)

Now, Ruanda-Urundi had Hutus in the north, and Tutsis in the south—and both tribes hated each other. The Belgians decided that, instead of trying to keep both peoples together in the same country, they would divide Ruanda-Urundi into two. The north would be Rwanda, where the Hutu would rule and would elect a Hutu president. The south would become a Tutsi monarchy, called Burundi.

That was in 1962.

Rwanda was now a republic governed by Hutus. But many Tutsi still considered it their rightful home. Tutsi who had been driven from Rwanda formed a political party in exile, called the Rwandan Patriotic Front. They wanted their country back.

In 1994, the Hutu president of Rwanda was killed in a plane crash. Immediately, some Hutus began to blame the crash on the Tutsis, saying that the Rwandan Patriotic Front had sabotaged the plane. All the hostility that had been temporarily bottled up by the division of the country into two suddenly boiled back over again. Hutus picked up weapons and begin to kill Tutsi neighbors who had lived beside them for years and years. Half a million Tutsi died at the hands of people they knew, who had lived near them, invited them for meals, played with their children and helped in their gardens.

In revenge, the Tutsi of the Rwandan Patriotic Front invaded Rwanda and began to drive the Hutu out of Rwanda. At least a million Hutu had to flee Rwanda and live in camps in Zaire. At the worst part of their flight, six hundred people were crossing over the border into Zaire every *minute*. With so many people in the camps, food and water were scarce; people died from hunger, thirst, and disease. Tens of thousands died.

The European occupation had made the hostility between the tribes worse, until it erupted into genocide.

Now for a story that is a little more hopeful, also from Africa. In South Africa, in the same year that the Hutu and Tutsi were battling with each other in the center of Africa, the first black South African president took office.

We've read about South Africa and apartheid. Apartheid— the practice of separating whites and nonwhites into different spaces, different buses, even different benches in waiting rooms—was designed to keep all of the power of a country in white hands. We read about the Unjust Laws, the apartheid laws that were established after World War II. We also read about the beginnings of resistance, how the African National Congress began to use Gandhi's techniques of nonviolent resistance, and how this brought little change to South Africa for years and years and years.

As a matter of fact, the ANC finally decided that nonviolent protest wasn't going to work. Instead, they began to set off bombs and make threats. This didn't work either. ANC leaders, including one named Nelson Mandela, were arrested for their illegal acts and put into prison.

But the unrest in South Africa did begin to finally attract the attention of the rest of the world. The UN put an embargo on weapons, so that no one could sell guns or ammunition to South Africa. All around the world, people began to suggest that not buying things made in South Africa (a "boycott"; do you remember reading about this word in the chapter on

Ireland?) would make South Africa poorer and force the government to reject apartheid.

In response, the South African government, led by P. W. Botha, declared that South Africa was in a state of emergency—and cracked down on the freedoms of black South Africans even more. Many were arrested. Newspapers were forbidden to write about the arrests, and South African TV stations couldn't cover them.

Nelson Mandela, anti-apartheid activist
and president of South Africa

But the outcry from the rest of the world did not stop. Desmond Tutu, an Anglican priest from South Africa, spoke out to the rest of the world, telling them about the evils of apartheid. In response, the United States refused to lend money to South Africa or to buy South African goods. So did other nations.

In 1989, at last, P. W. Botha resigned. The man who came to power after him, F. W. de Klerk, finally began to change the system.

In 1991, the South African Parliament repealed the laws of apartheid. F. W. de Klerk ordered Nelson Mandela released from prison. Together, Mandela and de Klerk tried to work out a plan for South Africa. They agreed that elections should be held—the first "open election" in South African history, in which any candidate, white or black, could be elected by all of the voters.

In 1994, Nelson Mandela was elected the first black president of South Africa. Archbishop Tutu became head of the Truth and Reconciliation Commission, which began to uncover the wrongs done to blacks in the past.

"The changes in South Africa," wrote one editorial in the magazine *Commonweal*, "happened in no small measure because of moral pressures exerted from abroad." The rebuilding of South Africa will go on for many years. But it is one of the few times in the history of the twentieth century in which countries have united together to force change for the better—instead of a government seizing power and exercising it for the worse.

Afterword

This history of the world ends in the twentieth century, not the twenty-first; its final chapter deals with events in 1994.

On September 11, 2001, two American airplanes, hijacked by radical Muslim terrorists, crashed into the World Trade Center towers in New York City. A third crashed into the Pentagon. A fourth, apparently headed for Washington DC, went down in a field in Pennsylvania.

I have not brought this history up to 2001, because I don't understand how 9/11 will play into history. At the time that I write this, the war that the event spawned is still going on. The administration that took us into the war is still in power. Reconstruction in the countries shattered by that war has only just begun. These are current events, not history; they are acts that cannot yet be interpreted. Only now can we interpret World War II, and in many ways the Vietnam War still evades our understanding. Instead of ending with 2001 (or later), I have instead tried to give the historical background that led up to the current chaos. If we can begin to understand the background of that chaos, we may find ourselves understanding a little more about the chaos itself.

Table of Dates

A Chronology of the Modern Age

Below are the events from Volume 4 of *The Story of the World*. Following each entry is the chapter in which it can be found. Entries without chapter numbers are not included in Volume 4, but are included as a contextual aid in your study of history. If you are searching for specific events within Volume 4, check the index (immediately following this chronology, on page 489).

1856–1860 Second Opium War

1857   Livingstone writes *Missionary Travels* [3]

1857–1858 The Sepoy Rebellion [1]

1859   Charles Darwin publishes *On the Origin of Species*

1860   The Taipings march towards Shanghai [4]

1861   Victor Emmanuel II crowned king of Italy [4]

1861   Italian states are united under King Victor Emmanuel [24]

1861–1865 The American Civil War [5]

1862   Francisco Solano López comes to power in Paraguay [6]

1863   Dost Mohammad Khan drives foreign invaders from Afghanistan [3]

1864   The Qing army retakes Nanjing [4]

1864   Prussia and Austria attack Denmark [7]

1864–1870 The War of the Triple Alliance [6]

1865   John Wilkes Booth assassinates U.S. President Abraham Lincoln [5]

1865   U.S. Congress bans slavery in the United States [5]

1867   The Dominion of Canada forms [6]

1867   The North German Confederation is created [7]

1868   Japan re-opens during the Meiji era [8]

1868–1912 Meiji Restoration [8]

1869   The first transcontinental railroad in the U.S. is completed [8]

1869   The Suez Canal opens [10]

1870   France becomes a republic [7]

1870–1871 The Franco-Prussian War [7]

1871–1918 The Second Reich [7]

1873–1903 Acheh War [9]

1876   Bulgarian revolutionaries rebel against the Turks [9]

1876   Abdul Aziz is assassinated [9]

1876	The Battle of Little Bighorn [16]
1876	Alexander Graham Bell submits a patent for the telephone
1877	The Satsuma Revolt in Japan [8]
1877–1878	The Russo-Turkish Wars [9]
1877–1879	The Zulu-British Wars
1878	Umberto I becomes king of Italy [24]
1878–1880	The Second Afghan War
1879	Thomas Edison invents the electric light [8]
1879	The War of the Pacific begins in South America [10]
1880	Police arrest Ned Kelly [11]
1880–1881	The First Boer War [12]
1881	Assassins kill Czar Alexander II [14]
1882	The Triple Alliance forms [24]
1883	The U.S. adopts time zones [8]
1884	The Berlin Conference [11]
1886	Parliament votes against the Home Rule Bill [12]
1889	Brazil is declared a republic; Pedro II leaves Brazil [13]
1889	Menelik takes control of Ethiopia [14]
1892	Abbas II named *khedive* of Egypt [24]
1894	The Armenians rebel against the Ottoman Turks [13]
1894	Nicholas II becomes czar of Russia [14]
1894–1895	The Sino-Japanese War [15]
1895	The creation of Rhodesia [12]
1896	Italy recognizes Ethiopian independence [14]
1898	The Spanish-American war begins [15]
1899–1902	The Second Boer War [12]
1895	The "Young Turks" try to reform the Ottoman Empire [13]
1900	The Boxer Rebellion in China [17]
1901	The Commonwealth of Australia is established

1902	Alfonso XIII is crowned king of Spain [27]
1903	Macedonians declare themselves independent from Turkish rule [18]
1903	Phan Boi Chau forms *Duy Tan Hoi*—The Restoration Society [19]
1903	Wright brothers make the first powered and controlled flight
1904–1905	The Russian-Japanese War [17]
1905	Irish Catholics form Sinn Féin [22]
1906	The first *Majles* begins after Liberal rebellion [18]
1908	Empress Cixi dies [19]
1908	Phan Boi Chau leaves Japan [19]
1910	Mexican Revolution begins [20]
1911	The end of the Qing dynasty [19]
1911	Delhi becomes capital of India [22]
1912	Sun Yixian flees to Canton [25]
1912	The *Titanic* sinks
1912	Arizona becomes a state [16]
1912	The First Balkan War [18]
1912	Sun Yixian forms the Kuomintang [25]
1913	The Second Balkan War [18]
1914	World War I begins [18, 20]
1914	Russia enters WWI [21]
1914	Egypt becomes a British protectorate [24]
1915	Italy joins Allied Forces [24]
1915	A German submarine sinks the Lusitania [20]
1916	Rasputin is killed [21]
1916	Easter Uprising in Ireland [22]
1916	Yuan Shikai dies [25]
1917	The U.S. joins WWI [20, 21]

1917	Kerensky takes over Russia's Provisional Government [21]
1917	Bolshevik Revolution [21]
1917	Bolsheviks renamed "Communist Party" [21]
1917	Ahmad Fuʿad becomes sultan of Egypt [24]
1918	Germany surrenders to the Allied Powers [21]
1918	Germany signs armistice to end fighting of World War I [21]
1918	Romanov family assassinated [21]
1918	Great Britain gives women right to vote [21]
1918	White Army forms [23]
1918	Egyptian delegates visit England in *wafd* [24]
1918–1921	Russian Civil War [23]
1919	Sinn Féin sets up Irish Assembly [22]
1919	Treaty of Versailles is signed [23]
1919	League of Nations forms [23]
1919	Amritsar massacre in India [22, 30]
1919	Fascist Party is formed in Italy [24]
1920	U.S. Congress gives women the right to vote [21]
1921	Sinn Féin and Great Britain reach peace agreement [22]
1921	Mohandas Karamchand Gandhi is elected head of the Congress Party [22]
1921	Chinese Communist Party is formed [25]
1922	Mussolini marches to Rome [24]
1922	Michael Collins assassinated during Irish Civil War [22]
1922	Lenin suffers stroke; Stalin takes control of Russia [23]
1922	Britain grants Egypt independence [24]
1923	Chiang Kai-shek starts Kuomintang military academy [25]
1923	Irish Free State begins to govern itself [22]
1923	Italy under control of the Fascists [24]

1924	Lenin dies; Petrograd renamed Leningrad [23]
1924	Henry Puyi leaves China [25]
1925	Sun Yixian dies [25]
1926	Emperor Hirohito ascends the Japanese throne [25]
1926	Mao Zedong and CCP members rebel against Kuomintang [25]
1928	Kuomintang takes control of China's government [25]
1929	The Wall Street Crash [26]
1930	Gandhi leads thousands on Salt March [22]
1930–1960	Russian Gulag in operation [23]
1931	Japan withdraws from League of Nations [25]
1932–1933	Famines in Russia kill up to 5 million people [23]
1933	Franklin Roosevelt becomes President [26]
1933	Hitler takes power in Germany [26]
1934–1935	Mao Zedong's Long March [25]
1936	Berlin hosts the Olympics; Jesse Owens wins four gold medals [28]
1936–1939	Spanish Civil War [27]
1937	Japanese capture Shanghai and Beijing [28]
1938	*Kristallnacht* [28]
1939	Germany invades Poland; World War II begins [27]
1939	General Franco gains control of Spain [27]
1940	Japan joins the Axis powers [28]
1940	The Dunkirk Evacuation [29]
1941	U.S. enters WWII after Japan bombs Pearl Harbor [28]
1942	The Battle of Midway [28]
1943	Italian troops in North Africa surrender [29]
1943	Juan Perón leads a revolt in Argentina [34]
1944	D-Day: Allied soldiers land at Normandy [29]
1945	Six million Jews have been killed in the Holocaust [28]

1960	Nigeria and Zaire become independent [34]
1961	Berlin Wall is built [31]
1961	Russian cosmonaut, Yuri Gagarin, first man to orbit the Earth [35]
1962	Cuban Missile Crisis [35]
1962–1966	Civil rights protests [36]
1962	Ruanda-Urundi is divided into Rwanda and Burundi [42]
1963	John F. Kennedy assassinated [36]
1964–1975	Vietnam War [37]
1965	U.S. enters Vietnam War [37]
1966	Beginning of the Cultural Revolution in China
1967	Six-Day War [37]
1967–1970	Civil war in Nigeria
1968	Martin Luther King, Jr., is assassinated [36]
1968	Soviet troops invade Czechoslovakia [38]
1969	American astronauts walk on the moon [35]
1969	IRA starts to campaign for a united Ireland [38]
1969	ARPANET, the predecessor to the Internet, is created
1971	Bangladesh becomes independent [39]
1972	Black September takes hostages at Olympics [38]
1973	U.S. signs treaty to withdraw from Vietnam [37]
1973	Yom Kippur War [37]
1973–1974	OPEC increases oil prices; gas shortages result [37]
1975	Mozambique is free from Portuguese control [42]
1975	General Franco dies in Spain, ends dictatorship
1976	Mao Zedong dies [41]
1978	Begin and Sadat win the Nobel Peace Prize [37]
1978	Rebel group assassinates king of Afghanistan [38]
1979	Shah of Iran overthrown [39]

1979	USSR invades Afghanistan [38]
1979	Nuclear accident at Three Mile Island [40]
1980–1988	Iran-Iraq War [39]
1982	Israel invades Lebanon
1983	Argentinian government overthrown in favor of democracy
1984	Indira Gandhi assassinated [39]
1984	Factory gas leak in Bhopal, India [39]
1985	Gorbachev becomes leader of USSR [40]
1986	Chernobyl nuclear disaster [40]
1986	Space shuttle *Challenger* explodes during liftoff
1987	U.S. and USSR sign the INF treaty [40]
1987	Hole in the ozone layer confirmed
1989	Tiananmen Square massacre [41]
1989	Berlin Wall comes down [41]
1989	Ceaucescu is overthrown in Romania
1990	Iraq invades Kuwait [42]
1990	Tim Berners-Lee creates the World Wide Web
1990	East and West Germany are reunited [41]
1991	Nelson Mandela is released from prison [42]
1991	Gorbachev resigns; Communist Party outlawed in USSR [41]
1991	America goes to war with Iraq [42]
1994	Genocide begins in Rwanda [42]
1994	Nelson Mandela is elected the first black president of South Africa [42]
2001	Terrorists attack World Trade Center in New York, Pentagon in Washington DC [Afterword]

Index

S

parents who use our books say ...

My daughter is 6½, and the lessons are perfect for her attention span. I love how *The Story of the World* includes history from places that are often overlooked for this age group—places like China, India, and Africa. *The Activity Books* are the perfect accompaniment! The maps and activities not only help my daughter understand and retain what she is learning but also help her enjoy it! I love the extra resources, like additional history reading and literature suggestions. To have maps available for her to color and projects for us to do together are the icing on the cake!

I am so thrilled that your books are working so well for us. They have taken away the headache of building my own curriculum and gathering my materials. Just keep your noses to the grindstone, now, because I'm going to want more! I've got 11 more years of school ... you can quit then!

— Maria R. • Darlington, WI

I know *The Story of the World* is written for grades 1–4, but I personally have learned more from reading them to my children than I *ever* did in school. The *Activity Books* add so much to the program, and truly bring the series alive. What a brilliant series!

— Linda M. • Booleroo Centre, Australia

The *Story of the World* saved our homeschool! I can't express my gratitude enough! The *Activity Books* are a comprehensive list of great ideas, categorized by chapter to go along with the books. It is such a tremendous help to have literature suggestions for each of my children (at different grade levels 2nd–6th) all at my fingertips. The activities are simple to do, yet make history come alive for the kids. They make what we are studying meaningful, instead of a boring memorization of dull facts. You know you have a great curriculum when your kids ask to read their history book as a bedtime story!

— Jennifer S. • Northern VA

The Story of the World and *Activity Book* have been extremely easy to implement with my boys. The variety of activities allows us to choose from several great resources immediately. The *Activity Book* has saved much time and work for this busy mom!

— Amy H. • San Antonio, TX

"You know you have a great curriculum when your kids ask to read their history book as a bedtime story!"
— Jennifer S.

My children love *The Story of the World.* They have a better grasp on world history than I ever did. The best part is what I am learning along the way! The *Activity Book* is what makes my children beg for history even on days when we are not doing school. The projects cement the learning and my kids retain what we have read. We use every part of the *Activity Book.*

— Mindy B. • Spokane, WA

I started my 9-year-old daughter on *Story of the World*, Volume 1 this year and assigned her a chapter to read every week or so. About halfway through it she said to me "This is great!" and she proceeded to read on through it. Then she begged me to buy the next two volumes. I told her she could keep reading but we would need to go back to some of the previous chapters and learn more in depth. She said, "Great, I want to read them again anyway!" She went on to read Volumes 2 and 3 in her free time in the next two or three weeks and is on her second round of reading them all the way through, by herself. She will come to me and tell me things she has learned that she thought were really interesting. Thanks so much for getting her excited about history!

— Wendy A. • Carrollton, TX